Social Entrepreneurship and Business Ethics

Social entrepreneurs are changemakers who aim to solve society's unsolved problems. Not surprisingly, social entrepreneurship has thus created high expectations. To better understand the potential as well as the limitations of social entrepreneurship, however, a more nuanced approach is needed in two ways.

First, social entrepreneurship is a multi-level phenomenon. It spans macro-level questions as well as meso-level questions and, finally, micro-level questions. If we really want to understand social entrepreneurship, we need to bring together all three levels of analysis and see how they are connected.

Second, although social entrepreneurship can certainly produce socially desirable outcomes, we also need a critical perspective to capture potential undesirable effects that social entrepreneurship can cause, often unintendedly, in society, in markets, in organizations, and for individuals. To this end, an ethical perspective can help complement the positive analysis of social entrepreneurship with a discussion of the normative implications of its potential 'dark side'.

Looking at social entrepreneurship from both a multi-level analysis and an ethical perspective, *Social Entrepreneurship and Business Ethics* takes the reader on a journey through the 'bright side' as well as the potential 'dark side' of social entrepreneurship for societies, organizations, and individuals. Highlighting both, this book not only seeks to provoke researchers and students to advance their understanding of social entrepreneurship; it also hopes to help practitioners to better realize the positive contributions of social entrepreneurship for society.

Anica Zeyen is a senior lecturer (associate professor) in Strategy and Sustainability at the Centre for Research into Sustainability (CRIS) at Royal Holloway University of London, UK.

Markus Beckmann is the chair of Corporate Sustainability Management at the School of Business and Economics at Friedrich-Alexander-Universität Erlangen-Nürnberg, Germany.

Routledge Studies in Entrepreneurship

Edited by
Susan Marlow and Janine Swail
University of Nottingham, UK

This series extends the meaning and scope of entrepreneurship by capturing new research and enquiry on economic, social, cultural and personal value creation. Entrepreneurship as value creation represents the endeavours of innovative people and organisations in creative environments that open up opportunities for developing new products, new services, new firms and new forms of policy making in different environments seeking sustainable economic growth and social development. In setting this objective the series includes books which cover a diverse range of conceptual, empirical and scholarly topics that both inform the field and push the boundaries of entrepreneurship.

For a full list of titles in this series, please visit www.routledge.com

Social Entrepreneurship and Business Ethics

Understanding the Contribution and Normative Ambivalence of Purpose-driven Venturing

Anica Zeyen and Markus Beckmann

Routledge
Taylor & Francis Group

NEW YORK AND LONDON

First published 2019
by Routledge
605 Third Avenue, New York, NY 10017

and by Routledge
2 Park Square, Milton Park, Abingdon, Oxon, OX14 4RN

First issued in paperback 2020

Routledge is an imprint of the Taylor & Francis Group, an informa business

Library of Congress Cataloging-in-Publication Data
A catalog record for this title has been requested

ISBN 13: 978-0-367-73279-0 (pbk)
ISBN 13: 978-1-138-07994-6 (hbk)

Typeset in Sabon
by Apex CoVantage, LLC

To our families

Contents

Tables and Figures

Tables

Figures

Author Biographies

Anica Zeyen is a senior lecturer (associate professor) in Strategy and Sustainability at the Centre for Research into Sustainability (CRIS) at Royal Holloway University of London, UK. Prior to her current position, Anica worked as a post-doc researcher at Friedrich-Alexander University of Erlangen-Nuremberg (Germany) and as a research assistant and lecturer at the Centre for Sustainability Management (CSM) at Leuphana University Lüneburg (Germany). Anica completed her PhD on scaling strategies of social entrepreneurial ventures at Leuphana University Lüneburg in 2014 and has been involved in research on social entrepreneurship ever since. Often together with Markus Beckmann, Anica has been designing and teaching classes on social entrepreneurship at undergraduate, postgraduate, and executive levels for the last ten years. They have further supported numerous student social entrepreneurs in their start-up adventures.

Markus Beckmann is the chair of Corporate Sustainability Management at the School of Business and Economics at Friedrich-Alexander-Universität Erlangen-Nürnberg, Germany. He began researching social entrepreneurship during his PhD in business ethics, which he completed at University of Halle-Wittenberg in 2009. Before going to Nuremberg, he was assistant professor for Social Entrepreneurship at Leuphana University Lüneburg, Germany. Often in collaboration with Anica Zeyen, Markus has been designing and teaching classes on social entrepreneurship and business ethics at undergraduate, postgraduate, and executive levels for the last ten years.

Preface

In a way, this book has been ten years in the making. For the past ten years, we have researched social entrepreneurship together; we have taught social entrepreneurship at more than ten universities from undergraduate to postgraduate and executive levels, worked with numerous national and international social entrepreneurial ventures, and supported numerous students in starting up their own social ventures.

Over these ten years, our passion for social entrepreneurship, and especially our appreciation for the incredible work many social entrepreneurs do, has never wavered and has actually grown steadily. Exactly for that reason, we consider it extremely important to talk about the shadows within the field of social entrepreneurship. We feel that the often overly positive narrative used in the field impedes its growth and development. Only if we understand the shadows as well as the light within social entrepreneurship will we be able to harness its full potential.

This book combines insights from our own ten-year research collaboration on social entrepreneurship as well as research we conducted with other co-authors. It also builds on practitioner discussions, live case study work, social enterprise consultation, practitioner conferences, numerous classroom discussions, and personal relationships we have with social entrepreneurs. This makes this book slightly different from other research monographs. It is rooted in rigorous research that aims at objectivity yet also includes subjective insights we gained through our own experience in the field of social entrepreneurship research, practice, and education.

It covers social entrepreneurship from many different angles, starting at a societal (macro-level) viewpoint and descending via an organizational (meso-level) perspective to understanding the light and shadows for individuals involved in social entrepreneurship (micro-level perspective).

We are very excited about the opportunity to publish this book because it gave us an opportunity to link all of these different perspectives on social entrepreneurship into a comprehensive story. We sincerely hope you enjoy reading this book as much as we enjoyed working on it.

Acknowledgments

We want to first and foremost thank our families for their patience and support throughout the last ten years but especially over the last few months of intensive writing.

We want to further thank the numerous social entrepreneurship practitioners we met over last decade. We want to thank all of them for the insightful and fruitful discussions and collaborations.

We would further like to thank Jens Heidingsfelder for his constructive and valuable comments on earlier drafts of this book.

1 Introduction

Why Social Entrepreneurship and Business Ethics?

Where there is much light, there is also shadow.
(Goethe 1773)

1.1. What Is Social Entrepreneurship?

Social entrepreneurs are changemakers who aim to solve society's unsolved problems. People like Muhammad Yunus from Bangladesh, founder of the Grameen Bank and inventor of modern microcredits, turn societal challenges such as poverty into an opportunity for innovation and positive social change. Around the world, social entrepreneurs use diverse organizational forms and strategies to innovate and implement novel solutions for equally diverse problems and target groups.

In Africa, Katherine Lucey and Neha Misra founded Solar Sisters, a social venture that uses clean technology solutions to empower women through economic opportunity. Having aided thousands of women to become micro-entrepreneurs, Solar Sisters not only creates income but helps shift economic development onto an ecologically sustainable path. In Europe, Danish Thorkil Sonne's venture Specialisterne builds upon the special skill set often linked to autism (such as attention to detail). By training people on the autism spectrum to become specialized IT business consultants, Specialisterne enables them to become valuable experts in jobs ranging from data entry to software testing. German social entrepreneur Rose Volz-Schmidt, on the other hand, has founded Wellcome. Her nonprofit company helps young families adapt to the disruptive changes that come along when a baby is born. In India, Govindappa Venkataswamy founded Aravind Eye Care System, a network of hospitals and support facilities that revolutionized the provision of urgently needed eye care services. Focusing especially on poor people, Aravind delivered more than six million surgeries to people who would otherwise most likely have gone blind. In Latin America, Brazilian Rodrigo Baggio founded the Center for Digital Inclusion that brings information and communication technology (ICT) into slums, thus creating opportunities for education and local entrepreneurship. In the United States,

Wendy Kopp founded Teach for America, which puts smart college seniors in some of the country's worst high school classrooms. In only a few years, Kopp expanded her idea onto a global scale and by now operates in more than twenty countries. With an even more global scale, Jimmy Wales is the well-known founder of Wikipedia. His idea to use a peer-operated platform transformed the global sharing and verifying of knowledge, thus democratizing the use and access of information.

Social entrepreneurs thus operate on all continents and address diverse issues ranging from education and economic empowerment via health and disability to sustainability and environmental stewardship. In so doing, they use nonprofit organizations (like the Center for Digital Inclusion), for-profit companies (like Specialisterne), nonprofit enterprises (like Wellcome), or foundations (like Wikipedia). At the same time, they can create a positive impact through their product for their direct customers (like Grameen or Aravind), through work opportunities for their employees (like Specialisterne), or for third parties and society at large (like Teach for America). Similarly, their funding may include market income, subsidies, fees, and donations.

Social entrepreneurship is, in short, a diverse (and fascinating!) phenomenon. Yet, despite their diversity, these examples illustrate what social entrepreneurs have in common. As entrepreneurs, they apply the skills, mind-sets, and practices of entrepreneurial venturing to identify opportunities for change, to devise innovative solutions to reap these opportunities, as well as to acquire necessary resources and take risks to implement their innovation. As *social* entrepreneurs, their primary motivation is not the realization of financial profits but to contribute to positive societal change. Social entrepreneurs are, thus, public-purpose changemakers.

Public-purpose changemakers have existed for a long time (Bornstein 2007). Florence Nightingale, for instance, was a remarkable social entrepreneur in nineteenth-century Britain. She innovated, implemented, and scaled the foundations of modern nursing, thus saving millions of lives through higher medical standards. In the early twentieth century, Maria Montessori founded kindergartens for working families in Italy. Her reform ideas soon transformed education and pedagogy worldwide.

The phenomenon of social entrepreneurship is thus not new. What is of more recent origin, however, is the vibrant discourse about it. A key figure in this regard is Bill Drayton. In 1980, Drayton founded Ashoka, an organization that supports social entrepreneurs. The idea of Ashoka is simple: If social entrepreneurs do an important job for society, they shall try to find, support, and connect these people. Ashoka supports these so-called Ashoka Fellows with a stipend and additional support. Starting in India in 1981, Ashoka soon expanded its work with the nominations of the first Ashoka Fellows in Brazil in 1986 and then Bangladesh, Mexico, and Nepal in 1987. During the 1990s, Ashoka added countries in Asia, Africa, Latin America, and Central and Eastern Europe. It was only during the 2000s that Ashoka expanded its program to the United States, Canada, and Western Europe (as of 2005). In this book, we will frequently draw on example social entrepreneurs who are Ashoka Fellows.

The systematic emergence of the social entrepreneurship movement thus started primarily with a focus on the Global South and was driven largely by practitioners and activists like Bill Drayton. Around the turn of the new millennium, however, this dynamic changed when both journalists and academics in the Global North discovered social entrepreneurship as an inspiring phenomenon. On the one hand, researchers started an academic discussion about the meaning of social entrepreneurship (Dees 1998) or its new business models (Seelos and Mair 2005), thus increasingly exploring social entrepreneurship research as a "source of explanation, prediction, and delight" (Mair and Martí 2006). On the other hand, a number of popular science books promoted the idea to a broader public (Leadbeater 1997; Bornstein 2007; Elkington and Hartigan 2008).

This increasing attention for social entrepreneurship has various reasons. With regard to the demand for social entrepreneurship, there is an increasing awareness that innovative solutions are urgently needed in light of pressing social and environmental challenges (Nicholls 2006). Although capitalist markets, public-sector institutions, and welfare organizations provide many people on this planet with a high standard of living (Rosling, Rönnlund, and Rosling 2018), many others are left behind—not only in the developing world but in industrialized countries as well. At the same time, climate change, loss of biodiversity, soil erosion, or air and water pollution are just a few problems in the ecological domain. In fact, the world is in many domains in very unsustainable equilibriums, thus creating the need for entrepreneurial solutions to creatively destroy the unsustainable status quo and pave the way for a better world (Schaltegger, Beckmann, and Hockerts 2018). With regard to the supply side, on the other hand, a number of developments ranging from the fall of the Iron Curtain via new means of information and communication to rising levels of affluence and education allow more and more individuals to engage in social entrepreneurship. As summed up by Bornstein (2007, 7), "more people today have the freedom, time, wealth, health, exposure, social mobility, and confidence to address social problems in bold new ways."

Against this background, the past two decades have witnessed the rapid emergence of ever more encompassing ecosystems for social entrepreneurs. Organizations like Ashoka, Schwab, Skoll, or Synergos identify, award, support, and connect promising social entrepreneurs. In the field of finance, venture philanthropy organization and their platforms like the European Venture Philanthropy Association (EVPA) promote and provide specific forms of funding for social entrepreneurs (Manuel et al. 2006). Closely linked, new approaches have emerged to measure the impact of social ventures (Nicholls 2005, 2009). At the same time, universities and schools have begun to integrate social entrepreneurship into their curricula, thus opening up the ever broader field of social entrepreneurship education (Tracey and Phillips 2007).

Though the research on social entrepreneurship is still fairly young, it has seen a highly productive and rapid development (Dees, Emerson, and Economy 2002; Seelos and Mair 2009; Hockerts, Mair, and Robinson 2006; Dacin, Dacin, and Matear 2010; Seelos and Mair 2005; Nicholls 2006). In fact, in academia, in addition to social entrepreneurship scholarship published in established journals, new journals have emerged with an explicit dedication to the issue such as the *Journal of Social Entrepreneurship*, the *Social Enterprise Journal*, or the *Stanford Social Innovation Review*. This research has yielded exciting findings and can, by now, fill entire libraries. So why do we think that there is not only room but arguably the need for yet another book on social entrepreneurship?

1.2. Bringing Together Social Entrepreneurship and Business Ethics

This book seeks to bring together the fascinating field of social entrepreneurship with a business ethics perspective. At first sight, the value of this linkage is not obvious. After all, social entrepreneurship and business ethics seem to be only remotely related. Business ethics focuses traditionally on conventional for-profit businesses. It then looks at potential conflicts between profit-seeking and societal interests, discussing the social responsibility of capitalist firms (Crane and Matten 2016). In contrast, social entrepreneurship, as just discussed, does not primarily focus on profit maximization but takes societal interests as the key objective for economic venturing. As a consequence, both perspectives seem to look into different directions (Beckmann 2011; Zeyen, Beckmann, and Akhavan 2014). In fact, so far there is little overlap between both discourses, both in the academic debate and the practitioner's world (for an exception see Chell et al. 2016; Dey and Steyaert 2016).

Upon closer inspection, however, the picture becomes more complicated. After all, ethical scandals and crises have occurred in social entrepreneurship as well. To illustrate, take the case of microcredits shortly introduced at the very beginning of this chapter. After this poster case of social entrepreneurship received abundant appraisal (including the Nobel Peace Prize), the diffusion of microcredits led to a borrowing crisis among various communities. With thousands of people overly indebted, a high number of them ended up committing suicide (Ashta, Khan, and Otto 2011; Seremani 2013). An innovative idea with noble intentions thus ended up creating misery instead of positive change. Cases like this one drastically underline that ethical problems are obviously not limited to for-profit venturing (Bouckaert and Vandenhove 1998).

We suggest that applying a business ethics perspective can add a valuable contribution for social entrepreneurship theory and practice. However, many business ethics approaches differ in their conceptual perspective. Some conceptual perspectives evaluate the moral quality of a behavior, decision, or phenomenon based on the underlying intentions (Crane and Matten 2016). From this perspective, the other-regarding, prosocial intentions of social entrepreneurs would obviously seem praiseworthy. The case of microcredits, however, illustrates that even well-intended ideas can lead to highly questionable results. How can ethics help understand this problem and improve these outcomes?

Against this background, this book builds upon a perspective that looks not at intentions but consequences. The starting point for our business ethics approach is to focus on the *un*intended ethical challenges that can emerge as the result of intentional behavior (Pies, Beckmann, and Hielscher 2014, 7), no matter whether the intentions for the latter are driven by profit or nonfinancial motives. A key insight from the business ethics literature is that not only intentions (such as the profit motive) but many other phenomena (such as competition or self-interest) are neither inherently good nor inherently bad. Instead, profit-seeking or competition are normatively ambivalent: Depending on the situational conditions, they can lead to socially highly desirable or highly undesirable consequences (Pies, Hielscher, and Beckmann 2009). This particular business ethics perspective thus shifts the attention toward analyzing the *situational context* to investigate under which conditions a self-interest, altruism, profit-seeking, or a phenomenon like social entrepreneurship lead to desirable or undesirable outcomes (Beckmann 2012).

We believe that such a business ethics perspective offers fruitful insights for the social entrepreneurship debate. Given its many fascinating examples, the literature often embraces social entrepreneurship as an inherently positive phenomenon with "univocally positive effects" (Dey 2006, 121). Social entrepreneurs are heralded as "as the real-life superheroes of our society" (Kickul and Lyons 2016, 2). Similarly, Yunus sees "social business entrepreneurs [as] the solution" to build the "future of capitalism" (Yunus 2013, 2009). By the same token, many elements of social entrepreneurship such as innovation or social mission orientation as well as many practices of social entrepreneurship such as scaling or the use of impact measurement are often presented as inherently desirable (see Seelos and Mair (2012) for a critical comment on the tendency to see innovation as inherently desirable).

What our business ethics perspective can contribute to this debate is to show that not only profit-seeking or good intentions but also most issues discussed in social entrepreneurship are normatively ambivalent. To use a metaphor, we suggest to view social entrepreneurship as a *tool*—an instrument to solve certain problems (Beckmann 2012). In everyday life, nobody would claim that a hammer or a knife is inherently good. It rather depends on the situation—how you use the tool. Although a knife can help a surgeon to save a life, it can also take a life. By analogy, we suggest viewing not only the very phenomenon of social entrepreneurship but also many of its features (mission orientation, innovation, entrepreneurial agency) and related practices (hybrid business models, scaling, measurement) as a tool: Depending on the context and how well they are used, they can lead to both desirable and undesirable consequences.

A key benefit of this conceptual perspective is not only that it can guide us toward a more balanced understanding of the contribution and limitations—the bright and dark side so to speak—of social entrepreneurship. Moreover, the concept of normative ambivalence shifts the focus toward the conditions for managing these tensions constructively, that is, how to improve the usage of the social entrepreneurship tools.

The purpose of this book is thus twofold. First, although social entrepreneurship can certainly produce socially desirable outcomes, we want to capture potential undesirable effects that social entrepreneurship can cause, often unintendedly, thus advancing critical perspectives in the field (Dey and Steyaert 2018).

Second, because our ethical perspective highlights the importance of situational conditions, this book seeks to analyze social entrepreneurship in context. Social entrepreneurship, however, is a multi-level phenomenon. It spans macro-level questions (which role does social entrepreneurship play in society, and how does it interact with the institutions of the market, the state, and civil society?) as well as meso-level questions (what are the implications of social entrepreneurship for organizing, business models, and management?) and micro-level questions (what are the effects on individuals in social entrepreneurship?). If we want to fully understand social entrepreneurship and its normative ambivalence, we need to bring together all three levels of analysis and see how they are connected.

1.3. How This Book Is Organized

In accordance with the overall objectives of this book, this volume is structured into four main parts, which are in turn subdivided into chapters.

Part I lays the conceptual foundations for this book. Here, Chapter 2 will not only define social entrepreneurship but will also deduce the key features that differentiate social entrepreneurship from other approaches. These key characteristics are then the basis for the analysis in the subsequent book parts. In addition to this *positive* analysis, Part I also introduces key ethical concepts to clarify the *normative* perspective that is needed to critically discuss the inherent ambivalence or the potential 'dark side' of social entrepreneurship. To this end, Chapter 3 briefly reviews candidate ethical theories, makes transparent why we chose a consequentialist approach, and refines this consequentialist perspective with a conceptual framework that develops the concept of *normative ambivalence*. Here, we substantiate this idea to analyze social entrepreneurship and its components and practices as ambivalent *tools*. This ambivalence perspective will guide us throughout the rest of this book.

Part II addresses social entrepreneurship from a macro-level perspective. We thus take a helicopter view and analyze the general role of social entrepreneurship in society for innovating and delivering solutions that address social and environmental needs. To this end, Chapter 4 first takes a generic sectoral perspective that compares social entrepreneurship as a problem-solving tool with the alternative tools of the state, the market, and the third sector, irrespective of a specific national context. Chapter 5 then looks at how specific differences in the macro-level context impact the potential role of social entrepreneurship. Focusing on how different types and degrees of institutionalization influence the supply and demand of social entrepreneurship, we discuss differences between community institutions, formal and informal economies, and welfare state systems. Looking at the interplay of different sectors, we then address the importance of entrepreneurial ecosystems for social ventures.

Part III shifts our attention from the macro to the meso-level, thus turning toward the organization and the organizing of social entrepreneurship. Here, we review key strategies and organizational concepts typically embraced in the social entrepreneurship debate and discuss them as principally ambivalent tools. Chapter 6 starts by addressing social entrepreneurship business models. As our discussion shows, social entrepreneurs can devise unique business models thanks to their social mission that allows them access to diverse resources from hybrid sources. At the same time, this tool can lead to unintended consequences, such as limiting a solution to a niche or reducing its adaptiveness in the face of environmental change. Chapter 7 then addresses the question of impact measurement. Again, after reviewing prominent options as well as the pros and cons for impact measurement, we show that the use of metrics is highly ambivalent. Particularly when linked to incentives, impact measurement should be used with extreme care or not at all. Completing our meso-level discussion, Chapter 8 looks at the issue of scaling social entrepreneurship. Based on a review of different instruments social entrepreneurs can use to scale their impact, we discuss the ambivalence of this tool and show that there can also be reasons not to use scale or limit scaling.

Part IV moves down to the micro-level of analysis. It thus sheds light on the individual within social entrepreneurship. In Chapter 9, we look at how specificities of social entrepreneurship—particularly the wedding of a social mission orientation on the one hand and individual entrepreneurial agency on the other hand—can affect, both negatively and positively, individual well-being. From a well-being perspective, these features are ambivalent tools. Building our analysis on the concept of calling, we focus our discussion not only on the entrepreneurs themselves but other individuals such as employees and their families. Chapter 10 then takes up the question as to whether (and how) social entrepreneurship education can teach individuals to become social entrepreneurs. After reviewing typical personality traits, skills, and intentions of social entrepreneurs, we discuss the possibilities and limitations of teaching social entrepreneurship. We also show that if used unwisely, this tool can, again, lead to undesirable consequences.

Chapter 11 serves both to conclude the book and to bring the three levels of our analysis together. Taking a critical look at narratives in the social entrepreneurship debate, we question the widespread portrayal of social entrepreneurs as successful hero-like individuals in two regards. First, hagiographies that applaud successful social entrepreneurs overlook the huge importance of failed social entrepreneurs and social ventures. Second, with their focus on the individual, social entrepreneurship hagiographies neglect the importance of team and community enterprising. We show how uncritical social entrepreneurship narratives can lead to unintended consequences through misallocations on the macro-level, isomorphic distortions on the meso-level, and potential conflicts on the micro-level. They can also limit the effectiveness of academic research. Against this background, the chapter ends by discussing future perspective for social entrepreneurship research and practice.

We have thus organized this book along a story line that starts with the conceptual foundations and then builds our argument from the macro-level context to the micro-level of the individual. Nevertheless, we have tried to write each chapter such that it can be read as a stand-alone contribution. Readers who are interested in any particular issue might therefore jump directly into what interests them most. At the same time, organizing each chapter this way may have led to some minor redundancies. Yet, we are confident that these areas of overlap actually serve to illustrate how different aspects and levels in this book are conceptually intertwined. To highlight these relations between different concepts and links to real-life examples, we have also added various cross references in each chapter and an index at the end of the book.

Finally, as this outline shows, the motivation of this book is not to provide a comprehensive review of social entrepreneurship scholarship. In fact, our choice of topics has been deliberatively selective. Nor does this volume intend to be (yet another) textbook or a how-to-manual for social start-ups. What we do want to achieve, instead, is to offer a fresh perspective on some of the often-overlooked blind spots in social entrepreneurship. We hope to inspire a critical debate. Therefore, we welcome any feedback, particularly critical voices who point out our own blind spots.

In short, looking at social entrepreneurship from both a multi-level analysis and an ethical perspective, this book takes the reader on a journey through the 'bright side' as well as the potential 'dark side' of social entrepreneurship for societies, organizations, and individuals. As Goethe put it, "where there is much light, there is also shadow" (Goethe 1773). Highlighting both, this book not only seeks to provoke researchers and students to advance their understanding of social entrepreneurship. It also hopes to help practitioners to better realize the positive contributions of social entrepreneurship for society.

Even though we both have been doing research in this field for an entire decade, we are still fascinated by social entrepreneurship as an exciting tool to solve societal problems. Discussing the limitations and dark sides of using this tool in the wrong way does not question the potential value and promise of social entrepreneurship. On the contrary, by taking a critical perspective that seeks to understand the concept's normative ambivalence, we hope to shed light *on* social entrepreneurship in way that helps to better bring out the light *in* social entrepreneurship.

References

Ashta, Arvind, Saleh Khan, and Philipp Otto. 2011. "Does Microfinance Cause or Reduce Suicides." *Personnel* 104: 287.

Beckmann, Markus. 2011. "The Social Case as a Business Case: Making Sense of Social Entrepreneurship from an Ordonomic Perspective." In *Corporate Citizenship and New Governance: The Political Role of Corporations*, edited by Ingo Pies and Peter Koslowski, 40: 91–115. Studies in Economic Ethics and Philosophy. Dordrecht, Netherlands: Springer. https://doi.org/10.1007/978-94-007-1661-2.

———. 2012. "The Impact of Social Entrepreneurship on Societies." In *Understanding Social Entrepreneurship & Social Business—Be Part of Something Big*, edited by Christine Volkmann, Kim Oliver Tokarski, and Kati Ernst, 235–54. Wiesbaden: Gabler Verlag.

Bornstein, David. 2007. *How to Change the World: Social Entrepreneurs and the Power of Ideas*. New York, NY: Oxford University Press.

Bouckaert, Luk, and Jan Vandenhove. 1998. "Business Ethics and the Management of Non-Profit Institutions." *Journal of Business Ethics* 17: 1073–81. https://doi.org/10.1023/A:1006071416514.

Chell, Elizabeth, Laura J. Spence, Francesco Perrini, and Jared D. Harris. 2016. "Social Entrepreneurship and Business Ethics: Does Social Equal Ethical?" *Journal of Business Ethics* 133 (4): 619–25. https://doi.org/10.1007/s10551-014-2439-6.

Crane, Andrew, and Dirk Matten. 2016. *Business Ethics: Managing Corporate Citizenship and Sustainability in the Age of Globalization*. Oxford, UK: Oxford University Press.

Dacin, Peter A., M. Tina Dacin, and Marggret Matear. 2010. "Social Entrepreneurship : Why We Don' t Need a New Theory and How We Move Forward From Here." *Academy of Management Perspectives*, 37–58.

Dees, J. Gregory. 1998. "The Meaning of 'Social Entrepreneurship." www.caseat duke.org/documents/dees_sedef.pdf.

Dees, J. Gregory, Jed Emerson, and Peter Economy. 2002. *Enterprising Nonprofits: A Toolkit for Social Entrepreneurs*. Vol. 186. New York, NY: John Wiley & Sons.

Dey, Pascal. 2006. "The Rhetoric of Social Entrepreneurship: Paralogy and New Language Games in Academic Discourse." *Entrepreneurship as Social Change: A Third Movements in Entrepreneurship Book* May: 121–42.

Dey, Pascal, and Chris Steyaert. 2016. "Rethinking the Space of Ethics in Social Entrepreneurship: Power, Subjectivity, and Practices of Freedom." *Journal of Business Ethics* 133 (4): 627–41. https://doi.org/10.1007/s10551-014-2450-y.

———, eds. 2018. *Social Entrepreneurship: An Affirmative Critique*. Cheltenham, UK: Edward Elgar Publishing.

Elkington, John, and Pamela Hartigan. 2008. *The Power of Unreasonable People: How Social Entrepreneurs Create Markets That Change the World*. Boston, MA: Harvard Business Press.

Goethe, Johann Wolfgang von. 1773. *Götz von Berlichingen*. Leipzig, Germany: Reklam.

Hockerts, Kai, Johanna Mair, and Jeffrey Robinson. 2006. *Social Entrepreneurship*. London, UK: Palgrave Macmillan.

Kickul, Jill, and Thomas S. Lyons. 2016. *Understanding Social Entrepreneurship: The Relentless Pursuit of Mission in an Ever Changing World*. New York, NY: Routledge.

Leadbeater, Charles. 1997. *The Rise of the Social Entrepreneur*. London, UK: Demos.

Mair, Johanna, and Ignasi Martí. 2006. "Social Entrepreneurship Research: A Source of Explanation, Prediction, and Delight." *Journal of World Business* 41 (1): 36–44. https://doi.org/10.1016/j.jwb.2005.09.002.

Manuel, Douglas G., Kelvin Lam, Sarah Maaten, and Julie Klein-Geltink. 2006. "Venture Philanthropy and Social Entrepreneurship in Community Redevelopment." *Nonprofit Management and Leadership* 16 (3): 345–68. https://doi.org/10.1002/nml.

Nicholls, Alex. 2005. "Measuring Impact in Social Entrepreneurship: New Accountabilities to Stakeholders and Investors?" ESRC Research Seminar. Local Government Research Unit. London.

———. 2006. "Social Entrepreneurship" *Financial Times*, Prentice Hall, Inc.

———. 2009. " 'We Do Good Things, Don't We?': 'Blended Value Accounting' in Social Entrepreneurship." *Accounting, Organizations and Society* 34 (6–7). Elsevier Ltd: 755–69. https://doi.org/10.1016/j.aos.2009.04.008.

Pies, Ingo, Markus Beckmann, and Stefan Hielscher. 2014. "The Political Role of the Business Firm: An Ordonomic Concept of Corporate Citizenship Developed in Comparison with the Aristotelian Idea of Individual Citizenship." *Business and Society* 53 (2): 226–59. https://doi.org/10.1177/0007650313483484.

Pies, Ingo, Stefan Hielscher, and Markus Beckmann. 2009. "Moral Commiments and the Societal Role of Business: An Ordonomic Approach to Corporate Citizenship." *Business Ethics Quarterly* 19 (3): 375–401.

Rosling, Hans, Anna Rosling Rönnlund, and Ola Rosling. 2018. *Factfulness: Ten Reasons We're Wrong about the World—and Why Things Are Better Than You Think*. New York, NY: Flatiron Books.

Schaltegger, Stefan, Markus Beckmann, and Kai Hockerts. 2018. "Sustainable Entrepreneurship: Creating Environmental Solutions in Light of Planetary Boundaries." *International Journal of Entrepreneurial Venturing* 10 (1): 1–16.

Seelos, Christian, and Johanna Mair. 2005. "Social Entrepreneurship: Creating New Business Models to Serve the Poor." *Business Horizons* 48 (3): 241–6. https://doi.org/10.1016/j.bushor.2004.11.006.

———. 2009. "Hope for Sustainable Development : How Social Entrepreneurs Make It Happen." In *An Introduction to Social Entrepreneurship: Voice, Preconditions and Context*, edited by Rafael Ziegler, 228–46. Cheltenham, UK: Edward Elgar Publishing.

———. 2012. "Innovation Is Not the Holy Grail." *Stanford Social Innovation Review* Fall: 44–9.

Seremani, Tapiwa Winston. 2013. "The Microfinance Paradox: The Questions That Social Entrepreneurship Theory Needs to Answer." In *Social Entrepreneurship as a Catalyst for Social Change*, edited by Charles Wankel and Larry E. Pate, 165–80. Charlotte, NC: Information Age Publishing.

Tracey, Paul, and Nelson William Phillips. 2007. "The Distinctive Challenge of Educating Social Entrepreneurs : A Postscript and Rejoinder to the Special Issue on Entrepreneurship Education." *Academy of Management Learning & Education* 6 (2): 264–71. https://doi.org/10.5465/AMLE.2007.25223465.

Yunus, Muhammad. 2009. *Creating a World without Poverty: Social Business and the Future of Capitalism*. New York, NY: Public Affairs.

———. 2013. "Social Business Entrepreneurs Are the Solution." In *The Future Makers. A Journey to People Who Are Changing the World—and What We Can Learn from Them*, edited by Joanna Hafenmayer Stefanska and Wolfgang Hafenmayer, 219–25. London: Routledge.

Zeyen, Anica, Markus Beckmann, and Roya Akhavan. 2014. "Social Entrepreneurship Business Models: Managing Innovation for Social and Economic Value Creation." In *Managementperspektiven Für Die Zivilgesellschaft Des 21. Jahrhunderts*, edited by Camillo Müller and Claas-Philip Zinth, 107–32. Wiesbaden: Springer Gabler.

Part I

Social Entrepreneurship and Business Ethics

The Foundations

2 What Is Social Entrepreneurship (Not)?

The probably most frequently cited and well-known definition of social entrepreneurship is Dees' (1998): "Social entrepreneurs play the role of change agents in the social sector by: adopting a mission to create and sustain social value (not just private value); recognizing and relentlessly pursuing new opportunities to serve that mission; engaging in a process of continuous innovation, adaptation, and learning; acting boldly without being limited by resources currently in hand and exhibiting a heightened sense of accountability to the constituencies served and for the outcomes created." In his seminal work, Dees (1998) was one of the first to attempt to define the then newly emerging research phenomenon: social entrepreneurship. In the two decades since, numerous additional definitions have emerged (P. A. Dacin, Dacin, and Matear 2010; Lee 2015; Zahra et al. 2009), fueling an ongoing debate about conceptual boundaries of social entrepreneurship.

The purpose of this chapter is not to resolve this definitional debate nor to offer yet another novel definition. Rather, we aim to highlight some of the key characteristics of social entrepreneurship that are relevant to the discussion within this book. We further wish to delineate social entrepreneurship from related concepts such as corporate social responsibility (CSR) or social activism. We feel that the latter is necessary because we have personally experienced many heated debates among practitioners, students, and academics that were rooted in different understandings of the boundaries of these concepts.

2.1. Social + Entrepreneurship = Social Entrepreneurship?

In this subsection, we will dive deep into the meaning of social entrepreneurship. To this end, we will figuratively pull apart social entrepreneurship into its components *social* and *entrepreneurship*. By so doing, we will highlight some of the origins of the definitional divergence and conceptual blurriness of the social entrepreneurship concept.

2.1.1. *The Social Mission: Front and Center?*

The first question that we need to ask ourselves is: What is different about social entrepreneurship that renders it necessary to delineate it from traditional commercial entrepreneurship (Carraher, Welsh, and Svilokos 2016; Letaifa 2016)? The vast majority of the literature on social entrepreneurship agrees that its key distinguishing factor is its social mission (Alvord, Brown, and Letter 2004; Austin, Stevenson, and Wei-Skillern 2006; Bacq and Janssen 2011; Albert, Dean, and Baron 2016; Moss et al. 2011; Weerawardena and Mort 2006; Chell et al. 2016; Short, Moss, and Lumpkin 2009; Dees 1998; Zahra et al. 2009; P. A. Dacin, Dacin, and Matear 2010). As a consequence, to understand social entrepreneurship, we need to first understand the *social* of social entrepreneurship.

An admittedly broad answer to this question is the argument that social entrepreneurs follow the principle of beneficence—actively doing good—rather than the principle of nonmaleficence—doing no harm (Fisscher et al. 2015) or that social entrepreneurship is more about altruism and empathy than self-interest (Petrovskaya and Mirakyan 2018). If we rephrase this slightly, social entrepreneurship is not about value capture but about the intentional value devolution to beneficiaries (Agafonow 2015). These more abstract insights reemphasize the *centrality of the social mission* for the social venture.

The idea of a *social mission* highlights that the feature of actively doing good does not exclusively or primarily relate to the external *consequences* of entrepreneurial behavior but systematically to the primary internal *intentions* that drive it. To illustrate, take the example of telecommunication providers like AT&T, T-Mobile, Telefónica, or Vodafone. In their pursuit of outcompeting their market rivals, these companies have continuously lowered their prices for phone calls and other services. Although this behavior has negatively affected the firms' profit margins, it has, as a consequence, strongly helped many people to get (cheaper) access to communication. Despite these positive social consequences, we would hardly consider these firms to be social entrepreneurs. The reason is that the beneficial social effects of lowering the price of their own products is not the primary intention of profit-seeking firms but rather a secondary or even unintended side effect of their competitive behavior. Social entrepreneurs, in contrast, are driven by the primary intention to bring about positive social effects. Put differently, the 'social' in social entrepreneurship does not refer primarily to the consequences of entrepreneurship but to its underlying motivation (a feature that we will come back to in Section 2.2.1 when discussing the difference to CSR). The centrality of the social mission thus highlights that social entrepreneurship is not only about *helping others* but also about *primarily intending* to do so. Interestingly, in the seemingly straightforward notion of helping others also lie some of the ambiguities of the *social* in social entrepreneurship.

For one, *helping others*—the subject matter of social entrepreneurship—is not clearly defined. In fact, because it remains open who or what these 'others' are, researchers debate the breadth of issues that fall within this concept. For some, *social* exclusively or primarily refers to sustainable development challenges directly linked to human beings such as poverty, healthcare, or human rights (Seelos and Mair 2005). By this logic, the 'social' in social entrepreneurship distinguishes "helping other people" from "helping the environment." Seen from this perspective, entrepreneurs that primarily intend to address environmental issues, such as clean-tech start-ups, are then part of the remit of environmental entrepreneurship or ecopreneurship (Schaltegger 2002).

Other scholars argue that social can also mean societal in a wider sense (P. A. Dacin, Dacin, and Matear 2010). Following this line of thought, any entrepreneurial behavior addressing issues that a group of individuals—that is, society or a societal subgroup—perceives as relevant and in need of change would therefore be part of the phenomenon (P. A. Dacin, Dacin, and Matear 2010), regardless whether these issues are social (linked to individual human beings), environmental (linked to nature), or both. Despite the divergence on which issues are part of the realm of social entrepreneurship, researchers are in agreement that the issues addressed are those so far overlooked or insufficiently addressed by conventional businesses, traditional nonprofit organizations, and/or governments (Squazzoni 2008).

Second, research widely accepts the social mission of social ventures to be their key distinguishing factor (Lee 2015; P. A. Dacin, Dacin, and Matear 2010). Yet, extant literature diverges as to *how central* the social mission needs to be, particular in relation to financial objectives such as self-sustainability or profit realization. The key point of debate here is whether financial objectives should have significantly lower priority than the social mission or whether financial and social objectives can be of equal importance to the venture (Wry and York 2017). Those organizations that follow a dual mission that combines social with financial objectives are most often referred to as hybrid organizations (Johansen et al. 2015; Dufays and Huybrechts 2015; Haigh and Hoffman 2014; Grassl 2012; Battilana and Dorado 2010) and sometimes as organizations operating in the so-called gray sector (Agafonow 2015). Hybridity thus brings in shades of gray that question the boundaries of a social mission orientation. Controversial debates—not only within the academia but often also within many social ventures themselves—then circle around the question as to whether an organization still qualifies as a social venture if it issues profits to its owners, if it accepts investments from conventional financiers or if it pays above-market wages or bonuses to its employees. In all these cases, financial objectives clearly play a strong role, with some voices then asking how much financial mission is acceptable in social entrepreneurship.

So what are the implications of market-oriented financial objectives for defining the boundaries of social entrepreneurship? There are two perspectives to answer this question. Figures 2.1 and 2.2 serve to illustrate this point. The first perspective (Figure 2.1) sees mission as a one-dimensional construct in which social and financial objectives define the two opposing

Figure 2.1 Social mission and financial mission (profit) orientation as two opposing ends of the same spectrum

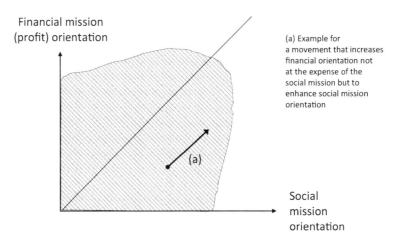

Figure 2.2 Social and financial mission orientation as a two-dimensional space

ends on the same spectrum (Dees 1996), with purely socially oriented intentions (nonprofits) being on one end of the spectrum and purely financially oriented intentions (for-profits) on the other. Hybrid organizations (but also CSR and many other phenomena) would then fall into middle positions on this spectrum.

Although categorizing missions between two such poles definitely has some value, a one-dimensional understanding suggests that financial and social objectives are purely substitutive: The more a mission focuses on financial objectives, the less it must care about social objectives and vice versa. We feel that such a one-dimensional understanding is too narrow. Entrepreneurs are often driven by various motivations simultaneously (Zeyen 2014). In our experience, we have seen some for-profit organizations that are more mission-driven to help others than self-absorbed nonprofits, thus indicating that social and financial motivations are not mutually exclusive. Moreover, a one-dimensional perspective fails to account for cases in which a stronger financial mission orientation does not substitute but actually serves the social mission (see (a) in Figure 2.2), for example when the successful integration of outside capital is used to scale an organization's social impact.

By this logic, a second perspective on hybridity sees mission as a two-dimensional construct (see Figure 2.2) in which a venture may become more financially oriented (e.g., by wanting to be attractive for investors) in its mission without necessarily losing its social mission (e.g., wanting to help others) and its centrality. Though the discussion on mission drift (Ebrahim, Battilana, and Mair 2014) shows that managing such hybridity is not easy, a two-dimensional approach allows for a richer analysis that investigates not only the strength of a venture's financial orientation but also whether or not and to what degree the financial mission serves the social mission. In this book, we will follow this second perspective. Instead of defining the social dimension in terms of a strong absence of a *financial orientation*, we do so by underlining the *social mission's presence and centrality* (illustrated by the space below the diagonal in Figure 2.2 in which the social mission is always more central than the financial orientation). In fact, as social entrepreneurs often innovate solutions that draw on resources from various sectors such as market income, public monies, or community support, their central social mission is typically paired with a certain hybridity that involves either financial or other objectives as well (Pache and Chowdhury 2012).

In short, the social in social entrepreneurship refers to intentionally solving societal problems through a central social mission.

2.1.2. *Entrepreneurship: Innovation or Market-Orientation?*

Based on the extant definitional discussion, we argue that the point of greatest divergence within the literature on social entrepreneurship revolves around the meaning of *entrepreneurship* in the context of social entrepreneurship. If we synthesize the ongoing discussion, we can identify three different interpretations of entrepreneurship. To avoid conceptual ambiguity, we consider it crucial to explicitly carve out these different notions.

1. *Entrepreneurship as enterprising.* Here, the term entrepreneurship exclusively refers to a specific funding strategy called 'earned income.' "Enterprising non-profits" (Dees, Emerson, and Economy 2002) that follow such an earned-income strategy aim to set themselves apart from traditional donor-dependent NPOs by engaging in business-like activities that create market revenue (Khieng and Dahles 2015; Swanson and Di Zhang 2010; Lepoutre et al. 2011; Mair and Martí 2006; Weerawardena and Mort 2006). Employing business-like behaviors then serves to sell products and services and thereby create the resources for pursuing a social mission. Put differently, the earned-income perspective thus equates entrepreneurship with market-revenue oriented *enterprising*. This form of social enterprising evolved due to increasingly scarce government grants and reductions in donations (Dees, Emerson, and Economy 2002). Thus, enterprising NPOs strive to create greater independence and

financial sustainability (Swanson and Di Zhang 2010). Dees and Anderson (2006) coined this the Social Enterprise School. An 'ideal' case here is the concept of a social business as developed by Muhammed Yunus (Beckmann, Zeyen, and Krzeminska 2014). For Yunus, a social business is fully independent from donations because it earns all of its income through market mechanisms. At the same time, it pursues a social purpose and reinvests any profits back into the organization to advance its social mission (Yunus 2007, 2008; Yunus, Moingeon, and Lehmann-Ortega 2010).

2. *Entrepreneurship as innovation*. In contrast to the Social Enterprise School, the Social Innovation School (Dees and Anderson 2006) understands entrepreneurship in a Schumpeterian way. For Joseph Schumpeter (1934), the godfather of entrepreneurship theory, innovation—defined as the recombination of existing materials, processes, means of production, or other factors—is the core element of entrepreneurship. Therefore, this school of thought places innovation at the core of the entrepreneurial dimension of social entrepreneurship (Hossain, Saleh, and Drennan 2017; Albert, Dean, and Baron 2016; Weerawardena and Mort 2006; Dees and Anderson 2006; Beckmann, Zeyen, and Krzeminska 2014). In comparison to the Social Enterprise School, the sources of funding are of lesser importance for this view of social entrepreneurship. This is not to say that the funding strategy is irrelevant but rather that the choice of funding follows the requirements of the innovation implemented. Whereas the Social Enterprise School thus defines a specific funding strategy (market income) as inherently desirable, the Social Innovation School takes a pragmatic approach also with regard to legal and organizational forms. If an innovation can be implemented more efficiently or effectively by using donations, the social venture would choose a nonprofit organizational form, whereas it might choose a for-profit form if that best suits its needs. In this innovation-oriented school of thought, social ventures lie on a continuum of organizational forms ranging from for-profit via hybrid to nonprofit (Khieng and Dahles 2015).

To illustrate, take the example of Jimmy Wales—the founder of Wikipedia. The innovation that Jimmy Wales had in mind was to create an open-access online encyclopedia that makes the world's knowledge available to everybody in an unbiased way. To implement this innovation, Wikipedia is built as a crowd-sourcing platform on which millions of users freely share, edit, and check content voluntarily. Although Wikipedia thus largely lives from its voluntary contributors, some financial resources are needed to operate the servers and cover overhead costs. According to the Social Enterprise School, Wikipedia should generate those funds through market income— such as usage fees or paid advertisement. Such strategies, however, would have conflicted with the innovation itself: Usage fees would restrain free access and paid advertisement could threaten the platform's independence and the volunteers' motivation to contribute. In addition, because Wikipedia needs comparably little funds, the fastest and easiest way to raise the necessary resources was to regularly ask its users for individual donations.

Fitting to Wikipedia as a crowd-based platform, this crowd-donation-based strategy was therefore the more effective and efficient instrument to achieve their mission.

The entrepreneurship-as-innovation perspective characterizes the understanding of some of the most influential organizations in the social entrepreneurship field such as Ashoka, the Skoll Foundation, and others.[1] Ashoka understands social entrepreneurs as 'change makers' that offer "new ideas for systems-level change" (Ashoka 2018) while the Skoll Foundation wants to "drive large-scale change" by investing in social entrepreneurs so as to help them "solve the world's most pressing problems" (Skoll 2018). Given grand challenges like poverty, social inequality, climate change, pollution, human rights abuse, and many more, innovations are seen as the force that can bring about large-scale positive social change through the 'creative destruction' (Schumpeter 1934) of unsustainable or unfair market, government, and bureaucracy failures (Schaltegger, Beckmann, and Hockerts 2018). It is thus this potential to "change the world" (Bornstein 2007) that connects the innovation perspective with the high expectations social entrepreneurship has created.

3. *Entrepreneurship as agency and process.* Although the entrepreneurship-as-innovation perspective focuses on the outcome that entrepreneurship generates, the third perspective analyzes entrepreneurship by specifying how and by whom innovations are brought about. In this view, the process and agency involved in opportunity recognition receive significant attention (e.g., Robinson 2006). In this context, scholars draw on the distinction between effectuation and causation (Perry, Chandler, and Markova 2012) where the former refers to shaping an opportunity based on available resources and the latter to recognizing opportunities and then searching for necessary resources to implement them. Social entrepreneurs are most commonly described as effectuating opportunities (Corner and Ho 2010; Christopoulos and Vogl 2015; Bacq and Janssen 2011). Additionally, some scholars define entrepreneurship very broadly by linking it to the founding process of a new venture (Sternberg and Wennekers 2005; Bacq, Hartog, and Hoogendoorn 2016). The entrepreneurship-as-agency-and-process perspective is thus closely related to the social innovation perspective insofar as the realization of novel opportunities is often based on or leads to innovations. At the same time, the agency-and-process-oriented perspective highlights that entrepreneurship occurs when individual actors (or groups of actors) find or invent opportunities, take risks to seize them, and start processes and often new organizations to implement innovations.

In short, there are three ways of understanding entrepreneurship in the context of social entrepreneurship: as a specific funding strategy, as innovation, or as the process of recognizing and acting on opportunities. Although the first is too narrow for the purpose of this book, we will draw on both the entrepreneurship-as-innovation and entrepreneurship-as-agency-and-process perspective in our analysis. As this book intends to show, both the oft-discussed bright side of social entrepreneurship as well as many of its ethical ambivalences are strongly connected not only to the social mission but also to the focus on innovation and individual change agents who bring them about.

2.1.3. *Social Entrepreneurship: Key Points for This Book*

Against the foregone discussions, we consider the following key characteristics of social entrepreneurship most relevant for our future discussions: (1) central social mission; (2) societal problem can be social or environmental (or both); (3) innovative solution to address set societal challenge; (4) nonprofit, hybrid, or for-profit organization founded; and (5) entrepreneurial agency. Though we concede that these characteristics are quite broad, we nonetheless believe that they will enable us to gain greater insights into the normative ambivalences of social entrepreneurship. Moreover, a degree of conceptual openness is necessary to allow for cross-country and cross-cultural analysis of social entrepreneurship as a global definition is not possible (Bidet, Eum, and Ryu 2018).

To illustrate the interplay of the key characteristics just described, take the example of Dialogue Social Enterprises (Heinecke and Sonne 2012; Heinecke 2011; Dialogue in the Dark India 2013 for more; see also Chapter 8). Andreas Heinecke, the founder of Dialogue Social Enterprises, originally worked in a news agency. One day, he was assigned to supervise a blind trainee. He describes this moment as overwhelming because he had no experience of engaging with people living with vision impairment. Based on his own experience and the desire to change the status quo, Heinecke decided to found Dialogue Social Enterprises (DSE) in Hamburg, Germany (characteristic 5). DSE uses exhibitions in complete darkness to raise public awareness about living with blindness and to provide qualified jobs for people with visual impairments. DSE met a societal need (characteristic 2) that was so far unaddressed in the German context. Moreover, the concept of using exhibitions in the dark with blind guides was highly innovative (characteristic 3). DSE chose a socially oriented for-profit business as its legal form (characteristic 4) and reinvests all profits back into furthering its social mission (characteristic 1).

These five key characteristics inform the discussions in the remainder of the book. In order to gain a deeper understanding into how social entrepreneurs, their mission, and innovations affect society, Part II of this book will closely analyze social entrepreneurship from a macro-environmental perspective. The specific mission as well as the corresponding diversity of funding sources and organizational forms lead to unique management challenges for social ventures. These range from their business model (Chapter 6) to internal performance (impact) measurement (Chapter 7) and growth (scaling) strategies (Chapter 8). Thus, Part III will take a meso-level view and shed light on these questions from an organizational level. As just highlighted from the entrepreneurship-as-agency-and-process perspective, the entrepreneur or entrepreneurial team are key actors in the process of entrepreneurship because they are the ones recognizing and shaping opportunities and engaging in the entrepreneurial process. To further our understanding on the individuals involved in social entrepreneurship, Part IV of this book follows a micro-level perspective.

2.2. Same-Same but Different: Social Entrepreneurship Is Not. . .

Before diving into an in-depth analysis of social entrepreneurship at a macro-, meso- and micro-levels, we deem it essential to delineate social entrepreneurship from two concepts that it is often conflated with: corporate social responsibility and activism or social movements.

2.2.1. Social Entrepreneurship Is Not Corporate Social Responsibility

Although *social* entrepreneurship and corporate *social* responsibility (CSR) share their emphasis on the societal dimension of economic endeavors, there are important differences between them (Zeyen and Beckmann 2018; Beckmann and Zeyen 2015). CSR is the voluntarily pursuit of social and/or environmental actions by for-profit firms (Crane, Matten, and Spence 2013). As discussed earlier, social entrepreneurship uses innovation to solve societal problems so far not properly addressed (Dacin, Dacin, and Tracey 2011; Dees 1998; Short, Moss, and Lumpkin 2009) and can manifest itself in both nonprofit and for-profit forms. So where is the conceptual difference?

On a more abstract level, CSR and social entrepreneurship differ in their means and ends—their *tools* and *objectives*, so to speak—with regard to the role of economic value creation and the satisfaction of societal needs (Beckmann 2011; Zeyen, Beckmann, and Akhavan 2014). For profit-seeking corporations, the creation (and capture) of economic value represents the formal *objective* of the firm: The corporate objective function is profit or value maximization (Jensen 2002). CSR then constitutes a qualifier of *how* companies obtain economic value. The CSR concept reflects that respecting and meeting societal needs is instrumental for a firm to be able to create value in the long term. CSR thus describes the *tools* of how to achieve the objective of economic value in an ethical, social, and environmentally friendly way. In comparison, the *objective* of social entrepreneurship is solving or alleviating a societal problem. Social entrepreneurship then constitutes a qualifier of *how* this mission is implemented. The social entrepreneurship approach reflects that generating economic value is instrumental for delivering and scaling innovative solutions that meet societal needs. For social entrepreneurs, economic value creation is not an objective in itself but rather a *tool* to further their social mission. They use innovation and economic value creation—either through nonprofit or for-profit resources—to achieve their mission (Zeyen and Beckmann 2018).

Table 2.1 Conceptual differences between social entrepreneurship and CSR

	Social Entrepreneurship	Corporate Social Responsibility
"Social" refers more to	What (target)	How (means)
Actor focus is on	Person	Organization
Width of the thematic focus	Narrow	Wide
Role of external expectations	Low	High
Degree of institutionalization	Low	High

(adapted from Zeyen and Beckmann (2011))

Based on the abstract distinction between social entrepreneurship and CSR, we can derive further differences (Beckmann and Zeyen 2015) which table 2.1 serves to summarize.

First, social entrepreneurship has a much stronger focus on *individual actors* and their agency. This is reflected in the ever expanding literature on social entrepreneurial motivation and personality (e.g., André and Pache 2016; Boluk and Mottiar 2014; Zeyen 2014; Christopoulos and Vogl 2015; McMullen and Bergman 2017). In comparison, CSR takes an organizational viewpoint that highlights the role of *corporate actors*.

Second, the breadth of topics addressed by social ventures and CSR vary significantly (Beckmann and Zeyen 2015). Social entrepreneurs innovate solutions to address specific societal challenges. As a consequence, most social ventures have a very specialized, often single-issue focus (for more see Section 6.3.3). For instance, Specialisterne, a Danish social venture, supports people with autism in acquiring jobs in the IT industry (Specialisterne 2013 and see Section 9.3) whereas Comfort Cases—a US-based social venture—provides special suitcases to children in the foster care system to provide them with essential care and to avoid the continued, yet humiliating, use of garbage bags to store and transport the children's belongings (comfort case 2018). In comparison, CSR looks at how corporate activities along the entire value chain interact with the entire breadth of the sustainable development goals (SDGs) (SDG 2018). As a result, CSR has by nature a broad perspective that addresses economic, social, and environmental goals simultaneously (Porter and Kramer 2011; Porter and Kramer 2006; Crane, Matten, and Spence 2013). Thus, CSR is a generalist approach whereas social entrepreneurship is a specialist approach.

Third, external expectations affect social entrepreneurship and CSR differently (Beckmann and Zeyen 2015). Social entrepreneurs often have not yet formed a significant public appearance and thus face fewer expectations by various stakeholder groups (Zeyen, Beckmann, and Akhavan 2014). In comparison, firms engaging in CSR activities often face more expectations from external stakeholders (Freeman and Reed 1983; Agle et al. 2008; Freeman 1984; Wicks, Gilbert, and Freeman 1994; Balzarova and Castka

2012; Jensen 2002). This is not least the case due to the breadth of topics they address. Moreover, CSR is much more concerned with the principle of "do no harm." As illustrated by Carroll's (1991) famous CSR pyramid, the lower foundations of CSR are first to avoid doing harm by violating legal or ethical norms before doing good by contributing philanthropically to the community. Social entrepreneurship, on the other hand, starts with actively doing good, which is often desired by society but less expected than avoiding harm.

Fourth, CSR has a higher degree of institutionalization. In contrast, there are no established standards for social entrepreneurship. Although various impact measurement tools have been developed in the field of social entrepreneurship (Bengo et al. 2016; Chmelik, Musteen, and Ahsan 2016 and see Chapter 7), their degree of institutionalization is low. In comparison, the CSR field has developed many standards ranging from those issued by the International Organization of Standards (ISO) like ISO 26.000 (Castka et al. 2004; Moratis 2017) to multi-stakeholder initiatives such as the Marine Stewardship Council (MSC) (Zeyen, Beckmann, and Wolters 2016; Mena and Palazzo 2012; Rasche 2012; Sethi and Schepers 2013; Potoski and Prakash 2009) or the Global Reporting Initiative that spells out areas and metrics for CSR in detail.

In sum, social entrepreneurship and CSR are two related, yet uniquely distinct concepts that investigate different empirical phenomena. Although CSR looks at firm-level broad sustainability-related activities, social entrepreneurship research investigates mostly single-issue activities driven by individual actors.

2.2.2. Social Entrepreneurship Is Not Activism!?

As briefly shown in Section 2.2.1, the distinction between social entrepreneurship and CSR has reasonably clear boundaries. In the context of social entrepreneurship and social movements/activism, the boundaries are slightly more blurred.

Analogous to the distinction between CSR and social entrepreneurship, the analysis of the respective tools and objectives can help to clarify the difference between activism and social entrepreneurship. With regard to the pursued objective, both concepts share the same goals: to bring about positive societal change (Martin and Osberg 2007). With regard to the employed tools, however, both concepts differ in how they try to achieve this. Whereas social entrepreneurs use their own agency to found organizations and to *directly* provide the solutions to the problems they identified (P. A. Dacin, Dacin, and Matear 2010), activists use an *indirect* strategy by appealing to third parties to bring about systemic change or to change their behavior (Martin and Osberg 2007). Common examples are calls to boycott certain companies to coerce them to change their operations or demonstrations and protests to demand changes in laws and policies. Take the example of the anti-nuclear power movement in Germany. After the tsunami devastated Fukushima (Japan), German energy users organized protests against the use of nuclear power, which eventually led to Germany phasing out nuclear power completely (Strunz 2014). This is a prime example of traditional activism. Protestors could not simply go up to a nuclear power station and turn it off directly. Leaving aside the legal implications of such behaviors, it would have been highly risky because turning off nuclear power stations needs to follow strict protocols. Therefore, they chose an indirect strategy and pressured others who held the power to enact change—in this case, the German federal government—to change their policies. In this scenario, going through the process of founding an organization that directly provides the novel solutions or the desired change would not have been possible. Against the background of such examples, the line between social entrepreneurship and activism is clear-cut. Social entrepreneurs address the need for societal change by directly providing their own solution whereas activists choose the indirect means of pressuring others to deliver the desired societal change (Martin and Osberg 2007).

The above notwithstanding, there are certain types of activism where the boundaries between both concepts are fuzzier. In these cases, social entrepreneurship and activism go hand in hand, and it is therefore challenging to clearly point to where one type of social change activity ends and where the other one starts. A case in point is the Arab Spring (Elsayed 2018). Elsayed argues that social entrepreneurship is a way of directly enacting political change in developing countries. During this turbulent time in Egypt, human rights activists would not only protest for changes to governmental policies but simultaneously engage in social entrepreneurship. They would provide medical and financial care to protestors and their families as well as take care of food and legal proceedings in case of arrests. An example here is the movement "OpAntiSH"—a movement against sexual harassment, a problem very common during the protests on Tahrir Square. This group started as an online campaign to raise awareness but then 'spilled over' into the offline world by directly offering interventions on the ground. These intervention teams would wear similarly looking T-shirts and help women who felt harassed by taking them to safe places (Azer 2016). In this and similar situations, the social entrepreneurship arm of the movement was a prerequisite for the activism to be feasible (Azer 2016).

Social entrepreneurship and activism thus often complement each other. On the one hand, as seen in the Arab Spring example, social entrepreneurs can directly provide services such as education, human rights, or communication training and medical and legal care that contribute to building the civil society capacities needed for social activism. On the other hand, social activism may be necessary to change the political and legal landscape in a way that creates the freedoms and opportunities social entrepreneurs need to innovate and deliver their solutions. One example that illustrates this interplay is the case of Ursula Sladek and EWS Schönau, a German cooperative that has innovated renewable energy solutions since the late 1990s (Schwartz 2012, chapter 1). Inspired by the anti-nuclear social movement, Ursula Sladek and other citizens in Schönau, a small town in southwestern Germany, protested that their local energy provider forced them to use and support electricity generated by nuclear power. Given the market regulation at the time, however, alternative energy providers were not allowed, thus making it impossible for Sladek and her fellow social entrepreneurs to directly offer renewable energy services. As a consequence, Sladek and other citizens of Schönau first engaged in social activism by starting (and eventually winning) several plebiscites that changed local market regulation and allowed the citizens to take over the municipal energy provider as a cooperative. After this legal change was brought about, Sladek and her cooperative could now engage in social entrepreneurship by directly implementing the local transition toward renewable energies.

Social activism and entrepreneurship are thus closely related, yet differ in the way they bring about societal change. In this book on social entrepreneurship, we focus on how change can be brought about by the direct provision of innovative solutions. For this purpose, we also include new forms of social movements that are linked to direct services as part of the social entrepreneurship debate but exclude traditional forms of activism and movements. In other words, we include social activism if it includes activities that go beyond pressuring others but include those that entail on the ground service provision for beneficiaries.

2.3. Conclusion

This chapter started off by pulling apart the term 'social entrepreneurship' into its components to pinpoint some of the definitional debates in extant research. We have highlighted that the 'social' in social entrepreneurship relates to the primary intention or mission of helping others, raising follow-up questions about both the content of this mission and its relationship to other objectives. Similarly, we have reviewed three understandings of 'entrepreneurship' within the literature on social entrepreneurship and that this is one of the main causes of the ongoing definitional debate. In a second step, we elaborated on how social entrepreneurship differs from corporate social responsibility and social activism. In both regards, we introduced the distinction between tools and objectives to show how these concepts, though closely related, differ from social entrepreneurship in how they define either the ultimate objectives pursued or the instruments used to achieve them.

Based on these discussions, we identified five key characteristics for social entrepreneurship that are most relevant for the purpose of this book: (1) central social mission to solve or alleviate a societal problem; (2) societal problem can be social, environmental, or both; (3) innovative solution to directly address their societal challenge; (4) nonprofit, hybrid, or for-profit organization founded; and (5) entrepreneurial agency including willingness to take risks.

Defining social entrepreneurship, this way does not pretend to present the one, true way to understand this phenomenon. In fact, we have left out certain elements of the definitional debate and put specific emphasis on others. We have done so with regard to the specific purpose of this book. Social entrepreneurship has gained attention as an exciting and powerful force for good. And, of course, who could be against changemakers who solve pressing societal problems? The starting point of this book, however, is that social entrepreneurship—just like almost any other phenomenon—not only has positive features but also has its limitations and potential downsides. We will show how the very definitional components discussed in this chapter—such as the social mission or the focus on innovation, risk-taking, and just-do-it individual agency—contribute to social entrepreneurship being a normatively ambivalent phenomenon: with a bright side but also a dark side of the force. In the following chapter, we introduce this concept of normative ambivalence in more detail and show how it can guide both our scholarly analysis and practical management of social entrepreneurship.

Note

1. See www.ashoka.org and skoll.org.

References

Agafonow, Alejandro. 2015. "Value Creation, Value Capture, and Value Devolution: Where Do Social Enterprises Stand?" *Administration and Society* 47 (8): 1038–60. doi:10.1177/0095399714555756.

Agle, Bradley R., Thomas Donaldson, R. Edward Freeman, Michael C. Jensen, Ronald K. Mitchell, and Donna J. Wood. 2008. "Dialogue: Toward Superior Stakeholder Theory." *Business Ethics Quarterly* 18 (2): 153–90. doi:10.5840/beq200818214.

Albert, Lumina S., Thomas J. Dean, and Robert A. Baron. 2016. "From Social Value to Social Cognition: How Social Ventures Obtain the Resources They Need for Social Transformation." *Journal of Social Entrepreneurship* 7 (3). Taylor & Francis: 289–311. doi:10.1080/19420676.2016.1188323.

Alvord, S. H., L. David Brown, and Christine W. Letter. 2004. "Social Entrepreneurship and Societal Transformation: An Exploratory Study." *Journal of Applied Behavioral Science* 40 (3): 260–82. doi:10.1177/0021886304266847.

André, Kevin, and Anne-Claire Pache. 2016. "From Caring Entrepreneur to Caring Enterprise: Addressing the Ethical Challenges of Scaling up Social Enterprises." *Journal of Business Ethics* 133 (4): 659–75. doi:10.1007/s10551-014-2445-8.

Ashoka. 2018. "Social Entrepreneurship | Ashoka | Everyone a Changemaker." June 24. www.ashoka.org/en/focus/social-entrepreneurship.

Austin, James, Howard Stevenson, and Jane Wei-Skillern. 2006. "Social and Commercial Entrepreneurship: Same, Different, or Both?" *Entrepreneurship Theory and Practice* 47 (3): 1–22. doi:10.5700/rausp1055.

Azer, Evronia. 2016. "A Different Type of Responsible Entrepreneurship: Interview on Activism in Egypt." Interview done by Anica Zeyen. London, UK. Not published.

Bacq, Sophie, Chantal Hartog, and Brigitte Hoogendoorn. 2016. "Beyond the Moral Portrayal of Social Entrepreneurs: An Empirical Approach to Who They Are and What Drives Them." *Journal of Business Ethics* 133 (4). Springer Netherlands: 703–18. doi:10.1007/s10551-014-2446-7.

Bacq, Sophie, and F. Janssen. 2011. "The Multiple Faces of Social Entrepreneurship: A Review of Definitional Issues Based on Geographical and Thematic Criteria." *Entrepreneurship & Regional Development* 23 (5–6): 373–403. doi:10.1080/089 85626.2011.577242.

Balzarova, Michaela A., and Pavel Castka. 2012. "Stakeholders' Influence and Contribution to Social Standards Development: The Case of Multiple Stakeholder Approach to ISO 26000 Development." *Journal of Business Ethics* 111 (2): 265–79. doi:10.1007/s10551-012-1206-9.

Battilana, Julie, and Silvia Dorado. 2010. "Building Sustainable Hybrid Organizations: The Case of Commercial Microfinance Organizations." *Academy of Management Journal* 53 (6): 1419–40.

Beckmann, Markus. 2011. "The Social Case as a Business Case: Making Sense of Social Entrepreneurship from an Ordonomic Perspective." In *Corporate Citizenship and New Governance: The Political Role of Corporations*, edited by Ingo Pies and Peter Koslowski, 40: 91–115. Studies in Economic Ethics and Philosophy. Dordrecht, Netherlands: Springer. doi:10.1007/978-94-007-1661-2.

Beckmann, Markus, and Anica Zeyen. 2015. "Social Entrepreneurship und Corporate Social Responsibility." In *CSR—ein integraler Bestandteil der Management- und Managerausbildung*, edited by Andreas Schneider and René Schmidpeter, 161–76. Berlin, Heidelberg: Springer. doi:0.1007/978-3-662-43483-3_11.

Beckmann, Markus, Anica Zeyen, and Anna Krzeminska. 2014. "Mission, Finance, and Innovation: The Similarities and Differences between Social Entrepreneurship and Social Business." In *Social Business*, edited by Andrea Grove and Gary A. Berg, 23–41. Berlin, Heidelberg: Springer. doi:10.1007/978-3-642-45275-8_2.

Bengo, Irene, Marika Arena, Giovanni Azzone, and Mario Calderini. 2016. "Indicators and Metrics for Social Business: A Review of Current Approaches." *Journal of Social Entrepreneurship* 7 (1). Taylor & Francis: 1–24. doi:10.1080/1942067 6.2015.1049286.

Bidet, Eric, Hyungsik Eum, and Jieun Ryu. 2018. "Diversity of Social Enterprise Models in South Korea." *VOLUNTAS: International Journal of Voluntary and Nonprofit Organizations*, January. Springer US. doi:10.1007/s11266-018-9951-8.

Boluk, Karla Aileen, and Ziene Mottiar. 2014. "Motivations of Social Entrepreneurs: Blurring the Social Contribution and Profits Dichotomy." *Social Enterprise Journal* 10 (1): 53–68. doi:10.1108/SEJ-01-2013-0001.

Bornstein, David. 2007. *How to Change the World: Social Entrepreneurs and the Power of Ideas*. New York, NY: Oxford University Press.

Carraher, Shawn M., Dianne H. B. Welsh, and Andrew Svilokos. 2016. "Validation of a Measure of Social Entrepreneurship." *European J. International Management* 10 (4): 386–402. doi:10.1504/EJIM.2016.077421 M4 — Citavi.

Carroll, Archie B. 1991. "The Pyramid of Corporate Social Responsibiiity: Toward the Moral Management of Organizational Stakeholders." *Business Horizons* 34: 39–48. doi:10.1177/0312896211432941.

Castka, Pavel, Christopher J. Bamber, David J. Bamber, and John M. Sharp. 2004. "Integrating Corporate Social Responsibility (CSR) into ISO Management Systems—in Search of a Feasible CSR Management System Framework." *The TQM Magazine* 16 (3): 216–24. doi:10.1108/09544780410532954.

Chell, Elizabeth, Laura J. Spence, Francesco Perrini, and Jared D. Harris. 2016. "Social Entrepreneurship and Business Ethics: Does Social Equal Ethical?" *Journal of Business Ethics* 133 (4): 619–25. doi:10.1007/s10551-014-2439-6.

Chmelik, Erin, Martina Musteen, and Mujtaba Ahsan. 2016. "Measures of Performance in the Context of International Social Ventures: An Exploratory Study." *Journal of Social Entrepreneurship* 7 (1). Taylor & Francis: 74–100. doi:10.1080/19420676.2014.997781.

Christopoulos, Dimitris, and Susanne Vogl. 2015. "The Motivation of Social Entrepreneurs: The Roles, Agendas and Relations of Altruistic Economic Actors." *Journal of Social Entrepreneurship* 6 (1): 1–30. doi:10.1080/19420676.2014.954254.

Comfort Cases. 2018. "Comfort Cases—Homepage." June 1. https://www.comfort cases.org/.

Corner, Patricia Doyle, and Marcus Ho. 2010. "How Opportunities Develop in Social Entrepreneurship." *Entrepreneurship Theory and Practice* 34 (4): 635–59. doi:10.1111/j.1540-6520.2010.00382.x.

Crane, Andrew, Dirk Matten, and Laura J. Spence. 2013. *Corporate Social Responsibility: Readings and Cases in a Global Context.* 2nd ed. London: Routledge.

Dacin, M. Tina, Peter A. Dacin, and Paul Tracey. 2011. "Social Entrepreneurship: A Critique and Future Directions." *Organization Science* 22 (5): 1203–13. doi:10.1287/orsc.1100.0620.

Dacin, Peter A., M. Tina Dacin, and Marggret Matear. 2010. "Social Entrepreneurship : Why We Don't Need a New Theory and How We Move Forward From Here." *Academy of Management Perspectives*, 37–58.

Dees, J. Gregory. 1996. "The Social Enterprise Spectrum: Philanthropy to Commerce." *Harvard Business Review* May: 1–7.

———. 1998. "The Meaning of 'Social Entrepreneurship'." www.caseatduke.org/documents/dees_sedef.pdf.

Dees, J. Gregory, and Beth Battle Anderson. 2006. "Framing a Theory of Social Entrepreneurship: Building on Two Schools of Practice and Thought." In *Research on Social Entrepreneurship: Understanding and Contributing to an Emerging Field*, edited by Rachel Mosher-Williams, 39–66. Indianapolis, IN: ARNOVA.

Dees, J. Gregory, Jed Emerson, and Peter Economy. 2002. *Enterprising Nonprofits: A Toolkit for Social Entrepreneurs.* Vol. 186. New York, NY: John Wiley & Sons.

Dialogue in the Dark India. 2013. "Home." May 15. www.dialogueinthedarkindia.com/.

Dufays, Frédéric, and Benjamin Huybrechts. 2015. "Where Do Hybrids Come from? Entrepreneurial Team Heterogeneity as an Avenue for the Emergence of Hybrid Organizations." *International Small Business Journal* 34 (6): 777–96 doi:10.1177/0266242615585152.

Ebrahim, Alnoor, Julie Battilana, and Johanna Mair. 2014. "The Governance of Social Enterprises: Mission Drift and Accountability Challenges in Hybrid Organizations." *Research in Organizational Behavior* 34. Elsevier Ltd: 81–100. doi:10.1016/j.riob.2014.09.001.

Elsayed, Yomna. 2018. "At the Intersection of Social Entrepreneurship and Social Movements: The Case of Egypt and the Arab Spring." *VOLUNTAS: International Journal of Voluntary and Nonprofit Organizations.* Online first. Springer US: :1–13. doi:10.1007/s11266-017-9943-0.

Fisscher, Olaf, David Frenkel, Yotam Lurie, and Andre Nijhof. 2015. "Stretching the Frontiers: Exploring the Relationships between Entrepreneurship and Ethics." *Journal of Busines Ethics* 60 (3): 207–9.

Freeman, R. Edward. 1984. *Strategic Management: A Stakeholder Approach*. Boston, MA: Pitman.

Freeman, R. Edward, and David L. Reed. 1983. "Stockholders and Stakeholders: A New Perspective on Corporate Governance." *California Management Review* XXV (3): 88–106.

Grassl, Wolfgang. 2012. "Business Models of Social Enterprise : A Design Approach" 1 (1): 37–60.

Haigh, Nardia, and Andrew J. Hoffman. 2014. "The New Heretics: Hybrid Organizations and the Challenges They Present to Corporate Sustainability." *Organization & Environment* 27 (3): 223–41. doi:10.1177/1086026614545345.

Heinecke, Andreas. 2011. "Interview with Andreas Heinecke, Founder of Dialogue Social Enterprise." Interview done by Anna Krzeminska, Vienna, Austria: unpublished.

Heinecke, Andreas, and Tholkil Sonne. 2012. "Meeting Notes from a Meeting with the Founders of Dialogue Social Enterprise and Specialisterne." Interview done by Anna Krzeminska, at the premises of Dialogue in the Dark in Hamburg.

Hossain, Sayem, M. Abu Saleh, and Judy Drennan. 2017. "A Critical Appraisal of the Social Entrepreneurship Paradigm in an International Setting: A Proposed Conceptual Framework." *International Entrepreneurship and Management Journal* 13 (2): 347–68. doi:10.1007/s11365-016-0400-0.

Jensen, Michael C. 2002. "Value Maximization, Stakeholder Theory, and the Corporate Objective Function." *Business Ethics Quarterly* 12 (2): 235–56.

Johansen, Svein T., Trude H. Olsen, Elsa Solstad, and Harald Torsteinsen. 2015. "An Insider View of the Hybrid Organisation: How Managers Respond to Challenges of Ef? Ciency, Legitimacy and Meaning." *Journal of Management & Organization* 21 (6): 725–40. doi:10.1017/jmo.2015.1.

Khieng, Sothy, and Heidi Dahles. 2015. "Commercialization in the Non-Profit Sector: The Emergence of Social Enterprise in Cambodia." *Journal of Social Entrepreneurship* 6 (2). Taylor & Francis: 218–43. doi:10.1080/19420676.2014.954261.

Lee, I. 2015. "A Social Enterprise Business Model for Social Entrepreneurs: Theoretical Foundations and Model Development." *International Journal of Social Entrepreneurship And Innovation* 3 (4).

Lepoutre, Jan, Rachida Justo, Siri Terjesen, and Niels Bosma. 2013. "Designing a Global Standardized Methodology for Measuring Social Entrepreneurship Activity: The Global Entrepreneurship Monitor Social Entrepreneurship Study." *Small Business Economics* 40 (3): 693–714. doi:10.1007/s11187-011-9398-4.

Letaifa, Soumaya Ben. 2016. "How Social Entrepreneurship Emerges, Develops and Internationalises during Political and Economic Transitions." *European Journal of International Management* 10 (4): 455. doi:10.1504/EJIM.2016.077424.

Mair, Johanna, and Ignasi Martí. 2006. "Social Entrepreneurship Research: A Source of Explanation, Prediction, and Delight." *Journal of World Business* 41 (1): 36–44. doi:10.1016/j.jwb.2005.09.002.

Martin, Roger L., and Sally Osberg. 2007. "Social Entrepreneurship : The Case for Definition." *Stanford Social Innovation Review* Spring: 29–39.

McMullen, Jeffery S., and Brian J. Bergman. 2017. "Social Entrepreneurship and the Development Paradox of Prosocial Motivation: A Cautionary Tale." *Strategic Entrepreneurship Journal* 11 (3): 243–70. doi:10.1002/sej.1263.

Mena, Sebastien, and Guido Palazzo. 2012. "Input and Output Legitimacy of Multi-Stakeholder Initiatives." *Business Ethics Quarterly* 22 (3): 527–56. doi:10.5840/beq201222333.

Moratis, Lars. 2017. "The Credibility of Corporate CSR Claims: A Taxonomy Based on ISO 26000 and a Research Agenda." *Total Quality Management & Business Excellence* 28 (1–2): 147–58. doi:10.1080/14783363.2015.1050179.

Moss, Todd W., Jeremy C. Short, G. Tyge Payne, and G. T. Lumpkin. 2011. "Dual Identities in Social Ventures: An Exploratory Study." *Entrepreneurship Theory and Practice* 35 (4): 805–30. doi:10.1111/j.1540-6520.2010.00372.x.

Pache, A. C., and I. Chowdhury. 2012. "Social Entrepreneurs as Institutionally Embedded Entrepreneurs: Toward a New Model of Social Entrepreneurship Education." *Academy of Management Learning & Education* 11 (3): 494–510. doi:10.5465/amle.2011.0019.

Perry, John T., Gaylen N. Chandler, and Gergana Markova. 2012. "Entrepreneurial Effectuation: A Review and Suggestions for Future Research." *Entrepreneurship Theory and Practice* 36 (4): 837–61. doi:10.1111/j.1540-6520.2010.00435.x.

Petrovskaya, Irina, and Araksya Mirakyan. 2018. "A Mission of Service: Social Entrepreneur as a Servant Leader." *International Journal of Entrepreneurial Behaviour and Research* 24 (3): 755–67. doi:10.1108/IJEBR-02-2016-0057.

Porter, Michael E., and Mark R. Kramer. 2006. "Strategy and Society. The Link between Competitive Advantage and Corporate Social Responsibility." *Harvard Business Review* 84 (12): 78–92.

———. 2011. "Creating Shared Value." *Harvard Business Review* January–February: 1–17.

Potoski, Matthew, and Aseem Prakash. 2009. *Voluntary Programs: A Club Theory Perspective*. Cambridge, MA: MIT Press.

Rasche, Andreas. 2012. "Global Policies and Local Practices: Loose and Tight Couplings in Multi-Stakeholder Initiatives." *Business Ethics Quarterly* 22 (4): 679–708.

Robinson, Jeffrey. 2006. "Navigating Social and Institutional Barriers to Markets: How Social Entrepreneurs Identify and Evaluate Opportunities." In *Social Entrepreneurship*, 95–120. London: Palgrave Macmillan. doi:10.1057/9780230625655_7.

Schaltegger, Stefan. 2002. "A Framework for Ecopreneurship: Leading Bioneers and Environmental Managers to ecopreneurship." *Greener Management International* 38: 45–58.

Schaltegger, Stefan, Markus Beckmann, and Kai Hockerts. 2018. "Sustainable Entrepreneurship: Creating Environmental Solutions in Light of Planetary Boundaries." *International Journal of Entrepreneurial Venturing* 10 (1): 1–16.

Schumpeter, Joseph. 1934. *The Theory of Economic Development*. Cambridge, MA: Harvard University Press.

Schwartz, Beverly. 2012. *Rippling: How Social Entrepreneurs Spread Innovation throughout the World*. Hoboken, NJ: John Wiley & Sons.

SDG. 2018. "United Nations Sustainable Development Goals." September 13, https://www.un.org/sustainabledevelopment/sustainable-development-goals/

Seelos, Christian, and Johanna Mair. 2005. "Social Entrepreneurship: Creating New Business Models to Serve the Poor." *Business Horizons* 48 (3): 241–6. doi:10.1016/j.bushor.2004.11.006.

Sethi, S. Prakash, and Donald H. Schepers. 2013. "United Nations Global Compact: The Promise—Performance Gap." *Journal of Business Ethics* 122 (2): 193–208.

Short, Jeremy C., Todd W. Moss, and G. T. Lumpkin. 2009. "Research in Social Entrepreneurship: Past Contributions and Future Opportunities." *Strategic Entrepreneurship Journal* 3 (2): 161–94. doi:10.1002/sej.69.

Skoll. 2018. "Skoll | Social Entrepreneurs Driving Large Scale Change." August 3. http://skoll.org/.

Specialisterne. 2013. "Specialisterne." May 3. http://specialisterne.com/.

Squazzoni, F. 2008. "Social Entrepreneurship and Economic Development in Silicon Valley: A Case Study on The Joint Venture: Silicon Valley Network." *Nonprofit and Voluntary Sector Quarterly* 38 (5): 869–83. doi:10.1177/0899764008326198.

Sternberg, Rolf, and Sander Wennekers. 2005. "Determinants and Effects of New Business Creation Using Global Entrepreneurship Monitor Data." *Small Business Economics* 24 (3): 193–203.

Strunz, Sebastian. 2014. "The German Energy Transition as a Regime Shift." *Ecological Economics* 100. Elsevier BV: 150–8. doi:10.1016/j.ecolecon.2014.01.019.

Swanson, Lee A., and David Di Zhang. 2010. "The Social Entrepreneurship Zone." *Journal of Nonprofit & Public Sector Marketing* 22 (2): 71–88. doi:10.1080/10495140903550726.

Weerawardena, Jay, and Gillian Sullivan Mort. 2006. "Investigating Social Entrepreneurship: A Multidimensional Model." *Journal of World Business* 41 (1): 21–35. doi:10.1016/j.jwb.2005.09.001.

Wicks, Andrew C., Daniel R. Gilbert, and R. Edward Freeman. 1994. "A Feminist Reinterpretation of the Stakeholder Concept." *Business Ethics Quarterly* 4 (4): 475–97. doi:10.2307/3857345.

Wry, Tyler, and Jeffrey G. York. 2017. "An Identity-Based Approach to Social Enterprise." *The Academy of Management Review* 42 (3): 437–60. doi:10.5465/amr.2013.0506.

Yunus, Muhammad. 2007. *Creating a World Without Poverty: How Social Business Can Transform Our Lives: Social Business and the Future of Capitalism.* New York, NY: PublicAffairs.

———. 2008. "Economic Security for a World in Crisis." *World Policy Journal*, 5–12.

Yunus, Muhammad, Bertrand Moingeon, and Laurence Lehmann-Ortega. 2010. "Building Social Business Models: Lessons from the Grameen Experience." *Long Range Planning* 43 (2–3). Elsevier Ltd: 308–25. doi:10.1016/j.lrp.2009.12.005.

Zahra, Shaker A., Eric Gedajlovic, Donald O. Neubaum, and Joel M. Shulman. 2009. "A Typology of Social Entrepreneurs: Motives, Search Processes and Ethical Challenges." *Journal of Business Venturing* 24 (5): 519–32. doi:10.1016/j.jbusvent.2008.04.007.

Zeyen, Anica. 2014. *Scaling Strategies of Social Entrepreneurship Organizations— an Actor-Motivation Perspective.* Lueneburg: Leuphana University.

Zeyen, Anica, and Markus Beckmann. 2011. *Social Entrepreneurship and Institutional Logics.* Lueneburg: Centre for Sustainability Management.

———. 2018. "Exploring the Global Potential of Social Entrepreneurship and Small Business Social Responsibility for Tackling Societal Value Creation." In *Research Handbook on Small Business Social Responsibility*, edited by Laura J. Spence, Jedrzej G. Frynas, Judy N. Muthuri, and Jyoti Navare, 267–91. Cheltenham, UK: Edward Elgar Publishing. doi:10.4337/9781784711825.00021.

Zeyen, Anica, Markus Beckmann, and Roya Akhavan. 2014. "Social Entrepreneurship Business Models: Managing Innovation for Social and Economic Value Creation." In *Managementperspektiven Für Die Zivilgesellschaft Des 21. Jahrhunderts*, edited by Camillo Müller and Claas-Philip Zinth, 107–32. Wiesbaden: Springer Gabler.

Zeyen, Anica, Markus Beckmann, and Stella Wolters. 2016. "Actor and Institutional Dynamics in the Development of Multi-Stakeholder Initiatives." *Journal of Business Ethics* 135 (2). Springer Netherlands: 341–60. doi:10.1007/s10551-014-2468-1.

3 Refining Our Ethical Perspective on the Light and Shadows in Social Entrepreneurship

The Concept of Normative Ambivalence

This book strives to bring together research on social entrepreneurship with conceptual perspectives from business ethics. By analyzing not only the positive contributions of social entrepreneurship but also its potential dark sides, ethical perspectives can help to better understand and also to manage the potential of purpose-driven venturing. When it comes to defining the perspective of business ethics, however, there is no generally agreed upon position. On the contrary, business ethics encompasses both descriptive and normative approaches, with the latter building on various, often competing normative theories (Crane and Matten 2016).

Against this background, the purpose of this chapter is to conceptually introduce, define, and elaborate the ethical perspective used in this book. To this end, our argument will proceed in the following seven steps. In the first step, we will start by asking what we mean by ethics and why the analysis of and debate about social entrepreneurship would benefit from the explicit integration of an ethical perspective. In our second step, we will then identify and discuss relevant features that our ethical perspective should have in order to live up to the purpose of the book. Next, in our third step, we will briefly review key ethical theories and argue that a consequentialist ethics perspective is best suited to fulfill the features desired for our analysis. In the fourth step, we will refine the consequentialist perspective with an analytical framework that helps us distinguish and relate normative and positive assumptions. This framework, the so-called practical syllogism, can guide our analysis of social entrepreneurship across different levels and contexts. In the fifth step, we will take the deepest dive into ethical theory in order to reflect as how and to what extent we can justify normative assumptions. Here, we will make the case for a procedural approach to ethics that sees consensus about rules and general principles as the ultimate source of moral justification. Building upon these foundations, we will then, in our sixth step, develop the concept of normative ambivalence. The ambivalence perspective argues against a tendency to see diverse phenomena as inherently good or bad. Rather, it highlights the contingency of consequences: Depending on the problem perspective and the relevant alternatives as well as on the contextual application, the same action, motivation, or principle can lead to either positive or negative outcomes. The ambivalence perspective thus shifts the focus toward analyzing these contingency conditions—and the question of how these conditions could be changed to bring out the bright outcomes instead of the dark ones. Finally, in the seventh step, we will conclude this chapter with a short summary.

So how to read this chapter? This chapter covers a lot of conceptual ground. For readers interested in (ethical) theory building, the full chapter should serve to make our ethical perspective transparent, including its normative foundations (Section 3.5), thus opening it up to further debate. We acknowledge, however, that the affection for ethical theory is not equally distributed. Still, this chapter introduces useful concepts for application in various fields. Those readers who are primarily interested in these practical applications may jump directly into Section 3.4, where we introduce the practical syllogism and, more importantly, into Section 3.6, in which we explain the concept of normative ambivalence.

3.1. Why Does This Book Need an Ethical Perspective?

A starting premise of this book is that the debate about social entrepreneurship can benefit from explicitly applying an ethical perspective. Yet, why do we think so? After all, most scholarly articles on social entrepreneurship do not engage in open discussion about ethics (for exceptions, see, for example, Zahra et al. 2009; Chell et al. 2016; Dey and Steyaert 2016). So why do we think that ethics matter here?

To answer this question, it is useful to start by clarifying the definition of ethics and how it differs from morality. Although the literature distinguishes between those two concepts in multiple ways, we draw on the distinction offered by the sociologist Niklas Luhmann (1991, 1996). For Luhmann (1991, 84), morality is "a special form of communication which carries with it indications of approval or disapproval." Therefore, in contrast to the academic discipline of ethics, which is often quite abstract and theoretical, morality is a concrete, real-life, daily phenomenon. Politicians who criticize their opponent's behavior as irresponsible express disapproval and thus engage in moral communication; as do children when they call each other names or stakeholders who assess a management proposal as unfair. Morality thus describes all forms of societal communication that use a 'moral code' to distinguish between good and bad, right and wrong, or legitimate and illegitimate (Luhmann 1992).

Morality thus denotes the empirical phenomenon of how societal communication divides the world into good and bad, approval and disapproval, and so on. Yet, it does not explain how these moral distinctions can be rationally justified. In fact, as research in moral psychology documents (Haidt 2001, 2007; Graham et al. 2013), in everyday life, moral statements are typically based on intuition and emotions rather than on conscious deliberation. To provide the ground for a rational discourse about morally charged issues, it is therefore necessary to take one step back and look at morality with a critical distance.

This is where ethics comes into play. For Luhmann (1991, 90), ethics has the task of providing "a theoretical reflection of morality." By this logic, philosophical ethics has traditionally sought to engage in a rational discourse about how to decide what counts as good or bad. In doing so, a key purpose of ethical discourse is to have a reasonable debate that makes implicit arguments explicit, thus allowing for criticism, learning, and ideally consensus.[1]

So where is the relevance of these considerations for this book? We argue that, seen from the perspective of Luhmann's sociology, much of the debate about social entrepreneurship is rife with diverse forms of moral communication. Social entrepreneurs follow normative missions that they perceive to be "good." In society, on the other hand, many writers, politicians, and academics herald social entrepreneurs as praiseworthy moral heroes, thus expressing esteem and approval. Similarly, the very concept of social entrepreneurship is embraced by many as something good or desirable. This praise also extends to its elements such as innovation or the other-regarding social mission (see Chapter 2). At the same time, there are also critics who seek to 'problematize' social entrepreneurship (Dey and Steyaert 2012) to point out its dark sides, which call for disapproval and critique.

In short, the debate on and analysis of social entrepreneurship have strong normative dimensions and involve moral statements. Whether or not social entrepreneurship is 'desirable' and whether certain aspects of this phenomenon deserve criticism (or not) amounts to a matter of value judgments. Such value judgments, however, do not reflect objective truths that can be scientifically proven (Weber 2017) but depend on subjective, personal criteria with which we define what is desirable, good, or bad. Ethical reasoning can reflect these normative criteria, discuss their plausibility, make them transparent, and open them up for a critical debate.

We therefore think that the explicit consideration of ethics is fruitful for social entrepreneurship, too. Consequently, this chapter serves to introduce our ethical perspective used in this book. By laying open its underlying assumptions, we want to give reasons for our conceptual choices and allow others to criticize them. But before we come to the ethical perspective itself, the next section will discuss what kind of features a candidate ethical perspective should fulfill for the purpose of this book.

3.2. Identifying Key Features That Our Ethical Perspective Should Fulfill

Just as there is moral pluralism in society, there is conceptual pluralism in philosophical ethics. In fact, philosophers have debated diverse and competing ethical theories for literally thousands of years. It goes without saying that we cannot (and do not want to) end this debate by somehow claiming which of the diverse candidate theories is 'true' and which is 'false.'

Still, we need to decide which ethical approach to choose and on what basis to ground this choice. This decision is crucial because every conceptual choice has consequences for how one can use a theory. Theories are tools for solving problems. Following this idea, we seek to define our conceptual ethical perspective, such that it can give us constructive guidance for the problem and specific purposes this book seeks to address. With this book's purpose in mind, we identify the following five requirements that can inform the conceptual choices for our ethical perspective:

1. Social entrepreneurship is a *multi-level phenomenon*. It spans macro-level questions (how does social entrepreneurship interact with the institutions of the market, the state, and civil society?) as well as meso-level questions (what are the implications of social entrepreneurship for organizing, business models, and management?) and micro-level questions (what are the roles of and the effects on individuals in social entrepreneurship?). If we want to be able to address normative questions in all these regards, we need an ethical perspective that can be equally applied on all three levels.

2. This book seeks to introduce social entrepreneurship as an interesting *field of research*. Although ethical perspectives are important to discuss normative questions, it should also be possible to relate them productively to positive analyses that scholars can undertake in their empirical research. We therefore see it as a plus when an ethical theory can generate productive research questions for positive analysis.

3. A central premise of this book is that social entrepreneurship is a phenomenon where there is not only *light but also shadow*. Our conceptual perspective should thus be able to analyze both elements equally and simultaneously, without fixed notions about or a preconceived preference for any of the two sides.

4. This book wants to not only describe what is good or bad about social entrepreneurship but also provide *conceptual guidance* as to how social entrepreneurship or certain aspects of it can *be managed constructively*. To this end, an ethical perspective should not only critique what is good or bad but also identify relevant levers for how things can be changed and improved.

5. Finally, social entrepreneurship is a *global phenomenon* and takes place in different countries, cultures, and religions. This book seeks to acknowledge the underlying diversity that social entrepreneurs share. As a consequence, this favors an ethical perspective that refrains from drawing on strong, yet culturally contingent normative positions but rather uses a framework that can be applied universally.

In the next section (Section 3.3), these five considerations can help us to sort through the available ethical pluralism and chose a candidate ethical theory before we then refine this perspective in the subsequent sections (Sections 3.4–3.6).

3.3. Comparing Ethical Approaches and Choosing This Book's Perspective

In philosophical ethics, Immanuel Kant (1998) famously put the key problem of ethics into the form of a question: What should I do? For the purpose of this book, Kant's original formulation has certain limitations because it focuses on individual behavior (what should *I* do?) whereas our analysis focuses on social phenomena, including organizations and macro-effects as well. Still, Kant's classical question of ethics can serve to start our analysis. The doing part in "what should I *do*?" highlights that the original focus of philosophical ethics is concerned with the problem of how to *act* morally. How does ethics, then, assess whether an action can be morally justified? In the Western[2] philosophical tradition, three major normative theories address this question: (1) deontology or non-consequentialism, (2) consequentialism, and (3) virtue ethics. We focus above all on the first two, which can be compared with the following framework (Crane and Matten 2016) that Figure 3.1 serves to illustrate. For each action, we can distinguish between the motivations and principles that led a decision-maker to choose that action and the outcomes that resulted as a consequence of that action. We first introduce the three theories (Section 3.3.1) and then discuss which one fits best for this book (Section 3.3.2).

3.3.1. A Very Brief Review of Candidate Ethical Theories

1. When assessing whether an action is morally right, *non-consequentialist* theories focus on the left side of Figure 3.1 and ask whether the underlying motivations (love, greed, etc.) and principles (e.g., always telling the truth, respecting rights and duties) that lead to an action are morally right—regardless of the consequences the action produces.

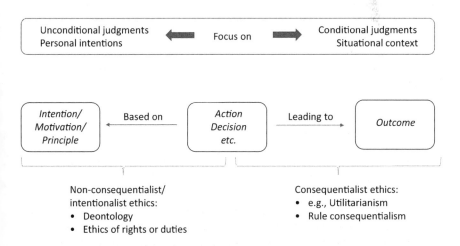

Figure 3.1 Non-consequentialist versus consequentialist ethics

There are different strands of non-consequentialist theories (Crane and Matten 2016). A first strand of theories focuses on the notion of (universal) *rights* that all actions have to respect. A prominent example is John Locke's philosophy of natural rights. Here, the premise is that every action should respect and protect these rights, irrespective of context and consequences.

A second strand of non-consequentialist theories focuses on (universal) *duties*. The arguably most famous proponent of this non-consequentialist thinking is Immanuel Kant himself. His 'deontology' (from the Greek word for 'duty') postulates a duty to act in accordance with *principles* that are universally desirable. How can we find such universal principles? For Kant, a universal principle must have an unconditional form: It must not be conditional on situational consequences. This is captured in Kant's famous '*categorical* imperative.' In comparison, in daily life, imperatives are typically hypothetical, that is, conditional on additional hypotheses: *If* you do not want to get a sunburn, *then* put on sunscreen. The categorical imperative, in contrast, postulates a command that is unconditional on additional hypotheses. Just do it. Kant (1993, 30) formulates this categorical imperative in three 'maxims,' of which the first is probably most well-known: "act only in accordance with that maxim through which you can at the same time will that it become a universal law." Kant's *universality* perspective thus provides a test for every possible action by scrutinizing whether the underlying principle can be universalized. Only principles that can be universalized then qualify as morally right.

Kant's universality principle is highly influential yet was criticized early on for refusing to look at the desirability of the *actual* consequences of applying universal principles in a concrete situation. In a response to that criticism, Kant (1949) commented on a drastic example. Imagine that a murderer knocks on your door. Further imagine that the potential victim is hiding inside your house. If the murderer asked you about the whereabouts of the victim, would it be morally right to lie to save the victim? (Or put more drastically: Do you have a duty to tell the truth to a Nazi searching for Anne Frank?) Though Kant acknowledges the worry about the victim, he argues that taking into account the potential consequences for the victim would make any universal principle conditional on the situation, thus ending its universality. At the same time, the alternative maxim of lying cannot be universalized. Kant (cited in Varden 2010, 405) therefore comes to the conclusion: "To be truthful (honest) in all declarations is therefore a sacred command of reason prescribing unconditionally, one not to be restricted by any conveniences." According to most Kant interpretations, Kant thus suggests that there is a moral duty to *reveal* the victim's whereabouts to the murderer (for a divergent interpretation, see Varden 2010).

2. For non-consequentialism, actual consequences thus do not count. The exact opposite perspective on ethics is taken by *consequentialist* theories. Consequentialist theories focus on the right side of Figure 3.1 and base their moral judgment on the *outcomes* of an action. According to this perspective,

an action is morally right if the consequences produced by it are desirable. If an action, however, leads to undesirable outcomes, the action is morally wrong. Moral rightness and wrongness thus relate to whether the effects of an action result in care or harm. In the case of the murderer asking you for the whereabouts of the victim, consequentialists would therefore argue that it is not only morally right to lie but that it would be morally wrong to tell the truth because it would or could have the consequence of Anne Frank being sent to death.

Just like non-consequentialism, consequentialist theories fall into different strands. Here, the most well-known consequentialist theory is the philosophy of utilitarianism. Utilitarianism is associated with the British philosophers Jeremy Bentham and John Stuart Mill. Utilitarianism also builds on universal assumptions, namely that all human beings experience pleasure as desirable and pain as undesirable. As pleasure produces and pain reduces 'utility' (a slightly awkward word for what others describe us 'happiness' or relate to *eudaimonia*), Mill (2016, 333) argued that the Utilitarian "creed [. . .] holds that actions are right in proportion as they tend to promote happiness, wrong as they tend to produce the reverse of happiness." Following the "Greatest Happiness Principle" (Mill 2016), Utilitarians then seek to maximize the utility of humankind (for a modern interpretation and case for Utilitarianism see Greene 2014).

In the Utilitarian view, something thus qualifies as morally right if its outcomes result in the greatest amount of good for the greatest amount of people. Note that this 'something' can refer both to an action but also to other things such as a rule or institution that requires or incentivizes certain acts, thus leading to desirable consequences. As a result, a Utilitarian perspective (and consequentialist thinking more generally) can easily look not only at individual behavior but also at the consequences produced by organizations, institutions, systems, and so on.

Compared to non-consequentialist perspectives, a major difference of consequentialism is that it shifts the perspective away from abstract, unconditional principles (inalienable rights, universal desirability) to concrete situational consequences that are conditional on a specific context. As a result, consequentialism emphasizes the need to consider those contextual factors that can influence which effects dominate in a given situation.

A further strand of consequentialism can be linked to Adam Smith. We will come back to Smith in more detail below. At this point, it suffices to call attention to his shift toward analyzing mechanisms that cause certain consequences. In his classical *Inquiry into the Nature and Causes of Wealth of Nations*, Smith (1776) famously shows that the individual intention of self-interest can lead to desirable outcomes on a societal level.

3. The third major normative theory that we want to review very briefly does not fall easily into Figure 3.1 and its non-consequentialism- consequentialism dichotomy.[3] Strongly based on the philosophy of Aristotle, *virtue ethics* does not focus on actions in terms of the principles that guide

them or in terms of the consequences that result from them but rather looks at the development of *character*. Moral behavior then refers to virtuous actions that exercise (and thereby train) virtues that constitute a character. These virtues can include patience, courage, or friendliness. Note, that these virtues are considered desirable not because of certain universal duties or effects on others but for developing one's own potential. In his Nicomachean Ethics (see McKeon 2009), Aristotle starts his argument by referring to the human desire to strive for *eudaimonia* (something like true happiness, flourishing, or well-being). To this end, one has to self-perfect the function of being human and bringing out one's potential (Pies, Beckmann, and Hielscher 2014). Virtuous behavior as the development and exercise of virtue then assists this striving for excellence.

3.3.2. Which Ethical Theory Best Fits the Purposes of This Book?

Our short review shows that the three ethical theories above highlight very different questions. Deontology focuses on (unconditional) rights and duties, consequentialism on (conditional) outcomes, and virtue ethics on the self-perfection of character. As the rich ethical tradition illustrates, *all* three theories can guide toward interesting questions. What we want to do next, however, is to discuss which theory best suits the specific purposes of our book. Coming back to the five features discussed in Section 3.2, we will make the *case for consequentialism* for the following reasons.

1. A consequentialist approach is well suited to analyzing social entrepreneurship as a multi-level phenomenon. As discussed earlier, the analysis of consequences can be applied to actions but also to organizations and institutions, thus covering both the micro- as well as the meso- and macro-levels. In contrast, with their focus on the intentions and principles that guide individual decisions or their emphasis on individual character, it is more difficult to apply deontology and virtue ethics to (system) phenomena. This is because there is no clear agent with a personal character or the intention to act on moral principles. After all, what are the 'intentions' or the 'character' of macro-level effects in society such as the diffusion of social innovation or competition for funding?
2. A consequentialist normative ethical perspective is well suited to generating productive research questions for empirical analysis. To assess the normative desirability of consequences, we first have to investigate, describe, and analyze them. Normative ethical reasoning thus calls for strong positive research. To be sure, this is also the case for deontology and virtue ethics. From a researcher's perspective, however, we have many elaborate tools to empirically identify, scrutinize, and test how causal mechanisms result in diverse outcomes. Investigating 'true intentions' that guide decision-makers or assessing the self-perfection

of character is a much narrower endeavor and difficult to investigate empirically.

3. As we will elaborate in more detail in our section on normative ambivalence, a consequentialist perspective allows analyzing the light, shadow, and shades of gray of a phenomenon like social entrepreneurship. Consequences can be desirable, undesirable, or—depending on the perspective—even both. Furthermore, they can change depending on the situation. Focusing on specific consequences can highlight these ambiguities. In contrast, the assumption of universal principles, whose implementation is always unconditionally desirable (and whose lack of implementation is equally unconditionally undesirable), tends to operate with a rather fixed black-and-white dichotomy that may not do justice to the complexity of social entrepreneurship.

4. A consequentialist perspective is further able to identify potential levers for change and improvement. To start with, the very ideas of management and reform are linked to a certain consequentialist thinking, because they seek to improve outcomes and results. Yet, even when taking an ethical perspective that intends to increase the moral rightness of an action, there is an important difference. If a deontological perspective qualifies a behavior or action as morally wrong because the decision-maker did not follow the right principle, a change toward moral rightness is only possible when the decision-maker changes his or her intentions. Changing the intentions of people, however, is hard (and may raise, in turn, ethical questions of paternalism, etc.). On the other hand, a consequentialist approach that qualifies a certain behavior as morally wrong because it creates harm has many more options to right that wrong. Consequences can be changed by appealing to the decision-maker's conscience (like in the deontological approach) but also by changing the incentives for the agent or by changing the situation in many other ways. Because consequences are always contingent on context, a consequentialist perspective does not only provide guidance for a rich prescriptive analysis but can also use the latter for practical learning and reform.

5. A consequentialist perspective is better suited for debate and learning that acknowledges cultural and international diversity. This is relevant because social entrepreneurship is a phenomenon that spans different cultural, religious, political, and social backgrounds. A consequentialist perspective focuses on the desirability of outcomes but, as we will elaborate in a moment, does not necessarily prescribe how to define desirability. Analyzing the consequences of alternative actions, institutions, or systems can pave the way for an open discussion about shared interests in certain outcomes. In contrast, ethical theories that presuppose the unconditional prevalence of universal principles make such an open learning process more difficult. Take the case of human rights. Historically speaking, the concept of human rights is a Western invention.

Outside Europe, critics therefore claim that the idea of universal and unconditional human rights neglects the role of Western culture in formulating them, thus making it inherently conditional (Cobbah 1987). The insistence on the *un*conditional authority of human rights is then often criticized as Euro-centrism. A consequentialist perspective, in contrast, could make the *conditional* case for human rights by analyzing the desirable consequences—both for the individual and for society—that result from having those rights (Scanlon 2003) and by investigating what kinds of conditions are necessary for these benefits to materialize.

In short, our review and discussion of the major ethical theories suggests that following a consequentialist perspective is well suited for the specific purposes of this book. A consequentialist approach looks at how certain actions, phenomena, or system properties lead to specific outcomes and then assesses their desirability. This raises the follow-up question: How do we assess desirability? To answer this question, the next section refines our consequentialist analysis by introducing the analytical framework of the practical syllogism.

3.4. Refining the Consequentialist Perspective: The Extended Practical Syllogism

Kant's *categorical* imperative expresses the assumption of universal principles that are *un*conditionally good. In contrast, by judging moral rightness as being conditional on consequences, consequentialism does not formulate categorical imperatives but *hypothetical* ones—with the hypotheses ('if. . .') specifying propositions for the contextual analysis. In philosophy, deriving conclusions from two or more such propositions is called a 'syllogism.' In the following, we want to elaborate this idea to refine our analysis.

In his *Nicomachean Ethics*, Aristotle (Crisp 2014) introduces the concept of the 'practical syllogism' as a three-proposition argument that consists of I) a major premise stating some universal truth, II) a minor premise stating some particular truth, and III) a conclusion derived from these two propositions. To illustrate, take Aristotle's example of assessing the healthiness of meat. For Aristotle, it is a universal truth I) that light meats are wholesome. When then acknowledging the particular truth II) that "This is light meat" (e.g., chicken), he logically concludes III) that this particular meat is wholesome.

Departing from Aristotle's original usage, we can refine the practical syllogism to use it as a general framework for our ethical analysis. In order to answer the question as to "what should I do?" or, more generally, "what kind of action, rule, system etc. would be morally desirable?," we need two kinds of ingredients. Figure 3.2 helps to illustrate this idea.

The first type of ingredients refers to the field of *normative* assumptions (I)). Normative assumptions express propositions about what is desirable.

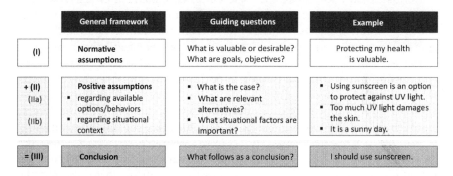

General framework	Guiding questions	Example
(I) Normative assumptions	What is valuable or desirable? What are goals, objectives?	Protecting my health is valuable.
+ (II) (IIa) **Positive assumptions** • regarding available options/behaviors (IIb) • regarding situational context	• What is the case? • What are relevant alternatives? • What situational factors are important?	• Using sunscreen is an option to protect against UV light. • Too much UV light damages the skin. • It is a sunny day.
= (III) Conclusion	What follows as a conclusion?	I should use sunscreen.

Figure 3.2 The extended practical syllogism

They answer the question as to what is valuable, what are the goals, ends, or objectives of an action. In contrast to Aristotle's 'major premises,' normative assumptions thus do not state objective, empirical truths but formulate value judgments.

The second type of ingredients refers to the domain of *positive* assumptions (II)). Positive assumptions describe the empirical context. They answer the question as to what is the case. This question contains two important subquestions. First, positive assumptions need to clarify the relevant alternatives that can be enacted or chosen as behavior (IIa)). What are the available actions, strategies, or practices that can be enacted or what kind of instruments, tools, or options can be used? Second, additional positive assumptions are needed to specify the context in which these options can be employed (IIb)). What are additional factors that define the situation? What are side parameters that constrain actions or influence the outcome they would produce?

We can use and extend this version of the practical syllogism to derive three important implications for our analysis.

1. The extended practical syllogism shows that to decide what we *should* do (or approve of as morally good) (III)) we need to clarify what we *want* to achieve (I)) and what we *can* do (IIa)) given a situational *context* (IIb)). Only by bringing *all* ingredients together—normative *and* positive assumptions—is it possible to deduce what one should do or whether a certain action or choice is desirable.

To illustrate, take the following simple example (see Figure 3.2). When you go to the beach, your normative assumptions could include "I do not want to get sunburned" or "Protecting my health is valuable." These normative assumptions alone do not allow clarifying what you should do. In this situation, positive assumptions need to describe your relevant options, for example, that you could use sunscreen (you know that it provides protection). Positive statements are also needed to describe relevant aspects of the situation—for example, that too much UV radiation is bad for your health and that it will be a sunny day with lots of UV radiation. Note how the conclusion depends on all three assumptions. *If* you want to protect your skin and *if* you have sunscreen available that protects you and *if* it is going to be a sunny day, then you should use sunscreen. Whether putting on sunscreen is desirable can thus be answered only conditionally. If the conditions change, so might the answer. If, for example, the normative assumption is not that it is desirable to protect the skin but rather to get a dark complexion as quickly as possible, then the conclusion will be different. Similarly, if the day is cloudy with no sunshine and UV radiation, putting on sunscreen would no longer be the most desirable action. Assessing the desirability of an action (or other options under consideration) is therefore possible only by considering *both* the normative goals/objectives *and* the situational context. Leaving out any of the propositions would change your conclusion or even render it impossible. If you have no normative assumptions, you do not know how to assess your choices. If you have no positive assumptions, you do not know which choice options are available.

2. When assessing what we should do and whether an action/tool/decision produces desirable consequences, the answer depends on the *relevant alternatives* available. In *Political Liberalism*, John Rawls (2005, 88) maintains: "We strive for the best we can attain within the scope of this world."[4] Reflecting upon what we actually can attain highlights that the yard stick for our analysis is not the 'best we could think of' in an ideal world but the best we could actually do given a real-life situation. Striving for the most desirable consequences thus does not refer to the most desirable outcomes that are theoretically thinkable but practically possible.

To illustrate, take the example of triage. Triage describes a procedure used to decide "what we should do" in case of accidents or catastrophes that involve a large number of casualties. The normative assumptions for the medical services are straightforward: It is valuable to save (as many) lives (as possible). In an ideal world with unlimited rescue workers and doctors, it would be possible to treat all casualties simultaneously, thus saving most lives and producing the best outcome. Yet, although this choice alternative (treat all of them) is theoretically conceivable, it is not practically available. In a situation with many more casualties than can be treated (positive assumptions about context), the medical emergency services thus need to decide how to prioritize and ration their services. So, whom should they treat? In this situation, triage refers to the assignment of degrees of urgency to wounds to sort all casualties into three groups: a) the lightly wounded who are likely to survive if not treated, b) the severely wounded who are likely to die even if they receive a lot of care, and c) the significantly wounded where medical care would most increase their likelihood of survival. Put differently, to treat group a, b, *or* c are then the relevant alternatives. With the aim of saving lives, the triage system then prioritizes the casualties of group c where the limited care that is possible would have the biggest effects.

There is an interesting lesson to be learned from the triage example. Identifying, discussing, and structuring the relevant alternatives can be an important part of the ethical analysis. Without the triage system and the guidance it provides, rescue workers would find it much more difficult to decide what they should do in a morally relevant issue (of literally life and death).

3. The categorization of the practical syllogism's components is a matter of perspective. What counts as normative assumptions, positive assumptions, and conclusion is not absolutely given but depends, again, on context. The practical syllogism can thus be used on different cascading levels. Figure 3.3 illustrates this idea.

To illustrate this important idea, let us go back to the beach example. Having concluded that we should use sunscreen to protect our skin, we realize that we do not have any sunscreen at home. So, what should we do next? Again, we can answer this question with the help of the practical syllogism. Interestingly, what we deduced as the conclusion earlier (you should use sunscreen) now informs the normative assumptions for our new problem. When clarifying here what is desirable, what we want, or what the guiding objectives and ends are, the normative assumptions (I)) could state something like "I *want* to use sunscreen" or "Having (and using) sunscreen is desirable." In terms of the positive assumptions (II)), the relevant alternatives could include "I *can* buy sunscreen at the drugstore next door" and the context assumption "The drugstore sells sunscreen and is open today."

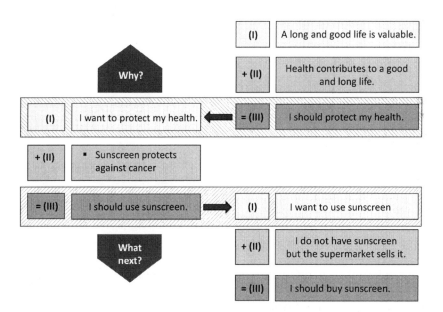

Figure 3.3 The extended practical syllogism in a multi-level perspective

Bringing together all assumptions could then result in the conclusion (III)) that we *should* buy some sunscreen at the drugstore.

The example thus highlights that what counts as a conclusion in one context (we should use sunscreen) can serve as a normative assumption for a different problem perspective (we want to use sunscreen). This change of perspective also works the other way around when a normative assumption can be reconstructed as the conclusion of a practical syllogism. Let us return to the sunscreen example. In our initial application of the practical syllogism, the normative assumptions were "I want to protect my health" or "My health is valuable." We could then ask *why* do we want to protect our health? Why is good health valuable or desirable? The answer to this question could then result from using the practical syllogism at a higher level. Here, positive assumptions (II)) could include "A good health prolongs life," "Illnesses cause pain," and "I can make lifestyle choices that affect my health" whereas normative assumptions could state "I want to live a long life" and "Avoiding pain is desirable." Bringing all assumptions together then leads to the conclusion (III)) that we should protect and nurture our health.

By asking "why" and "what follows from here" we can thus "*move up and down*" between different levels on which to apply the practical syllogism. This change in perspective changes the status of the components involved. Note, for example, how 'being healthy' was initially a normative goal that seemed desirable in itself and then turned into an instrument for leading a good life in our final application. The multi-level application of the practical syllogism thus shows that both goals and ends and instruments and tools are categories that do not ontologically describe the inherent nature of, say, health or sunscreen but rather provide methodological distinctions that are contingent on context.

This ability to distinguish between different levels of analysis is relevant for our discussion of social entrepreneurship. In this book, we want to analyze social entrepreneurship, its key features, and related concepts on different levels and from different perspectives. As a preview, let us look briefly at the notion of innovation (see Figure 3.4). As Chapter 2 highlighted, innovation is seen as a defining feature of social entrepreneurship. In certain contexts, innovation (and encouraging innovation) is then seen as a praiseworthy end in itself (normative assumption) (see, critically, Seelos and Mair 2012). From this perspective, the practical syllogism would ask how innovation (I)) can be achieved and would therefore discuss potential options for fostering innovation (II)). Depending on the specific context, these positive assumptions could include, for example "social entrepreneurs need seed funding to innovate" (IIb)) and "We can create funding schemes for seed money" (IIa)). The practical conclusion could then maintain that we should create new funding schemes to foster more innovation. If we change the perspective, however, we can move up the staircase and ask *why* (and when) innovation is desirable and valuable. Here, one possible answer

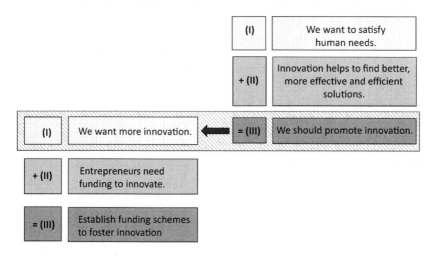

Figure 3.4 Innovation in the multi-level practical syllogism

could be that society wants to satisfy diverse human needs (I)) in a world of scarcity (IIb)). Here, innovation can create more efficient solutions, which is why we should foster them (III)). By changing the frame of reference, innovation thus changes from being a (contingent) societal end into being a societal means. As a consequence, we can then discuss innovation as a tool for satisfying human needs—and compare it with other alternatives (such as spending the money on publish health instead on entrepreneurial seed funding) to see what would work best.

3.5. The Will of the People—Defining Democratically What Ultimately Counts as 'Good'

Building upon the idea of the practical syllogism, we can now address the perhaps most challenging question for ethics: What is the ultimate criterion for desirability and thus the moral judgment of consequences?

As the practical syllogism shows, assessing desirability always requires normative assumptions. Yet, where do these normative assumptions come from and how can we justify them? Our multi-level application demonstrated that by questioning the taken-for-grantedness of normative assumptions we can often 'move up the staircase' to more abstract goals, for example, moving from sunscreen via health to a good life or from seed funding via innovation to satisfying human needs. Ultimately, at the highest levels, we then talk about *values* that people hold dear. As we discussed earlier, however, value judgments cannot be proven scientifically (Weber 2017). So how can the practical syllogism still help here? We want to distinguish two cases in this regard.

Let us start with the arguably easier case. In our experience, many moral 'ethical' discussions do not really reflect a conflict of values but rather a debate of how best to achieve them. In this case, 'moving up the staircase' can already help to open a more constructive discourse. Take the case of minimum wage. Proponents of minimum wage support it because they care about the poorest in the labor market. Motivated by this value, some minimum wage proponents then morally disapprove of minimum wage opponents because they feel that the latter do not care about the poor. However, if you ask *why* they oppose the minimum wage, many will answer that, in their analysis, minimum wage does not help but hurt poor people (e.g., by increasing unemployment or increasing the cost of living). Thus, moving up to a higher level highlights that there is no conflict of values (if and when both sides of the debate care about solutions for the poor) but rather that there are competing *positive* assumptions. In other words, this argument is a disagreement as to what works and not about the desirability of protecting the poor (value). This does not mean that the debate is therefore easy to settle. Yet, the discussion is now about empirical statements that can be tested and criticized with data and models—without the need for debating value judgments. Consequentialist reasoning can then change an 'ethical' problem into a matter of comparative policy analysis (Schelling 1981).

Let us now turn to the arguably more interesting case of dealing with value judgments: What can we do if 'moving up the staircase' of the practical syllogism does *not* lead to a shared value on a higher level? There are two variations of such a situation. First, as John Rawls (2005, 36–9) pointed out in *Political Liberalism*, a modern, free society is characterized by "the fact of reasonable pluralism." People follow diverse concepts of the good and differ in the values they hold. Second, even if people share the same values, there can be cases in which values may conflict with each other. This then raises the question of how to prioritize or link values. Take the normative goals of environmental protection and poverty alleviation. Most people would say that both goals are in line with their personal values. Yet, what do you do when the realization of one goal occurs at the expense of the other? Imagine that a social venture teaches poor farmers to use diesel generators to irrigate their crops. Although this might boost their productivity and income, it also contributes to climate change. So, how can we deal with this perceived underlying value conflict?

For many, these 'ethical dilemmas' constitute the core problem that ethics needs to address. Though there is much research on how individual decision-makers deal personally with ethical dilemmas in a given situation (Trevino 1986), we want to not only cover these intrapersonal value conflicts but also potential interpersonal value conflicts. We therefore use a broader perspective that also includes the meso- and macro-levels. Instead of asking what should *I* do, we thus ask: What should *we* do? (with the corresponding questions of what do *we* want; what can *we* do; and which facts do *we* have to take into account?). As already discussed, applying the practical syllogism and 'moving up the staircase' then ultimately leads to a discussion about what we see as valuable on the highest level. Given the fact of reasonable pluralism, however, there can be diverse highest-level values (e.g., protecting the environment, human rights, material well-being) that are incommensurable in direct comparison. What we therefore need is a meta-value or 'common currency' (Greene 2014) that provides a shared criterion for comparing, evaluating, and aligning diverse dimensions.

There are two alternatives to define such a shared criterion or meta-value. The first option is to define this 'common currency' in *material* terms, thus specifying the actual content of what counts as ultimately valuable. As already reviewed, this is the strategy taken by Utilitarianism. Utilitarian thinkers argue that utility is both the ultimate value and common currency for assessing ethical questions (Mill 2016; Greene 2014). Yet, critics point out that operationalizing utility is challenging (Who defines utility? Who should measure it and how?). Moreover, there are rival candidates other than utility that people embrace for defining what counts as ultimate normative criteria such as universal rights, liberty, or the holiness of sacred entities (Graham et al. 2013). Choosing utility over other candidate common currencies would therefore amount, again, to a (debatable) value judgment.

Against this background, we follow a second option to define a shared criterion or meta-value. Instead of defining 'common currency' in material terms, the alternative is to refrain from specifying the actual content of what counts as ultimately valuable but rather refine common currency in *procedural* terms. Our procedural approach has two important elements: first, to use consensus as the ultimate normative criterion, and second, to use the rules of the game (not a single move in it) as the frame of reference.

Let us start with the first element of our procedural perspective—the core concept of *consensus*. Although there are many variants of procedural consensus-oriented ethics (Bayertz 1994), we interpret it from our consequentialist perspective. The starting point for our argument is thus simple: *If all actors involved and affected by the issue under consideration agree that the resulting outcome (consequences) is superior to (more desirable than) the relevant alternatives, then their voluntary consent legitimizes procedurally this outcome as morally acceptable.* If everyone agrees, who can still be against it?[5]

Although a moral consensus would obviously seem desirable (again: a normative assumption), the follow-up question is whether (or what kind of) a moral consensus is actually possible (which would be a matter of positive assumptions). Clearly, given the fact of reasonable pluralism, a consensus about personal values is not possible. Just try to have a vegan and a steak-lover come up with a common ranking for the value of animal rights. Similarly, it would not be feasible to generate a factual or hypothetical consensus for each concrete situation or with regard to every particular action or decision. After all, if the police fine somebody for speeding, that person is likely not to be happy about this specific act when viewed in isolation.

The solution to this impasse lies in shifting the perspective away from a single decision or action in a particular situation toward principles that would govern social interactions in general. The literature mirrors such a shift in perspective in various ways, ranging from Rawls' (1999)[6] idea of the original position via social contract theory (Donaldson and Dunfee 1994) to the concept of discourse ethics (Habermas 2015). As engaging in these different theory traditions would go beyond the scope of this chapter, we want to focus on the conceptual foundations that inform our analysis most significantly, that is, the perspective of constitutional economics (Brennan and Buchanan 2000; Buchanan 1990, 2000).

Constitutional economics provides the following fruitful distinction for business ethics (for current applications see, for example, Beckmann 2016; Beckmann and Pies 2016; Hielscher, Beckmann, and Pies 2014): We can analyze each social interaction on two levels. To illustrate, take the case of football. Within a given football game, we can focus on the level of the *moves in a game*. How do the players play the game? Here, the players follow their individual interests that often diverge in important regards. (Team A does not want that Team B score a goal.) When looking at the game itself and alternative ways to organize it, however, the perspective changes. How can the game be organized in alternative ways? Here, the players focus on their collective interests that often converge in important regards. (Nobody should get hurt. The game should be fun.) To achieve these shared interests, we need to move to the level of the *rules of the game*. What kind of game would the players prefer to play? This change in perspective thus allows identifying consensus by 'moving up the staircase' from the moves of the game to the rules that govern it.

The key idea of *constitutional* economics, then, is that this change in perspective by moving up to the level of rules can be iterated: There are rules for how we create the rules for football (e.g., through a discussion and vote by the representatives in the football federation), and there are rules for how to organize and elect the football federation's representatives, and so on. With each move up to a higher level and to more abstract rules, the prospect of consensus increases (Brennan and Buchanan 2000). A factual or hypothetical consensus thus becomes possible, if necessary by moving up to the highest level of the most general—that is, constitutional—rules (for a more detailed elaboration see Brennan and Buchanan (2000, 35) as well as Beckmann (2010, 133–7) and Hielscher, Beckmann, and Pies (2014)).

In summary, we thus do not define what is 'good' from the standpoint of any external ethical authority or absolute material viewpoint but from within the democratic discourse.[7] Based on this discussion, we believe that our business ethics perspective not only draws on a solid conceptual foundation but it also provides a pragmatic approach for the social entrepreneurship debate. In fact, whereas foundational discussions about ethics can be fairly abstract and complex, it is our experience that many practical phenomena do not require a complicated ethical debate. After all, if social entrepreneurs innovate a solution that allows slum dwellers to lift themselves out of poverty, we typically observe that there is a broad factual consensus that, for example, helping the poor is desirable. From the perspective of a consensus-oriented ethics, there is thus no need for a sophisticated analysis of whether or not helping the poor is desirable. In a second set of cases, there may be controversial discussions about particular strategies or practices, yet 'moving up the staircase' in the practical syllogism shows that there is no real disagreement about ends, but a debate about the effectiveness of means. (How can we best help the poor?) Finally, in a third set of cases, there may be conflicting values or competing value rankings. (Is it more important to help the poor or to protect the environment?) In this scenario, ethics can help to ask how conditions and rules can be changed such that—given the relevant alternatives—diverse values and objectives can be best reconciled. This final scenario thus highlights the importance of understanding context—and how changing the context can change the desirability of the resulting consequences. (What can we change so that helping the poor also protects the environment?) This brings us to the final component of our conceptual perspective to be discussed in the next section: the concept of normative ambivalence.

3.6. The Concept of Normative Ambivalence

To navigate through complexity, human beings have the tendency to organize the world into clear-cut categories. This is particularly true when it comes to the distinction between good versus bad, desirable versus undesirable and others. From an evolutionary perspective, this makes sense. You want to recognize quickly what (or who) hurts and benefits you.

Against this background, humankind has often been portrayed as pattern-recognizing animals. A challenge that arises from this human inclination to categorize things as good or bad is that pattern recognition can lead to wrong conclusions. This is above all the case when a pattern observed in a specific situation is then interpreted as the general nature of the phenomenon under consideration.

To illustrate, take the following example. If whenever a child goes to a dentist, the dentist needs to use the drill and the child experiences pain, the child will soon consider not only the pain but also going to the dentist per se as something inherently bad. In a way, this process reflects some form of syllogistical learning. Here, the normative assumptions (I)) include "pain is bad," the positive assumptions are (II)) "I can go to the dentist" and "The dentist causes pain," thus leading to the conclusion (III)) "going to the dentist is bad."

The problem with this conclusion is, of course, that the child deduces a *false* judgment about the *general* nature of going to the dentist from a *specific* situation. After all, the dentist needed to use the drill only because the child had caries. If the child's teeth had been okay, the child would have experienced the visit to the dentist very differently. The desirability of going to the dentist thus does not depend primarily or exclusively on the nature of the dentist but on the contingency of the situation. Understanding this difference leads to very different conclusions: Instead of wanting to go to the dentist less often, the child should brush their teeth more often.

Although the dentist example looks trivial, we argue that the underlying issue has important implications for business ethics in general and our discussion about social entrepreneurship in particular. When it comes to normative discussions about what is good/desirable or bad/undesirable, there is a strong human tendency to use this distinction to classify how things 'really are'—irrespective of situational context. Good and bad are then used as *ontological* distinctions that serve to describe the true nature of being. Ontological features describe inherent qualities that things have per se, thus being *un*conditional on context. As discussed earlier (see Section 3.3), some strands of ethics base much of their theory on the idea that there are such universal principles that are unconditionally good. Take again, Kant's assumption that speaking the truth is inherently good—no matter the consequences.

Seen from this perspective, both the business ethics and the social entrepreneurship debates include many concepts, phenomena, or principles that are often discussed as being inherently desirable or good. As we will discuss in detail throughout this book, social entrepreneurship itself is often seen as a praiseworthy and even superior approach to societal problem-solving (Chapters 4 and 5). Similarly, there are often implicit or explicit notions that appraise not only phenomena like innovation, initiative, entrepreneurship but also principles such as following a social mission or concrete strategies and practices such as having a business model (Chapter 6), measurement (Chapter 7), or scaling (Chapter 8), as well as social entrepreneurship education (Chapter 10), as something to be encouraged, fostered, and promoted—thus implying that these concepts are per se and always desirable.

Similarly, in business ethics and more so in the public moral communication about business, there is often a tendency to see phenomena like profit-seeking, greed, or competition as bad or at least with skepticism while cooperation, trust and transparency are seen as inherently good (see, for example, Hosmer (1995) and Solomon (1992)).

In this subsection, we now want to challenge these ontological tendencies and make the case for a *situational* concept of *normative ambivalence*, that is, the notion that, seen from a consequentialist perspective, most phenomena can lead to negative *and* positive consequences depending on situational context. We develop this argument in the following two steps and start by looking at key origins of ambivalence thinking.

3.6.1. Back to the Roots: Deriving the Ambivalence Concept from Adam Smith

The perhaps most influential shift away from assuming unconditional desirability or undesirability of certain principles or intentions toward the analysis of context-specific consequences can be traced back to the work of Adam Smith. In his capacity as a *moral philosopher* (who unintendedly laid one of the cornerstones of economics as an academic discipline), Smith observed that the pursuit of self-interest (an intention or principle) can result in both desirable *and* undesirable consequences for society.

This nuanced perspective on self-interest in Smith's work is often overlooked (for a critique of the general Smith reception, see Kennedy (2009)). In fact, much of the literature reduces Smith to the famous *invisible hand* passage. Here, Smith (1776) explains certain welfare gains of trade by referring to a self-interested merchant who "intends only his own gain, and he is in this, as in many other cases, led by an invisible hand to promote an end which was no part of his intention." Smith thus shows that in *this* case—in this situational context—the pursuit of self-interest *can* make society better off.

Smith, however, did not claim that the pursuit of self-interest is *per se* good for society. (Note that even in this famous quote Smith adds "as in many other cases" not "as in *all* other cases.") Smith was well aware that, given other situational conditions, the same phenomenon of self-interest can lead to socially *un*desirable effects. For example, Smith (1776) argues in another well-known quote in *The Wealth of Nations*: "People of the same trade seldom meet together, even for merriment and diversion, but the conversation ends in a conspiracy against the publick, or in a contrivance to raise prices."[8] Far from being an uncritical proponent of egoism (Crane and Matten 2016) or profit-seeking behavior, Smith is thus well aware of the ambivalent societal effects of the pursuit of self-interest. In fact, just in book I and II of *The Wealth of Nations*, Smith gives more than sixty (!) examples of the *malign* effects of self-interest while mentioning the *benign* invisible hand just once (Kennedy 2009).[9]

The discussion as to how the pursuit of self-interest (either by individuals or in form of corporate profit-seeking) can be reconciled with the realization of societal 'moral' objectives lies at the heart of business ethics (Pies, Hielscher, and Beckmann 2009). Smith shows that it is not fruitful for this debate to ask whether self-interested behavior is in itself good or bad. Instead, he highlights that the pursuit of self-interest is morally *ambivalent*: It can produce *both* a *positive* and *negative value*, depending on context. For Smith as a moral philosopher, self-interest is, thus, a mirror with two faces. Seen from the perspective of just a subset of situations, one might then be led to perceive that one face in this mirror represents the true nature of self-interest. Figure 3.5 serves to illustrate this point.

When looking at cases in which self-interest goes at the expense of others only, the relationship between self-interest and moral (other regarding, societal) objectives appears to be a pure trade-off relationship (Figure 3.5b). Self-interest is, then, something bad. In this perception, furthering societal objectives is consequently only possible by limiting the profit motive. When looking, in contrast, only at cases in which self-interest promotes

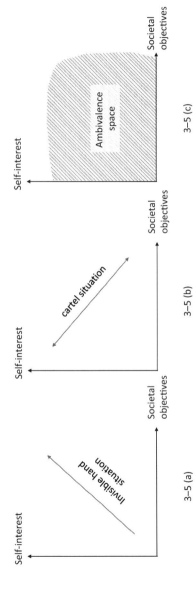

Figure 3.5 The ambivalent relationship between self-interest and societal objectives

moral (other-regarding, societal) objectives, then the relationship appears to be one of pure harmony (Figure 3.5a). Self-interest then appears to be something inherently good. In this perception, furthering societal objectives would consequently call for more or welcome self-interested behavior.

Though both perceptions point toward very different directions, they share an important commonality. Both ontological views (self-interest *is* good or *is* bad) see the relationship between self-interest and moral objectives as *one-dimensional*—as just one line on which self-interest or moral objectives can change. Smith, however, shows in his analysis that the relationship between self-interest and societal objectives is *two-dimensional*: it can work in many ways. Depending on the situation, there can be conflict or harmony, thus opening the context-dependent *ambivalence space* as illustrated in Figure 3.5c. The ambivalence space illustrates that both a trade-off and a harmony relationship are possible. Which effect prevails then does not depend on the ontological nature of self-interest but on the situational conditions that define the link between self-interest and moral objectives. As a result, ambivalence thinking thus focuses the analysis toward these conditions and to the question: Which conditions are needed and how can they be created to bring out the positive face of the self-interest mirror? In fact, Adam Smith spent much of his life educating people and advocating policy options to guide reforms to steer the British economy into that direction (Kennedy 2009).

3.6.2. A Useful Tool? Refining the Ambivalence Concept

We can refine Smith's specific analysis of the ambivalence of self-interest as a basis for deriving a general concept of ambivalence. As a professor of moral philosophy, Smith reflected upon the relationship between self-interest and the greater good. Upon closer inspection, it is possible to argue that Smith reflects upon the relationship of *two values*. On the one hand, helping others or promoting the greater good qualifies as a normative value. Yet, so does pursuing one's interest, on the other hand. Following one's own interests expresses values like liberty, autonomy, or the pursuit of happiness.

From an ambivalence perspective, we can thus derive that seemingly incommensurable values are not necessarily incommensurable. The relationship between values is rather characterized by ambivalence. Whether values can be reconciled or are in conflict with each other depends, again, on the situational conditions. There is an important implication here: Given the two-dimensional ambivalence space, each value can be analyzed in its capacity to either promote or hinder the other value—and vice versa! Equity and efficiency can be in conflict—but also reinforce each other. Protecting the environment can cost money—or save it. Economic growth, in turn, may erode ecological resources—or help guard them. Security concerns may go at the expense of civil rights—or may defend them. Civil rights, in turn, can contribute to security—or can hinder it. Depending on the perspective taken, *all* 'values' thus do not only have a bright but, potentially, also a *dark* side.

If we generalize this idea, we can develop the claim that basically *all phenomena are potentially ambivalent*. Practically all phenomena, principles, practices, and so on can have effects on something else—with the quality of these effects (whether they are desirable or not) being subjective to change with the situational conditions. Seen from this 'something else' perspective, everything is then ambivalent because it can lead to better or worse outcomes.

We argue that the ambivalence viewpoint outlined here provides a useful framework for our analysis and discussion of the social entrepreneurship agenda in this book. Switching from an ontological "how things are" to a situational "how things can be" perspective allows three worthwhile contributions: (1) to highlight that potentially useful tools only lead to intended desirable outcomes when used properly, (2) to create awareness for otherwise overlooked unintended 'dark sides' in social entrepreneurship, and (3) that the comparative assessment of any tool depends on the relative alternatives available. In the following, we will describe these three contributions in principle and briefly apply them to the discussion about entrepreneurship.

1. Because an ambivalence perspective does not view any practice or phenomenon as an end in itself but as a contingent means or instrument, it shifts the focus toward analyzing the appropriate instrumental application of these means. If social entrepreneurship can produce positive outcomes for society, then it presents an instrument—a tool that society can use for its goals. (Similarly, if we judge innovation, a social mission, initiative, altruism, measurement, cooperation, scaling, trust, or transparency in their capacity to produce desirable outcomes, we do not consider them as independent goals but as potentially useful tools.)

Tools, however, are never inherently good or bad. Most would agree that it seems absurd to ask whether a knife is good or bad. After all, you can use a knife to perform a surgery that saves a life, or you can use a knife to kill a person and destroy a life. The knife is therefore a tool with a normatively ambivalent potential. What really matters is the knife's *usage*. The ambivalence perspective thus shifts the focus toward how a particular phenomenon is *used*: how it is embedded in context and which conditions bring out its bright or dark side.

To illustrate, take the example of entrepreneurship. Entrepreneurship is often viewed as an important force to promote innovation, growth, and economic development (Acs, Desai, and Hessels 2008). If we see entrepreneurship as tool for economic development, however, an ambivalence perspective invites to ask whether there can be instances in which the usage of this tool can go wrong. Just as we can think of examples in which a knife does not save but end human life, we can analyze under which conditions entrepreneurship can actually destroy economic value and hinder development. In fact, in his seminal paper, Baumol (1990) showed that entrepreneurship can not only be productive but also unproductive or even destructive. If entrepreneurial activities are allocated toward rent-seeking or organized crime, entrepreneurship actually hinders economic development. Societies therefore need to enact adequate policies to 'use' entrepreneurship wisely. More generally speaking, an ambivalence perspective thus emphasizes the need to understand how a tool needs to be handled to achieve its *intended* consequences.

2. By questioning the assumptions that things can be inherently good, the ambivalence principle guides the analysis to look for potential *unintended* dark sides that may otherwise be overlooked. Because any evaluation depends on the perspective taken, the ambivalence concept thus encourages to ask: Are there potentially relevant perspectives on a phenomenon that have been overlooked? Can there be negative outcomes that materialize as unintended consequences in a different dimension than the one that focuses on the intended ones?

To illustrate, take again the concept of entrepreneurship. In terms of the societally intended effects, entrepreneurship can, under the right conditions, indeed serve as a driver of economic development. Yet, focusing alone on this economic dimension runs the risk of overlooking unintended consequences that may result in other dimensions. In fact, entrepreneurial venturing that does create value and drive economic development might have undesirable social effects (such as increases in inequality) or ecological effects (degradation of resources), thus expressing a "dark side of entrepreneurship" (Kets de Vries 1985; Wright and Zahra 2011). An ambivalence perspective would encourage to ask which perspective might be missing in the debate to uncover overlooked blind spots.

3. By assessing a phenomenon as a tool that can produce certain (ambivalent) outcomes, the ambivalence concept invites wedding an instrumental perspective with a comparative one. This is of relevance for the social entrepreneurship debate. In our community, we have heard time and again excited voices who appraise concepts like social business, innovation, or having a social mission as the better way to problem-solving (Yunus 2013). Understanding social entrepreneurship and other phenomena not as an (inherently desirable) end but instrumentally—as a tool to achieve desirable outcomes—underlines, however, that any such discussion is ultimately a comparative assessment: a comparison of the usefulness of *alternative* tools. (Note there that there is a strong link to the practical syllogism discussed earlier, which underlines the importance to clarify what the *relevant* alternatives are.) The ambivalence concept thus warns against the tendency of unconditionally acclaiming certain tools and practices such as social business entrepreneurs as *the* solution (Yunus 2013) or the more desirable "future of capitalism" (Yunus 2009).

The analogy of a real-life toolbox can demonstrate our point. If a friend of yours emphatically argued that the screwdriver is *the* solution or that the carpet cutter is *the* future, it would probably seem strange. Instead of discussing which tool is inherently 'the best' or 'superior,' you would probably object that the answer depends on the problem you want to solve. If you want to fix a loose screw, using a screwdriver is certainly the better solution than using the carpet cutter. Yet, if you want to open a cardboard box, the carpet cutter would be more useful. Furthermore, you might want to add that it also depends on what is available in the toolbox. If you want to cut some wrapping paper to wrap a present, having a pair of scissors would be great. But if there is no pair of scissors, using the carpet cutter might be the best *relevant* alternative (cutting the paper with a carpet cutter can still be better than using a screwdriver or no tool at all). At the same time, we all know that tools need to be used properly. After all, no parent would give a carpet cutter to their three-year-old because this tool, if used wrongly, can also create harm. In short, we are well aware of the ambivalence concept in real life. For judging the right thing to do, it all depends—on the problem, on the relevant alternatives, and on context and usage.

Let us again turn to the concept of entrepreneurship to illustrate that any instrumental judgment always needs to bear in mind the relevant alternatives. As mentioned previously, entrepreneurship and its promotion have been embraced as a driver for growth and economic development (Acs, Desai, and Hessels 2008). Understanding entrepreneurship as a societal tool helps to raise the question about potentially relevant alternatives. Seen from this perspective, foreign direct investment by multinational corporations can be—again: under adequate conditions—an alternative instrument for the creation of growth, transfer of knowledge, and economic development (Hansen and Rand 2006). Evaluating and managing the societal role of entrepreneurship thus benefits from taking the relevant alternatives into account (and even combining them).

3.7. Conclusion

In this chapter, we have argued that the social entrepreneurship discussion can benefit from integrating an ethical perspective. Social entrepreneurship and many of its related components, such as innovation or having a social mission, are often appraised as socially desirable. Ethics can help to make transparent, question, and justify the normative assumptions underlying these claims.

After discussing the features that an ethical perspective should fulfill for the purpose of this book, we have reviewed key strands of ethical theories. Based on this discussion, we have argued that a consequentialist paradigm is well suited to research and judge the desirability of outcomes that social entrepreneurship can produce on the macro, meso, and micro-levels.

We then refined the consequentialist perspective with the analytical framework of the extended practical syllogism that distinguishes between normative and positive assumptions. Here, we have shown that this methodological distinction can be applied to different levels, thus highlighting the contingency of how we define desirability.

To identify a common currency for assessing desirability at the highest level, we made the case for a consensus-oriented normative theory that does not aim at a consensus of values but at a procedural approach that looks for a consensus about rules and general principles that allows different actors to realize their diverse values and interests.

Finally, we introduced the concept of normative ambivalence. Because everything that produces consequences can be viewed as a tool or a means, the ambivalence perspective questions all attempts to categorize things as inherently good (or bad). It rather highlights that all tools can create ambivalent outcomes depending on how we use them. The ambivalence perspective thus encourages to clarify the problem perspective, to take into account the relevant alternatives, and to analyze the context conditions that bring out the dark or bright side of a phenomenon.

We argue that our ethical perspective and the concept of normative ambivalence can provide valuable guidance for discussing social entrepreneurship. The ambivalence perspective highlights that social entrepreneurship (and many of its buzz co-phenomena) is not an end in itself but a fascinating, powerful tool that can produce highly desirable results, yet that should not be romanticized. This book serves to appraise the social entrepreneurship tool, its limitations, and context conditions. In Part II, we will discuss social entrepreneurship as a *societal* tool for problem-solving, first in general terms (Chapter 4) and then in specific societal contexts (Chapter 5). Part III then discusses the value, limitations, and dark sides of much-acclaimed *organizational* tools in social entrepreneurship, such as social business models (Chapter 6), measurement (Chapter 7), and scaling (Chapter 8) before Part IV looks at how concepts of entrepreneurial agency and motivation (Chapter 9) as well as social entrepreneurship education (Chapter 10) serve as powerful, yet ambivalent tools on the micro-level. Chapter 11 then critically looks at the dominant social entrepreneurship narrative and argues that also our language and framing of phenomena are ambivalent tools to be used with care.

Notes

1. In contrast to traditional philosophical ethics, Luhmann (1991, 90) is skeptical whether philosophical ethics achieves this objective. He therefore sees the role of *theoretical* ethics to go one step further and to question whether the use of the moral code is justified in the first place, thus fulfilling ethic's perhaps most radical "task [. . .] to warn against morality" (see also Moeller 2011).
2. For the sake of brevity and, quite frankly also due to our limited knowledge, we focus our brief discussion on selected ethical theories most common in the Western tradition. We concede that this Euro-centric focus might leave out interesting and valuable perspectives and encourage others to critically fill this gap.

3. Just like the two other major normative theories, virtue ethics builds upon a rich tradition with diverse subtheories. Given the specific purpose of our book, however, this chapter only highlights the general focus of the theory, thus ignoring the intense debate about contemporary conceptions of virtue ethics. For an influential position in this regard, see MacIntyre (2007) or Bruni and Sugden (2013).

4. Note how his quote can be interpreted as mirroring the different elements of our practical syllogism. We "strive" expresses what we should do. The "best" refers to the normative assumptions according to which we judge our options. "We can attain" refers to the available choice options. Finally, "within the scope of this world" highlights the importance of the empirical situation.

5. Note how such a procedural understanding changes the status of ethics. Material approaches such as Utilitarianism or deontology see ethics as something like an external observer who knows and defines what is right and wrong and then applies this outside perspective to society. A procedural perspective, in contrast, sees ethics as a way to structure a discourse *within* society, without pretending to know, defining, and prescribing the content of what is valuable. Rather, society can and needs to engage in open ethical discourse and learning, thus exercising what Rorty (1988) called the "priority of democracy to philosophy."

6. Rawls (1999, 508–9) maintains: "It is perfectly proper, then, that the argument for the principles of justice should proceed from some consensus. This is the nature of justification."

7. Along these lines, Buchanan (2000, 210) thus defines as "good that which emerges from agreement among free men, independent of intrinsic evaluation of the outcome itself."

8. This brief example shows why "cooperation" is a normatively ambivalent phenomenon. Cartel behavior illustrates that cooperation (between competitors to raise prices) can go at the expense of others and make society worse off.

9. Here is another example in which Smith clearly highlights the conflict between self-interest and the wider public, namely with regard to the interests of merchants to limit competition at the expense of consumers. Smith (1776, 267) highlights:

> The interest of the dealers, however, in any particular branch of trade or manufactures, is always in some respects different from, and even opposite to, that of the public. To widen the market and to narrow the competition, is always the interest of the dealers. To widen the market may frequently be agreeable enough to the interest of the public; but to narrow the competition must always be against it, and can serve only to enable the dealers, by raising their profits above what they naturally would be, to levy, for their own benefit, an absurd tax upon the rest of their fellow-citizens. The proposal of any new law or regulation of commerce which comes from this order, ought always to be listened to with great precaution, and ought never to be adopted till after having been long and carefully examined, not only with the most scrupulous, but with the most suspicious attention. It comes from an order of men, whose interest is never exactly the same with that of the public, who have generally an interest to deceive and even to oppress the publick, and who accordingly have, upon many occasions, both deceived and oppressed it.

References

Acs, Zoltan J., Sameeksha Desai, and Jolanda Hessels. 2008. "Entrepreneurship, Economic Development and Institutions." *Small Business Economics* 31 (3): 219–34. doi:10.1007/s11187-008-9135-9.

Baumol, William J. 1990. "Entrepreneurship: Productive, Unproductive, and Destructive." *Journal of Political Economy* 98 (5): 893–921.

Bayertz, Kurt. 1994. "The Concept of Moral Consensus." In *The Concept of Moral Consensus: The Case of Technological Interventions in Human Reproduction*, edited by Kurt Bayertz, 41–57. Dordrecht, Netherlands: Springer.

Beckmann, Markus. 2010. *Ordnungsverantwortung. Rational Choice Als Ordonomisches Forschungsprogramm*. Berlin: wissenschaftlicher Verlag Berlin.

———. 2016. "Sustainability from an Order Ethics Perspective." In *Order Ethics: An Ethical Framework for the Social Market Economy*, edited by Christoph Luetge and Nikil Mukerji, 293–310. Wiesbaden, Germany: Springer. doi:10.1007/978-3-319-33151-5.

Beckmann, Markus, and Ingo Pies. 2016. "The Constitution of Responsibility: Toward an Ordonomic Framework for Interpreting (Corporate Social) Responsibility in Different Social Settings." In *Order Ethics: An Ethical Framework for the Social Market Economy*, edited by Christoph Luetge and Nikil Mukerji, 221–50. Wiesbaden, Germany: Springer. doi:10.1007/978-3-319-33151-5.

Brennan, Geoffrey, and James M. Buchanan. 2000. *The Reason of Rules*. Indianapolis, IN: Liberty Fund.

Bruni, Luigino, and Robert Sugden. 2013. "Reclaiming Virtue Ethics for Economics." *The Journal of Economic Perspectives* 27 (4): 141–63. doi:10.1257/jep.27.4.141.

Buchanan, James M. 1990. "The Domain of Constitutional Economics." *Constitutional Political Economy* 1 (1): 1–18.

———. 2000. *The Limits of Liberty: Between Anarchy and Leviathan*. The Collection. Indianapolis, IN: Liberty Fund.

Chell, Elizabeth, Laura J. Spence, Francesco Perrini, and Jared D. Harris. 2016. "Social Entrepreneurship and Business Ethics: Does Social Equal Ethical?" *Journal of Business Ethics* 133 (4): 619–25. doi:10.1007/s10551-014-2439-6.

Cobbah, Josiah A. M. 1987. "African Values and the Human Rights Debate: An African Perspective." *Human Rights Quarterly* 9 (3): 309–31. doi:10.2307/761878.

Crane, Andrew, and Dirk Matten. 2016. *Business Ethics: Managing Corporate Citizenship and Sustainability in the Age of Globalization*. New York, NY: Oxford University Press.

Crisp, Roger. 2014. *Aristotle: Nicomachean Ethics*. Cambridge: Cambridge University Press.

Dey, Pascal, and Chris Steyaert. 2012. "Social Entrepreneurship: Critique and the Radical Enactment of the Social." *Social Enterprise Journal* 8 (2). Emerald Group Publishing Limited: 90–107.

———. 2016. "Rethinking the Space of Ethics in Social Entrepreneurship: Power, Subjectivity, and Practices of Freedom." *Journal of Business Ethics* 133 (4): 627–41. doi:10.1007/s10551-014-2450-y.

Donaldson, Thomas, and Thomas W. Dunfee. 1994. "Toward a Unified Conception of Business Ethics: Integrative Social Contracts Theory." *Academy of Management Review* 19 (2). Academy of Management Briarcliff Manor, NY 10510: 252–84.

Graham, Jesse, Jonathan Haidt, Sena Koleva, Matt Motyl, Ravi Iyer, Sean P. Wojcik, and Peter H. Ditto. 2013. "Moral Foundations Theory: The Pragmatic Validity of Moral Pluralism." *Advances in Experimental Social Psychology* 47. Elsevier: 55–130.

Greene, Joshua David. 2014. *Moral Tribes: Emotion, Reason, and the Gap between Us and Them*. New York, NY: Penguin.

Habermas, Jürgen. 2015. *Between Facts and Norms: Contributions to a Discourse Theory of Law and Democracy.* Cambridge, MA: Polity Press.

Haidt, Jonathan. 2001. "The Emotional Dog and Its Rational Tail: A Social Intuitionist Approach to Moral Judgment." *Psychological Review* 108 (4). American Psychological Association: 814.

———. 2007. "The New Synthesis in Moral Psychology." *Science* 316 (5827): 998–1002.

Hansen, Henrik, and John Rand. 2006. "On the Causal Links between FDI and Growth in Developing Countries." *World Economy* 29 (1). Wiley Online Library: 21–41.

Hielscher, Stefan, Markus Beckmann, and Ingo Pies. 2014. "Participation versus Consent: Should Corporations Be Run According to Democratic Principles?" *Business Ethics Quarterly* 24 (4): 533–63. doi:10.5840/beq2014111919.

Hosmer, La. T. 1995. "Trust: The Connecting Link between Organizational Theory and Philosophical Ethics." *Academy of Management Review* 20 (2): 379–403. doi:105465.

Kant, Immanuel. 1949. "On a Supposed Right to Lie from Altruistic Motives." In *Critical of Practical Reason and Other Writings*, 346–50. Chicago, IL: University of Chicago Press.

———. 1993. *Grounding for the Metaphysics of Morals: With on a Supposed Right to Lie Because of Philanthropic Concerns.* Indianapolis, IN: Hackett Publishing.

———. 1998. *Critique of Pure Reason.* Cambridge: Cambridge University Press.

Kennedy, Gavin. 2009. "Adam Smith and the Invisible Hand: From Metaphor to Myth." *Econ Journal Watch* 6 (2): 239–63.

Kets de Vries, Manfred F. R. 1985. "The Dark Side of Entrepreneurship." *Harvard Business Review* 63 (6): 160–7.

Luhmann, Niklas. 1991. "Paradigm Lost: On the Ethical Reflection of Morality: Speech on the Occasion of the Award of the Hegel Prize 1988." In *Thesis Eleven* 29 (1), 82–94. Thousand Oaks, CA: Sage Publications.

———. 1992. "The Code of the Moral." *CARDOzo L. REv.* 14. HeinOnline: 995.

———. 1996. "The Sociology of the Moral and Ethics." *International Sociology* 11 (1). Sage Publications: 27–36.

MacIntyre, Alasdair. 2007. *After Virtue: A Study in Moral Theory.* 3rd ed. Notre Dame, IN: University of Notre Dame Press.

McKeon, Richard. 2009. *The Basic Works of Aristotle.* New York, NY: Modern Library.

Mill, John Stuart. 2016. "Utilitarianism." In *Seven Masterpieces of Philosophy*, 337–83. New York, NY: Routledge.

Moeller, Hans-Georg. 2011. *The Radical Luhmann.* New York, NY: Columbia University Press.

Pies, Ingo, Markus Beckmann, and Stefan Hielscher. 2014. "The Political Role of the Business Firm: An Ordonomic Concept Corporate Citizenship Developed in Comparison with the Aristotelian Idea of Individual Citizenship." *Business & Society* 53 (2): 226–59. doi:10.1177/0007650313483484.

Pies, Ingo, Stefan Hielscher, and Markus Beckmann. 2009. "Moral Commiments and the Societal Role of Business: An Ordonomic Approach to Corporate Citizenship." *Business Ethics Quarterly* 19 (3): 375–401.

Rawls, John. 1999. *A Theory of Justice: Revised Edition. A Theory of Justice.* Cambridge, MA: The Belknap Press of Harvard University Press.

———. 2005. *Political Liberalism*. Columbia Classics in Philosophy. New York, NY: Columbia University Press.

Rorty, Richard. 1988. "The Priority of Democracy to Philosophy." In *The Virginia Statute for Religious Freedom: Its Evolution and Consequences in American History*, edited by Merrill D. Peterson and Robert C. Vaughan, 257–82. New York, NY: Cambridge University Press.

Scanlon, Thomas Michael. 2003. "Rights, Goals, and Fairness." In *The Difficulty of Tolerance. Essays in Political Philosophy*, 26–41. Cambridge: Cambridge University Press. doi:https://doi.org/10.1017/CBO9780511615153.003.

Schelling, Thomas C. 1981. "Economic Reasoning and the Ethics of Policy." *The Public Interest* 63. National Affairs, Inc: 37.

Seelos, Christian, and Johanna Mair. 2012. "Innovation Is Not the Holy Grail." *Stanford Social Innovation Review* Fall: 44–49.

Smith, Adam. 1776. *An Inquiry into the Nature and the Causes of the Wealth of Nations. The Glasgow Edition of the Works and Correspondence of Adam Smith*. Reprint 20. Basingstoke: Palgrave Macmillan. doi:10.1057/9780230291652.

Solomon, Robert C. 1992. *Ethics and Excellence: Cooperation and Integrity in Business*. Oxford: Oxford University Press.

Trevino, Linda Klebe. 1986. "Ethical Decision Making in Organizations: A Person-Situation Interactionist Model." *Academy of Management Review* 11 (3). Academy of Management Briarcliff Manor, NY 10510: 601–17.

Varden, Helga. 2010. "Kant and Lying to the Murderer at the Door??? One More Time: Kant's Legal Philosophy and Lies to Murderers and Nazis." *Journal of Social Philosophy* 41 (4): 403–21. doi:10.1111/j.1467-9833.2010.01507.x.

Weber, Max. 2017. *Methodology of Social Sciences*. New York, NY: Routledge.

Wright, Mike, and Shaker Zahra. 2011. "The Other Side of Paradise: Examining the Dark Side of Entrepreneurship." *Entrepreneurship Research Journal* 1 (3). doi:10.2202/2157-5665.1043.

Yunus, Muhammad. 2009. *Creating a World without Poverty: Social Business and the Future of Capitalism*. New York, NY: Public Affairs.

———. 2013. "Social Business Entrepreneurs Are the Solution." In *The Future Makers: A Journey to People Who Are Changing the World—and What We Can Learn from Them*, edited by Joanna Hafenmayer Stefanska and Wolfgang Hafenmayer, 219–25. London: Routledge.

Zahra, Shaker A., Eric Gedajlovic, Donald O. Neubaum, and Joel M. Shulman. 2009. "A Typology of Social Entrepreneurs: Motives, Search Processes and Ethical Challenges." *Journal of Business Venturing* 24 (5): 519–32. doi:10.1016/j.jbusvent.2008.04.007.

Part II

Society, Economy, and Social Entrepreneurship

A Macro-perspective

4 The Societal Function of Social Entrepreneurship

Innovating in the Voids Between Market and State

Social entrepreneurship is often heralded as *the* solution to societal problems (Seelos and Mair 2009) or even as the pioneer of a new type of capitalism (Yunus 2007). This discussion sometimes implies that social entrepreneurship is a—if not *the*—better tool to solve societal problems if compared to the conventional tools (government, commercial ventures, and traditional nonprofits) society uses to address diverse societal needs. And indeed, there are impressive examples of social entrepreneurship (Bornstein 2007; Elkington, Harding, and Litovsky 2010). For instance, consider Wikipedia, which changed the provision and collection of knowledge internationally; Sekem, who developed a new form of biodynamic agriculture in Egypt (Seelos and Mair 2009); or Aravind (Rangan, Thulasiraj, and Rangan 2007 and see Chapter 7), who revolutionized eye healthcare provision in India.

Without a doubt, all of these and many other social ventures have a societal impact and create necessary and significant social change. Yet, it would be presumptuous to use these examples to subsume generic conclusions on the overall impact of social entrepreneurship on entire societies or whole economies. As elaborated in Chapter 3, the conceptual perspective taken in this book does not look at social entrepreneurship as an end in itself but as an exciting tool—as an instrument whose positive and negative effects need to be analyzed (a) by considering the context in which the tool is used and (b) in comparison with alternative tools available. With regard to context, this chapter aims to understand the role social entrepreneurship plays on a macro-level. With regard to relevant alternatives, the question then is: What makes social entrepreneurship distinct from alternative problem-solving tools such as conventional for-profits, nonprofits, and the state?

Due to its unique nature, social entrepreneurship lies between the logic of the market, the state, and the third sector. In other words, it typically makes use of mechanisms of at least two of the three sectors (Ridley-Duff and Bull 2015). Whereas the social sciences help us to understand, assess, and compare the logics and societal contributions of pure market, pure state, and pure nonprofit organizations in the third sector, the question arises as to how the 'in-betweenness' of social entrepreneurship affects the role it plays for society at large.

To this end, Chapter 4 starts analyzing the macro-context for social entrepreneurship by taking a sectoral perspective that focuses on general differences between the public (state), private/for-profit (market), and voluntary third (nonprofit) sector. Building upon this sectoral perspective to understand the 'in-betweenness' of social entrepreneurship, we distinguish between the static contribution of social entrepreneurs (filling governance and service provision gaps) and their dynamic contribution (triggering change in the way other actors in the state, the market, and the third sector provide solutions) (Beckmann 2012). Following this general analysis of the societal role of social entrepreneurship, we will dive deeper into its inherent normative ambivalence. For conceptual clarity, the sectoral perspective of this chapter applies a rather idealized view of the four problem-solving tools under investigation. Building upon this generic analysis, Chapter 5 will then specify our macro perspective and look at differences within sectors and between societies. We will then discuss specific contextual differences such as the level of welfare state prevalence and level of development.

4.1. Social Entrepreneurship—The Better Solution?

Prior to presenting our analysis of the macro-level role of social entrepreneurship, we deem it necessary to understand the underlying assumptions that sometimes lead to a presumed superiority of social entrepreneurship. To this end, we will use Yunus' concept of social business as an illustration of the underlying argument. (For a more detailed discussion of the overlap and difference between the social business and social entrepreneurship concept, see Beckmann, Zeyen, and Krzeminska 2014). We merely utilize Yunus as an example. There are many other scholars who use similar lines of justification (see, for example, Kickul and Lyons 2016).

Yunus presents the social business concept as a novel, hybrid organizational form between the conventional for-profit firm (in the market) and the traditional nonprofit organization (in the third sector). His case for the social business approach argues that this hybrid construct can combine the advantages of both for-profit and nonprofit organizations: In terms of organizational objectives, just like nonprofit organizations, social businesses follow a motivation allegedly superior to commercial ventures as the former place other-regarding motives (social impact) above self-interested motives (profit) (Yunus 2007). If we rephrase this in line with our conceptual framework (Chapter 3), Yunus claims that social ventures follow normatively superior *objectives* (Beckmann 2011, 2012). In terms of organizational resources, however, Yunus perceives market-generated income as used by commercial ventures superior to donations traditionally used by nonprofit organizations (Yunus 2003; Yunus, Moingeon, and Lehmann-Ortega 2010; Yunus 2007). In other words, he perceives business-like *tools* superior to charitable *tools* while he argues that charitable *objectives* are superior to business-like *objectives* (Beckmann 2012). According to Yunus, the 'in-betweenness' of social business thus uses hybridity to combine the best of two worlds by linking superior objectives (other regarding motives) with superior tools (self-sustaining market income and efficiency of private business).

We acknowledge that part of the fascination and attractiveness of the social business and social entrepreneurship concept lies in the hybrid logic as described by Yunus or others who assert that "social entrepreneurship represents the best of the private and public sectors" (Kickul and Lyons 2016, 4). For the purpose of this chapter, however, we claim that a closer look at this argument points to a very important oversight. Rather than taking a societal view, Yunus' assessment of the hybridity of social business actually investigates *organizational* tools and objectives (Beckmann 2012). Yet, if we wish to understand the role of social entrepreneurship on a macro-level—seen from a *societal* point of view—we need to redefine social entrepreneurship not as the organizational *objective* but as a *tool* for society (Beckmann 2012). Whether social entrepreneurship is an effective tool for society, then, ultimately does not depend on the internal motivation but the external impact it creates. Moreover, by considering social entrepreneurship as a tool to achieve societal objectives, we can see that social entrepreneurship is only one of many tools that society has at its disposal to problem-solve. As a consequence, we conjecture that it is more theoretically stimulating to ask under which conditions or for which type of problem, social entrepreneurship is a promising solution rather than stipulating that a specific organizational form is per se the best solution regardless the problem. Such an instrumental assessment thus encourages considering both the problem context and the alternative instruments available (also see Chapter 3). Bringing both aspects together allows phrasing the question slightly differently: Are there problems that are better solved by other tools than social entrepreneurship?

4.2. A Societal View on Social Entrepreneurship as a Tool for Impact

To analyze social entrepreneurship as a tool, we first need to clarify both the problem it seeks to solve and the perspective from which we assess the solution. As elaborated in Chapter 2, the problem that social entrepreneurship seeks to address for society is to generate positive *social change* through the *direct provision* of solutions for diverse societal challenges. To assess social entrepreneurship as a problem-solving tool, we therefore need to compare it with the alternative societal instruments available in the public, private business, and third sector that directly provide diverse goods and services. To this end, the following subsection will thus compare social entrepreneurship with the public sector, commercial ventures, and traditional third sector organizations in regard to their impact and respective role within society.

When assessing these solutions, however, we need to refine how we understand impact. As widely acknowledged in both economics and system theory, analyzing the macro-level impact of certain system elements such as competition benefits from distinguishing a static perspective from a dynamic one (Melcher and Melcher 1980; Blaug 2001). A *static* perspective focuses on the efficiency effects in a given state or (momentary) equilibrium. A *dynamic* perspective, in contrast, analyzes the effects of innovation, change, and development. Following this distinction, we first take a static perspective (Section 4.2.1) and start our discussion by comparing social entrepreneurship from an efficiency perspective. Section 4.2.2 then shifts the perspective from efficiency to innovation and learning, thus looking at the dynamic impact of social entrepreneurship on societies.

4.2.1. A Static View on Social Entrepreneurship and Societal Impact

To analyze the static impact of social entrepreneurship as a hybrid solution to directly address societal needs, we compare it with the idealized ways of how public sector, private (market), and nonprofit organizations directly provide goods and services. For each sector, we briefly highlight certain characteristics and describe their underlying logic. As social entrepreneurship shares its other-regarding mission with traditional nonprofits, we start our analysis with the third sector (nonprofits) before looking at the market and public logic.

a) Comparing Traditional, Charitable NPOs and Social Entrepreneurship—A Static View

Within the third sector, charitable NPOs traditionally engage in the direct provision of diverse goods and services to beneficiaries in need. The main source of funding for these activities are voluntary donations (Littlewood and Holt 2015). Therefore, to compare the static impact of social entrepreneurship with that of traditional NPOs, we need to understand in what situations donation-based solutions are the most effective and efficient tool to problem-solve. To do so, we need to take a step back and understand the underlying mechanisms of donations. Donations are rooted in 'spontaneous'—that is, in a Hayekian sense (Hayek 1988), emergent, bottom-up—solidarity and as such have a deep-rooted place in most cultures and religions (e.g., concept of Zakat in Islam: Almarri and Meewella 2015; Christianity and Hinduism: Ranganathan and Henley 2008; Christianity and Judism: Bird 1982). So in which situations is spontaneous solidarity an effective means to problem-solve? As Figure 4.1 illustrates, we can distinguish two dimensions for this analysis (Beckmann 2012).

The first dimension we can draw upon is time. From a static perspective, this temporal dimension does not look at how situations dynamically change over time but rather focuses on the frequency of how often and

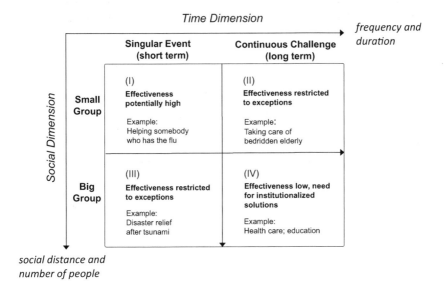

Figure 4.1 The effectiveness of spontaneous solidarity in different social settings
Source: Adapted from Beckmann (2012)

long support is needed in a given situation. Spontaneous solidarity is an emotional state and requires both actual or perceived urgency as well as actual or perceived closeness to the subject. As such, various reasons make it difficult to sustain solidarity and therefore ongoing donations for a longer period of time.

First, given the usual news half-life of six weeks, both news agencies and the public tend to turn their attention to something new, thus making it difficult to sustain a sense of urgency for enduring crises. Second, giving a donation once requires fewer resources than permanently supporting a cause, thus creating increasing incentive issues for frequent or permanent solidarity. As a consequence, spontaneous solidarity is a tool more potent for singular events or short time periods.

Next to time, number and social distance of people affected (social) dimension influence the effectiveness of spontaneous solidarity (Beckmann 2012). As human beings, we find it harder psychologically to empathize with people we do not know (cf. Hogg 1992). This is because we are prone to think in the dichotomy of in-group and out-group and have a tendency to favor in-group members (Tajfel 1974). In the social dimension, we can thus distinguish between small groups (micro-cosmos) and big groups (macro-cosmos) where the former is based on informal face-to-face personal relationships such as family or friendship groups and the latter based on large-scale societal relationships that are anonymous, formal, and rule-based (Hayek 1988 and see Section 8.2.2 for an application to scaling). Along this dimension, people are more willing to display solidarity in the micro-cosmos, while increasing social distance reduces spontaneous solidarity in the macro-cosmos.

Let us now combine both the temporal and social dimension: Spontaneous solidarity occurs most naturally—and typically does not need formal organizing—when situations of urgent (short-term) need happen within the micro-cosm in which people share strong small-group ties (box I in Figure 4.1). For such *single-event small-group* challenges, not only family members but also friends and neighbors will be willing to help. Take the example of a friend who has come down with the flu. For a number of days, many people who are socially close would be willing to assist them by doing the shopping, picking up medication from the pharmacy, and even cooking for them.

Yet, what happens if this flu turns into a chronic disease or disability confining the person to their bed and in need of care for many years? In this case (box II in Figure 4.1) it is less obvious that spontaneous solidarity will provide a sustainable solution. Within the very small group of the immediate family, people may permanently take care of their children and, to a lesser extent, of their elderly parents. Yet, most other people—even with a personal relationship to the one in need—would not provide the same care in the long term as compared to a short crisis. This example illustrates that emergent bottom-up solidarity is much more difficult to activate on a permanent basis compared to a temporary one. Therefore, *long-term small-group* needs are in a gray zone where spontaneous solidarity can still be effective, but in a much more limited way.

In contrast to the small-group micro-cosmos, solidarity in the anonymous big group macro-cosmos typically requires more formal organizing. Let us start with *single-event big-group* problems (box III in Figure 4.1) such as a natural disaster like the devastating 2004 tsunami in Southeast Asia. In such an exceptional (and therefore temporary) instance, many of us are ready to give donations for people we have never met, even at the other side of the world. Charitable third-sector actors then provide the organizational infrastructure to mobilize and orchestrate such spontaneous solidarity on a societal level. Given the context of such crisis situations, already existing charitable organizations such as disaster relief NPOs can be a very effective instrument to provide much needed services. This example challenges, however, Yunus' underlying assumption that donations are per se inferior to earned-income strategies. In fact, compared to self-sustaining social entrepreneurship ventures, raising donations for disaster relief is arguably more effective and efficient than innovating a new social entrepreneurial organization. What is needed in such a crisis is typically not novel solutions but the fast mobilization of resources—which, in certain contexts, established third-sector charities can organize quicker and more effective through donations.

To complete the discussion, we now turn our attention to *long-term big-group* issues in the macro-cosmos (box IV in Figure 4.1) such as taking care of the elderly or people with special needs, providing education, or healthcare. These questions have a systemic character because they need to be dealt with permanently and throughout society. How adequately could spontaneous solidarity address these systemic issues based on voluntary donations? There are multiple underlying issues here. First, voluntary donations are inherently volatile and fluctuate with the level of economic and household income growth (Hughes and Luksetich 2008). Therefore, the aggregated value of available funding would not be consistent which would make long-term planning challenging if not impossible. Just imagine trying to plan a nation's education system without any certainty about funds available in the next quarter. Second and more importantly, as discussed earlier, the willingness to donate decreases over time and with social distance. The challenge for bottom-up, spontaneous solidarity is that there are few incentives in the anonymous macro-cosmos for the individual to permanently give voluntary donations for people they do not know. Though it might be collectively desirable that everybody makes significant voluntary donations, there is an individual incentive to freeride on the solidarity of others (Olson 2009). As a consequence, spontaneous solidarity expressed as voluntary donations will not provide sufficient resources for the system-wide provision of goods and services. What is needed here are solutions that replace spontaneous solidarity with *institutionalized* solidarity that aligns collective problem-solving with individual incentives. Such solutions can either draw on the public-sector logic of the state (see Section c) and thus enforce mandatory contributions (such as taxes) for collective solutions or build upon the for-profit logic of the market such as in the case of private insurances that also organize institutionalized solidarity in regard to hardship situations.

In short, charitable NPOs that rely on voluntary donations can organize spontaneous solidarity for society. This can be effective for providing relief in single-event situations or for rather specialized services. For certain contexts, such as a humanitarian crisis, organizing spontaneous solidarity through donations is arguably more effective than social entrepreneurship ventures that seek to innovate complex business models. The limits of spontaneous solidarity, however, lie where long-term, system-wide solutions are needed. In these instances, the sectoral in-betweenness of social entrepreneurship can transcend these limits. By tapping into the public- and private-sector logic, social entrepreneurs can innovate financially sustainable business models that allow scaling beyond the limits of spontaneous solidarity. Social entrepreneurship business models thus organize institutionalized solidarity to address systemic societal needs. To further analyze this potential, we now turn to the market and the public sector as alternative approaches for the system-wider provision of goods and services.

b) Comparing Social Entrepreneurship and Commercial Ventures—A Static View

Modern society and the capitalist system as we know it today evolved only around 150–200 years ago but has grown ever since (Luhmann 2012). Despite lots of criticism regarding the capitalist system (for more see du Gay and Morgan 2014), the rise of capitalism has gone hand in hand with increased standards of living, rising life-expectancy, and improved working conditions (William J. Baumol 2002; Rosling, Rönnlund, and Rosling 2018). Reflecting upon how these dramatic improvements in social welfare can emerge in a system characterized by the pursuit of individual self-interest and profit-seeking goes back to Adam Smith (1776) and his famous idea of the invisible hand. For our purpose, these considerations about the societal function of the profit motive are relevant because they allow analyzing for-profit firms as an instrument for addressing societal needs—and then contrasting this tool (and its limitations) with the social entrepreneurship approach.

So why (and how) is the profit principle a potentially useful tool for making society better off? For brevity, we focus on just two ideas that highlight the static and also dynamic potential of the profit motive. First, in a competitive market system, companies can realize superior profits only if they outperform their competitors through better, cheaper, and above all novel products and services (see Section 4.3 and Baumol 2002). Second, from the static point of view that we primarily focus on in this subsection, the profit motive creates incentives for realizing efficiency gains for society. The link to the profit principle is simple: Companies realize a profit only when their revenues—that is, the value of the resources they have produced—are higher than their costs—that is, the value of the resources they have consumed (Jensen 2002). Under the right conditions—properly functioning institutional frameworks that we critically reflect on in a moment—profit-seeking thus induces companies to create value for society: to combine resources in a way that gives society more valuable options (measured in a company's revenues) than it consumes (measured in a company's costs). In a world with scarce resources, yet abundant needs, such efficiency gains are highly important. For-profit firms are then instruments that society uses to organize the provision of private goods and services in a value-creating way. Business' organizational objective of profit-seeking then serves as a tool for societal value creation.

As already conceded, however, the potentially positive societal effects of private profit-seeking are not automatically given but hinge upon adequate enabling conditions (also see Section 3.6.1). Companies realize profits when the value—expressed in market prices—of their products is higher than the value—expressed in market prices—of the resources consumed. Ideally, these market prices reflect 'real' societal scarcity and thus indicate which kind of costs and benefits are relevant for society as a whole. Corporate profits and societal value creation are then well aligned. In order to fulfill this function, however, the price mechanism requires adequate regulation including well-defined property rights. If property rights are poorly defined, companies may not consider all societal costs, for example when polluting the environment saves costs for the firm but creates costs for society. In fact, to perfectly align the profit motive with societal value creation requires working markets with the absence of any market failure, including functioning competition, no externalities, well-designed property rights, no abuse of power or coercion, no exclusion of underprivileged groups with free access to labor and product markets, capital, education, and legal justice for everyone.

For-profit companies are thus a powerful, yet ambivalent instrument for addressing societal needs. Given the idealized conditions just discussed above, for-profit firms are the most powerful machine for delivering diverse private goods and service. In fact, we argue that in a situation of well-functioning markets, for-profit firms are *more* effective than social entrepreneurship in terms of creating value for society through the direct provision of private goods and services. Compared to social entrepreneurship's other-regarding mission, the for-profit motive can be more impactful for various reasons.

For one, if (!) profits signal value creation, they not only reward those companies that already create value for society but also direct other firms to redirect their activities to where societal needs are greatest. At the same time, the profit-principle would punish those firms that destroy value as they would suffer financial losses. The profit-principle thus allocates resources on a macro-level toward societal needs. Second, profits can help an organization decide which internal projects to pursue. It gives a clear performance criterion that allows constant internal optimizing and accountability. Third, profits also provide signals to investors by showcasing which areas create most value, thus providing the resources to scale good solutions. The latter is something that the social entrepreneurship field is still struggling with (see Chapter 8). While there are many performance measurement schemes, they are still ambiguous and not easily comparable (Chmelik, Musteen, and Ahsan 2016; Arena, Azzone, and Bengo 2015; Andersson and Ford 2015; and see Chapter 7).

Similar to our analysis of donation-based NPOs, we can thus identify conditions under which the in-betweenness of social entrepreneurship would not automatically be an advantage from a societal viewpoint. On the contrary, in well-functioning markets, departing from the profit motive to embrace a hybrid mission could make it more difficult to create value for society because of system-wide and organizational efficiency losses. In these instances, for-profit firms would be the first-best solution to provide private goods and services with social entrepreneurship only being a second-best option.

The above notwithstanding, it is essential to remember that the societal functionality of the profit-principle is contingent upon strict context conditions. If and only if markets are organized by perfect institutional frameworks with no market failure (Beckmann 2012) is it possible that the invisible hand (Smith 1776) driven by profits is the first-best solution rather than the visible hand of the social entrepreneur. The reality of markets, however, is often far from perfect. Thus, commercial ventures are likely to not achieve their full potential and might therefore not be available as the first-best solution for societal impact. In this situation, social entrepreneurs can become a relevant second-best solution. Thanks to their hybrid in-betweenness, social entrepreneurs can depart from the pure profit principle to intentionally internalize externalities, provide access to otherwise excluded groups, and create value where commercial ventures are not (Santos 2012).

In short, compared to the ideal world of perfect markets, social entrepreneurship provides only a second-best solution—but so do real-life markets with their imperfections. Whether social entrepreneurship or imperfect for-profit ventures are more effective for society then ultimately amounts to an empirical question. Instead of following a 'nirvana approach' (Demsetz 1969) that takes idealized solutions as the reference point, the appraisal of social and commercial ventures then needs to take a comparative look at the *empirically relevant alternatives* in a given context. With regard to many examples of real-life market failure, such an analysis suggests that social entrepreneurship can well be the best available tool for society.

c) Comparing Government Provision and Social Entrepreneurship—A Static View

In this final step, we turn our attention to government and the public sector. Although commercial ventures typically provide private goods, governments are primarily tasked with public and common goods provision. Public goods are those goods that are nonrival and nonexcludable (Nordhaus 2006). Nonrivalry means that while one person is using the good, other people can still use it. Nonexcludability states that everyone can make use of the good provided. Take the example of clean air. If one person breathes in clean air, it does not hinder someone else from doing the same. Analogous, it is hardly possible to exclude someone from breathing the air outside. While nonexcludability and nonrivalry sound good on paper—everyone can enjoy it—it becomes a challenge when considering the incentives for providing them (Samuelson 1954). If you cannot exclude someone from using a product or service, then no one will be willing to pay for it. As a consequence, markets are not likely to evolve to offer public goods efficiently and effectively. Yet, some of the most significant sustainable development challenges (SDG 2018) include public goods such as infrastructure, functioning legal systems, education, the eradication of poverty, or basic public health.

To systematically tackle this challenge, societies have developed various mechanisms to organize the provision of public goods (Cornes and Sandler 1996; Olson 2009). Whereas for smaller or traditional communities such solutions can be informal and based on social norms (Ostrom 2015), modern societies use above all the formal institutions of the state, government, and public-sector organizations, respectively, to organize the system-wide provision of public goods (Beckmann 2012; Cornes and Sandler 1996).

When it comes to providing public goods throughout society, public-sector institutions build upon various advantages. First, one key role that the state plays in public goods provision is to level the playing field. An inherent problem in public goods is free-riding, that is, some people use the good—because they cannot be excluded—without contributing any resources for its provision (Olson 2009). To overcome this pitfall of public goods, states can force contributions by all users, for example, through collecting taxes. What is important here is that the government does not necessarily have to provide the public good itself but can contract it to NPOs or even private firms (as in the case of army base security for US forces).

Second, if we assume efficiently functioning state bureaucracies, the state is able to effectively disseminate new solutions through existing sophisticated infrastructures. Take the example of the National Health Service (NHS) in the UK. This nation-wide system allows for quick implementation of, say, a new vaccination for children. Here, they can draw not only on their previous experience with vaccinations but also on the available clinics, storage facilities and trained nursing staff. If in comparison, a newly formed social enterprise would intend to vaccinate every child in the UK, it would take up many resources and much time to achieve that objective.

Finally, in a democratic state, the public can hold their governments accountable for success and failures and vote them out of office. Whereas taxation coerces the citizens to fund public expenditures, democratic checks and balances allow them to control that these expenditures are according to the preferences of the public (Friedman 1970). From a political science perspective, this then provides feedback to the government on where to spend finite and scarce resources (Przeworski, Stokes, and Manin 1999).

The complex institutional infrastructure of the state thus provides elaborate mechanisms for effectively funding, efficiently administering, and democratically controlling the provision of public goods. Particularly when it comes to providing public goods solutions for long-term, system-wide needs (compare box IV in Figure 4.1), ideal-type governments are arguably the first-best instrument for this purpose. In fact, we argue that, compared to well-functioning state institutions, social entrepreneurship is a systematically inferior instrument to provide public goods. In light of permanent, societal needs for public goods, social entrepreneurs cannot tap into systematic means to organize collective action for an entire society. They further have no or very limited access to comparable existing and sophisticated infrastructure. Finally, feedback mechanisms within social entrepreneurship are likely to be less well developed than those of functioning democratic states (Beckmann 2012).

In short, compared to ideal-type public institutions, social entrepreneurship would be less effective, efficient, and democratic to systematically provide public goods. With ideally functioning government being the first-best solution, social entrepreneurship would then be a second-best option only. Analogous to markets, however, such an idealized perspective hinges on certain, critical conditions: a well-functioning state, a fair and effective tax system, no corruption, minority voices are not ignored, and all citizens are well informed about their choice when voting.

Yet, herein lies the crux of the matter. Similar to real-life markets, real-life states do not fulfill the perfect criteria assumed for ideal types. In fact, government and public institutions often fail to provide much needed public goods, particularly with regard to local community or minority needs. Although social entrepreneurs might find it hard to organize the provision of nation-wide, encompassing public goods, their in-betweenness enables them to innovate mission-driven business models that provide rather focused public goods. This can range from the community-oriented provision of education (like in the case of Rodrigo Baggio, who created the Center for Digital Inclusion to provide high-tech skills to slum dwellers in Brazil—see Santos (2012)) to the protection of natural resources (like in the case of Durukan Dudu whose organization, Anatolian Grasslands, teaches farmers in Turkey to use regenerative techniques that protect the soil from erosion (Ashoka 2018)). In all these instances, social entrepreneurship plays a crucial role of pointing to so far unmet needs, in gathering resources to address it, and providing solutions to such needs.

In short, compared to the ideal world of perfect state institutions, social entrepreneurship is only a second-best solution to provide public goods—but so are real-life state institutions with their imperfections. Whether social entrepreneurship or imperfect state institutions are more effective for society then ultimately amounts, again, to an empirical question. With regard to many examples of real-life state failure, however, social entrepreneurship has proven to be the best available tool for society.

In summary, a static perspective shows that social entrepreneurship is a potentially important, yet not perfect instrument for organizing the direct provision of socially needed goods and services. In fact, compared to idealized sectoral solutions by the state, the market, and charitable nonprofits, social entrepreneurship is *systematically* only the second-best solution for many problems. In an idealized world, pure ideal-type solutions would be more efficient and effective than the hybrid solutions that characterize social entrepreneurship's in-betweenness. In the real world, however, neither markets nor state nor charitable institutions are perfect. Given the relevant empirical alternatives, social entrepreneurship may then be a second-best solution in theory but the better or even best solution available on the ground. In these instances, the very hybridity of social entrepreneurships allows going into the gaps and blind spots created by the real-life imperfections of the state, market, and third sector.

The static contribution of social entrepreneurship to societies therefore lies, in short, in *compensating* the imperfections of existing public, private, and third-sector institutions. Social entrepreneurs fill in the gaps left by others. This static contribution can be important. The next section, however, argues that the impact of social entrepreneurship does not stop here. From a dynamic perspective, social entrepreneurship can also contribute to *reducing* the imperfections of existing institutions by inducing them to *change*— so that certain gaps no longer open up in the first place.

4.2.2. A Dynamic View on Social Entrepreneurship and Social Impact

As elaborated in our definitional Chapter 2, social entrepreneurship aims at positive social change through the direct provision of socially or ecologically needed solutions. To analyze the immediate impact of these direct provisions, the previous Section 4.2.1 took a macro-view on social entrepreneurship to discuss its static impact on society. In this section, we will now elaborate social entrepreneurship's ability to generate *social change* by taking a dynamic perspective. Although social entrepreneurs create change directly by filling in the gaps left by conventional institutions, they also change society indirectly by triggering learning processes that change these very institutions. In other words, our analysis now goes beyond merely looking at the direct effect social entrepreneurship ventures have on their beneficiaries. Instead we now also include the *in*direct influence of social entrepreneurs that can change the entire field and may lead other actors to adapt and adopt their solutions. We thus now move away from a focus on efficiency and effectiveness (a static view) to a focus on innovation and diffusion (dynamic perspective).

The purpose of this subsection is to substantiate our claim that social entrepreneurship often has a systematic and important comparative advantage for creating a dynamic impact (Beckmann 2012). To this end, we follow a similar process as in the previous subsection—we will compare social entrepreneurship to its relevant alternatives: traditional NPOs, commercial ventures, and the state.

a) Comparing Traditional NPOs and Social Entrepreneurship—A Dynamic View

Earlier in this book, in our definitional Chapter 2, we highlighted that NPOs and social entrepreneurship do not necessarily exclude each other. Though NPOs are defined as a mission-driven organizational form that does not issue profits, social entrepreneurship is about the mission-driven, pragmatic use of innovations to directly provide societal solutions. Because social entrepreneurs may (but need not) use a nonprofit form to do this and because

NPOs are often innovative, both concepts overlap in real life. (In fact, most of Ashoka's award-winning social entrepreneurs operate their venture as a nonprofit.) Still, there are differences between traditional, purely philanthropic NPOs and social entrepreneurs that pragmatically combine different logics. To carve out these differences more clearly, this subsection contrasts social entrepreneurship with, again, idealized traditional nonprofits, that is, to purely philanthropic organizations that fund themselves through voluntary donations and that provide their products and services charitably—for free—to their needy beneficiaries. Instead of analyzing the efficiency and effectiveness of the direct provision of these offers, our dynamic analysis now scrutinizes how these differences affect the capacity to innovate new solutions and the potential to diffuse them throughout the system.

Taking this dynamic innovation and diffusion perspective, we posit that the often hybrid in-betweenness of social entrepreneurship has multiple systematic advantages compared to a purely charitable logic. To illustrate this claim, our subsequent discussion will make use of the example of a philanthropic NPO that relies on donations and provides charitable aid to beneficiaries in a developing nation.

First, the development of innovative solutions is not an easy one-off quick process but often requires ample iterations of trial and error. This trial-and-error process requires feedback, particularly from the users or beneficiaries whose needs the solutions seeks to address. Despite their attempts to gather feedback, however, aid organizations often find it difficult to fully evaluate their societal impact and the quality of their solutions. This is not least due to the fact that they offer their products and services for free. To start with, a purely philanthropic logic creates a power asymmetry between the benevolent donor and the dependent recipient—making it less likely that the latter criticizes the product or suggests (let alone demands) improvements. Furthermore, beneficiaries also have little incentive to provide feedback because their personal investment was minimal. To make this point clearer, take the example of Acumen Fund (Batavia et al. 2011), a US nonprofit social venture capital firm that, among many other things, tackled malaria prevention, in particular, the provision of mosquito nets. Acumen queried the situation that although aid organizations had provided millions of people with mosquito nets for free, they were not really used. Through the process of selling the mosquito nets rather than giving them away, Acumen was able to not only provide employment to locals and drive down the costs of providing the mosquito nets but to also gather feedback from their customers. As Acumen's founder and CEO Jacqueline Novogratz maintained, departing from a purely philanthropic logic and bringing in a market logic allowed using "the market as a listening device that reveals how to tailor services and products to the preferences of low-income people who are viewed as consumers, not victims" (Novogratz 2010). Empowered to change from the role of dependent recipients to market customers, their users stated that mosquito nets had significant disadvantages given the tropical climate because it was often too hot underneath them to sleep. Furthermore, users pointed out that as soon as someone would need to get up at night, they would still face the mosquitos in their houses. Users themselves suggested mosquito-secure paint or windows so that they could still move around the house and be less hot while sleeping.

This example shows that due to their in-betweenness that weds a mission-driven approach with market-elements, social entrepreneurs were able to gather valuable feedback, particularly with regard to product development and improvement. This is not to say that social ventures are free from the pitfalls of gathering feedback. Indeed, impact and performance measurement are some of the most demanding challenges in running a social venture (see Chapter 7). Nonetheless, social ventures are able to access feedback channels that are closed off to many aid organizations. Furthermore, through the process of empowering their stakeholders and integrating them into their business model, they operate more at arm's length, which is vital to gather rich feedback and innovate for the users.

Second, after effective solutions are innovated, purely charitable solutions correspond with inherent limits for scaling them throughout the system (see the earlier discussion on spontaneous solidarity). To be scalable in the long term, a solution needs to have a sustainable base, that is, it needs to be self-sufficient and secure the resources it requires (Beckmann 2012). Here, a systematic challenge arises with philanthropic NPOs. Aid at its core implies dependence, most often on an external foreign provider, with grants and donations being a limited resource. Though we do not deny that foreign transfer aid can lead to self-sustaining projects in the long run, empirical evidence strongly suggests that the road there is arduous (Easterly 2006). Innovations that purely rely on aid and donations thus limit their scalability.

In comparison, the very idea of social entrepreneurship and especially social business (see Chapter 2) is self-sufficiency. Thus, social ventures acquire their resources *within* the system they wish to influence rather than relying on external resource inputs. This is possible through their focus on innovative solutions that wed a social mission with elements that tap into the logic of the market or the public sector, thus securing additional inputs, for example, through business models that integrate local beneficiaries and other actors into their value chain. As a consequence, these business models are more easily transferable to other actors, even if the latter do not equally share the social entrepreneurs' mission drive. For instance, for-profit firms could copy social entrepreneurial solutions and adapt them to their business or governments could scale them through their systems.

Third, there might be unintended, negative dynamic effects. The provision of aid can crowd out or even destroy local systemic solutions by commercial ventures or local governments (Thielke 2005; Kubania 2015). For instance, if an NPO delivers basic healthcare to a developing country, the local government might not feel the need to develop the relevant capabilities. This potential effect is well documented for food aid (Thielke 2005) as well as for the potentially destructive nature of second-hand clothing markets (Alexander 2018; A. Brooks 2015b; J. Brooks 2017; Rodgers 2015; A. Brooks 2015a; Kubania 2015). In the context of food aid, Western donations may be well intended and help lower the costs for poor people in the short term. At the same time, however, these market interventions risk undercutting any price local farmers could achieve (Thielke 2005), thus driving them out of business and exacerbating food crises in the long term. In the case of textiles, we will briefly turn to Kenya as an example. Kenya's textile industry used to employ about half a million people in the 1980s. This number has fallen to roughly 2,000 (Kubania 2015). This drop is mostly due to the opening of the Kenyan market and the influx of second-hand clothing from Western countries. According to Oxfam, about 70 percent of second-hand clothes donated end up on the African continent (Kubania 2015). Their original look and better quality then pushed most local products out of the market. Ironically, simply banning Western imports to Kenya would not solve the problem—or at least would create others. This is because many Kenyans now rely on second-hand textile trade as their source of income (Kubania 2015).

If we link this back to our discussion in Section 4.2.1, we can again see the importance of a temporal dimension in understanding the effectiveness of various societal tools. Though aid is highly potent for disaster relief, that is, to help out starving populations in the short run, it is not as potent and can even be destructive in the long run.

Moreover, charitable aid can even set perverse incentives. Corrupt governments can benefit from keeping their country in crisis because this means the continuation of foreign aid (Harvey 2015; Thielke 2005). Corruption is a challenging topic in humanitarian aid. For instance, there are estimates that the vast majority of aid going into Afghanistan was lost through corruption (Danish 2016). Needless to say, social ventures are not immune to these challenges. However, they have certain characteristics (see Chapter 2) that help them better deal with these challenges. For one, to the extent that they source their resources within the system, they are less prone to corruption that tries to grab its share from resources inflowing from outside donors. Also, social entrepreneurship ventures often aim to create and develop markets rather than crowding them out. These initiatives then often turn into blueprints for commercial ventures to follow and adapt. Last but not least, social entrepreneurs often find themselves in a better position to influence local governments. A study on Ashoka Fellows found that about half of them impacted policy-making within their first five years (Sen 2007).

b) Comparing Commercial Ventures and Social Entrepreneurship—A Dynamic View

In our static analysis of the profit principle, we maintained that company profits can signal that a firm creates something of high value for society.

Over time, this signal will induce other firms to follow the profit signal and redirect their activities, thereby expanding the supply for these products. With firms competing over price, the market will eventually reach a new equilibrium at which products and services are provided with highest efficiency and at lowest costs for the consumers. From a societal point of view, this process is highly desirable. For companies, however, imitation and price competition by their rivals means that it becomes very difficult to maintain sustainable and above-market profits in the long term (Baumol 2002).

As competition brings down profits for existing products over time, companies who seek to secure or increase their profits therefore need to outcompete their rivals with new, better, or cheaper products. Seen from a dynamic viewpoint, the profit principle paired with competition thus incentivizes firms to constantly innovate (Baumol 2010). Innovation allows firms to escape competition temporarily, thus creating attractive innovation rents. These innovation rents, in turn, induce competitors to follow suit. Innovation-oriented competition then shifts the economy toward yet another new equilibrium.

The profit motive can thus be a powerful incentive for innovative entrepreneurship that changes society. As Schumpeter (1934) famously noted, entrepreneurship describes a process of "creative destruction," with innovation creating new solutions that render existing structures obsolete. To illustrate, take the example of smartphones. Their invention has rendered other portable audio devices like the Sony Discman or MP3 player obsolete because most people would not bother carrying two separate devices. As such, the impact of commercial ventures on our daily lives is significant and so is the impact of their innovations. Just pause to consider the progress in information and communication technology over the last twenty years or the progress made in pharmaceuticals.

Particularly when paired with competition, profit-seeking companies can thus be powerful engines to address societal needs through innovation. Despite their impressive track record of innovation that has in many ways made our lives easier, however, commercial ventures have failed to innovate solutions for certain customer groups or problems. The reason is that the societal contribution of purely profit-driven innovation hinges upon critical context conditions including: open competition, a functioning price system that monetarizes relevant costs and benefits, as well as the ability of beneficiaries to express their needs with effective purchasing power. In the real world, these idealized assumptions are often not given. We argue that in these cases their hybrid in-betweenness can provide social ventures with comparative advantages in innovating and in thereby setting up more inclusive markets for at least four reasons.

First, as the saying goes "time is money," and setting up new and more inclusive markets often takes time and thereby can incur significant costs. Moreover, for some solutions it might take many years before they turn profitable or become self-sufficient. This is particularly the case at the base of the pyramid, that is, the market of and for the poor in developing economies, where companies need to address multiple challenges simultaneously, including poor infrastructure, access to finance or education (Batavia et al. 2011). Here, social ventures have the advantage that their time horizon of investment is long term instead of the mostly short-term driven horizon of commercial ventures or funders. It is important to note here that this short-termism is not necessarily of the commercial ventures' choosing but often a result of demands by external stakeholders such as stockholders. Moreover, with the median CEO tenure now being as low as five years (Marcec n.d.), individual top managers have no or little incentives to invest in projects whose success materializes only after their tenure ends. Social ventures, in contrast, often have the luxury of 'patient capital' (Novogratz 2007, 2010) thanks to impact investors. This allows them to invest in riskier approaches, which are, however—if successful—more likely to create new markets or overcome deadlocks.

Second, social entrepreneurs tend to be highly committed to their mission to a point where it could be considered obsessive (see Chapter 9). This clear, often single-issue focus provides them with a specific search heuristic. To be clear, we are not arguing that commercial ventures do not innovate for social needs. Numerous examples show they do. However, they identify a social need as a potential new business opportunity. Yet, if addressing this social need does not allow them to create and capture sufficient value, they will drop it and move on to the next. Social entrepreneurs, in contrast, are stuck with their mission, thus forcing them to continue trial-and-error processes in the domain in which they started.

Third, the social mission of social ventures can help overcome the public goods problem inherent to the innovation process. Knowledge, novel ideas, or inventions are public goods. If everybody can freely use them, there are few incentives to invest in their development. This is why research and development by for-profit firms is incentivized through patents while the government subsidizes basic research by financing universities with tax money. Where such schemes do not exist, social ventures often mobilize the necessary resources by cooperating with traditional NPOs, community groups, or local governments (Choi 2015; André and Pache 2016). This provides them with access to nonmonetary resources such as volunteer work or in-kind donations (Zeyen, Beckmann, and Akhavan 2014). As a consequence, these hybrid models can pool the resources needed for innovating (see Chapter 6).

Fourth, the social mission can help overcome instances of market failure that occur because of the newness of innovations. Note that newness is not only a positive feature but also a liability (Stinchcombe 1965). Two problems are relevant here. First, switching to a new product that only the first-mover in the market provides can make the user dependent on this provider, thus creating the risk that the firm later exploits this dependence (e.g., by raising the price). Second, if a solution is really new and unknown, potential customers find it difficult to assess its quality, thus creating the risk that a firm misleads the consumer and exploits such information asymmetries. Given both challenges, purely profit-driven companies could then be seen as having an incentive to exploit dependencies and information asymmetries at the expense of the poor. A well-known example in this regard is Nestlé's infant formula controversy (Sethi 2012). Here, Nestlé was criticized for aggressively targeting uneducated poor people with the claim that Nestlé's instant formula product was a superior substitute for breast-feeding. According to its critics, however, feeding instant baby milk is not only more expensive for the poor but also less healthy than natural breast-feeding. Given such information asymmetries and vulnerabilities, particularly of disenfranchised groups, purely profit-driven firms might therefore fail to convince the targeted beneficiaries or other important stakeholders that innovative solutions really benefit the poor. Thanks to their strong social mission, social ventures are, in contrast, often perceived as trustworthy, credible, and, legitimate (Beckmann 2012). The social mission then serves as some form of assurance that can stabilize stakeholder cooperation. In other words, social ventures can help to overcome a lack of transparency, reduce information asymmetries, and develop underdeveloped markets. Interestingly, after social ventures have helped to increase transparency about a new product by educating consumers, commercial ventures can then enter the market and offer similar products and face fewer challenges.

In short, their hybrid in-betweenness endows social entrepreneurs with certain advantages for creating positive social change from a dynamic perspective. Thanks to their longer-term perspective, their almost irrational issue persistence, and the perceived trustworthiness of their mission orientation, social entrepreneurs can not only innovate new products and services. Their dynamic impact also results from the creation of new markets and the process of competitors adopting and diffusing novel value-creating practices. Finally, the lack of competition is a challenge in many markets—both at the base of the pyramid (Prahalad 2010) as well as in the quasi-markets of Western welfare states (Brandsen 2004 and see Chapter 5). To the extent that social entrepreneurs offer new alternatives, they increase competition for incumbent ventures, thus inducing them to innovate themselves.

c) Comparing Governments and Social Entrepreneurship—A Dynamic View

We do not wish to insinuate that governments are unable to innovate. On the contrary, competition between governments as well as competition within governments creates incentives for 'policy entrepreneurs' (Mintrom 2000) to develop and implement innovations in the public sector. Still, countless societal problems fall into the blind spot of this process. With regard to many of these issues, we claim that social entrepreneurship has at least three comparative advantages to create social change by illuminating these blind spots.

First, to create dynamic impact we require significant learning through trial and error. Douglas North (2005) argued that the 'adaptive efficiency' of these types of learning processes is equally dependent on the number and diversity of trial and error as it is on the quality of the feedback generated. Government organizations, however, are not ideally set up for adaptive efficiency. They are often centralized organizations with strict bureaucratic procedures. Although these are highly efficient for disseminating tried and tested approaches, they tend to be too stiff for innovation purposes. Furthermore, even if experimentation is feasible within a government setting, it is often rudimentary and does not allow for fast, iterative processes of adaptive efficiency. Though, in the market, customers give constant product feedback through their buying behavior, feedback mechanisms in the public sector need to be organized in more complex ways. To be sure, elections and polls do provide citizen feedback, yet in a less instant, less incremental, and less informative way. As Chapter 7 will discuss, devising alternative feedback channels through impact measurement is challenging for social issues, too. In short, the hierarchical organization of the state faces difficulties when it comes to engaging in iterative learning processes that require decentralized knowledge, feedback, and adaptation.

Here, the advantage of social entrepreneurship lies in its bottom-up rather than top-down approach because it is able to increase adaptive efficiency by mobilizing decentralized experimentation and feedback. Given their hybrid in-betweenness, social ventures are not constricted by well-established systems and processes but can move between different system logics in order to create and start up whichever solution works best for their current experiment. On top, their arm's-length approach provides them with richer feedback as they often have relationships with their beneficiaries (André and Pache 2016).

Second, modern democracies are based on majority rule. Yet, many societal challenges are specific to certain subgroups of individuals—often minorities— or local areas. Against this background, policy entrepreneurs face incentives to direct their engagement toward issues that can win elections or woo important donors. As a consequence, government authorities are less likely to address a problem that would not (positively) impact the next election (e.g., too small, or nonvoter beneficiaries). Given their bottom-up approach, social entrepreneurship is not constrained by these mechanisms. Social entrepreneurs can thus innovate in niches deemed too irrelevant by other actors. From a dynamic perspective, they can then demonstrate how supporting a minority may benefit the majority and thereby support governments in finding rationales to implement new policies.

Third, innovation entails risk. New ideas can fail. Governmental organizations, however, tend to be inherently risk averse. As both the media and voters focus more on negative news about failure than on reports about things that work just fine, governments often provide funding only to solutions that have a so-called proof of concept, that is, they have shown that it works. As a result, the public sector is hesitant toward disruptive change and rather favors incremental changes of the status quo. Here, social entrepreneurship can take the risk and then provide evidence that a novel solution really works. This in turn then allows government organizations to implement this new solution. Take again the example of Rodrigo Baggio and his Center for Digital Inclusion. Influenced by Baggio's success, the Brazilian government launched a national program of digital inclusion to scale the underlying idea throughout the country (Santos 2012). The dynamic effects of social entrepreneurship thus go significantly beyond the direct provision of their new solutions.

In sum, if we compare our discussion on the static and dynamic view of social entrepreneurship, we can see that from a static point of view, social entrepreneurship may not be the most efficient, first-best solution in an idealized world, yet does provide important second-best contributions in the real world. By directly providing much needed solutions, social entrepreneurs compensate for some of the shortcomings of the existing institutions in the state, market, and third sector. From a dynamic perspective, however, the arguably even more relevant contribution of social entrepreneurship lies in its innovations triggering broader learning processes for the state, market, and third sector. Our discussion on dynamic impact thus shows that key features of social entrepreneurship (mission orientation, innovation focus, hybrid logic, risk-taking preference, etc.) not only endows them with specific advantages to innovate novel solutions. Their in-betweenness also often opens up pathways for traditional sectoral actors to adopt and adapt these solutions more easily.

The direct provision of much needed solution thus sums up the static contribution of social entrepreneurship. The systematic contribution to positive social change then results' from the direct and indirect dynamic impact of social entrepreneurship. Against this backdrop, it is possible to argue that social entrepreneurship is the research and development (R&D) department of society. Indeed, some scholars go as far as to argue that the societal role of social entrepreneurship is not to solve societal problems (as most authors argue) but to provide ideas and linkages between organizations that previously did not exist (Carraher, Welsh, and Svilokos 2016). If solutions work, governmental, conventional nonprofit, or commercial actors are then likely to adopt and adapt them and thereby scale them to a wider audience.

4.3. A Mission-Driven, Societal R&D Department—That's Good, Isn't It?

As outlined in more detail in Chapter 3, key elements of the conceptual perspective taken in this book include the concept of unintended consequences and the idea of ambivalence. The concept of unintended consequences encourages us to focus the analysis on both the direct as well as indirect effects of purposeful behavior. The idea of ambivalence maintains that it is often of limited value to discuss whether a certain phenomenon or construct is per se inherently good or bad. Instead, it highlights that most phenomena can be embedded in different contexts that may, in turn, trigger both desirable or undesirable consequences, respectively. The ambivalence perspective then shifts the focus toward analyzing these conditions and how they can be managed to bring out the bright side instead of the dark.

Seen from this conceptual perspective, this entire chapter has already discussed social entrepreneurship in terms of its contextual ambivalence on a macro-level. Instead of assessing social entrepreneurship in absolute terms or appraising it as a per se desirable approach, we have assessed social entrepreneurship as a societal tool and compared its relative potential advantages and disadvantages with regard to different contexts and different alternative tools.

At the end of this chapter, we now want to take our ambivalence analysis one step further. Instead of looking at the potential ambivalence of social entrepreneurship as a whole, we refine our discussion by examining the potential ambivalence of some selected features that typically define social entrepreneurship (see Chapter 2). In much of the social entrepreneurship debate, a common subtext implicitly appraises these features as inherently positive and desirable per se—praising individual agency, approving of the social mission, celebrating innovativeness, and applauding how social entrepreneurships fill in the gaps left by other actors. In the following, we challenge this assumption and want to briefly show how individual agency, social-mission orientation, innovation, and filling in the gaps can lead to undesirable phenomena on a macro-level.

4.3.1. Grass-Roots versus Venturing: Serving Minorities without a Mandate—The Ambivalence of Entrepreneurial Agency

Social entrepreneurship is based on individual or small-group agency (Robinson 2006; Dacin, Dacin, and Matear 2010; Lee 2015), that is, social entrepreneurship is about individuals acting on their beliefs to achieve a social mission. Social entrepreneurship thus describes a decentral, bottom-up approach in which individual agency includes identifying a problem, devising a solution, and implementing it with the necessary resources. Compared to a rather hierarchical political process, social entrepreneurship's bottom-up contribution to society can offer a voice to those overlooked by the political mainstream. This occurs when prospective beneficiaries are part of a minority group—be it based on ethnicity, race, sexual orientation, or disability—or because the issue is too niche to be relevant on a national or even regional political arena. In these situations, social ventures can be a potent vehicle to offer minority groups access to certain rights. Indeed, a quick look through the Ashoka Fellow database clearly supports this. Many social ventures deal with issues such as disability or support groups of individuals that are oppressed in their freedom—for example, women or minority ethnic groups.

To illustrate the potential of individual agency, take the example of Specialisterne from Denmark (Specialisterne 2013). This social venture serves a very specific and small group of beneficiaries (people living with certain types of high-functioning autism). Due to their unique needs but relative small size in terms of the overall population, people with autism are a group that conventional for-profit firms are unlikely to consider as workforce or customers and that is unlikely to receive full-fledged governmental attention. This is not to say that the respective government does not 'care,' but rather that there are many issues a government needs to take care of and very specialized or small minorities easily fall through the cracks. In the case of Specialisterne, its founder, Thorkil Sonne, wanted to bridge these cracks because his son was diagnosed with autism and therefore displayed individual agency in innovating a novel solution. Trained as a software engineer, Thorkil Sonne's had the idea to transform autism into a competitive advantage by employing people with autism for software testing where they have significantly lower fault rates than average workers. Knowing the field, he then founded Specialisterne to offer the new solution to business customers. Individual agency was thus instrumental in identifying the problem (personal affectedness because of his son), devising the solution (thanks to his software expertise), and implementing it (within the business context Thorkil Sonne knew).

From a societal perspective, individual agency thus has many advantages. It can draw on decentral knowledge, tap into widely dispersed resources, and allow for parallel innovating in different domains. It is therefore hardly surprising why many are fascinated by the individual agency in social entrepreneurship. (So are we!) Yet, individual agency is ambivalent. Under certain conditions, its underlying characteristics can also lead to questionable or undesirable consequences on a macro-level. We want to highlight three potential challenges in this regard.

1. First, individual agency for social entrepreneurship is not equally dispersed in society and for different issues—thus addressing some challenges while ignoring others. As the example of Thorkil Sonne illustrates, individual agency requires that the people who know and care about relevant problems also have the skills and can acquire the resources to solve a problem (see Chapter 10). An often-unspoken underlying assumption of social entrepreneurship is that people always have the agency to engage in such grassroots activities. Yet, some groups do not have that agency due to lack of legal rights, lack of knowledge, lack of self-esteem, or lack of other capabilities. Because social entrepreneurs often act in areas they are familiar with (Belz and Binder 2017), this is yet another reason why certain topics might be overlooked by social entrepreneurs because those who have the experience might not have sufficient agency to go forward. As a consequence, individual agency might then be least available in the communities who most need it. In fact, a look at the Ashoka Fellow database in a country like Germany reveals that most social entrepreneurs operate in big cities

whereas only few come from smaller cities and almost none from economically deprived rural areas. One additional reason for this phenomenon is that individual agency benefits from a supportive ecosystem (see Chapter 5), thus limiting decentral, bottom-up contributions where these conditions are lacking.

Moreover, the decentral mobilization of resources is arguably easier for some societal issues than it is for others. To illustrate, we will briefly compare two organizations. First, take Guide Dogs for the Blind Association UK (Guide Dogs 2018), who breed and train guide dogs. Within the UK, they are one of the charities that is very successful in collecting donations—not least because of the adorable puppy pictures they use in their adverts. In comparison, take *hand-in* (JAS 2018), a German-based venture that provides personal development training through boxing to youth offenders. In an interview with the first author, one of the founders discussed their struggles to find sponsors because most individual or corporate sponsors do not wish to link their name or brand with youth offenders. Thus, hand-in finds it harder to fund their youth rehabilitation program than Guide Dogs does to fund their life-changing dog partnerships.

Although we compared two separate social ventures, it nonetheless helps to highlight an important challenge in macro-level social entrepreneurial agency. Though filling blind spots of other societal problem-solving tools, social entrepreneurship might face its own blind spots, that is, they might themselves overlook certain groups or topics because the motivation and skills for individual initiative as well as the availability of resources are unevenly dispersed.

2. Second, and closely related, decentral individual agency lacks coordination—thus risking the misallocation of resources Social entrepreneurship features a bottom-up approach to problem-solving. Yet, figuratively speaking, you cannot see much from the bottom. As a consequence, social ventures lack the oversight of governments about general distribution systems and the status quo of society. To be sure, networking and cooperation play an important role for social entrepreneurs (Montgomery, Dacin, and Dacin 2012). Yet, we have personally witnessed that social entrepreneurs often compete for scarce resources like funding, volunteers, or attention despite the fact that they sometimes pursue rather similar ends. This is not least due to the fact that individual agency often comes from strong personalities who value their individual autonomy. Instead of pooling the resources to scale impact, multiple individual projects then seek to (re-) invent the wheel. Furthermore, without coordination, it is easily possible that similar ideas are tested in various areas without any mutual learning. As such, similar mistakes could happen in different areas, which waste scarce resources. Decentralization enables innovation but does not guarantee system-wide learning and feedback.

3. Third, individual agency seeks to change society without an explicit and democratically controlled mandate. Social entrepreneurs want to change

society but decide individually how this change should look like. Some critics therefore point out that social entrepreneurs do not automatically have the societal mandate to act, that is, they act in areas often assigned as core governmental tasks but were not elected by the public. Decentral, bottom-up processes therefore not only raise questions of coordination but also of accountability.

In short, the macro-level effects of individual agency are inherently ambivalent. Although there are many advantages of decentral, bottom-up individual agency, uncoordinated individual agency can also create blind spots, lead to resource misallocation, and raise issues of accountability. Whether the goals and practices of a social entrepreneur's individual agency are really in the interest of society is then an open question and also depends on the specific mission pursued. The next section therefore looks at the ambivalence of having a social mission.

4.3.2. Ideology and Paternalism—The Ambivalence of a Social Mission

As shown in Chapter 2, the key characteristic of social entrepreneurship is its social mission (Zahra et al. 2009; Dacin, Dacin, and Matear 2010; Lee 2015). Much of the fascination and appraisal of social entrepreneurship circles around this altruistic motivation to help others. In fact, the social mission is often seen as inherently desirable for society as being other-oriented is perceived to be more noble and effective than being merely self-interested or profit-oriented.

In this section, we want to challenge such a romanticized notion of the social mission. Just as individual agency, a social mission can have ambivalent consequences on a macro-level. Three issues can play a role here: (1) the normative content of the mission, (2) unintended consequences and potential discrepancies between normative objectives and the ability to achieve them, and (3) the structural asymmetry involved in helping others that can lead to paternalism. We will first briefly elaborate each of these issues and then (4) use one example to illustrate all three.

1. Social entrepreneurs have a vision of what is good for society and what is good for their beneficiaries. When defining this mission, social entrepreneurs follow their positive assumptions of how the world works and their normative assumptions that reflect their values. Yet, this guarantees neither that these factual assumptions are actually true nor that the underlying values are shared in society. In fact, social entrepreneurs might pursue objectives that are not necessarily in line with a societal consensus on what is right (desirable) and what is wrong (undesirable). Although this can push boundaries and challenge society's view on certain topics, it can also create significant harm and be viewed by many as undesirable. Just take organizations like the Taliban and their mission to create a strictly Islamic society. By building madrasahs, funding religious hospitals, and organizing Sharia law, they directly provide solutions for this kind of social change and finance

them through the entrepreneurial cultivation and sales of heroine. From their own internal perspective, the Taliban surely follows a social mission, with a missionary drive to build a better society and help others. Yet, many people will disagree with this vision. Whether a *social* mission is widely viewed as desirable depends on its normative content and the societal (and historical) context.

An important learning here is that it would be short-sighted and naïve to give social entrepreneurs and their ventures a free reign simply because they follow a social mission. This, however, is what sometimes happens in practice. When social entrepreneurs emphasize their social mission and signal that they are not (primarily) profit-oriented, they are often considered trustworthy. Whether their mission and impact is truly socially desirable, however, requires further scrutiny.

2. A social mission expresses the *intention* to help others. Yet, it does not necessarily say anything about whether the social entrepreneur has the knowledge and skills to do so. This is highly delicate when it comes to helping others. When the pursuit of a social mission is glorified as something per se valuable (see Chapter 11), potentially inexperienced social entrepreneurs may end up in areas where they work with potentially highly vulnerable people without the necessary skills. Any well-intended social mission can therefore lead in its implementation to negative unintended consequences. This is particularly relevant from a macro-level perspective because the eventual impact on a system level is fairly detached from the social entrepreneur's direct intention but rather results from the interplay of manifold additional factors.

3. The very notion of helping others raises the potential issue of paternalism. It rests on the structural asymmetry between the one who helps and the one who receives help. To be sure, many social ventures do operate at arm's length with their beneficiaries. And in doing so, they both treat their beneficiaries with respect and are able to collect rich feedback from them to improve their solutions. Yet, this is not a guaranteed feature. In effect, some social ventures do take a very paternalizing view in that they know best and do not need to engage in processes of adaptive efficiency (Dey 2006).

Proponents of social entrepreneurship might argue, rightly so, that the challenge of paternalism is much less of a problem for social entrepreneurs than for traditional charitable organizations. Although both have a mission to help others, social entrepreneurs often innovate solutions that empower their beneficiaries by integrating them into a value chain or engaging them in some sort of win-win exchange. Empowerment, however, depends not only on whether a beneficiary is better off materially but also on whether someone's ability to freely choose has improved. This raises the question of power and dependency. In many cases, there is a power asymmetry between social entrepreneurs who provide a solution and those who depend on it. This can be a power asymmetry in terms of money or material resources, in terms of status, or in terms of knowledge (see Section 6.3).

4. The following, admittedly stark, example may illustrate all three instances of the ambivalence of a social mission. In Uganda,[1] 'social entrepreneurs' have set up gay conversion centers that are tasked with 'curing' homosexual men from their sexual orientation (Onyulo 2017). Funded through donations by American evangelical Christians, these centers employ innovative campaigns and 'therapies' to achieve their social mission. Their organizational purpose is to promote a Christian life and help homosexual men to overcome their "sinful lifestyle choices." These gay conversion centers fulfill, in other words, all the characteristics of social entrepreneurship. Instead of pursuing financial profits, these organizations are driven by a very clear social mission: to cure people of what they consider to be an unnatural sexual tendency.

However, just because the mission is social, that is, it aims to help people, it does not mean—and in the authors' view, it definitely does not in this case of gay conversion centers—that the work of these organizations is socially desirable. Many people would disagree with the underlying values of the organization (1)). Furthermore, according to most psychologists, the notion that homosexuality is a disease that can (and should) be cured is factually wrong. In fact, instead of helping gay men, conversion theory causes depression, anxiety, and even drives 'patients' into suicide. Although the mission intends to help gay men, the lack of psychological expertise results in the (unintended) effect of hurting them (2)). Finally, with American donor money involved and the influence of US evangelical missionaries, there are various issues of power discrepancies in terms of money, status, and knowledge. After all, it is unlikely that conversion theory participants—regardless if they went voluntarily or were coerced—had access to all information to make an informed decision. It is doubtful that they would have been given and read all the research that disproves claims that homosexuality is a lifestyle choice.

In short, from a societal perspective, having a social mission is not per se desirable and inherently ambivalent. The normative content of a mission may well reflect goals that are widely shared in society but also objectives that are controversial or seen as undesirable. Even if the intentions reflect a societal consensus, the implementation can fail or lead to negative unintended consequences. Finally, having a mission to help others may raise issues of power, dependency, and paternalism.

4.3.3. Real Progress or a Fetishized Fad? The Ambivalence of Innovation

In Chapter 2, we have elaborated that the idea of innovation is a defining feature of social entrepreneurship—be it in the scholarly Social Innovation School or when organizations like Ashoka aim for a society that makes "everyone a changemaker." And indeed, as shown in this chapter from a macro-view, there are many positive effects of social entrepreneurial innovation. Yet, there is a tendency in the social entrepreneurship debate to see innovation as something inherently good, consequently seeing innovation only as part of the solution. In this section, we want to challenge this unreflected notion of innovation and show that innovation can also be part of the problem. Innovation, again, is an inherently ambivalent phenomenon. We will point to three issues: the content of an innovation, its creative destruction, and the effects of fetishizing innovation.

1. Innovation just means that something new was not only invented but also successfully implemented. Whether this factual change counts as positive societal progress depends on the content of the innovation and how it is later used. For terrorists, suicide bombing is an innovation. The Nazis innovated a method to use Cyclone B, a cyanide-based poison, to murder approximately one million people in gas chambers such as Auschwitz-Birkenau. Innovation is, therefore, again, a tool to be used with care. Whether innovation leads to ethically desirable results depends on what you do with it.
2. Schumpeter famously described entrepreneurial innovation as a process of 'creative destruction.' Innovation creates new things. But it is also a source of destruction. Often, destruction can be socially desirable, for example, when innovation destroys a market failure. But there can also be (unintended) consequences that add shadow to the light of innovation. Take again the example of Ursula Sladek (Chapter 2) who innovated solutions for renewable energy services. Such innovations are now rapidly destroying the nuclear- and fossil-fuel-based energy industry in Germany, thus creating follow-up problems in communities in which nuclear power plants used to be the biggest employer in town. Here, people have to retrain to get a new job and relocate to other places. Innovation is therefore an important driver for structural change. Even if the societal benefits of such structural change are net positive, innovation often creates not only winners but also losers.
3. If innovation is fetishized as an objective in itself, this can lead to a misallocation of resources on many levels. The underlying issue here goes beyond an individual social venture but includes the entire field of social entrepreneurship, the macro-environment. Many organizations—public and private—that support social ventures support only innovative projects. Just consider, for instance, the rhetoric and narratives used by some of the largest supporters in the field such as Ashoka or the Skoll foundation (see Chapter 2). Therefore, social ventures who seek external support need to demonstrate that they innovate. What is more, the majority of available funding is for one- to three-year projects after which the social venture needs to reapply with yet another innovative project. As a consequence, many projects have just started running or are just past a pilot stage before they are 'killed' to start another project. This is problematic because some projects might not even reach the proof-of-concept stage necessary for governments or commercial

ventures to adopt and adapt the idea. Second, a social venture might need to spend a significant amount of time to identify new opportunities and arenas for innovation. Third, solutions that prove successful might not continue because they have to give way to innovation. In other words, the way that the social entrepreneurship field is set up and the narrative and rhetoric that evolved around social entrepreneurship (e.g., society's R&D department) bear the risk of creating a context in which organizations innovate for the sake of innovation.

In short, from a macro-perspective, innovation is inherently ambivalent. On the one hand, it can create significant and positive societal change. On the other hand, innovations can have negative consequences. Moreover, fetishizing innovation as an objective in itself can lead to a misallocation of resources, both within social ventures and with regard to donor monies.

4.3.4. Doing Their Job Too Well? Unintended Consequences of Successfully Filling in the Gaps

The final point we would like to address here is the risk that the rise of social entrepreneurship organizations lets other actors off the hook, particular in the public sector. Social ventures may not only prove that certain ideas are working but also successfully run the provision of a specific public good. In such a scenario, it is an open question as to how governments then react to successful social entrepreneurship. One option that we discussed earlier is that governments learn from successful innovations and use them to improve and expend their own services. However, an alternative pathway would be that public institutions decide to pull back from certain mandates (Cook, Dodds, and Mitchell 2003) and to let externals such as social entrepreneurs 'run the ship.'

More recently, critical discussions on social entrepreneurship emerged that take a Foucauldian perspective on neoliberal governmentality as their argument's starting point (Dey and Steyaert 2016). According to Dey and Steart, governmentality strives toward an inherent market logic that in turn aims to create responsible subjects that take matters into their own hands. For some this is the reason why many governments actively aim to support and encourage social entrepreneurship as a means to govern civil society (Carmel and Harlock 2008). In their critical paper, Dey and Steyaert (2016) further argue that this view pushes the notion of competition, flexibility, and managerialism onto civil society. Here, the argument is that this 'high-jacking' of social entrepreneurship by governments pushes out the value of pure prosocial values in favor of those stated above (cf. Eikenberry 2009). In particular, some policies and programs on social entrepreneurship support the idea of a Social Enterprise School understanding of social entrepreneurship, that is, every civil society organization should follow business-like behaviors (Parkinson and Howorth 2008). Based on these developments, some critics argue that social entrepreneurship is used as a scapegoat to justify a governmental pull back from providing public goods and a tendency to push this responsibility onto individual agents (Mason 2012). Though this debate is primarily based on a UK and Australian context, it highlights how the relationship between social entrepreneurship and governments is also a political one.

4.4. Conclusion

This chapter discussed social entrepreneurship as a societal instrument to provide much-needed services and foster positive social change. To this end, it kicked off with a static view on social entrepreneurship and its efficiency to directly provide solutions. Compared to other problem-solving tools such as idealized charitable NPOs, commercial ventures, or public-sector institutions, social entrepreneurship may not be the first-best solution in an ideal world but often provides a second-best solution in the real world. A dynamic view then highlighted the role of social entrepreneurship for societal change. Compared to other approaches, social entrepreneurship has certain advantages to innovate where others do not. In this vein, social ventures can then be regarded as a research and development department for society. In a third step, we pointed to some of the inherently ambivalent issues of social entrepreneurship. From a macro perspective, key features of social entrepreneurship can have not only positive but also negative implications.

Note

1. We want to highlight that many countries have gay conversion centers and that in most countries these are not outlawed (see recent article by BBC News (2018) for the UK; or the documentary "This Is What Love Looks Like" by Fox (2011) for the US context). We picked Uganda as the consequences of homosexuality there are much more severe than in other countries.

References

Alexander, Jessica. 2018. "Please Don't Send Your Old Shoes to the Philippines: Survivors of Typhoon Haiyan Need Your Help. But Send Money, Not Your Hand-Me-Downs." *The Slate.*

Almarri, Jasem, and John Meewella. 2015. "Social Entrepreneurship and Islamic Philanthropy." *International Journal of Business and Globalisation* 15 (3): 405–24. https://doi.org/10.1504/IJBG.2015.071.

Andersson, Fredrik O., and Michael Ford. 2015. "Reframing Social Entrepreneurship Impact: Productive, Unproductive and Destructive Outputs and Outcomes of the Milwaukee School Voucher Programme." *Journal of Social Entrepreneurship* 6 (3). Taylor & Francis: 299–319. https://doi.org/10.1080/19420676.2014.981845.

André, Kevin, and Anne-Claire Pache. 2016. "From Caring Entrepreneur to Caring Enterprise: Addressing the Ethical Challenges of Scaling up Social Enterprises." *Journal of Business Ethics* 133 (4): 659–75. https://doi.org/10.1007/s10551-014-2445-8.

Arena, Marika, Giovanni Azzone, and Irene Bengo. 2015. "Performance Measurement for Social Enterprises." *Voluntas* 26 (2): 649–72. https://doi.org/10.1007/s11266-013-9436-8.

Ashoka. 2018. "Durukan Dudu | Ashoka | Everyone a Changemaker." July 24. www.ashoka.org/en/fellow/durukan-dudu#intro.

Batavia, Hima, Justin Chakma, Hassan Masum, and Peter Singer. 2011. "Market Minded Development." *Stanford Social Innovation Review* 9 (1): 66–71.

Baumol, William J. 2002. *The Free-Market Innovation Machine. Analyzing the Growth Miracle of Capitalism*. Princeton, NJ: Princeton University Press.

———. 2010. *The Microtheory of Innovative Entrepreneurship*. Princeton, NJ: Princeton University Press.

BBC News. 2018. "Fresh Call to Ban 'Gay Conversion Therapy'." January 25. www.bbc.co.uk/news/uk-politics-42817947.

Beckmann, Markus. 2011. "Social Entrepreneurship—Altes Phänomen, Neues Paradigma Moderner Gesellschaften Oder Vorbote Eines Kapitalismus 2.0?" In *Social Entrepreneurship—Social Business: Für Die Gesellschaft Unternehmen*, edited by Helga Hackenberg and Stefan Empter, 67. Wiesbaden: VS Verlag für Sozialwissenschaften. https://doi.org/10.1007/978-3-531-92806-7.

———. 2012. "The Impact of Social Entrepreneurship on Societies." In *Understanding Social Entrepreneurship & Social Business—Be Part of Something Big*, edited by Christine Volkmann, Kim Oliver Tokarski, and Kati Ernst, 235–54. Wiesbaden: Gabler Verlag.

Beckmann, Markus, Anica Zeyen, and Anna Krzeminska. 2014. "Mission, Finance, and Innovation: The Similarities and Differences between Social Entrepreneurship and Social Business." In *Social Business*, edited by Andrea Grove and Gary A. Berg, 23–41. Berlin, Heidelberg: Springer. https://doi.org/10.1007/978-3-642-45275-8_2.

Belz, Frank Martin, and Julia Katharina Binder. 2017. "Sustainable Entrepreneurship: A Convergent Process Model." *Business Strategy and the Environment* 26 (1): 1–17. https://doi.org/10.1002/bse.1887.

Bird, Frederick B. 1982. "A Comparative Study of the Work of Charity in Christianity and Judaism Author (s) : Frederick B. *Bird Source : The Journal of Religious Ethics*, 10 (1). Spring: 144–69. Published by Blackwell Publishing Ltd on Behalf of Journ. *The Journal of Religious Ethics* 10 (1): 144–69.

Blaug, Mark. 2001. "Is Competition Such a Good Thing? Static Efficiency versus Dynamic Efficiency." *Review of Industrial Organization* 19 (1). Springer: 37–48.

Bornstein, David. 2007. *How to Change the World: Social Entrepreneurs and the Power of Ideas*. New York, NY: Oxford University Press.

Brandsen, Taco. 2004. *Quasi-Market Governance: An Anatomy of Innovation*. Utrecht: Lemma Publishers.

Brooks, Andrew. 2015a. *Clothing Poverty: The Hidden World of Fast Fashion and Second-Hand Clothes*. London, UK: Zed Books Ltd.

———. 2015b. "The Hidden Trade in Our Second-Hand Clothes given to Charity." *The Guardian*, February 13. www.theguardian.com/sustainable-business/sustainable-fashion-blog/2015/feb/13/second-hand-clothes-charity-donations-africa.

Brooks, Julia. 2017. "Want to Help after a Disaster? Give Your Cash, Not Your Clothing." *The Guardian*, September 25.

Carmel, Emma, and Jenny E. Harlock. 2008. "Instituting the 'third Sector' as a Governable Terrain: Partnership, Procurement and Performance in the UK." *Policy and Politics* 36 (2): 155–71. https://doi.org/10.1332/030557308783995017.

Carraher, Shawn M., Dianne H. B. Welsh, and Andrew Svilokos. 2016. "Validation of a Measure of Social Entrepreneurship." *European J. International Management* 10 (4): 386–402. https://doi.org/10.1504/EJIM.2016.077421 M4 — Citavi.

Chmelik, Erin, Martina Musteen, and Mujtaba Ahsan. 2016. "Measures of Performance in the Context of International Social Ventures: An Exploratory Study." *Journal of Social Entrepreneurship* 7 (1). Taylor & Francis: 74–100. https://doi.or g/10.1080/19420676.2014.997781.

Choi, Youngkeun. 2015. "How Partnerships Affect the Social Performance of Korean Social Enterprises." *Journal of Social Entrepreneurship* 6 (3). Taylor & Francis: 257–77. https://doi.org/10.1080/19420676.2014.965723.

Cook, Beth, Chris Dodds, and Wiliam Mitchell. 2003. "Social Entrepreneurship-False Premises and Dangerous Forebodings." *Australien Journal of Social Issues* 38 (10): 57–72. www.samhallsentreprenor.glokala.se/wp-content/uploads/false-premises.pdf.

Cornes, Richard, and Todd Sandler. 1996. *The Theory of Externalities, Public Goods, and Club Goods*. Cambridge: Cambridge University Press.

Dacin, Peter A., M. Tina Dacin, and Marggret Matear. 2010. "Social Entrepreneurship: Why We Don't Need a New Theory and How We Move Forward From Here." *Academy of Management Perspectives*, 37–58.

Danish, Jamil. 2016. "Afghanistan's Corruption Epidemic Is Wasting Billions in Aid." *The Guardian*, November 3.

Demsetz, Harold. 1969. "Information and Efficiency: Another Viewpoint." *The Journal of Law and Economics* 12 (1). The University of Chicago Law School: 1–22.

Dey, Pascal. 2006. "The Rhetoric of Social Entrepreneurship: Paralogy and New Language Games in Academic Discourse." *Entrepreneurship as Social Change. A Third Movements in Entrepreneurship Book* May: 121–42.

Dey, Pascal, and Chris Steyaert. 2016. "Rethinking the Space of Ethics in Social Entrepreneurship: Power, Subjectivity, and Practices of Freedom." *Journal of Business Ethics* 133 (4): 627–41. https://doi.org/10.1007/s10551-014-2450-y.

Easterly, William Russell. 2006. *The White Man's Burden: Why the West's Efforts to Aid the Rest Have Done so Much Ill and so Little Good*. New York, NY: Penguin.

Eikenberry, Angela M. 2009. "Refusing the Market." *Nonprofit and Voluntary Sector Quarterly* 38 (4): 582–96. https://doi.org/10.1177/0899764009333686.

Elkington, John, Rebecca Harding, and Alejandro Litovsky. 2010. "From Enterprise to Ecosystem: Rebooting the Scae Debate." In *Scaling Social Impact: New Thinking*, edited by Paul N. Bloom and Edward Skloot, 84–102. New York, NY: Palgrave Macmillan.

Fox, Morgan Jon. 2011. *This Is What Love Looks Like*. Sawed-Off Collaboratory Productions.

Friedman, Milton. 1970. "The Social Responsibility of Business Is to Increase Its Profits." *The New York Times Magazine*, September.

Gay, Paul du, and Glenn Morgan. 2014. *New Spirits of Capitalism? Crisis, Justifications, and Dynamics*. Oxford: Oxford University Press.

Guide Dogs. 2018. "About Us."

Harvey, Paul. 2015. "Evidence on Corruption and Humanitarian Aid." *Reliefweb*. https://reliefweb.int/report/world/evidence-corruption-and-humanitarian-aid.

Hayek, Friedrich A. 1988. *The Fatal Conceit: The Errors of Socialism*. Edited by W. W. Bartley. Chicago, IL: University of Chicago Press.

Hogg, Michael A. 1992. *The Social Psychology of Group Cohesiveness: From Attraction to Social Identity.* New York, NY: Harvester Wheatsheaf.

Hughes, Patricia, and William Luksetich. 2008. "Income Volatility and Wealth: The Effect on Charitable Giving." *Nonprofit and Voluntary Sector Quarterly* 37 (2): 264–80. https://doi.org/10.1177/0899764007310416.

JAS. 2018. "Über Uns."

Jensen, Michael C. 2002. "Value Maximization, Stakeholder Theory, and the Corporate Objective Function." *Business Ethics Quarterly* 12 (2): 235–56.

Kickul, Jill, and Thomas S. Lyons. 2016. *Understanding Social Entrepreneurship: The Relentless Pursuit of Mission in an Ever Changing World.* New York, NY: Routledge.

Kubania, Jacqueline. 2015. "How Second-Hand Clothing Donations Are Creating a Dilemma for Kenya." *The Guardian,* July 6. www.theguardian.com/world/2015/jul/06/second-hand-clothing-donations-kenya.

Lee, I. 2015. "A Social Enterprise Business Model for Social Entrepreneurs: Theoretical Foundations and Model Development." *International Journal of Social Entrepreneurship And Innovation* 3 (4). www.inderscienceonline.com/doi/abs/10.1504/IJSEI.2015.069351.

Littlewood, David, and Diane Holt. 2015. "Social and Environmental Enterprises in Africa: Context, Convergence and Characteristics." In *The Business of Social and Environmental Innovation: New Frontiers in Africa,* edited by V. Bitzner, R. Hamann, M. Hall, and E. W. Griffin EL, 27–47. Wiesbaden, Germany: Springer International Publishing. https://doi.org/10.1007/978-3-319-04051-6_2.

Luhmann, Niklas. 2012. *Theory of Society.* Stanford, CA: Stanford University Press.

Marcec, Dan. n.d. "CEO Tenure Rates." July 9, 2018. https://corpgov.law.harvard.edu/2018/02/12/ceo-tenure-rates/.

Mason, Chris. 2012. "Up for Grabs: A Critical Discourse Analysis of Social Entrepreneurship Discourse in the United Kingdom." Edited by Simon Teasdale. *Social Enterprise Journal* 8 (2): 123–40. https://doi.org/10.1108/17508611211252846.

Melcher, Arlyn J., and Bonita H. Melcher. 1980. "Toward a Systems Theory of Policy Analysis: Static versus Dynamic Analysis." *Academy of Management Review* 5 (2). Academy of Management Briarcliff Manor, NY 10510: 235–48.

Mintrom, Michael. 2000. *Policy Entrepreneurs and School Choice.* Washington: Georgetown University Press.

Montgomery, A. Wren, Peter A. Dacin, and M. Tina Dacin. 2012. "Collective Social Entrepreneurship: Collaboratively Shaping Social Good." *Journal of Business Ethics* 111 (3). Springer: 375–88.

Nordhaus, William D. 2006. "Paul Samuelson and Global Public Goods." In *Samuelsonian Economics,* 88–98. Oxford: Oxford University Press.

North, Douglass C. 2005. *Understanding the Process of Economic Change.* Princeton, NJ: Princeton University Press.

Novogratz, Jacqueline. 2007. "Meeting Urgent Needs with Patient Capital." *Innovations: Technology, Governance, Globalization* 2 (1–2). MIT Press: 19–30.

———. 2010. *The Blue Sweater: Bridging the Gap between Rich and Poor in an Interconnected World.* New York, NY: Rodale.

Olson, Mancur. 2009. *The Logic of Collective Action: Public Goods and the Theory of Groups, Second Printing with New Preface and Appendix.* Vol. 124. Cambridge, MA: Harvard University Press.

Onyulo, Tonny. 2017. "Uganda's Other Refugee Crisis." *PRI*, July 17. www.pri.org/stories/2017-07-12/ugandas-other-refugee-crisis.

Ostrom, Elinor. 2015. *Governing the Commons*. Cambridge: Cambridge University Press.

Parkinson, Caroline, and Carole Howorth. 2008. "The Language of Social Entrepreneurs." *Entrepreneurship and Regional Development* 20 (3): 285–309. https://doi.org/10.1080/08985620701800507.

Prahalad, Coimbatore Krishna. 2010. *The Fortune at the Bottom of the Pyramid: Eradicating Poverty through Profits*. Upper Saddle River, NJ: Wharton School.

Przeworski, Adam, Susan C. Stokes, and Bernard Manin. 1999. *Democracy, Accountability, and Representation*. Vol. 2. Cambridge: Cambridge University Press.

Rangan, Kasturi V., R. D. D. Thulasiraj, and V. Kasturi Rangan. 2007. "Making Sight Affordable (Innovations Case Narrative: The Aravind Eye Care System)." *Innovations: Technology, Governance, Globalization* 2 (4). MIT Press: 35–49. https://doi.org/10.1162/itgg.2007.2.4.35.

Ranganathan, Sampath Kumar, and Walter H. Henley. 2008. "Determinants of Charitable Donation Intentions: A Structural Equation Model." *International Journal of Nonprofit and Voluntary Sector Marketing* 13 (1): 1–11. https://doi.org/10.1002/nvsm.297.

Ridley-Duff, Rory, and Mike Bull. 2015. *Understanding Social Enterprise: Theory and Practice*. London, UK: Sage Publications.

Robinson, Jeffrey. 2006. "Navigating Social and Institutional Barriers to Markets: How Social Entrepreneurs Identify and Evaluate Opportunities." In *Social Entrepreneurship*, 95–120. London, UK: Palgrave Macmillan. https://doi.org/10.1057/9780230625655_7.

Rodgers, Lucy. 2015. "Where Do Your Old Clothes Go?" *BBC News Magazine*, February. www.bbc.co.uk/news/magazine-30227025.

Rosling, Hans, Anna Rosling Rönnlund, and Ola Rosling. 2018. *Factfulness: Ten Reasons We're Wrong about the World—and Why Things Are Better Than You Think*. London, UK: Spectre.

Samuelson, Paul A. 1954. "The Pure Theory of Public Expenditure." *The Review of Economics and Statistics*. JSTOR, 387–9.

Santos, Filipe M. 2012. "A Positive Theory of Social Entrepreneurship." *Journal of Business Ethics* 111 (3): 335–51. https://doi.org/10.1007/s10551-012-1413-4.

Schumpeter, Joseph. 1934. *The Theory of Economic Development*. Cambridge: Harvard University Press.

SDG. 2018. "United Nations Sustainable Development Goals." September 13, https://www.un.org/sustainabledevelopment/sustainable-development-goals/

Seelos, Christian, and Johanna Mair. 2009. "Hope for Sustainable Development : How Social Entrepreneurs Make It Happen." In *An Introduction to Social Entrepreneurship: Voice, Preconditions and Context*, edited by Rafael Ziegler, 228–46. Cheltenham, UK: Edward Elgar Publishing.

Sen, Pritha. 2007. "Ashoka's Big Idea: Transforming the World through Social Entrepreneurship." *Futures* 39 (5): 534–53. https://doi.org/10.1016/j.futures.2006.10.013.

Sethi, S. Prakash. 2012. *Multinational Corporations and the Impact of Public Advocacy on Corporate Strategy: Nestle and the Infant Formula Controversy*. Vol. 6. New York, NY: Springer Science & Business Media.

Smith, Adam. 1776. *An Inquiry into the Nature and Causes of the Wealth of Nations: The Glasgow Edition of the Works and Correspondence of Adam Smit.* Basingstoke: Palgrave Macmillan.

Specialisterne. 2013. "Specialisterne."

Stinchcombe, Arthur L. 1965. "Social Structure and Organizations." In *Handbook of Organizations*, edited by James G. March, 7: 142–93. New York, NY: Routledge.

Tajfel, Henri. 1974. "Social Identity and Intergroup Behaviour." *Information (International Social Science Council)* 13 (2), 65–93. Thousand Oaks, CA: Sage Publications.

Thielke, Hilo. 2005. " 'For God's Sake, Please Stop the Aid!'—Interview with James Shikwat." *The Spiegel.* www.spiegel.de/international/spiegel/spiegel-interview-with-african-economics-expert-for-god-s-sake-please-stop-the-aid-a-363663.html.

Yunus, Muhammad. 2003. *Banker to the Poor: Micro-Lending and the Battle against World Poverty.* New York, NY: Public Affairs.

———. 2007. *Creating a World Without Poverty. How Social Business Can Transform Our Lives: Social Business and the Future of Capitalism.* New York, NY: Public Affairs.

Yunus, Muhammad, Bertrand Moingeon, and Laurence Lehmann-Ortega. 2010. "Building Social Business Models: Lessons from the Grameen Experience." *Long Range Planning* 43 (2–3). Elsevier Ltd: 308–25. https://doi.org/10.1016/j.lrp.2009.12.005.

Zahra, Shaker A., Eric Gedajlovic, Donald O. Neubaum, and Joel M. Shulman. 2009. "A Typology of Social Entrepreneurs: Motives, Search Processes and Ethical Challenges." *Journal of Business Venturing* 24 (5): 519–32. https://doi.org/10.1016/j.jbusvent.2008.04.007.

Zeyen, Anica, Markus Beckmann, and Roya Akhavan. 2014. "Social Entrepreneurship Business Models: Managing Innovation for Social and Economic Value Creation." In *Managementperspektiven Für Die Zivilgesellschaft Des 21. Jahrhunderts*, edited by Camillo Müller and Claas-Philip Zinth, 107–32. Wiesbaden: Springer Gabler.

5 From Informal Economies to Welfare States
Social Entrepreneurship in Different Macro-level Contexts

Extant research frequently discusses the hybrid nature of social entrepreneurship (Mitra, Byrne, and Janssen 2017; Molina 2009) and the idea that it operates between different societal systems (Beckmann 2011, 2012). To better understand this, Chapter 4 took a simplified sectoral perspective and compared social entrepreneurship to the three ideal-type instruments of societal problem-solving in the market, the state, and civil society (NGOs). As social entrepreneurs operate in and between these sector logics (Ridley-Duff and Bull 2015), it was helpful to first understand the sectoral division of labor between the state, the market, and civil society as the *generic* context for social entrepreneurship.

The *specific* contexts in which social entrepreneurs operate around the globe, however, are characterized by diverse, heterogeneous state, market, and civil society environments. Any analysis of the macro-environment of social entrepreneurship would therefore lack nuance if it were to ignore differences among national or regional contexts. The importance of context also becomes apparent in the sheer number of country-specific studies on social entrepreneurship (Bhatt, Qureshi, and Riaz 2017; Rivera-Santos et al. 2015; Denyer and Neely 2004; Goodwin, Costa, and Adonu 2004; Mair and Marti 2009). These and other studies discuss how the particularities of a context impact the configuration of social entrepreneurship, that is, how social entrepreneurship needs to respond to context-specific challenges and advantages.

Given our definition of social entrepreneurship (Chapter 2) and conceptual perspective (Chapter 3), the relevance of the specific societal context for influencing the role and opportunities of social entrepreneurship is not surprising. As discussed earlier, social entrepreneurs seek to address the blind spots of existing institutions with innovative solutions and mobilize the necessary resources to implement them directly. The specific societal environment thus defines important *demand-* and *supply-side conditions* for social entrepreneurship (Nicholls 2006; Mair 2010).

In terms of the *demand side*, social entrepreneurs address unaddressed societal needs. At a very basic level, the social needs within a specific context thus determine the realm of opportunities for social entrepreneurship organizations (Santos 2009; Rivera-Santos et al. 2015). For instance, studies indicate that the dominant sustainable development topics in the Global North differ from those in the Global South. Although the former focuses on issues such as climate change, the latter places more emphasis on social issues like poverty (Barkemeyer, Figge, and Holt 2013). More generally, specificities of how states, markets, and civil societies work (or do not work) delineate where there is a demand for social entrepreneurship and what kind of solutions are needed.

At the same time, the societal context also defines the *supply side* for entrepreneurial initiative and the available resources that social entrepreneurs can mobilize for their solutions. These resources can be material as in the case of funding options or immaterial as in the case of the legal framework that determines the availability of social entrepreneurship-specific legal forms (Defourney and Nyssens 2010; Kerlin 2006, 2012), the effectiveness of governments and quality of infrastructure (Partzsch and Ziegler 2011), or cultural preferences for individual or collective action (Montgomery, Dacin, and Dacin 2012).

In this chapter, we will discuss how specific societal contexts influence social entrepreneurship through diverse supply-side and demand-side effects. Because it is impossible and frankly conceptually not interesting to discuss the specificities of each country and its impact on social entrepreneurship, we will group countries for the purpose of our discussion. Yet, rather than grouping countries based on their geographical position (Rivera-Santos et al. 2015), we will distinguish countries based on similar macro-environmental criteria. Otherwise, if we were to take Sub-Saharan Africa as an example, it would include South Africa as a strong emerging economy as well as Eritrea as one of the poorest countries in the world.

The question thus arises of how to best distinguish countries so as to gain a conceptually rich understanding of the macro-environmental influence on social entrepreneurial configurations. Here, we will draw on key ideas of institutional theory and in particular the concept of institutionalization (DiMaggio and Powell 1983; Zilber 2002; R. Greenwood et al. 2009). For the purpose of this book, we understand institutions in a broad sense as suggested by Douglas North. According to North (2008), institutions are all informal and formal human-made rules that guide human behavior. With this distinction in mind, our focus shifts toward different *types of institutionalization*. Here, we can distinguish low versus high levels of formal (informal) institutionalization, on the one hand, and different varieties of formal (informal) institutionalization, on the other hand.

We conjecture that analyzing the type of institutionalization within different market economies, different states, and different civil societies offers a much more nuanced and conceptually interesting differentiation between countries for at least two reasons. First, it allows us to discuss context conditions independent of geographical location or the often-used distinction between developing and developed countries. The latter—though potent in many research studies—groups large numbers of countries that are very different in regard to their culture, their political systems, ideologies/faiths, and economic development. Secondly, an institutionalization perspective allows one to differentiate not only between countries on a more abstract level but also within countries between the respective level of institutionalization of the state, market, or civil society.

In short, Chapter 5 adds an additional layer of complexity to the discussion of the macro-environment of social entrepreneurship. We will develop the argument in five steps. Mirroring the sectoral perspective used in Chapter 4, the first three steps (Section 5.1–5.3) introduce and discuss how variations in the development and institutionalization of civil society, the market, and the state impact social entrepreneurship through specific demand and supply side conditions. In the fourth step (Section 5.4), we transcend the single-sector perspective and introduce the idea of social entrepreneurial ecosystems to look at the interdependencies and synergies between different sector actors. The fifth step (Section 5.5) serves to summarize and conclude.

5.1. Social Entrepreneurship and the Institutionalization of Civil Society

The third sector is built on the idea of reciprocity (Ridley-Duff and Bull 2015) or solidarity (see Chapter 4). Although this is an attribute that civil society shares globally, the way in which civil society manifests itself can vary significantly across contexts. Depending on the effectiveness of existing third-sector institutions, the resulting gaps in social value provision left by civil society thus influence the demand side for social entrepreneurship. At the same time, depending on how a civil society is organized, the means available to social ventures would likely alter as well, thus impacting input factors on the supply side.

To provide a more fine-grained analysis, we will distinguish between the level of institutionalization of formal institutions and informal institutions. The inclusion of informal institutions is necessary to provide a more comprehensive view as it also includes interpersonal or community-based institutions such as tribal structures (Rivera-Santos et al. 2015) that are common in countries of the Global South.

5.1.1. Social Entrepreneurship and the Formal Institutionalization of Civil Society

Formal institutions within the context of civil society include laws and regulations that govern organizational-level questions such as organizational forms, tax exemptions, and accountability standards as well as the granting or oppression of civil rights. What is important to note here is that a high level of formal institutionalization of civil society does not necessarily correlate with its functionality. In line with our conceptual perspective discussed in Chapter 3, we will rather show that the formalization of institutions (and the lack thereof) is an ambivalent phenomenon that can have positive and negative implications.

With regard to supply-side inputs for social entrepreneurship, a high level of formal institutionalization can offer valuable tools to social ventures. The perhaps most well-known formal institution in this regard is the legal status of nonprofit organizations and the corresponding tax exemption of charitable NPOs. These legal organizational forms provide clearly defined vehicles for civil society actors that greatly reduce uncertainty or ambiguity about rights and obligations. The charity status not only allows signaling a social mission but tax exemptions also help to acquire donations.

Yet, at the same time, legal institutions that reduce ambiguity by distinguishing and formalizing different organizational logics can also turn from being an asset into being a liability. This is particularly relevant with regard to the sectoral in-betweenness of many social ventures. Take the example of a social venture that operates within civil society as a nonprofit organization and now wishes to engage in more business-like behavior. In this scenario, the social venture might have to set up an additional legal for-profit entity (Zeyen and Beckmann 2011). This is because many countries specify how much nondonation income a charity is allowed to have. Yet, running not one but two organizations that need to work together increases complexity and can raise organizational challenges for social ventures. In contrast, the same social venture would be easily able to move between funding structures in a less institutionalized civil society context, that is, it would be better able to configure the organization based on current needs.

This example thus illustrates that given their hybrid logic social entrepreneurs can both suffer or benefit from institutional ambiguity. Consequently, the relevant question is not how strongly institutions are formalized but rather how well they reflect the (heterogeneous) needs of social ventures. As a consequence, some countries have created specific legal forms that incorporate hybrid logics such as the Community Interest Company (CIC) in the UK (Defourney and Nyssens 2010), whereas other countries like Germany do not provide such options so far.

Although a low degree of formal institutionalization can result in a lack of barriers or of red tape for social entrepreneurs, it can limit social entrepreneurial agency if the most basic institutional options such as the ability to found an organization are absent. In the extreme, a poorly institutionalized third sector can lead to other actors' control over civil society activities. This can take many different forms. In the case of China, for instance, social ventures face a nonmunificent institutional environment that actively impedes social entrepreneurial engagement (Bhatt, Qureshi, and Riaz 2017). In this case, because the level of formal institutionalization is low, there are no or only limited procedures to oppose governmental practices for instance for fear of retribution (Bhatt, Qureshi, and Riaz 2017). Given the weakly institutionalization of civil rights and independent NPOs in China,

Chinese social entrepreneurs often choose organizational forms from business because, in comparison to civil society, the Chinese "socialist market economy" is more strongly institutionalized (Wong and Tang 1998).

However, the de facto control over a civil society can also be in the hands of foreign organizations. For instance, in the case of many countries in Sub-Saharan Africa, there have been many concerns that NGOs from the Global North are running the local civil society and its activities (Hearn 2007). As with everything, this is not per se a bad or good thing. It can be positive because they can help build up local civil societies (as is often their objective) and engage in skills transfer and capacity building. Yet, in addition to the risk of relying on foreign organizations to provide civil society activities, there is also the question of meeting local needs. Extant research suggests that non-locals often struggle to identify solutions in a context of poverty (Goyal, Sergi, and Jaiswal 2015). Thus, a desirable role of social entrepreneurship in weakly institutionalized civil societies would be to provide solutions from within, thereby shifting our attention to the demand side of social entrepreneurship.

As seen for the case of China, a weak institutionalization of a country's civil society sector often goes in parallel with limited civil rights, thus affecting supply conditions for social entrepreneurship. The poor provision of human rights also influences the demand for social entrepreneurial solutions. If certain social groups lack civil rights, this is a gap that social entrepreneurs can address. Indeed, ample examples of social ventures aim to provide civil rights to underprivileged groups. Take the examples of Terrawode (Terrawode 2018), which assists women in Uganda to exert more civil rights by helping them to own land, or Grupo Matizes (Grupo Matzies 2018), which supports the enforcement of LGBTQ rights in Brazil, or numerous social enterprises that help empower women in Pakistan (Venters and Wood 2007) or India (Haugh and Talwar 2016).

In short, the formal institutionalization of civil societies impacts both the demand side for social entrepreneurs who address institutional voids or shortcomings of the status quo. It also influences supply side factors by defining the liberties, legal forms, and other resources for social entrepreneurial activities.

5.1.2. Social Entrepreneurship, Civil Society, and the Role of Informal Institutions

Informal institutions are less rooted in legal frameworks or policies but rather in community structure and culture. As a consequence, we conjecture that these vary to a greater extent between and within countries than legal frameworks. This is not least due to the sheer diversity of smaller social groups such as tribes and ethnic or religious groups found around the globe.

In a context where formal institutionalization of civil society is low, informal institutionalization can become a key tool to solve societal problems.

This can occur in at least two ways. First, informal institutions can determine implementation aspects of social entrepreneurship ranging from the issues addressed (demand side) to the people (both entrepreneurs and beneficiaries) allowed to engage in these activities (supply side). A case in point is Islamic law that very clearly identifies what social entrepreneurship is allowed to do and what it is not (Almarri and Meewella 2015).

Second, informal institutions can shape the business model and become a resource in their own right (thus, again, affecting supply-side factors). In these situations, social ventures make use of tribal structures or other community-based structures to fulfill their mission. Put differently, social capital—that is, interpersonal relationship capital—becomes an important resource (Zeyen and Beckmann 2018; Rivera-Santos et al. 2015; and see Chapter 6).

A very prominent example here are microcredits because this concept highlights the relevance and importance of social capital for survival in a context of poverty (Coleman 1982; Sengupta, Sahay, and Croce 2017). Before going into the details on how microcredits work, we will briefly outline the background against which they were developed. One of the main challenges of the poor is that they find it difficult to save and therefore struggle to invest into any assets (Bauer, Chytilová, and Morduch 2012). Moreover, due to their lack of savings and subsistence lifestyle, they are unable to offer banks collaterals against which they could borrow money. As a consequence, the chance of breaking out of a cycle of poverty is very low. This is the social issue that microcredits wish to address (Yunus and Weber 2010; Yunus 1974; Yunus, Moingeon, and Lehmann-Ortega 2010; Yunus 2003). The key innovation that Muhammed Yunus introduced via his social business Grameen Bank is credit rings. These credit rings typically consist of five women. Each woman seeks to be granted a loan for a small investment (e.g., sewing machine). After the first two women received their loan and paid back their first installment, the next woman receives her loan. Then if the first two women pay back their second installment and the third woman pays back her first, the fourth woman receives her loan and so on. This group liability solves both the problem of adverse selection (how to avoid that people who are not creditworthy become borrowers) and moral hazard (how to make sure that once borrowers receive the money they pay it back as promised) that would otherwise undermine the credit relationship (Aghion and Morduch 2005, 8). However, this model works only because social capital is a crucial resource for survival in poor rural areas of Bangladesh and similar regions. In other words, rather than offering valuables like jewelry or stock options as collateral, these women offer their social capital as collateral to the microcredit institute. The women self-monitor each other and thereby ensure the nearly perfect repayment rate of 99 percent.

This model thus works not despite weak formal institutions but *because of strong informal* institutions within poor rural communities. However, therein also lies its normative ambivalence. In this case, strong informal institutions institute peer-group pressure as a powerful, yet precarious tool. One the one hand, peer-group mechanisms support self-monitoring and provide sanctioning for noncompliant individuals, which solves the problems of adverse selection and moral hazard. On the other hand, the sanctioning of noncompliant individuals can lead not only to social isolation and shunting but in its most drastic forms also to suicide (Biswas 2010). Note that these dark sides of the sanctioning mechanisms are rooted in the very same informal institutions that social entrepreneurs can use as a tool.

The case of microcredits thus demonstrates that informal institutions can be a potentially valuable resource or tool for social ventures to create social value; but the unintended repercussions need to be sufficiently considered to not create more harm than benefits. Moreover, we can further use microcredits as an example to illustrate how the effectiveness of this resource (social capital) is highly context-dependent. Microcredits have gained much interest around the world. As a consequence, organizations from the Global North started transferring the idea to their contexts. However, although the idea of providing small loans to people who wish to become entrepreneurs remains the same, the concept of credit rings is usually abandoned in any Western adaptation. This is due to multiple reasons but for the purpose of this argument we only highlight two. First, developed countries have highly formal, dense, and enforceable legal regulations in the financial sector that would often not even allow or render the implementation of a credit ring difficult. Second, and more importantly for our argument, social capital is not equally available and not as critical a resource for survival and everyday life as it is in other communities. For example, it is less likely that a woman in Paris would pay back a loan just because four other Parisian women would otherwise stop talking to her. This is not to say that this fictional French woman would not care about the relationship breakdown but that these interactions are not as essential for her livelihood. She would still be able to join in social activities with other people, have access to anything she needs to survive, and has, if required, the option to simply relocate to another area.

In sum, the level and type of institutionalization shape social entrepreneurship in any given context as it influences the resources available and who can engage in social entrepreneurship (thus affecting supply-side factors) as well as the subject matters social ventures address (thus affecting demand-side opportunities).

5.2. Social Entrepreneurship and the Institutionalization of the Market

In the literature, the discussion about "varieties of capitalism" highlights that whereas markets exist in practically all human societies, even capitalist markets differ significantly between each other (Hancké 2009). Two distinctions are particularly prominent in this regard: first, the difference between formal and informal economies (Rivera-Santos et al. 2015); and, second, the distinction between liberal and coordinated economies within formal capitalist markets (Hall and Soskice 2001).

Let us start by focusing on differences regarding the formal institutionalization of markets, that is, *the relative dominance of the informal economy versus the formal economy* (Zeyen and Beckmann 2018; Rivera-Santos et al. 2015). The informal economy includes a vast variety of activities that range from homeworkers to street vendors, garbage collectors, and even to small-scale manufacturing (Becker 2004). The core characteristic is that it is not regulated, or only to a limited degree, thus reducing the barriers to entry significantly (De Soto and others 1989; Feige 1990; Ram et al. 2017). Because regulation is limited in the informal sector, workers are not protected by labor laws or other standards. In comparison to developed countries, many developing nations rely much more on informal economies or shadow markets (Vanek et al. 2014). For instance, Zambia, Uganda, and Nicaragua rely to almost 70 percent on the informal economic sector compared to Slovakia that only has 7 percent of its workforce employed in the informal economy (ILO 2012). Informality is often closely linked with higher levels of poverty (ILO 2012) and/or weaker institutions (Julian and Ofori-dankwa 2013; Peng et al. 2009).

Thus, if we take the link between a weak formal institutionalization of the market and poverty as a given, we can identify clear gaps for social entrepreneurship to address, thus impacting the need and demand for social entrepreneurship. In fact, social ventures use various approaches to provide reliable income or safe consumption opportunities for impoverished people. In many instances, these social ventures then fill the need for a more institutionalized economy. An example here are farming cooperatives that aim to support farmers in developing their skills as well as providing them with sufficient income to sustain and grow their businesses. Here, social ventures substitute mechanisms of the formal economy (such as labor rights and job protection) and introduce them into the informal economy.

In comparison, social ventures in formal economy markets in parts aim to overcome market inefficiencies or market failures. Their attempts are thus corrective in nature. Instead of substituting the lack of formal market regulation, social ventures then complement it. What is important to note is that although these ventures correct market failures, they often use the mechanisms (as supply-side factors) that the formal economy provides. Take the example of many social enterprises in Europe that aim to support people living with disabilities in their efforts to enter the first labor market. Rather than entering relationships with potential employers as a nonprofit organization, these social enterprises operate as HR consultancy firms, thereby emulating the mechanisms of the formal economy rather than those of the civil society. Other examples are benefit corporations in the US context (Honeyman 2014). These types of businesses operate within the formal economy to solve societal needs.

Let us now turn to differences within formal economies and to the distinction between liberal and coordinated economies. According to Hall and Soskice (2001), in liberal market economies (e.g., such as in the United States), pure market relationships such as competition primarily coordinate firm activities whereas in coordinated market economies (e.g., countries in continental Europe) non-market relationships such as long-term collaboration in industrial relations or government regulation coordinate firm activities significantly. Each form of formal institutionalization can affect social entrepreneurship. Mair (2010) argues, for example, that social entrepreneurship is more likely in liberal economies because the latter typically demonstrate a more entrepreneurial mind-set. At the same time, one could make the opposite case and argue that coordinated market economies display themselves a certain degree of hybridity between the market and a social logic, thus being more favorable for the in-betweenness of social ventures. Either way, the type of formal institutionalization affects both the blind spots of and the resources available in the existing institutional setting, thus opening up interesting questions for further research.

In short, the different degrees and types of the market's formal institutionalization influence both the target problems but also the resources for mission-driven venturing.

5.3. Social Entrepreneurship and the Institutionalization of the State

Whether the state is organized as a totalitarian system, an autocratic regime, or a democratic government obviously impacts the prospects for social entrepreneurship. After all, social entrepreneurs need a minimum of civil liberties to display individual agency. In the following, we therefore limit our discussion to societies in which governments follow at least basic democratic principles and focus on different ways in which the state can address the issues relevant for social entrepreneurship. Just as there is a discussion about varieties of capitalism, there is research on varieties of welfare states that is informative in this regard (Section 5.3.1). We then discuss in more detail some selected implications for social entrepreneurs in fully developed welfare states (Section 5.3.2).

5.3.1. Variations in Welfare States

In parallel to the literature on varieties of capitalism, research on political economy looks at varieties of welfare states (Rudra 2007; Arts and Gelissen 2002; Esping-Andersen 1990; Hicks and Kenworthy 2003). Welfare state describes a specific approach to governing a country. Its rudimental principles of governance are rooted in the idea of equal opportunity, equitable distribution of wealth, and public responsibility for those who are unable to achieve a good life on their own (Castles et al. 2012; Arts and Gelissen

2002; Esping-Andersen 1990; Hicks and Kenworthy 2003). Although all welfare states follow these core principles in varying degrees, there are different forms of how they are implemented (Esping-Andersen 1990; Hicks and Kenworthy 2003).

There are many proposals of how to best distinguish different types of welfare states. For the purpose of this book, we do not wish to engage with this discussion because it is not in the focus of our analysis. Rather, we will follow the probably most established and frequently cited distinction between welfare states (Emmenegger et al. 2015): liberal, corporatist, and social democratic (Esping-Andersen 1990). These types vary depending on their emphasis on *decommodification*—the process of reducing the dependence on market income and of transforming certain basic services into citizen rights (Esping-Andersen 1990).

In a *liberal* welfare state (with the United States as a typical example), universal transfers are low to modest. Out of the three types of welfare states, the liberal model has the lowest level of decommodification, thus containing the realm of social rights guaranteed and administered by the state. The general logic is that the state provides only a minimum for those living in poverty. The difference in welfare provision then depends on the individual's income and is encouraged to be drawn from the market.

The *corporatist* welfare state embraces the idea of social rights, yet defines them primarily in conservative terms that seek to preserve existing status differentials and social structures. Historically, countries like Germany and Italy fall into this category. This model thus aims to preserve traditional family values. Consequently, the state would support individuals only after the means of the family (or community) are exhausted. This type of welfare state is not as focused on efficiency and commodification as the liberal model. The state is rather willing to substitute the market as welfare provider where deemed necessary.

The final model is the *social democracy* with Sweden being an often-cited example. This welfare state type provides social rights universally and places significant emphasis on decommodification. As a consequence, there is no duality between the state and the market because the principle of universalism demands that everyone has access to equally high standards of social rights. In other words, rather than putting the costs for social rights on the individual (liberal) or family (corporatist), it places it on the shoulders of the entire society.

The type of welfare state clearly influences both the blind spots that social entrepreneurs seek to address (thus influencing the demand for social entrepreneurial solutions) and the supply of potentially useful resources. For brevity, we will just pick the corporatist welfare state as an example. As the corporatist welfare state places emphasis on preserving traditional familyhood, modern family services such as day-care are typically underdeveloped in this context (Esping-Andersen 1990). Against this background, numerous social ventures in countries like Germany have created privately operated kindergartens whereas other social ventures such as Wellcome (see Chapter 9) address social needs that arise when traditional multi-generational family structures are no longer the norm. At the same time, the corporatist welfare state highly relies on third-sector organizations to deliver social services and provides public money to this end (Defourny and Nyssens 2010), thus offering social ventures pathways toward long-term funding for their solutions.

Interestingly, the vast majority of the literature on welfare states focuses on more developed countries. If, indeed, they refer to developing countries, they are grouped as one, and it is argued that none of the above-mentioned welfare state types are prevalent (Rudra 2007). In her seminal work, Rudra (2007) theoretically and empirically developed a more nuanced view of welfare states in developing countries. To explain their differences, we first need to look at the different background of developed and developing economies.

In developed economies, the welfare state emerged as a reaction to the phenomenon of proletarianization: As the labor force shifted from (largely self-sustaining) farming to manufacturing and services, human work became commoditized as wage labor which, in turn, lead to social inequalities within societies that the welfare state seeks to address (Esping-Andersen 2013). In developing countries, in contrast, most of the labor force is still in (self-subsistence) agriculture. Here, the key social question does not relate to internal divisions within a country—but to the external divisions between rich (developed) and poor (developing) countries (Rudra 2007). The focus of the welfare state then shifts toward bridging this development gap.

Against this background, Rudra's analysis yielded two main types, protective and productive, plus an additional weaker dual welfare state (Rudra 2007), of how developing countries define their welfare state. *Productive* welfare states have high levels of commodification with low levels of decommodification (Rudra 2007). These countries are concerned with opening up to international competition and being competitive within a global market. Their welfare efforts are focused on encouraging wage labor and on simultaneously serving workers and employers. Example countries are Malaysia and Costa Rica.

In contrast, *protective* welfare states have high levels of decommodification coupled with low levels of commodification. In some cases, decommodification began before any level of commodification was reached. These countries aim to shield themselves from international competition, often due to an inherent mistrust of international markets and colonial experiences of its citizens. In these countries, governments aim to achieve decommodification before achieving a full-scale market-dependent labor force. To this end, they might hire people into public contracts to reduce their dependence on market income and to counterbalance the low rates of growth in wage employment. Moreover, governments wish to have as much control over the economy as possible. In other words, protective welfare states are a combination of socialism and conservatism. Zambia and Zimbabwe are two examples of protective welfare states.

The third cluster (weak dual-welfare states) aims to engage in both protective and productive welfare states at the same time. As this model is less stable and contains a vast variety of models, we will look only at the two clearly distinguishable forms of protective and productive welfare states for the purpose of this book chapter.

Both the productive and the protective developing country welfare states can significantly influence the prospect for social entrepreneurship. As the productive welfare state seeks to integrate its citizens into market exchanges, it provides a stimulating environment for market-oriented social ventures. At the same time, productive welfare states typically invest in primary and secondary education as well as basic healthcare (Rudra 2007), thus reducing the need for social entrepreneurs to fill this specific gap. In contrast, protective welfare states focus more on public employment, tertiary education, and labor protection, thus often following policies that serve certain privileged groups (Rudra 2007), which opens opportunities for social entrepreneurs to address the underprivileged (e.g., in the informal economy).

In short, each type of welfare state—be it liberal, corporatist, social democratic, productive, or protective—leads to a unique set of institutions that govern policy-making and that influence both the demand and the supply conditions of social entrepreneurship.

5.3.2. *When Social Entrepreneurs Need to Be Policy Entrepreneurs*

The institutionalization of the welfare state has important implications for the ability of social entrepreneurs to innovate and diffuse their innovations throughout society. The existence of any type of welfare state means that most public goods—ranging from education via health to other welfare services—are provided or at least their provision is governed by the state and elaborate public policies. As a result of this policy dimension, social entrepreneurs who wish to innovate and diffuse novel solutions in a welfare state context typically need to interact with their policy environment and switch into what Mintrom (1997) called 'policy entrepreneurs' (Beckmann and Ney 2013).

To illustrate the relevance of policy entrepreneurship, let us compare the difference between social entrepreneurs who innovate a novel solution in the market with innovations in the publicly organized welfare system (table 5.1). On the market side, take the example of a social entrepreneur who innovates affordable antimalaria bed nets to be sold to villagers. In this case, the entrepreneur does not need a formal permit to approach the beneficiaries of their solution. The social entrepreneur rather needs to convince the beneficiaries directly. He or she thus approaches private decision-makers—for example, the consumers—who decide for themselves whether or not they like the product. The villagers' decision-making situation is one

Table 5.1 Differences between private-market and public-policy decisions

	Private Market Offers	*Public Policy Decisions*
Ability to directly approach beneficiary group (consumer)	Typically no systematic constraints	Often institutional constraints (permission needed)
Beneficiaries	Decide for themselves	Have someone decide for them
Decision as	Individual choice	Public decision
Legitimacy of decision	Derives from individual consent	To be justified with regard to public approval
Importance of gatekeepers	No central gatekeepers	Institutionalized gatekeepers

Source: Aadapted from Beckmann and Ney (2013)

Table 5.2 Two types of policy-making for social entrepreneurship

	Deliberative Collective Decision-Making	*Discretionary Individual Decision-Making*
Decision type	Procedural	Discretionary
Decision-maker	(Elected) Collective bodies	(Appointed) Individual officials
Governance level	Tends to be higher	Public decision
Policy output	Legislation, directives, etc.	Permissions, etc.
Success factor for policy decision	Coalition-building, public campaigns, network-alliances	Access to individual decision-makers
Example	Decision about inclusion into regulated quasi-markets	Permission to offer program in school

Source: Adapted from Beckmann and Ney (2013)

of individual choice. Moreover, there is no need to justify the decision to third parties. Because there are no formal gatekeepers, the social entrepreneur can freely innovate a solution and scale it throughout the system without further institutional constraints.

Let us now turn to the highly institutionalized context of the welfare state. Here, take the example of Alexander McLean, a UK Ashoka fellow whose African Prisons Project brings educational projects into African prisons (Ashoka 2018). In this case, the entrepreneur cannot just walk into the prison and offer his solution. He rather needs to approach third parties (the prison director) and secure the permit to approach his actual beneficiaries. The social entrepreneur thus approaches public decision-makers who decide on behalf of others and the general public. The decision-making situation is therefore one of a public policy choice: The prison director decides whether such new offers will become part of the prison policy. Moreover, the prison director needs to be able to justify the decision to third parties such as the ministry or, ultimately, the general public. The policy context thus creates formal gatekeepers. As a result, the social entrepreneur cannot freely innovate a solution and scale it throughout the system but needs to engage as a policy entrepreneur to secure the necessary opportunity space within a highly institutionalized environment.

In a welfare state context, social entrepreneurs can face the need to engage in policy entrepreneurship in different ways. As Beckmann and Ney (2013) distinguish, policy decisions can fall into a spectrum between (1) discretionary individual decisions and (2) deliberative collective decisions (see table 5.2).

1. *Deliberative collective decision-making* involves policy-making processes either at state or national level that result in system-wide policy outputs such as laws or directives. As such there is no single individual that makes the decision, but rather the decision is made collectively by elected members of parliament. To invoke a favorable decision, the social venture would need to engage in the democratic deliberative process and build coalitions to produce or change policies (Mintrom and Norman 2009), thus engaging what we discussed in Chapter 2 as social activism. Once the decision is made, the social venture is then granted the desired state- or nation-wide access to its beneficiary group or financing of its offer.

To illustrate, imagine the following situation. A social venture has developed a new service for ALS patients. To make the funding as easy for the beneficiaries as possible, the social venture wishes to fund this through the public care insurance. Whether this new service is to be part of the service catalogue in the public care insurance is a decision that typically no individual person can make in a democratic welfare state—not even the CEO of the insurance or the health secretary or minister. Instead, there will be a deliberative process in either a special committee or in parliament (Beckmann and Ney 2013). Such collective parliamentary decisions are particularly relevant for the democratic installment of quasi-markets (see Chapter 4) that play a huge role in welfare states for funding and scaling social innovations. These quasi-markets follow a market logic in that customers (beneficiaries) can choose which service provider they wish to use (Brandsen 2004). They are unlike markets in that prices are set by the government and that only the government can decide who can enter the market, thus underlining the relevance of the policy dimension.

For the ALS service social venture in our example, this access to the quasi-market is ambivalent. On the one hand, the process of gaining access is time- and resource-consuming. Because social ventures are often underresourced (Zeyen 2014), this can put significant strain on the organization. In the extreme, the venture might not survive long enough. Yet, entrance to the quasi-market allows for usually steady income streams. Furthermore, quasi-markets can also hinder the innovation capabilities of a social venture. This is due to the rigid nature of the market. The venture can only offer the services it was approved for and would need to get recertified for any changes or additional offerings. Furthermore, although the set price creates steady income streams, it often does not provide for high margins and therefore reduces the availability of risk capital that can be used to experiment with new ideas.

Quasi-markets do not only occur in social democracies but are also common in other welfare state systems. For instance, in the United States—a typically liberal welfare state—school vouchers are used to provide education (Tyre 2017). The difference is that the more a welfare state leans toward decommodification, the more institutionalized and encompassing quasi-markets are likely to become. For instance, although questions about health insurance would fall into quasi-markets within the German corporatist/social democracy, it would not in the United States as it (no longer) has universal healthcare. However, the example of US school vouchers also shows the ambivalence of quasi-market as they sometimes lack quality control and lack the feedback mechanisms of regular markets, and therefore can lead to lower quality of the services (Tyre 2017).

From a societal perspective, policy-negotiated quasi-markets are thus ambivalent, too. On the one hand, they promise efficiency gains by establishing a hybrid model that weds market and public sector mechanisms. On the other hand, the underlying policy process as just described creates formal gatekeepers in which the incumbent players (who sit, for example, on the relevant committees) keep out competition from innovative social entrepreneurs. In fact, empirical research indicates that many quasi-markets lack competition (Brandsen 2004).

2. *Discretionary individual decision-making.* Let us now turn to the other end of the spectrum of policy-making. Here, the decision does not require collective decision-making but rather relies on the decision-making discretion of individual actors (Beckmann and Ney 2013). Hence, the social venture would rely much more on personal relationships, access to, and networking with these relevant decision-makers.

To illustrate, take the example of a self-defense training for primary school children. Again, children that age are not allowed to decide on their own whether they want to participate in the training. Rather, the school would decide if it were to offer self-defense classes to all its students. Therefore, the social venture would need to engage with every individual principal or head teacher to gain access. Thus, although the decision-maker is at a relatively low level within the welfare state hierarchy, they nonetheless create bottlenecks and are significant gatekeepers. Moreover, the process of offering to other schools involves repeating the acquisition process over and over again.[1] In practice, some social ventures build networks with similar social entrepreneurs to overcome this problem (Beckmann and Ney 2013). Hence, instead of each individual social venture talking to a school, the network negotiates and then grants access to all its members. An example here is the Social Lab in Cologne, Germany (Beckmann and Ney 2013).

In both scenarios, social entrepreneurship needs to engage in policy entrepreneurship. To this end, social ventures require a set of specific skills. This in turn can create barriers for some social ventures that for whatever reasons are not able to access either interorganizational or interpersonal relationships. As a consequence, these ventures would then not be able to access their beneficiaries.

The dense institutionalization of the welfare state thus leads to resources as well as significant constraints for social entrepreneurs to innovate (see Chapter 4) and scale (see Chapter 9) their solutions. In comparison, consider both examples in a context of low or limited institutionalization. First, the social venture might be able to directly access both care patients and children (with all the ethical implications of such actions) or would be able to by-pass certain steps. On the other hand, there would be no established funding structure through quasi-markets, which in turn would most likely make the services less affordable for many people.

5.4. Social Entrepreneurship, Ecosystems, and Intersectoral Synergies

In the previous three sections, we took a sectoral perspective to look at the different institutional context conditions of civil society, the market, and the state in isolation. However, as already alluded at by the varieties of welfare capitalism debate, the type of institutionalization in one sector is often coupled with corresponding institutions in other sectors. In fact, from a societal viewpoint, it is generally desirable that all three sectors complement each other and work together to achieve optimal levels of social value creation. More specifically, the interplay of institutions, actors, and resources in the state, market, and civil society creates a societal environment that can hinder or promote social entrepreneurship synergistically.

Indeed, research clearly indicates that social entrepreneurial organizations require diverse forms of external support to strive, which can range from funding to full-fledged partnerships (Kodzi 2015). An increasingly influential way of thinking about these support structures is to understand them as ecosystems. As is the case in nature, in entrepreneurial ecosystems, each element plays a role for creating a viable context for (social) entrepreneurs to operate in (Isenberg 2011; Yusoff et al. 2018; Bloom and Dees 2008; Suresh and Ramraj 2012). Part of these ecosystems would be organizations like Ashoka, government agencies, further social entrepreneurs, funding organizations, and other relevant stakeholders.

Entrepreneurial ecosystems influence both the demand for social entrepreneurship solutions and the supply of relevant resources—be it financial, knowledge, or social capital. In terms of the demand for value-creating solutions, weakly institutionalized ecosystems can have as a consequence that social ventures can (and sometimes have to) provide more comprehensive solutions that address multiple blind spots simultaneously. For instance, Sekem (Bornstein 2007; Sekem 2018), an Egyptian social venture, started off by applying a new approach to biodynamic farming in the Sahara Desert and is now also offering healthcare and education to its workers and their families. In a more developed ecosystem, Sekem might have arguably built upon healthcare and education services already available, thus implementing a model more focused on biodynamic farming.

Though weakly developed ecosystems certainly create the demand for social entrepreneurial innovation, they significantly limit not only the supply of necessary resources but also of social entrepreneurs themselves. The supply of individuals willing and able to engage in social entrepreneurship clearly increases with the availability of various ecosystem features such as high-quality education, health services and rising life-expectancy, material well-being, and access to information and communication as well as civil rights and a supportive culture (Nicholls 2006).

To provide these diverse resources, supportive ecosystems for social entrepreneurship are therefore dependent on well-developed subsystems; that is, the development and institutionalization of all three sectors needs to be sufficiently elaborate. As a consequence, it is often developed countries that have such advanced ecosystems whereas they are less frequent in a developing country context where the supply-side conditions do not match the demand for social entrepreneurship.

To illustrate the synergistic interplay of different sectors in a complex ecosystem take the example of a Social Impact Bond (SIB) (Berndt and Wirth 2018; Whitfield 2015). A Social Impact Bond provides an innovative funding structure to social ventures in which the government, the market, and civil society operate jointly to address pressing societal issues. In this model, the government is the elected agent of the public who is in charge of providing tested solutions for societal problems. Take the example of young criminal offenders who have a high risk of reoffending. Here, there is a public interest to support programs that prevent and reduce recidivism. Yet, although the government can use taxes to effectively fund tested solutions, it is arguably less prone to innovate new solutions and to handle the risk involved in this process (see Chapter 4). Against this background, the government turns into a customer who signals which problem it wishes to be resolved and how much they are willing to pay for a viable and efficient solution. This is where (social) venture capitalists come in who agree with the government on a Social Impact Bond (also called pay-for-success contract). In such a scheme, the private funders (who can be for-profit and/or philanthropists) assume up front the financial risk of a new project with the promise of repayment (plus a return) from taxpayers only if the project has achieved the specific outcomes set by the government. Though these private funders are good at raising capital and handling risk, they are not experts in innovating social services. This is why the venture capitalists then look for an NGO or social enterprise that are able to offer an innovative and effective solution to the social problem. Because they have a vested interest in the project's success, the private funders, just like conventional venture capitalists, support these organizations in further developing their products or services not only financially but also often with their expertise. Once a social venture has proven its potential to solve the social issue within the efficiency and cost parameters set by the government, the SIB 'sells' the idea to the government and receives the previously agreed price for it.

As is apparent from the description, SIBs can function only if the three societal sectors are permeable and able to work together. However, this is much more challenging than it might seem at first glance. For one, each sector follows different institutional logics (Thornton and Ocasio 2008). As a consequence, communication can be challenging because each sector might communicate through different 'codes' (cf. Luhmann 1986). This can reduce the efficiency and effectiveness of a cross-sector tool. There are additional challenges with SIBs. SIBs are complex tools. Like any tool, they can produce ambivalent outcomes and need to be handled with care (see Chapter 3). For instance, performance-related funding builds upon the idea of outcome measurement. However, performance metrics can lead to mission drift, side-line the real interests, and can be gamed (Chapter 7), which are all playing a potential role in SIBs (Fraser et al. 2018). Moreover, as the social ventures need to be comparable in light of the government's parameter, there might be certain social issues that can be less easily addressed through the tool of Social Impact Bonds. On the other hand, once a social innovation has successfully passed through a Social Impact Bond, it can be scaled to a bigger constituency via governmental organizations.

5.5. Conclusion

This chapter refined our general-sectoral perspective on social entrepreneurship by discussing how specific conditions in the state, market, and third sector influence both demand and supply factors for social entrepreneurial solutions. Focusing on different types of institutionalization, we reviewed how the difference between formal and informal institutions in civil society and the market as well as varieties of capitalism and welfare states shape the macro-context for social entrepreneurs. Because social entrepreneurs typically operate in between different sectors, we emphasized the role of entrepreneurial ecosystems that capture the interplay of different actors, institutions, and resources. Whereas advanced ecosystems can enable high levels of social entrepreneurship, poorly institutionalized macro-contexts in less developed countries can result in the demand for social entrepreneurship significantly outweighing its limited supply.

Note

1. This is also what Alexander McLean experiences with his African Prison Project. As explicitly stated in his Ashoka profile, "Alexander's vision brings empathy into prisons *one by one*, working hand-in-hand with key staff as a leverage point" (Ashoka 2018, emphasis added).

References

Aghion, Beatriz Armendáriz de, and Jonathan Morduch. 2005. *The Economics of Microfinance*. Cambridge, MA: MIT Press.

Almarri, Jasem, and John Meewella. 2015. "Social Entrepreneurship and Islamic Philanthropy." *International Journal of Business and Globalisation* 15 (3): 405–24. doi:10.1504/IJBG.2015.071.

Arts, Wil, and John Gelissen. 2002. "Three Worlds of Welfare Capitalism or More?" 12 (5): 137–58.

Ashoka. 2018. "Alexander McLean | Ashoka | Everyone a Changemaker." July 27th. www.ashoka.org/en/fellow/alexander-mclean#intro.

Barkemeyer, Ralf, Frank Figge, and Diane Holt. 2013. "Sustainability-Related Media Coverage and Socioeconomic Development: A Regional and North-South Perspective." *Environment and Planning C: Government and Policy* 31 (4): 716–40. doi:10.1068/c11176j.

Bauer, Michal, Julie Chytilová, and Jonathan Morduch. 2012. "Behavioral Foundations of Microcredit : Experimental and Survey Evidence from Rural." *The American Economic Review* 102 (2): 1118–39.

Becker, Kristina Flodman. 2004. *The Informal Economy—a Fact Finding Study*. Sweden: Swedish International Development Cooperation Agency (Sida)

Beckmann, Markus. 2011. "Social Entrepreneurship—Altes Phänomen, Neues Paradigma Moderner Gesellschaften Oder Vorbote Eines Kapitalismus 2.0?" In *Social Entrepreneurship—Social Business: Für Die Gesellschaft Unternehmen*, edited by Helga Hackenberg and Stefan Empter, 67. Wiesbaden: VS Verlag für Sozialwissenschaften. doi:10.1007/978-3-531-92806-7.

———. 2012. "The Impact of Social Entrepreneurship on Societies." In *Understanding Social Entrepreneurship & Social Business—Be Part of Something Big*, edited by Christine Volkmann, Kim Oliver Tokarski, and Kati Ernst, 235–54. Wiesbaden: Gabler Verlag.

Beckmann, Markus, and Steven Ney. 2013. "Wenn Gute Lösungsansätze Keine Selbstläufer Werden: Vernetzung Als Skalierungsstrategie in Fragmentierten Entscheidungslandschaften Am Beispiel Des Social Labs in Köln." In *Sozialunternehmen in Deutschland: Analysen, Trends Und Handlungsempfehlungen*, edited by Stephan A. Jansen, Rolf G. Heinze, and Markus Beckmann, 253–84. Wiesbaden: Springer Gabler.

Berndt, Christian, and Manuel Wirth. 2018. "Market, Metrics, Morals: The Social Impact Bond as an Emerging Social Policy Instrument." *Geoforum* 90 (January). Elsevier: 27–35. doi:10.1016/j.geoforum.2018.01.019.

Bhatt, Babita, Israr Qureshi, and Suhaib Riaz. 2017. "Social Entrepreneurship in Non-Munificent Institutional Environments and Implications for Institutional Work: Insights from China." *Journal of Business Ethics* January. Springer Netherlands: 1–26. doi:10.1007/s10551-017-3451-4.

Biswas, Soutik. 2010. "India's Micro-Finance Suicide Epidemic." *BBC News Magazine*, December 16. www.bbc.co.uk/news/world-south-asia-11997571.

Bloom, Paul N., and Gregory Dees. 2008. "Cultivate Your Ecosystem." *Stanford Social Innovation Review* Winter: 47–53.

Bornstein, David. 2007. *How to Change the World: Social Entrepreneurs and the Power of Ideas*. New York, NY: Oxford University Press.

Brandsen, Taco. 2004. *Quasi-Market Governance. An Anatomy of Innovation.* Utrecht: Lemma Publishers.

Castles, Francis G., Stephan Leibfried, Jane Lewis, Herbert Obinger, and Christopher Pierson. 2012. *The Oxford Handbook of the Welfare State.* Oxford: Oxford University Press.

Coleman, James S. 1982. *The Assymetric Society.* New York, NY: Syracuse University Press.

De Soto, Hernando, and others. 1989. *The Other Path.* New York, NY: Harper & Row.

Defourny, Jacques, and Marthe Nyssens. 2010. "Conceptions of Social Enterprise and Social Entrepreneurship in Europe and the United States: Convergences and Divergences." *Journal of Social Entrepreneurship* 1 (1): 32–53. doi:10.1080/19420670903442053.

Denyer, David, and Andy Neely. 2004. "Introduction to Special Issue: Innovation and Productivity Performance in the UK." *International Journal of Management Reviews* 5–6 (3–4): 131–5. doi:10.1111/j.1460-8545.2004.00100.x.

DiMaggio, Paul J., and Walter W. Powell. 1983. "The Iron Cage Revisited: Institutional Isomorphism And Collective Rationality In Organizational Fields." *American Sociological Review* 48 (2): 147–60.

Emmenegger, Patrick, Jon Kvist, Paul Marx, and Klaus Petersen. 2015. "Three Worlds of Welfare Capitalism: The Making of a Classic." *Journal of European Social Policy* 25 (1): 3–13. doi:10.1177/0958928714556966.

Esping-Andersen, Gosta. 1980. *The Three Worlds of Welfare Capitalism.* Cambridge, UK: Polity Press.

Feige, Edgar L. 1990. "Defining and Estimating Informal Underground and Economies : The New Institutional Economics Approach." *World Development* 18 (7): 989–1002. doi:10.1016/0305-750X(90)90081-8.

Fraser, Alec, Stefanie Tan, Mylene Lagarde, and Nicholas Mays. 2018. "Narratives of Promise, Narratives of Caution: A Review of the Literature on Social Impact Bonds." *Social Policy and Administration* 52 (1): 4–28. doi:10.1111/spol.12260.

Goodwin, Robin, Patricia Costa, and Joseph Adonu. 2004. "Social Support and Its Consequences: 'positive' and 'Deficiency' Values and Their Implications for Support and Self-Esteem." *The British Journal of Social Psychology/the British Psychological Society* 43 (Pt 3): 465–74. doi:10.1348/0144666042038006.

Goyal, Sandeep, Bruno S. Sergi, and Mahadeo Jaiswal. 2015. "How to Design and Implement Social Business Models for Base-of-the-Pyramid (BoP) Markets?" *European Journal of Development Research* 27 (5): 850–67. doi:10.1057/ejdr.2014.71.

Greenwood, R., A. M. Diaz, S. X. Li, and J. C. Lorente. 2009. "The Multiplicity of Institutional Logics and the Heterogeneity of Organizational Responses." *Organization Science* 21 (2): 521–39. doi:10.1287/orsc.1090.0453.

Grupo Matzies. 2018. "Grupo Matizes." http://grupomatizespiaui.blogspot.com/.

Hall, Peter A., and David W. Soskice, eds. 2001. *Varieties of Capitalism. The Institutional Foundations of Comparative Advantage.* Oxford: Oxford University Press. doi:10.1093/0199247757.001.0001.

Hancké, Bob. 2009. *Debating Varieties of Capitalism: A Reader.* Oxford: Oxford University Press on Demand.

Haugh, Helen M., and Alka Talwar. 2016. "Linking Social Entrepreneurship and Social Change: The Mediating Role of Empowerment." *Journal of Business Ethics* 133 (4). Springer Netherlands: 643–58. doi:10.1007/s10551-014-2449-4.

Hearn, Julie. 2007. "African NGOs: The New Compradors?" *Development and Change* 38 (6): 1095–110. doi:10.1111/j.1467-7660.2007.00447.x.

Hicks, Alexander, and Lane Kenworthy. 2003. "Varieties of Welfare Capitalism." *Socio-Economic Review* 1 (1): 27–61. doi:10.1093/soceco/1.1.27.

Honeyman, Ryan. 2014. *The B Corp Handbook: How to Use Business as a Force for Good*. Oakland, CA: Berrett-Koehler Publishers.

ILO. 2012. "Statistical Update on Employment in the Informal Economy." Geneva, Switzerland. http://laborsta.ilo.org/informal_economy_E.html.

Isenberg, Daniel. 2011. *The Entrepreneurship Ecosystem Strategy as a New Paradigm for Economic Policy: Principles for Cultivating Entrepreneurship*. Vol. 1. The Babson Entrepreneurship Ecosystem Project. Wellesley, MA: Babson College

Julian, Scott D., and Joseph C. Ofori-dankwa. 2013. "Financial Resource Availability and Corporate Social Responsibility Expenditures in a Sub-Saharan Economy: The Institutional Difference Hypothesis." *Strategic Management Journal* 34 (11): 1314–30. doi:10.1002/smj.2070.

Kerlin, J. A. 2006. "Social Enterprise in the United States and Europe: Understanding and Learning from the Differences." *Voluntas* 17 (3): 246–62. doi:10.1007/s11266-006-9016-2.

———. 2012. "Defining Social Enterprise Across Different Contexts: A Conceptual Framework Based on Institutional Factors." *Nonprofit and Voluntary Sector Quarterly* 42 (1): 84–108. doi:10.1177/0899764011433040.

Kodzi, Emmanuel T. 2015. "The Clash of Missions: Juxtaposing Competing Pressures in South Africa's Social Enterprises." *Journal of Social Entrepreneurship* 6 (3). Taylor & Francis: 278–98. doi:10.1080/19420676.2014.981844.

Luhmann, Niklas. 1986. "The Autopoiesis of Social Systems." In *Sociocybernetic Paradoxes: Observation, Control and Evolution of Self-Steering Systems*, edited by Felix Geyer and Johannes van der Zouwen, 172–92. London, UK: Sage Publications.

Mair, Johanna. 2010. "Social Entrepreneurship: Taking Stock and Looking Ahead." *IESE Business School* 3: 11. doi:http://dx.doi.org/10.2139/ssrn.1729642.

Mair, Johanna, and Ignasi Marti. 2009. "Entrepreneurship in and around Institutional Voids: A Case Study from Bangladesh." *Journal of Business Venturing* 24 (5). Elsevier Inc.: 419–35. doi:10.1016/j.jbusvent.2008.04.006.

Mintrom, Michael. 1997. "Policy Entrepreneurs and the Diffusion of Innovation." *American Journal of Political Science* 41 (3): 738–70.

Mintrom, Michael, and Phillipa Norman. 2009. "Policy Entrepreneurship and Policy Change." *The Policy Studies Journal* 37 (4): 649–68.

Mitra, Paulami, Janice Byrne, and Frank Janssen. 2017. "Advantages of Hybrid Organising in Social Entrepreneurship: Evidence from Norway." *International Review of Entrepreneurship*, 15 (4): 519–36.

Molina, Alfonso H. 2009. *Understanding Multi-Sector Hybridity in Social Innovation*. Edinburgh, UK: The University of Edinburgh. http://www.mondodigitale.org/sites/default/files/paper_2.pdf

Montgomery, A. Wren, Peter A. Dacin, and M. Tina Dacin. 2012. "Collective Social Entrepreneurship: Collaboratively Shaping Social Good." *Journal of Business Ethics* 111 (3): 375–88. doi:10.1007/s10551-012-1501-5.

Nicholls, Alex. 2006. *Social Entrepreneurship: New Models of Sustainable Social Change: New Models of Sustainable Social Change*. Oxford: Oxford University Press.

North, Douglass C. 2008. "Institutions." *The Journal of Economic Perspectives*, 5 (1): 97–112.

Partzsch, Lena, and Rafael Ziegler. 2011. "Social Entrepreneurs as Change Agents: A Case Study on Power and Authority in the Water Sector." *International Environmental Agreements: Politics, Law and Economics* 11 (1): 63–83. doi:10.1007/s10784-011-9150-1.

Peng, M. W., S. L. Sun, B. Pinkham, and H. Chen. 2009. "The Institution-Based View as a Third Leg for a Strategy Tripod." *Academy of Management Perspectives* 23 (3): 63–81. doi:10.5465/AMP.2009.43479264.

Ram, Monder, Paul Edwards, Trevor Jones, and Maria Villares-Varela. 2017. "From the Informal Economy to the Meaning of Informality: Developing Theory on Firms and Their Workers." *International Journal of Sociology and Social Policy* 37 (7–8): 361–73. doi:10.1108/IJSSP-06-2016-0075.

Ridley-Duff, Rory, and Mike Bull. 2015. *Understanding Social Enterprise: Theory and Practice*. London, UK: Sage Publications.

Rivera-Santos, Miguel, Diane Holt, David Littlewood, and Ans Kolk. 2015. "Social Entrepreneurship in Sub-Saharan Africa." *The Academy of Management Perspectives* 29 (1): 72–91. doi:10.5465/amp.2013.0128.

Rudra, Nita. 2007. "Welfare States in Developing Countries: Unique or Universal?" *The Journal of Politics* 69 (2): 378–96. doi:10.1111/j.1468-2508.2007.00538.x.

Santos, Filipe M. 2009. "A Positive Theory of Social Entrepreneurship." INSEAD Working Papers. Paris, France: INSEAD.

Sekem. 2018. "40 Years of Sustainable Development." June 22, www.sekem.com/en/index/.

Sengupta, Subhanjan, Arunaditya Sahay, and Francesca Croce. 2017. "Conceptualizing Social Entrepreneurship in the Context of Emerging Economies: An Integrative Review of Past Research from BRIICS." *International Entrepreneurship and Management Journal* 5: 1–33. doi:10.1007/s11365-017-0483-2.

Suresh, Jayshree, and R. Ramraj. 2012. "Entrepreneurial Ecosystem: Case Study on the Influence of Environmental Factors on Entrepreneurial Success." *European Journal of Business and Management* 4 (16): 95–102.

Terrawode. 2018. "Terrewode."

Thornton, Patricia, and William Ocasio. 2008. "Institutional Logic." In *The Sage Handbook of Organizational Institutionalism*, edited by Royston Greenwood, C. Olivier, K. Sahlin, and R. Suddaby, 99–129. London, UK: Sage Publications.

Tyre, Peg. 2017. "Trump Administration Advances School Vouchers Despite Scant Evidence." *Scientific America*, August. www.scientificamerican.com/article/trump-administration-advances-school-vouchers-despite-scant-evidence/.

Vanek, Joann, Martha Alter Chen, Françoise Carré, James Heintz, and Ralf Hussmanns. 2014. "Statistics on the Informal Economy: Definitions, Regional Estimates and Challenges." *Working Informal Migrant Entrepreneurship And Inclusive Growth Migration Policy Series* 68.

Venters, Will, and Bob Wood. 2007. *Activist to Entrepreneur: The Role of Social Enterprise in Supporting Women's Empowerment*. Geneva, Switzerland: United Nations ESCAP & British Council

Whitfield, Dexter. 2015. *Alternative to Private Finance of the Welfare State: A Global Analysis of Social Impact Bond, Pay-for-Success and Development Impact Bond Projects*. Adelaide: Australian Workplace Innovation and Social Research Centre, The University of Adelaide.

Wong, Linda, and Jun Tang. 1998. "Dilemmas Confronting Social Entrepreneurs: Care Homes for Elderly People in Chinese Cities." *Pacific Affairs* 79 (4): 623–40.

Yunus, Muhammad. 1974. "Microcredit and Social Business for Poverty Reduction." 7–13.

———. 2003. *Banker to the Poor: Micro-Lending and the Battle against World Poverty*. New York, NY: Public Affairs.

Yunus, Muhammad, Bertrand Moingeon, and Laurence Lehmann-Ortega. 2010. "Building Social Business Models: Lessons from the Grameen Experience." *Long Range Planning* 43 (2–3). Elsevier Ltd: 308–25. doi:10.1016/j.lrp.2009.12.005.

Yunus, Muhammad, and Karl Weber. 2010. *Building Social Business. The New Kind of Capitalism That Serves Humanity's Most Pressing Needs*. New York, NY: Public Affairs.

Yusoff, Wan Fauziah Wan, Tan Shen Kian, Abdul Razak Ahmad, and Nuraniza Quantaniah Jusoh. 2018. "Fostering the Entrepreneurial Ecosystem: The Roles of Government Agencies in Malaysia." *Advanced Science Letters* 24 (5): 3079–84. doi:10.1166/asl.2018.11321.

Zeyen, Anica. 2014. *Scaling Strategies of Social Entrepreneurship Organizations—an Actor-Motivation Perspective*. Lueneburg: Leuphana University.

Zeyen, Anica, and Markus Beckmann. 2011. *Two Hearts Beat as One: How Social Entrepreneurs Use a Non-Profit-/for-Profit Organizational Mix to Deal with Multiple Institutional Logics*. Lüneburg: Leuphana University.

———. 2018. "Exploring the Global Potential of Social Entrepreneurship and Small Business Social Responsibility for Tackling Societal Value Creation." In *Research Handbook on Small Business Social Responsibility*, edited by Laura J. Spence, Jedrzej G. Frynas, Judy N. Muthuri, and Jyoti Navare, 267–91. Cheltenham, UK: Edward Elgar Publishing. doi:10.4337/9781784711825.00021.

Zilber, T. B. 2002. "Institutionalization as an Interplay between Actions, Meanings, and Actors: The Case of a Rape Crisis Center in Israel." *Academy of Management Journal* 45 (1): 234–54. doi:10.2307/3069294.

Part III

Social Entrepreneurship, Organizations, and Management

A Meso-perspective

6 Social Mission and Hybrid Resources
Business Models in Social Entrepreneurship

Mirroring the field of commercial entrepreneurship, social entrepreneurship practice has embraced the idea of business models (Kreutzer and Niendorf 2017; Zeyen, Beckmann, and Akhavan 2014). In contrast, research on business models in the field of social entrepreneurship—often called social business models—is so far comparatively scarce (Jokela and Elo 2015). The purpose of this chapter is to fill part of this research gap. We contribute to the discussion on social business models by highlighting some of their specificities and discuss them from an ambivalence perspective (Chapter 3). Like with any other tool, both business model thinking and the very use of a specific business model type can lead to both positive and negative results for both the social venture and its beneficiaries. We will pinpoint some of these inherent ambivalences.

To this end, we will first provide a brief introduction to the idea of business models and will highlight some key insights from the extant literature on social business models (Section 6.1). Following, we will then outline three selected social business model types (Section 6.2). In a final step, we will discuss how some of the characteristics of social entrepreneurship can create ambivalences when implementing various social business models (Section 6.3) before concluding this chapter (Section 6.4).

6.1. (Social) Business Models—An Introduction

The business model perspective emerged in the mid-1990s (Zott, Amit, and Massa 2011). It initially originated in the New Economy (Timmers 1998; Venkatraman and Henderson 1998; Mahadevan 2000a) and was then adapted across the business world. Due to its high uptake among practitioners, business model research also gained interest (Boons and Lüdeke-Freund 2013).

6.1.1. A Brief Introduction to Business Models

There is no clear consensus on the definition of a business model (Zott, Amit, and Massa 2011) or its components (Lee 2015). For some, business models are a strategy-building tool that helps a business to configure its knowledge leverage, customer interaction, and assets (Venkatraman and Henderson 1998) or value, logistic, and revenue streams (Mahadevan 2000b). Others focus on the notion that a business model needs to create value or benefits to all actors (stakeholders) involved in it (Timmers 1998). When combining these various viewpoints, a business model perspective thus takes apart an organization's operations, resources, and interactions with stakeholders to depict how these components work together to create value (Osterwalder, Pigneur, and Tucci 2005b; Afuah and Tucci 2001; Zott, Amit, and Massa 2011)—be it financial, social, or environmental (Schaltegger, Lüdeke-Freund, and Hansen 2012). Put differently, a business model perspective is a heuristic that aims to shed light on how resources and value link (cf. Chesbrough and Rosenbloom 2002; Morris, Schindehutte, and Allen 2005). Importantly, a business model is not limited to organizational boundaries but can include customers and suppliers in so-called value networks (Hamel 2000).

To systematically analyze business models, scholars have developed various tools (Zott, Amit, and Massa 2011). The most prominent here is the business model canvas developed by Osterwalder and colleagues (2005a, 2011) and Staehler (2002). Their conceptualization subdivides a business model into three categories: the value proposition, value architecture, and revenue model. Here, *value proposition* refers to what the organization offers to its specific customer segment. Note a key difference to a product or service focus: rather than asking what the product can do, a value perspective queries which *needs* customers have and then proposes how to satisfy these. To illustrate, take the example of a power drill. A traditional product perspective would emphasize its key product features like electric power (450 Watts), revolutions per minute (2600), or the range of included drill bits (20). A value proposition perspective, in contrast, would try to understand what kind of problem a typical nonprofessional wants to solve with a drill. In most cases, that would probably be drilling holes to hang pictures or affix shelves to the wall. Although this change in viewpoint might not seem much different at first glance, the difference emerges when we consider potential alternatives to solving the problem. To hang up pictures, for instance, high-performance adhesive tapes (such as Blu-Tack or Powerstrips) could also do the job while creating additional customer value because they are cheaper than a drill and easier to use with no noise or dirt problems. This shift in perspective thus sheds light on potential competitors that would have otherwise been overlooked. In addition, it allows considering new business models such as renting out drills rather than selling them.

The *value architecture* includes key resources, key activities, and customer relationships as well as key partnerships. In other words, the value architecture encompasses all components of the organization that enable it to create its value proposition. As such, the value architecture can also incorporate partner organizations or other external stakeholders. The *revenue model* then looks at how an organization earns its income as well how it spends it. The revenue model thus describes how and to what extent an organization *captures* value from the value created by the business model. In all business models, value proposition, value architecture, and value capture are thus intertwined.

Due to this holistic approach, it seems essential for managers and entrepreneurs to understand their business model to realize their organization's full potential (Zott, Amit, and Massa 2011). For profit-maximizing firms, the business model lens then allows analyzing how the value proposition and delivery for the customers can be optimized in a way that allows maximizing value capture.

6.1.2. Social Entrepreneurship and Business Models—A Brief Review

So how can this perspective help us to understand social entrepreneurship? We argue that there are at least five reasons why this perspective is useful to our purposes (Zeyen, Beckmann, and Akhavan 2014).

1. The business model perspective underlines that value delivery for beneficiaries and value capture to fund value creation cannot be separated. Even purely profit-maximizing firms can capture value only if they create desirable value propositions in the first place. Purely mission-driven organizations can, in turn, deliver value to their beneficiaries in the long run only if they capture enough value to be self-sustainable. For the often hybrid nature of social ventures (see Chapters 2 and 4), the business model concept thus provides a conceptual perspective illustrating how the social mission and economic objectives reinforce each other. For some researchers, the very essence of social entrepreneurship lies in a specific business model configuration: Although for-profit firms seek to maximize value *capture*, social entrepreneurs aim for solutions that use value capture as a tool to maximizing societal value *creation* (Santos 2012).
2. The value proposition concept shifts the emphasis away from products or services toward the solution that satisfies needs of various stakeholders. Because social entrepreneurship aims to fulfill needs that are so far overlooked or not satisfactorily resolved (Dacin, Dacin, and Matear 2010; Dees 1998), a value rather than product or service focus seems highly potent for social entrepreneurship.
3. The business model perspective highlights that value is often not created by only one organization but through the complex interplay of various actors (Hamel 2000), each providing different valuable resources. For instance, if we combine the concept of value architecture and revenue model, we can shed light on the fact that users of a product or service might not be those paying for it. A well-known example are online services like YouTube. People who watch videos do not pay for them.

Rather, YouTube finances itself through advertisements. YouTube thus has multiple customer groups (users and advertising agencies) with multiple value propositions. If we analyzed just the bilateral relationships between the users and YouTube or YouTube and advertising agencies, we would be unable to grasp the underlying interdependent value creation concept. Similarly, social entrepreneurship typically pushes the boundaries of organizations through linking stakeholders in a meaningful way. Moreover, social ventures frequently operate in situations where at least some of their beneficiaries might be unable to pay for the goods or services they receive (F. Santos, Pache, and Birkholz 2015). Moreover, social ventures often rely on other organizations to provide them with relevant resources (Yunus, Moingeon, and Lehmann-Ortega 2010; Wilson and Post 2013).

4. The concept of value architecture calls for business model designs that exploit unused resources. To illustrate, take the example of IKEA's business model innovation. Prior to IKEA, buying furniture meant going to a shop, choosing a piece, and waiting for eight to twelve weeks to get the furniture delivered and assembled. IKEA turned this model upside down because it uses its customers to provide valuable resources. Customers (mostly) commission the products from the warehouse, transport it home, and assemble it themselves, thereby providing valuable time and transportation resources to IKEA's value-creation process. Analogously, social entrepreneurship is able to tap into unused resources as in the case of Grameen Bank and women's social capital (for more, see Part II).

5. A business model perspective underlines the central role of design. In particular, it emphasizes the importance of designing every component of the organization to match its value-creation intention. Going back to our IKEA example, the design teams have to literally design furniture to fit the business model. The requirements for any new piece are that it can be packaged using flatpacks that fit average cars and that it is possible for a layperson to assemble it with only average household tools (IKEA 2013). If a new product does not fulfill these criteria, IKEA will not include it in its product range. As we discussed in Part II of this book, social entrepreneurs operate in between different sector logics where a solution's viability depends on its fit to the situational ecosystem. We therefore suggest that a design view is highly useful for reflecting and creating this fit.

Generally speaking, the literature on social entrepreneurial business models offers either abstract business model types (Dohrmann, Raith, and Siebold 2015; Mair and Seelos 2006; Kreutzer and Niendorf 2017) or elements that should be included in business models such as the centrality of the social mission, creating positive impact, being entrepreneurial, and establishing a competitive and market-oriented position (Grassl 2012).

There are various approaches in the literature to differentiate between social business models (F. Santos, Pache, and Birkholz 2015). Yet, for the purpose of this book chapter, we only outline two exemplary ones. We chose these because they offer two unique but complementary viewpoints. The first (1)) offers a distinction based on the role of the social mission for funding and value creation (Dohrmann, Raith, and Siebold 2015) whereas the second (2)) analyzes how resource groupings are used to create value (Kreutzer and Niendorf 2017). Thus, one takes the mission as a starting point to understand the business model whereas the other starts its analysis from a resource perspective.

1) Dohrmann and colleagues (2015) use the degree of social value monetization as their key differentiating factor. Specifically, they distinguish between value creation *for* the social mission and value creation *with* the social mission on one axis and between social missions requiring funds or generating funds on the other. Against this background, they distinguish four social business model types (a–d). The first (a) is the *one-sided* mission model that requires funds and generates value for the social mission. An example is a soup kitchen where beneficiaries are unable to pay for their meal, which is then offset by donations.

The second model (b) is a *two-sided social mission*. This model is nearly identical to the one-sided mission model. The main difference is that the social venture integrates beneficiaries not only as customers but also as producers. For example, Wheelmap uses Open Street Map's open source digital maps to mark the wheelchair accessibility of public places such as restaurants. Every user can also input new data to build a more comprehensive map (Wheelmap 2018). The beneficiaries thus receive and create social value without generating economic value.

In contrast, the third model (c), *market-oriented social mission*, generates economic value *with* the social mission. Dialogue Social Enterprise, which we have mentioned previously in this book, is an example. Its mission to support people living with visual and hearing impairment attracts customers. However, its exhibitions are designed for able-bodied customers and not for their beneficiaries. Thus, beneficiaries are only involved on the production and not on the consumption side.

The fourth model (d), *commercially utilized social mission*, again combines generating funds through market orientation with the mission, but does so by attracting beneficiaries on the consumption side as a mechanism to satisfy the needs of another consumer group. An example here are pay-as-you-go cafes (see Section 6.3.3.a).

(2) In contrast, Kreutzer and Niendorf (2017) differentiate their three social business models (e–g) based on how resources are used to create social and economic value. The first type (e) uses a pool of all resources to create both economic and social value. The second type (f) employs some resources exclusively to create economic or social value although some are used to create both. In their third type (g), each resource is exclusively allocated to either economic or social value creation. They use these configurations to carve out when hybridity-related tensions within social ventures are most pronounced (Kreutzer and Niendorf 2017).

In short, a business model perspective allows us to understand the active role of the social venture in bringing together resources that otherwise might not have been combined. Social ventures can thus function as matchmakers for different actors and resources (Zeyen, Beckmann, and Akhavan 2014).

6.2. Innovative Business Models Serve Special Needs—Three Generic Cases

For social entrepreneurship, different social business model designs represent entrepreneurial opportunities for engendering the *tools* for the organization's *objectives* (cf. Wilson and Post 2011; Mair and Schoen 2007). To illustrate, we will use the business model canvas (Osterwalder 2004; Staehler 2002; Osterwalder and Pigneur 2011) to showcase three generic social business models. In particular, we will outline how these leverage the specificities of social entrepreneurship as well as how they closely couple the social mission and its operationalization (Wilson and Post 2013).

6.2.1. Freemium—Some Pay, Others Don't

The freemium business model is not unique to the field of social entrepreneurship. Rather, it is well established within commercial entrepreneurship. Freemium combines the idea of 'free' and 'premium' by providing services for free to some customers whereas others pay in exchange for additional premium services (Liu, Yoris and Choi 2014). Figure 6.1 illustrates the freemium model. Organizations choose freemium models if their success relies on network effects, that is, the service or product becomes the more valuable

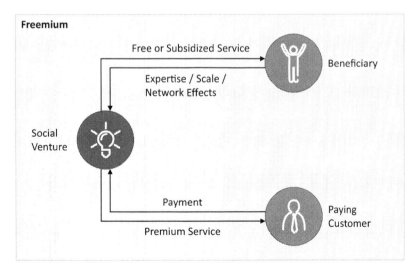

Figure 6.1 The freemium business model

the more people use it (Shapiro and Varian 1998). The organization then uses its free services to attract enough users to reach a critical mass. As a result, organizations can achieve economies of scale, learn from feedback, and refine their premium offers. This model is quite common in the information and communication technology industry with platforms like Dropbox, Spotify, and LinkedIn. In the LinkedIn case, for instance, premium users are willing to pay because the network includes the data of millions of free users.

An example of how the freemium model is applied in social entrepreneurship is Aravind Eye Care Hospitals in India. Cataract disease often leads to blindness in developing countries due to lack of financial resources and the inaccessibility of eye care hospitals. Against this background, Dr. Govindappa Venkataswamy founded Aravind to fight 'needless blindness' created by cataract disease. In the financial year 2016/2017 alone, Aravind performed over 460,000 surgeries of which 20 percent were free and 28 percent subsidized (Aravind Eye Care System 2017), thus saving more than 220,000 poor people from losing their sight. In addition to free surgeries, Aravind identified further challenges for the poor to access eye care. Most of the poorer population in India lives in rural areas without sufficient medical infrastructure. To overcome this logistical barrier, Aravind uses mobile eye care camps to screen people and then offers free bus transport to and from the hospital for those in need of surgery.

These activities reflect the vision (*value proposition*) of Aravind, which wishes to offer high-quality eye care to everyone (Aravind Eye Care System 2017). If we rephrase this, Aravind aims to achieve high quality while providing a service to as many people as possible. However, mass provision and high quality are often incompatible (cf. Porter 1980). So how did Aravind achieve this feat? How did it translate its ambitious value proposition into their value architecture?

In crude terms, Aravind achieves this through a combination of cost reduction through standardization, world-leading surgeons, and internal cross-subsidization (*value architecture*). The focus on only a small number of eye operation types allows Aravind to standardize its processes to a very high degree (Rangan and Thulasiraj 2007), which in turn reduces costs and allows for higher throughput, that is, more surgeries.

Due to this high volume of operations, Aravind's surgeons belong to the world's experts in cataract and related surgeries. This high skill level is then the reason why patients who can pay a premium price choose Aravind. Thus, paying customers at Aravind predominantly do not chose Aravind because of its social mission, but rather because of its highly skilled and world-leading surgical staff. Their payments then cross-subsidize surgeries and eye camps for those unable to pay (*revenue model*), who in turn provide the critical mass to further build Aravind's expertise. The 'premium' part of Aravind's freemium model stems from both the premium quality of surgeries, but also from additional services provided to paying patients such as a wider and more sophisticated choice of meals and nicer accommodation (Levine 2007; Rangan and Thulasiraj 2007).

This case illustrates how social ventures can adapt the freemium model to fit their individual purpose. For instance, rather than using it to attract paying customers (as is the case for LinkedIn), it does so to reach as many people as possible (Zeyen, Beckmann, and Akhavan 2014). We argue that this shift enables Aravind to attract additional resources. Though many social ventures make use of cross-subsidization (Cooney 2011), Aravind has found a very unique and intriguing way to do so. In fact, smart freemium models do not simply transfer value from one area into another but create value by linking two or more domains.

Note that the social mission plays an important role in how Aravind organizes its *value architecture*. In fact, Aravind is a typical example for how a social mission provides access to valuable social capital, in particular network and partnership capital (Zeyen, Beckmann, and Akhavan 2014). Some of the eye care camps are actually run by partner organizations such as the World Health Organization. If Aravind did not have a social mission and charged all of its patients, these organizations would arguably be less willing to partner.

In addition, the social mission not only allows Aravind to access partnerships, it also enables Aravind to get better access to its target group—the rural poor. They are more likely to trust a mission-driven organization than they would a commercial venture offering the same services (e.g., McGivering 2013). It is easily conceivable to argue that people would be far more skeptical of someone recommending them surgery for which they have to pay afterward or go to a distant city.

Furthermore, Aravind has access to relevant human resources for two reasons. First, there are some surgeons who work for Aravind due to its mission. However, most of their medical staff work for Aravind to receive training in the leading hospitals in the world (Rangan, Thulasiraj, and Rangan 2007). This sets Aravind apart from purely nonprofit hospitals that might not necessarily attract the best skilled staff because they often offer lower wages and a less stimulating environment. Because the high skill level attracts paying patients, we can rephrase this by arguing that only because Aravind has access to a unique human resource are they able to access relevant financial resources.

The case of Aravind demonstrates how the social mission as a specific characteristic of social entrepreneurship is a key enabler for combining unique resources in a business model. Without its social mission, Aravind would not gain access to its beneficiaries (the rural poor) and in turn would not have been able to build world-leading expertise in eye surgery that then provides essential financial resources.

6.2.2. The Catalyst Matchmaker—Tapping into
Unused Human Resources

This business model is best explained through the analogy with chemistry implied in its name (Zeyen, Beckmann, and Akhavan 2014). A catalyst is a

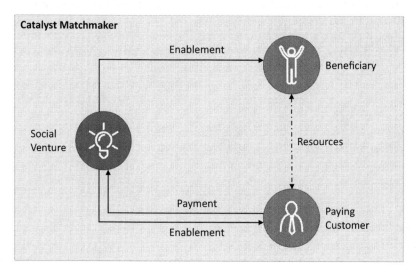

Figure 6.2 The catalyst matchmaker business model

substance that allows other substances to react with each other that otherwise would not have done so. Thus, in this business model the social venture functions as a catalyst for at least two other parties. These parties both have valuable resources to offer each other but are unable to establish this exchange on their own (see Figure 6.2).

We conjecture that this business model is particularly powerful for leveraging underutilized human resources. One reason for this under-utilization of human talent lies in societal preconceived ideas about certain groups. For instance, people living with disabilities are often considered less capable than their able-bodied counterparts (Baron-Cohen et al. 2009; Goddard and Morris 1990). However, many people with sensory or learning disabilities have special skills that would be valuable for other individuals or organizations. Some of those people require very specific conditions to fully exploit certain skills, which frequently leads to their skills being underutilized. In this situation, the catalyst steps in and creates the conditions so that both parties (individual with skills and other actors needing those particular skills) are able to engage. In contrast to the freemium model, beneficiaries of this business model are not service users but usually employees of the social venture.

The German social venture Discovering Hands is an example of the catalyst model. Its value proposition is twofold: to reduce the number of women dying from breast cancer and to provide blind women with meaningful employment. Here, Discovering Hands had identified two challenges. First, to increase survival chances of breast cancer patients, an early recognition of the cancer is crucial (Engel, Baumert, and Hölzel 2000). However, in most countries, breast cancer screening through mammography is—if at all—only offered to women over forty or even fifty years of age despite the fact that breast cancer is one of the top mortality reasons for women under forty. Other early-detection methods, such as tactile screening, are not as reliable when carried out by gynecologists with limited tactile sensitivity. Second, Discovering Hand's founder Frank Hofmann speaks about the loss of jobs specifically designed for people living with sight loss, such as telephone board operator. These jobs are often no longer required due to advances in ICT. In addition, many people living with disabilities are seen as only second-best choice and face discrimination (Foster and Wass 2012). In combination, however, both challenges provide an opportunity. Because people living with sight loss rely more on their other senses, their tactile awareness is often much higher than that of a fully sighted person. Therefore, Discovering Hand partnered with special vocational training centers for the blind to develop a training course for Medical Tactile Examiners (MTEs) (*value architecture*). This half-year course teaches blind women how to detect breast cancer through a sophisticated tactile screening procedure. Once MTEs are trained, women's health centers can then employ them as part of their breast cancer screening team. So far, research indicates that MTEs are more than twice as likely to detect early-stage cancer than trained gynecologists (Discovering Hands 2018). To finance their operations, Discovering Hands utilizes a hybrid *revenue model*. The training actually receives external funding, as it is done by specialist vocational training centers, which in turn receive funding from the tax payer. The income of the MTEs is provided by their employers, which in turn charge women for accessing this breast cancer screening either directly or indirectly through their healthcare.

Our example illustrates how two groups with complementary interests (meaningful employment and breast cancer detection) would have not been able to come together without the social venture (Zeyen, Beckmann, and Akhavan 2014). On the one hand, blind people cannot simply approach women to screen their breasts for cancer. On the other hand, even if other gynecologists had recognized the potential of blind women for early breast cancer detection, they might not have been able to act on it. For one, they would have needed to gain access to this very specific target group and then would have had to train them. However, just because a women's health expert has knowledge about breast cancer, they are not necessarily able to develop a vocational training for blind people, especially if potential trainees have additional and rather specific needs. Against this background, Discovering Hands served as an important catalyst creating the conditions that enable the interaction between both sides.

Similar to the Aravind case, Discovering Hands' social mission plays an important role in this business model. The social mission allows them both to engage with their beneficiaries as well as to gain access to other valuable resources such as the expertise and funding of vocational training centers. Without a social mission, discovering hands would have likely found it much harder to collaborate with some actors. In sum, the catalyst business model uncovers underutilized human resources by bridging the gap between those who possess a skill or skill set and those who can benefit from it. Further examples of the catalyst model include the already mentioned Dialogue Social Enterprises or Thorkil Sonne's Specialisterne, who create conditions that empower people with autism to be valuable software testers (see Chapters 4 and 10).

6.2.3. Expertise Broker—Use What You Know

As the name suggest, the expertise broker business model benefits from unique information resources that social ventures gain from working with specific beneficiary groups over a period of time (Zeyen, Beckmann, and Akhavan 2014). They then use this accumulated knowledge—some of which might be implicit or tacit—to either advocate (e.g., lobbying) on behalf of their beneficiaries or to support others in adapting their behavior or operations to better fit the needs of the beneficiary group (see Figure 6.3).

An example of this social business model is Väter ('fathers' in English). In a time where rigid gender roles are starting to breakdown, Väter's mission is to support fathers who wish to take a more active role in parenting, for example, through taking paternity leave. Its founder, Volker Baisch, started Väter after his own experience of facing prejudice and challenges when he wanted to engage more in raising his children while working. Through their

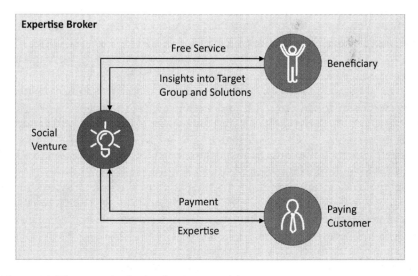

Figure 6.3 The expertise broker business model

work with fathers in this kind of situation, Väter acquired comprehensive knowledge on both the challenges working fathers face and on what works to address them. Capitalizing on this knowledge, Väter not only played a central role in changing parental leave regulations in Germany, they now also use this expertise to support companies on their human resource policies regarding parental leave. To facilitate this, Väter uses both a nonprofit and a for-profit legal form. The nonprofit arm works with fathers and engages in advocacy whereas the for-profit arm provides consultancy services to businesses (Vaeter 2013) (*value architecture*). Just as discussed earlier, the business model thus works by incorporating multiple customer groups (young fathers and for-profit businesses) with different *value propositions*. Furthermore, the case of Väter shows how social ventures can usefully articulate their hybrid identity by combining different legal forms in one overarching business model. Väter's nonprofit arm uses the implicit trustworthiness of mission-driven organizations to attract its beneficiary groups and to engage with governmental agencies. In contrast, it uses the for-profit arm to be perceived as professional within the business world. In other words, they translate their expertise into different logics (Zeyen and Beckmann 2011). Note that both arms of Väter's operations jointly create a feasible business model and that each arm could not stand alone. Without access to young fathers, the Väter consultancy would not have the same level of expertise. Without the for-profit consultancy, the nonprofit would not have sufficient funding (*revenue model*).

Expertise broker social ventures gain access to the necessary information resources through their social mission. Fathers are more likely to open up about personal experience to a mission-driven organization that aims to advocate on their behalf rather than to a company that would aim to monetize these insights.

To summarize, we want to outline three key learnings from the foregone discussion (Zeyen, Beckmann, and Akhavan 2014). First, the discussion underpins the centrality of resources for designing social business models. Some social business models are designed to leverage specific resources. The catalyst uncovers unused or underutilized human resources whereas the expertise broker generates and capitalizes on information resources. Furthermore, all three examples show how an innovative recombination of resources enables social mission delivery, as well as how this recombination can be the precondition for accessing latent resources in the first place. Second, we have shown how social ventures can adapt existing business models to fit their purpose. In so doing, they are able to generate greater societal impact than they would have with a traditional nonprofit model. Third, the above illustrations highlight that social ventures often need to engage with diverse stakeholders from different sectoral backgrounds so as to achieve their mission through integrating them into their business, thus underlining the in-betweenness of many social business models (see Chapter 4).

6.3. The Ambivalences in Social Entrepreneurship Business Models

The previous section illustrated how social ventures shape business models to harness the specific characteristics of social entrepreneurship as well as to create conditions that allow for otherwise improbable value creation. In fact, some of these social business models inspire other actors within the same industry to adapt their operations (Olofsson, Hoveskog, and Halila 2018).

Although we acknowledge the fascination and innovative potential of many social business models, we will now broaden the discussion by analyzing some of the inherent ambivalences of social business models. As Casadesus-Masanell and Ricart (2011) put it, businesses models are a combination of choices and consequences. Following this viewpoint, we will discuss how intentional social business model choices might lead to unintended negative or at least ambivalent outcomes. We will particularly focus on the role of the social mission within social business models because this is the key factor that differentiates social entrepreneurship (Dacin, Dacin, and Matear 2010) and is as such a key component of social business models (Hlady Rispal and Servantie 2017; Wilson and Post 2013).

6.3.1. *The Social Mission as a Tool to Acquire Relevant Resources*

As we discussed in the previous section as well as in parts I and II of this book, social ventures are, due to their social mission, able to access a broader variety of resources than for-profits including donations, volunteers, government support, or stakeholder cooperation. Yet, though this allows them to design innovative business models, we argue that these same resources can render a business model inherently fragile and may even open it up to misuse.

a) *Social Mission, Resources, and Inherent Fragility*

For instance, consider a social venture that requires volunteer engagement. Extant literature on volunteer management within the traditional nonprofit literature frequently discusses the challenges of volunteer acquisition and retention (Brudney and Meijs 2009; Hager and Brudney 2004). Let us assume that a social venture has already acquired the necessary numbers and skill levels of volunteers for currently running its business model and now needs to focus on volunteer management and retention. One challenge in this regard is the unpredictability of volunteer availability. Volunteers spend their free time to support a social mission. However, this also means that if other obligations—be it personal or work-related—emerge, volunteer engagements are often one of the first activities to be discontinued.

Depending on the individual level of commitment that each volunteer feels toward a social mission, that could even mean that they fail to come to a planned shift on their rota without or with only very short notice. In such situations, the social venture has no means of sanctioning such behavior. To avoid service disruptions, many social ventures frequently allocate more volunteers to specific services than would be necessary. This however can lead to dissatisfaction because there might be too little work if everyone comes to their shift.

Furthermore, most volunteers wish to interact with the beneficiary or with nature directly instead of engaging in administrative-type work (Kreutzer and Jager 2011b). Putting it bluntly, volunteers often desire to engage in the interesting rather than boring jobs. This can lead to conflicts between paid and volunteer staff. Paid staff might feel frustrated that they are less likely to engage with the social mission 'on the ground.' Furthermore, volunteers sometimes feel superior to paid staff members in their teams, because they perceive their voluntary work as more valuable than that of paid staff (Kreutzer and Jager 2011a).

This discussion addressed only one specific resource that social ventures can use. Yet it may illustrate how the very use of non-market resources can complexify and even destabilize a social business model. If the value architecture requires volunteers, their unpredictable availability or desire to take on only certain tasks within the organization can create significant managerial challenges for a social venture, especially in its early stages. As a consequence, the reliance on fairly uncontrollable resources such as donations or volunteers can make some social business models more vulnerable to shocks.

On a more general note, the downside of being able to access diverse resources from different logics (community, market, state, professions) is that it increases complexity as the business model needs to handle multiple institutional logics and various levels of hybridity.

b) Social Mission, Resources, and Misuse

In our past ten years observing the field, we have witnessed, unfortunately, that the credibility and trustworthiness given to social ventures up front is—though highly potent to support the social mission—also an aspect that opens social entrepreneurship up for misuse. To be precise, we are not referring to those cases where individuals actively seek to do harm to their beneficiaries or to nature but rather scenarios in which the social mission intentionally or unintentionally deceives external stakeholders and obscures fundamental shortcomings of some social business models.

To illustrate, we will briefly outline the example of John's Path, a real social venture whose name we altered to maintain anonymity. John's Path's mission was to support primary and secondary education in developing countries (especially Cambodia) through providing free schoolbooks to poor children. To finance the schoolbooks, the organization sold college binders to university students at a premium price. The social mission of John's Path enabled it to engage university students (ambassadors) on each campus to sell these college binders as volunteers. The one-to-one model of John's Path meant that one schoolbook was purchased for every college-binder sold. To this point, this 'buy-one-give-one' social business model is quite a common one, well known in the social entrepreneurship and non-profit field (Marquis and Park 2014).

A difference here was that rather than working with partner organiza-tions, John's Path prided itself on being independent and thereby avoiding corruption or other potential hazards that could occur when cooperating. Yet, what looked like a social entrepreneurship organization was, apart from the campus volunteers, pretty much a one-man show. In fact, John, the founder, would fly to Cambodia himself, travel the country to schools he somewhat randomly came across and handed out schoolbooks person-ally. As a consequence, most of the money earned through selling college binders went into airfares for the founder. Moreover, much of the rest was spent on a roadshow to present his social business model. These presenta-tions however focused more on him and his alleged moral heroism due to 'doing something good' rather than the actual venture, its social mission, the underlying theory of change, or information about impact performance (for more on measurement and accountability see Chapter 7).

The key point here is that this social venture was able to attract both enthusiastic volunteers and trusting buyers due to its social mission. How-ever, the social mission also blinded these volunteers to the fact that while the venture might have had the best intentions at heart, its approach was highly ineffective and inefficient. Moreover, the social mission further skewed the perception of the founder who seemed to be driven more by the narrative of social entrepreneurship than by a value-creating substance (see Chapters 9 and 11 for a more detailed discussion of the ambivalent effects of the social entrepreneurship narrative on individuals).

Similarly, Tracey and Jarvis (2007) investigated the failure of a previously successful UK social enterprise called Aspire. They conclude that one of the challenges that Aspire struggled with was a flaw in its business model. Aspire chose social franchising as a scaling strategy (for more on scaling see Chapter 8). When choosing social franchisees, they gave priority to organi-zations that had experience in working with homeless people, because this was Aspire's target beneficiary group. However, Aspire's core idea was to run a catalogue-ordering business that required good business skills from the organizations operating it. This flaw, however, did not become clear because most partners were blinded by the social mission as well as by the charisma of one of the founders (Tracey and Jarvis 2007).

Hence, the assumed credibility of social ventures rooted in their social mission is both a blessing and a curse. On the one hand, as our examples in the previous section have shown, it enables resource access and combination otherwise improbable or even impossible. On the other hand, however, the social mission can shift the attention away from problems within the business model. One of the challenges here is that people who share a social mission—be it the founders, volunteers, customers, or donors—want to believe in its effectiveness and then perceive criticism of the business model as questioning the underlying values. A social mission thus binds and blinds. Eventually, rather than combining resources to achieve superior societal impact, some social ventures bind resources that could elsewhere be used more effectively and efficiently.

6.3.2. *The Social Mission as a Barrier to Business Model Learning*

We now shift the perspective and consider the social mission as a resource in its own right rather than just the tool to acquire other resources. The resource-based view (RBV) argues that resources are strategically advantageous only if they are valuable, rare, difficult to imitate, and if the organization has the capabilities of exploiting the resource (Bacq and Eddleston 2016; Eisenhardt and Martin 2000; Wernerfelt 1984). Now assume that a social venture currently possesses a social mission that satisfies these criteria. The question then arises what happens if something changes, for example, through shifts in the external environment?

Just like any other resource, a social mission, when viewed instrumentally, can turn from a valuable asset into a liability for a social venture. To illustrate, let us take a current and perhaps controversial example. Let us start with the uncontroversial background. Many environmentally oriented social ventures engage in ecofriendly farming to preserve small-scale agriculture, local jobs, and biodiversity as well as natural soil and water systems. In fact, there are various Ashoka Fellows in this category. They all operate business models that integrate community actors, employees, funders, customers, volunteers, distribution partners, and other stakeholders who rally around an eco-agriculture social mission, thus turning it into a valuable resource. If the mission is to promote organic agriculture, it typically involves principles such as to refrain from using pesticides, artificial fertilizer, and genetically modified organisms (GMOs).

Now here comes the controversial part. In the past years, new developments in genetic engineering have led to a novel technology called CRISPR that is arguably much safer, faster, and more precise than traditional breeding techniques (Reardon 2016). Against this background, an increasing number of voices from scientists, journalists, and even environmental activists argue that CRISPR genetic editing could advance ecofriendly farming by offering solutions against soil degradation, water pollution, pesticide use, the spread of invasive organisms, and more (Gallegos 2018). Given this change in the external environment and the availability of new knowledge and technology, some would argue that social ecopreneurs should at least *consider* embracing CRISPR technology if it provides a more effective and safer approach to protect the environment. Yet, this would require revising the part of the social mission that bans the use of GMOs. How likely would be such a change?

The point of this example is *not* to make a case for GMOs (we would rather leave this debate to others more knowledgeable in the field). What we are interested in is how a business model built around a social mission can react to environmental changes that question key assumptions of the mission. Given the normative status of the social mission, we argue that not only a substantive change of the social mission (e.g., to embrace new forms of genetic engineering), but also an open, rational debate about a potential change (e.g., the CRISPR technology) would be rather unlikely because both would threaten the stability of the business model. Yet, at some point every social entrepreneur will likely be faced with the (at least partial) 'expiry date' of their social business model (Osterwalder 2016).

Argyris' (1977) seminal learning theory perspective can serve to substantiate this point by distinguishing between single- and double-loop learning. While single-loop learning is about adjusting one's actions to reach set goals and values (e.g., incrementally improving organic farming), double-loop learning requires an organization and individual to reconsider not only their actions but also their fundamental belief systems. Double-loop learning, however, is hard and becomes ever more unlikely the more a group shares and feels strongly about common values.

For our example, this would imply that if all organizational members follow the set belief system that any form of genetic engineering is bad and must not be used, new information about CRISPR technology cannot be easily accommodated. Because beliefs about genetic engineering touch upon the social venture's core values, intensive double-loop learning would be required, yet would be unlikely because it would challenge fundamental beliefs.

Note the importance of the business model dimension here. Individual actors already find it hard to question their individual beliefs. If in a business model, however, the self-selection of key partners as well as the value proposition is built on specific beliefs thus coordinating value creation through shared beliefs, questioning those beliefs is not only difficult but even dangerous for the business model's stability. Just imagine an eco-oriented social agribusiness that invites its stakeholders to an open debate about introducing GMOs. If the other partners in the business model, who were selected or self-selected themselves because they oppose GMOs, do not open up to double-loop learning, the mere debate might alienate them, undermine their support, and thus threaten the business model.

Against this background, business models built around a social mission can experience substantial learning rigidities. However, as Osterwalder's quote (Osterwalder 2016, ix) "business models and value propositions expire like a yogurt in the fridge" implies, business models and value proposition quickly outdate. Yet social entrepreneurship ventures who are applauded for their superior ability to innovate new public-purpose business models (see Chapter 2) might actually be *less prepared* to *adapt* business models built around a strong social mission if environmental changes demand double learning. From a learning perspective, the social mission then, again, binds and blinds. Note how this in parts contradicts the narrative of social entrepreneurship (see Chapter 11). For one, it shows how the *tools* of an organization can become their objective, thus somehow crowding out the centrality of the actual social mission (see Chapter 2). Second, it also raises the questions if social entrepreneurs would indeed step aside if better solutions to their chosen societal problems emerged (for more see Zeyen 2014).

6.3.3. Social Business Model and Limited Impact

Building a business model on a social mission is ambivalent. It can enable but also limit the creation of societal value creation. To underpin this statement, we will elaborate on three scenarios.

a) Social Business Model and the Niche

Certain social business models restrict a social venture to a niche. This niche position can benefit the social venture, yet it also limits its ability to reach high impact. TOMS is a US-based social venture that predominantly sells shoes, bags, and eyewear. These products are one-to-one linked to their social mission. Each shoe sold finances a pair of shoes for a child in need and each eyewear product sold pays for an eye surgery in a developing nation (TOMS 2018). What is unique in the value architecture of TOMS is that it deliberately decided against any form of formal marketing strategy and rather relies entirely on word-of-mouth advertising (Marquis and Park 2014). Although this a very cost-effective way of gaining new customers, it also limits the market potential of TOMS (Marquis and Park 2014). Moreover, it further does not constitute a replicable business model for other ventures. Word-of-mouth communication works only because TOMS' story is different from the rest of the industry. If every social venture or business adopted the one-to-one business model, however, TOMS' message would no longer be worth spreading (Marquis and Park 2014). Building a business model around the distinctiveness of the social mission might therefore work for the individual social venture in the niche but hinder adaptation and diffusion outside the niche.

Similarly, some social ventures employ a pay-as-you-want-strategy to combine their social and economic value creation activities (Mendoza-Abarca and Mellema 2016). The idea is that beneficiaries with limited financial resources can use the service for free, whereas those that can, pay for it. While this model is similar to freemium it differs in how the revenue is acquired. In the freemium model, customers pay premium prices because they receive premium products or services. In this pay-as-you-want approach, both customer groups obtain the exact same service.

This social business model is niche because it relies on people willing to pay for something because they wish to help others. This customer segment is limited. Furthermore, the model is often likely to require additional outside funding. Even if each customer pays, for a service, they are less likely to pay enough to cover not only their own consumption but also that of a beneficiary.

b) Social Business and the Integration of Beneficiaries

The expertise broker and catalyst social business models showed how beneficiaries of a social venture are integrated into the value architecture. Despite its potency, the integration of beneficiaries can also reduce an organization's social impact.

Business at the base of the pyramid (BOP) refers to value creation operations that serve and integrate individuals in the lowest income brackets of developing countries (Goyal, Sergi, and Jaiswal 2015; Prahald 2009, 2010). A core component of this approach is to empower economic interactions without pushing economic risk onto the target group. However, we argue that in some social business models, this transfer of risk to vulnerable groups inadvertently occurs.

Following the BOP logic, some social ventures work with locals as distributors in micro-franchising schemes (Sireau 2017). Here, the social venture utilizes their local knowledge and networks (social capital). These distributors often work outside the organization's boundaries as self-employed entrepreneurs or micro-franchisees. This can support the development of local economies and create a higher standard of living (Michelini and Fiorentino 2012). However, what happens if these local distributors are not actually entrepreneurs?

In her recent study, Rol (2018) found that many of the local micro-franchisees of social ventures who seek to promote income opportunities could not really live from this work, but needed to engage in multiple additional endeavors to earn their living. Moreover, their entrepreneurial sovereignty and bricolage were significantly limited because both the wholesale price at which they purchase the product as well as the sales price are fixed. Instead of empowering the beneficiaries to become independent entrepreneurs, the social business model then actually limits opportunities and creates new dependencies. Furthermore, in this situation, local distributors bear all the risk. They have to pay for the products upfront and need to cover these costs if they do not sell them or if the products get stolen. This transfer of risk onto the beneficiaries may cause harm despite the fact that micro-franchising is a tool developed with a social mission in mind (Sireau 2017).

In short, the very integration of beneficiaries into the value chain is an ambivalent tool to be used with care for the creation of social and economic value. Under certain conditions some business models can make beneficiaries even unintentionally worse off.

c) Social Mission as Blinkers

Social entrepreneurs often found social ventures to alleviate a societal problem that they have often personally or professionally experienced (see Chapter 2). This personal connection to the issue is the reason for their drive, expertise, and perseverance but also of their organization's blinkers.

Because social entrepreneurs seek to innovate solutions for very specific problems, most social ventures focus on only one single-issue domain (see Chapter 2). This specialization helps social ventures to achieve higher societal impact for their target beneficiary group. However, we conjecture that the stronger a social venture focuses on one issue, the more likely it is to have blind spots and to even tolerate harm in other areas.

To be clear, we are not arguing that each social venture should solve all sustainable development goals. Yet, some social ventures do not seem to care about any negative effect they might have outside the realm of their own social mission. During various discussions we have had with social entrepreneurs, we often received the same response when asking about their, say, environmental footprint: "We already do so much good in our field that we can hardly focus on all those other issues as well." To be sure, it might be perfectly reasonable for a social venture to prioritize where it wants to create value. What is striking, however, is that many social entrepreneurs gave the same answer to justify questionable practices (e.g., waste issues or negative HR practices for more see Chapter 9) that actually create harm.

In the psychology literature, this mechanism to justify less moral behavior (bad deeds) with existing moral behavior (good deeds) in a different domain is called moral licensing (Blanken, van de Ven, and Zeelenberg 2015; Kouchaki 2011). Moral licensing is a phenomenon that everybody can experience randomly after a good deed (e.g., to feel entitled to use the car more often after buying an ecofriendly hybrid car). Yet, when social entrepreneurs found an organization to do good systematically, the effect of moral licensing can spill over into the entire business model. As a result of these moral licensing processes, some social business models completely ignore other sustainability issues. For instance, they might provide support for people sleeping rough by handing out disposable plastic sheets against the rain but at the cost of the environment. Thus, some of their positive societal impact is offset by negative impacts in other areas. What is important here is that moral licensing is a subconscious phenomenon that social ventures neither intend nor are aware of. Again, the social mission can bind and blind, that is, bind to a single issue and blind to others.

In sum, the way social business models are designed can influence and ultimately limit their potential for social impact.

6.3.4. Social Business Models as a Narrative—Business Models for the Sake of It?

In the social entrepreneurship community, the business model concept has gained significant attention. As a consequence, social entrepreneurs are often expected to have a business model that they can explain when they pitch their ideas, seek funding, apply for awards, or communicate their impact. We insinuate that this very narrative of social business model can lead to ambivalent outcomes. For one, thinking in terms of business models can refine social value creation, make it transparent, and assist the scaling and diffusion of innovative ideas. On the other hand, the pressure to fit early on into well-defined business model categories can limit innovation and bind resources. Furthermore, the success of some social business models and the subsequent push toward their increased implementation may lead to mission drift or other organizational-level challenges within social entrepreneurship.

When support operations or funders push social ventures toward developing social business models, they often refer to earned-income strategies or specific templates such a social franchising schemes (see Chapter 8). Such isomorphic pressures (i.e., pressures to become more similar) within the social business model discourse can have at least two potential effects.

First, if a social venture is encouraged to design a social business model, it might spend more time working on reshaping its organization to fit a conceived ideal rather than fulfilling their social mission. Business models are just a tool to create value. Yet given a certain narrative glorification, the business model may be elevated to the organization's *objectives* rather than a *tool* to achieving it.

Second, if a social venture implements a business model for the sake of implementing it, the likelihood that it is not fully suitable for its purposes is high. Rock Your Life! is a German social venture whose idea is to engage university students as mentors for secondary school students who are unlikely to consider higher education (Rock Your Life 2018). After winning several awards and a lot of attention, the social venture was soon expected to develop a business model that can scale the idea nation-wide. To this end, Rock Your Life! developed a textbook business model built on a social franchising system in which groups of university students open local university chapters. These chapter receive training and support from the headquarters. To cover the costs, Rock Your Life! in turn charges each university chapter an annual fee. Although this allows the headquarters to run smoothly, it creates challenges for the chapters. Most students are inexperienced in fundraising or obtaining sponsorship agreements. As a consequence, they might spend more of their volunteer time finding sponsors than working as mentors. Thus, the desire to have a well-defined business model for Rock Your Life! as a social franchisor might shift the dependent franchisees and arguably the entire system away from its social mission and toward a strong focus on fundraising.

In short, although a business model narrative can help rethink social value creation and create highly impactful models, it can also lead to the development of suboptimal models or lock-in effects for beneficiaries.

6.4. Conclusion

In this chapter, we started off by outlining various definitions of business models and introduced some of the current research on social business models. We then introduced three distinct social business model types—freemium, catalyst, and expertise broker—to showcase how social ventures leverage their social mission to gain access to sometimes underutilized resources. In a third and final step, we then introduced our ambivalence viewpoint to analyze social business models. We pointed to the risk of fragility within social business models as well as the risk of misuse and learning rigidities that stem from strong mission focus. We further elaborated on three ways in which social business models can limit impact delivery. Finally, we discussed the inherent ambivalences of a business model narrative.

References

Afuah, Allan, and Christopher Tucci. 2001. "Internet Business Models and Strategies." *New York: McGraw-Hill* January 2015: 384. https://doi.org/10.1036/0072511664.

Aravind Eye Care System. 2017. "2016–2017 Activity Report | Vision: Eliminate Needless Blindness." www.aravind.org/content/downloads/AECS Report 201617.pdf.

Argyris, Chris. 1977. "Double Loop Learning in Organizations." *Harvard Business Review* 55 (5): 115–25. https://doi.org/10.1007/BF02013415.

Bacq, Sophie, and Kimberly A. Eddleston. 2016. "A Resource-Based View of Social Entrepreneurship: How Stewardship Culture Benefits Scale of Social Impact." *Journal of Business Ethics* September. Springer Netherlands, 1–23. https://doi.org/10.1007/s10551-016-3317-1.

Baron-Cohen, S., E. Ashwin, C. Ashwin, T. Tavassoli, and B. Chakrabarti. 2009. "Talent in Autism: Hyper-Systemizing, Hyper-Attention to Detail and Sensory Hypersensitivity. Philosophical Transactions of the Royal Society B." *Biological Sciences* 364 (1522): 1377–83.

Blanken, Irene, Niels van de Ven, and Marcel Zeelenberg. 2015. "A Meta-Analytic Review of Moral Licensing." *Personality and Social Psychology Bulletin* 41 (4): 540–58. https://doi.org/10.1177/0146167215572134.

Boons, Frank, and Florian Lüdeke-Freund. 2013. "Business Models for Sustainable Innovation: State-of-the-Art and Steps towards a Research Agenda." *Journal of Cleaner Production* 45 April: 9–19. https://doi.org/10.1016/j.jclepro.2012.07.007.

Brudney, Jeffrey L., and Lucas C. P. M. Meijs. 2009. "It Ain't Natural: Toward a New (Natural) Resource Conceptualization for Volunteer Management." *Nonprofit and Voluntary Sector Quarterly* 38 (4): 564–81. https://doi.org/10.1177/0899764009333828.

Casadesus-Masanell, R., and J. E. Ricart. 2011. "How to Design a Winning Business Model—Harvard Busines . . . How to Design a Winning Business Model

How to Design a Winning Business Model—Harvard Busines. . . " *Harvard Business Review* 89 (1–2): 100–7. http://esc-web.lib.cbs.dk/login?url=http://search. ebscohost.com/login.aspx?direct=true&db=bth&AN=56701295&site=ehost-live&scope=site.

Chesbrough, Henry, and Richard S Rosenbloom. 2002. "The Role of the Business Model in Capturing Value from Innovation: Evidence from Xerox Corporation's Technology Spin-off Companies." *Industrial and Corporate Change* 11 (3): 529–55.

Cooney, K. 2011. "An Exploratory Study of Social Purpose Business Models in the United States." *Nonprofit and Voluntary Sector Quarterly* 40 (1): 185–96. https:// doi.org/10.1177/0899764009351591.

Dacin, Peter A., M. Tina Dacin, and Marggret Matear. 2010. "Social Entrepreneurship: Why We Don 't Need a New Theory and How We Move Forward from Here." *Academy of Management Perspectives* 37–58.

Dees, J. Gregory. 1998. "The Meaning of 'Social Entrepreneurship'." www.caseat duke.org/documents/dees_sedef.pdf.

Discovering Hands. 2018. "Discovering Hands." July 6. www.discovering-hands. de/.

Dohrmann, Susanne, Matthias Raith, and Nicole Siebold. 2015. "Monetizing Social Value Creation—A Business Model Approach." *Entrepreneurship Research Journal* 5 (2): 127–54. https://doi.org/10.1515/erj-2013-0074.

Eisenhardt, Kathleen M., and Jeffrey A. Martin. 2000. "Dynamic Capabilities: What Are They?" *Strategic Management Journal* 21 (10–11). John Wiley & Sons: 1105–21. https://doi.org/10.1002/1097-0266(200010/11)21:10/11<1105:: AID-SMJ133>3.0.CO;2-E.

Engel, J., J. Baumert, and D. Hölzel. 2000. "Brustkrebsfrüherkennung in Deutschland." *Der Radiologe* 40 (2): 177–83.

Foster, D., and V. Wass. 2012. "Disability in the Labour Market: An Exploration of Concepts of the Ideal Worker and Organisational Fit That Disadvantage Employees with Impairments." *Sociology* 47 (4): 705–21. https://doi.org/10.1177/ 0038038512454245.

Gallegos, Jenna. 2018. "10 Ways CRISPR Will Revolutionize Environmental Science." *Cornell Alliance for Science*. July 10. https://allianceforscience.cornell.edu/ blog/2018/07/10-ways-crispr-will-revolutionize-environmental-science/.

Goddard, M., and J. Morris. 1990. "Putting Them in the Picture." *The Health Service Journal* 100 (5213): 1186. https://doi.org/10.1108/eb001883.

Goyal, Sandeep, Bruno S. Sergi, and Mahadeo Jaiswal. 2015. "How to Design and Implement Social Business Models for Base-of-the-Pyramid (BoP) Markets?" *European Journal of Development Research* 27 (5): 850–67. https://doi.org/10.1057/ ejdr.2014.71.

Grassl, Wolfgang. 2012. "Business Models of Social Enterprise : A Design Approach." *ACRN Journal of Entrepreneurship Perspectives* 1 (1): 37–60.

Hager, Mark A., and Jeffrey L. Brudney. 2004. "Volunteer Management: Practices and Retention of Volunteers." *The Urban Institute*. www.urban.org/uploaded PDF/411005_VolunteerManagement.pdf.

Hamel, Gary. 2000. *Leading the Revolution*. Boston, MA: Harvard Business School Press.

Hlady Rispal, Martine, and Vinciane Servantie. 2017. "Business Models Impacting Social Change in Violent and Poverty-Stricken Neighbourhoods: A Case Study in

Colombia." *International Small Business Journal: Researching Entrepreneurship* 35 (4): 427–48. https://doi.org/10.1177/0266242615622674.

IKEA. 2013. "Our Business Idea." December 15. www.ikea.com/ms/en_GB/about_ikea/the_ikea_way/our_business_idea/index.html.

Jokela, Päivi, and Maria Elo. 2015. "Developing Innovative Business Models in Social Ventures." *Journal of Entrepreneurship, Management and Innovation* 11 (1): 103–18.

Kouchaki, Maryam. 2011. "Vicarious Moral Licensing: The Influence of Others' Past Moral Actions on Moral Behavior." *Journal of Personality and Social Psychology* 101 (4). American Psychological Association: 702.

Kreutzer, Karin, and U. Jager. 2011a. "Volunteering Versus Managerialism: Conflict Over Organizational Identity in Voluntary Associations." *Nonprofit and Voluntary Sector Quarterly* 40 (4): 634–61. https://doi.org/10.1177/0899764010369386.

———. 2011b. "Volunteering Versus Managerialism: Conflict Over Organizational Identity in Voluntary Associations." *Nonprofit and Voluntary Sector Quarterly* 40 (4): 634–61. https://doi.org/10.1177/0899764010369386.

Kreutzer, Karin, and Elisabeth Niendorf. 2017. "Social Business Models—A Typology Based on Levels of Integration." *Die Unternehmung* 71 (2): 183–96. https://doi.org/10.5771/0042-059X-2017-2-183.

Lee, I. 2015. "A Social Enterprise Business Model for Social Entrepreneurs: Theoretical Foundations and Model Development." *International Journal of Social Entrepreneurship And Innovation* 3 (4). www.inderscienceonline.com/doi/abs/10.1504/IJSEI.2015.069351.

Levine, Ruth. 2007. *Case Studies in Global Health: Millions Saved*. Sudbury, MA: Jones and Bartlett Publishers.

Liu, Charles Zhechao, Yoris A. Au, and Hoon Seok Choi. 2014 "Effects of freemium strategy in the mobile app market: An empirical study of google play." *Journal of Management Information Systems*, 31 (3): 326–354.

Mahadevan, B. 2000a. "Business Models for Internet-Based E-Commerce: An Anatomy." *California Management Review* 42 (4): 55–69. https://doi.org/10.2307/41166053.

———. 2000b. "Business Models for Internet-Based E-Commerce: An Anatomy." *California Management Review* 42 (4): 55–69. https://doi.org/10.2307/41166053.

Mair, Johanna, and Oliver Schoen. 2007. "Successful Social Entrepreneurial Business Models in the Context of Developing Economies: An Explorative Study." *International Journal of Emerging Markets* 2 (1): 54–68. https://doi.org/10.1108/17468800710718895.

Mair, Johanna, and Christina Seelos. 2006. "Profitable Business Models And Market Creation In The Context Of Deep Poverty : A Strategy View Christian Seelos Profitable Business Models And Market Creation In The Context Of Deep Poverty : A Strategic View." Vol. 3. Working Paper Series. Barcelona, Spain.

Marquis, Christopher, and Andrew Park. 2014. "Inside the Buy-One Give-One Model." *Stanford Social Innovation Review* 28–33.

McGivering, Jill. 2013. "The Indian Women Pushed into Hysterectomies." *BBC News Magazine*, February. www.bbc.co.uk/news/magazine-21297606.

Mendoza-Abarca, Karla I., and Hillary N. Mellema. 2016. "Aligning Economic and Social Value Creation through Pay-What-You-Want Pricing." *Journal of Social Entrepreneurship* 7 (1). Taylor & Francis: 101–25. https://doi.org/10.1080/19420676.2015.1015437.

Michelini, Laura, and Daniela Fiorentino. 2012. "New Business Models for Creating Shared Value." *Social Responsibility Journal* 8 (4): 561–77. https://doi.org/10.1108/17471111211272129.

Morris, Michael, Minet Schindehutte, and Jeffrey Allen. 2005. "The Entrepreneur's Business Model: Toward a Unified Perspective." *Journal of Business Research* 58 (6): 726–35. https://doi.org/10.1016/j.jbusres.2003.11.001.

Olofsson, Sandra, Maya Hoveskog, and Fawzi Halila. 2018. "Journey and Impact of Business Model Innovation: The Case of a Social Enterprise in the Scandinavian Electricity Retail Market." *Journal of Cleaner Production* 175. Elsevier Ltd: 70–81. https://doi.org/10.1016/j.jclepro.2017.11.081.

Osterwalder, Alexander. 2004. *He Business Model Ontology: A Proposition in a Design Science Approach*. HEC 173. Lausanne, Switzerland: University of Lausanne, Ecole des Hautes Etudes Commerciales.

———. 2016. "Foreword." In *Customer Value Generation in Banking*, edited by Stefanie Auge-Dickhut, Bernhard Koye, and Axel Liebetrau. Imprint: Springer International Publishing.

Osterwalder, Alexander, and Yves Pigneur. 2011. "Aligning Profit and Purpose through Business Model Innovation." In *Responsible Management Practices for the 21st Century*, edited by Guido Palazzo and Maia Wentland, 61–75. Paris, France: Pearson International.

Osterwalder, Alexander, Yves Pigneur, and Chrsitopher L. Tucci. 2005a. "Clarifying Business Models: Origins, Present, and Future of the Concept Clarifying Business Models : Origins, Present, and Future of the Concept." *Communication of the Association of Information Systems* 15 May.

———. 2005b. "Clarifying Business Models: Origins, Present, and Future of the Concept." *Communications of the Association for Information Systems* 15 May.

Porter, Michael E. 1980. *Competitive Strategy*. New York, NY: The Free Press.

Prahald, Coimbatore Krishna. 2009. *Fortune at the Bottom of the Pyramid*. 5th ed. Upper Saddle River, NJ: Prentince Hall, Inc.

———. 2010. *The Fortune at the Bottom of the Pyramid: Eradicating Poverty through Profits*. Upper Saddle River, NJ: Wharton School.

Rangan, Kasturi V., and R. D. Thulasiraj. 2007. "Making Sight Affordable." *Innovations: Technology, Governance, Globalization* 1 (3): 35–49.

Rangan, Kasturi V., R. D. Thulasiraj, and V. Kasturi Rangan. 2007. "Making Sight Affordable (Innovations Case Narrative: The Aravind Eye Care System)." *Innovations: Technology, Governance, Globalization* 2 (4). MIT Press: 35–49. https://doi.org/10.1162/itgg.2007.2.4.35.

Reardon, Sara. 2016. "Welcome to the CRISPR Zoo." *Nature* 531 (7593): 160–3. https://doi.org/10.1038/531160a.

Rock Your Life. 2018. "Home." July 15. https://rockyourlife.de/sonstiges/international.

Rol, Kate. 2018. *Stable and Precarious: The Organisation and Experience of Work in BOP Development Programmesl*. Hong Kong: International Association for Business and Society.

Santos, Filipe M. 2012. "A Positive Theory of Social Entrepreneurship." *Journal of Business Ethics* 111 (3): 335–51. https://doi.org/10.1007/s10551-012-1413-4.

Santos, Filipe M., Anne-Claire Pache, and Christoph Birkholz. 2015. "Making Hybrids Work: Aligning Business Models and Organizational Design for Social Enterprises." *California Management Review* 57 (3): 36–59. https://doi.org/10.1525/cmr.2015.57.3.36.

Schaltegger, Stefan, Florian Lüdeke-Freund, and Erik G. Hansen. 2012. "Business Cases for Sustainability: The Role of Business Model Innovation for Corporate Sustainability." *International Journal of Innovation and Sustainable Development* 6 (2): 95. https://doi.org/10.1504/IJISD.2012.046944.

Shapiro, Carl, and Hal R. Varian. 1998. *Information Rules: A Strategic Guide to the Network Economy*. Cambridge MA: Harvard Business Press.

Sireau, Nicolas. 2017. *Microfranchising: How Social Entrepreneurs Are Building a New Road to Development*. New York, NY: Routledge.

Staehler, Patrick. 2002. *Geschäftsmodelle in Der Digitalen Ökonomie; Merkmale, Strategien Und Auswirkungen*. 2nd ed. Lohmar, Germany: Josef Eul Verlag.

Timmers, Paul. 1998. "Business Models for Electronic Markets." *Journal on Electronic Markets* 8 (2): 3–8. https://doi.org/10.1080/10196789800000016.

TOMS. 2018. "How We Give." July 12. www.toms.co.uk/what-we-give.

Tracey, Paul, and Owen Jarvis. 2007. "Toward a Theory of Social Venture Franchising." *Entrepreneurship Theory and Practice* 31 (5): 667–85.

Vaeter. 2013. "Väter. Werte, Die Tragen." June 23. http://vaeter-ggmbh.de/ueber-uns/.

Venkatraman, N., and John C. Henderson. 1998. "Real Strategies for Virtual Organizing." *Sloan Management Review* 40 (1): 33–48. https://doi.org/Article.

Wernerfelt, Birger. 1984. "A Resource-Based View of the Firm." *Strategic Management Journal* 5 (2): 171–80. https://doi.org/10.1002/smj.4250050207.

Wheelmap. 2018. "Home." May 22nd, https://wheelmap.org/en/map#/?zoom=14.

Wilson, Fiona, and James E. Post. 2011. "Business Models for People, Planet (& Profits): Exploring the Phenomena of Social Business, a Market-Based Approach to Social Value Creation." *Small Business Economics* 40 (3): 715–37. https://doi.org/10.1007/s11187-011-9401-0.

———. 2013. "Business Models for People, Planet (& Profits): Exploring the Phenomena of Social Business, a Market-Based Approach to Social Value Creation." *Small Business Economics* 40 (3): 715–37. https://doi.org/10.1007/s11187-011-9401-0.

Yunus, Muhammad, Bertrand Moingeon, and Laurence Lehmann-Ortega. 2010. "Building Social Business Models: Lessons from the Grameen Experience." *Long Range Planning* 43 (2–3). Elsevier Ltd: 308–25. https://doi.org/10.1016/j.lrp.2009.12.005.

Zeyen, Anica. 2014. *Scaling Strategies of Social Entrepreneurship Organizations—an Actor-Motivation Perspective*. Lueneburg: Leuphana University.

Zeyen, Anica, and Markus Beckmann. 2011. *Social Entrepreneurship and Institutional Logics*. Lueneburg: Centre for Sustainability Management.

Zeyen, Anica, Markus Beckmann, and Roya Akhavan. 2014. "Social Entrepreneurship Business Models: Managing Innovation for Social and Economic Value Creation." In *Managementperspektiven für die Zivilgesellschaft des 21. Jahrhunderts*, edited by Camillo Müller and Claas-Philip Zinth, 107–32. Wiesbaden: Springer Gabler.

Zott, C., R. Amit, and L. Massa. 2011. "The Business Model: Recent Developments and Future Research." *Journal of Management* 37 (4): 1019–42. https://doi.org/10.1177/0149206311406265.

7 Measuring Impact
Blessing or Curse?

In the context of performance measurement, Edwards Deming (2000, 35) once said: "it is wrong to suppose that if you can't measure it, you can't manage it—a costly myth." This quote reflects well one of the positions within the ongoing debate on impact measurement within the field of social entrepreneurship. Social impact measurement aims to evaluate and compare the effectiveness and efficiency of social ventures in their objective to achieve their social mission. For some researchers, impact measurement is a key topic of social entrepreneurship (Dacin, Dacin, and Matear 2010; Lumpkin et al. 2013; Grieco, Michelini, and Iasevoli 2015) despite its underdeveloped state (Salazar, Husted, and Biehl 2012; Rawhouser, Cummings, and Newbert 2017).

And indeed, many practitioners mirror this viewpoint, which has so far led a third of them to adopt formal impact measurement (Maas and Grieco 2017). This increase in relevance sparked the development of numerous impact measurement tools (Chmelik, Musteen, and Ahsan 2016). However, some social entrepreneurs mirror the view of Edwards Deming and even push it further to completely denounce the relevance and value of impact measurement. These social ventures try to resist increasing pressures to adopt formal impact measurement tools (Molecke and Pinkse 2017) by, for example, using delegitimization strategies. So what does this mean for impact measurement? Should social ventures measure impact or not?

In fact, this is a question that is frequently raised at practitioner events and can lead to heated debates. In this chapter, we want to contribute to this important debate within the field of social entrepreneurship. Yet, rather than siding with one of the positions, we argue that the question should not be whether or not to use social impact measurement but rather how and for what to use it. Applying our conceptual perspective discussed in Chapter 3, we highlight that social impact measurement is not an objective in itself but a *tool* that can produce ambivalent outcomes. Instead of debating the inherent (un)desirability of impact measurement per se, we need to clarify what kind of problems the tool should help solve, what the relevant alternatives are, and how the tool can be used. To this end, we start off by defining social impact and introducing two well-known impact measurement tools to illustrate how impact measurement can work in practice (Section 7.1). Following, we dive deeper into the debate on impact measurement and its benefits and challenges (Section 7.2). In a final step, we will then shift the perspective to how the ambivalence of social impact measurement can be managed by discussing options for using this tool more wisely (Section 7.3).

7.1. The Concept of Impact and Its Measurement Tools

Similar to the term social entrepreneurship (see Chapter 2), *social impact* has many definitions and faces contextual and terminological diversity (Rawhouser, Cummings, and Newbert 2017). In addition to the term *impact*, the literature also uses other often nearly synonymous terms such as social performance (Mair and Martí 2006; Nicholls 2008), social return (Emerson 2003), or social value (Moss et al. 2011; Santos 2009; Social Value UK 2018). For the purpose of this book and to be consistent, we will use the term social impact. So, what does impact mean?

7.1.1. Social Impact—What Is It?

One of the challenges of defining social impact is its conceptual proliferation (Grieco, Michelini, and Iasevoli 2015; Rawhouser, Cummings, and Newbert 2017). This proliferation stems from the wide spectrum of issues (e.g., environmental protection, education, human rights) (Stephan et al. 2016), contexts (macro-conditions, see Chapters 4 and 5), and types of organizations (nonprofit, for-profit, hybrid) impact measurement is applied to.

In its origin, the term was used in the international development context. Here, the OECD defined impact as "positive and negative, primary and secondary long-term effects produced by a development intervention, directly or indirectly, intended or unintended" (OECD 2002). The term was then transplanted to the field of social entrepreneurship. What is interesting to note here is that during this process, the meaning of the term was altered. To highlight this, take the example of a review-based definition by Rawhouser and colleagues (2017, 2) who define social impact as "beneficial outcomes resulting from prosocial behavior that are enjoyed by the intended targets of that behavior and/or by the broader community of individuals, organizations, and/or environments." The key differences to the earlier OECD definition are the omission of the notion of negative and unintended impact effects. We conjecture that this change in definition can be explained by the characteristics of and the narrative about social entrepreneurship (Chapter 11). First, the notion of intention and targeted groups clearly speaks to the entrepreneurial and agency-based nature of social entrepreneurship (Haugh and Talwar 2016). Second, as discussed in detail in Part II, social entrepreneurship is often seen as *the* solution to societal problems (Seelos and Mair 2009). Put differently, the change in definitional focus also highlights the often inherent success bias of social entrepreneurship (Andersson and Ford 2015) because it assumes greater efficiency and effectiveness of social entrepreneurship (Dey 2006). This narrative might explain why the definition of social impact in the context of social entrepreneurship discards negative and unintended effects. From the viewpoint of our conceptual framework, however, we claim that neglecting potential negative outcomes of social entrepreneurial activities ignores the inherent ambivalences of social entrepreneurship and therefore impedes learning. As a consequence, we re-integrate negative effects as part of the impact definition for this book.

The terms outcome and output are often used in conjunction with impact (Clark et al. 2004; SIBG 2014). Here, output refers to the actual service or product provided whereas outcome looks at the short-term results of those services or products (see Figure 7.1 and also Clark et al. 2004). For some, impact then refers only to the long-term results; for others, impact encompasses outcomes and even outputs (Rawhouser, Cummings, and Newbert 2017). Activity-based impact understandings implicitly assume that any prosocial or pro-environmental intended activity will sui generis lead to the expected results. We consider this view slightly short sighted because it does not acknowledge context conditions (see Chapter 3 and Part II) or other implementation-related deviances leading to unintended consequences. Furthermore, and following our consequentialist perspective (Chapter 3), as the core idea of impact is to understand the effects of social entrepreneurial activities (see definition earlier), we will exclude an understanding of impact measurement that only analyzes activities. Rather, we will focus on those impact notions that analyze short-term and long-term effects. This is also in line with an increasing preference for outcome-focused impact measurement in practice (Alexander and Brudney 2010).

The impact definition by Rawhouser and colleagues (2017, see previous) mentions not only the targeted group of beneficiaries but also their community and wider society. This is another point of contestation within the impact literature. In other words, some argue that impact should include only the target group (individual beneficiary perspective) whereas others argue that it should include the wider community (systemic context perspective) (De Ruysscher et al. 2017). We conjecture that both viewpoints are important. Most social and environmental problems are complex, and every change will have knock-on effects for other members of the community or even other societal issues. As such, completely ignoring these additional effects would offer a very narrow and limited understanding of social impact in the context of social entrepreneurship. Similarly, if an organization aims at an encompassing systemic viewpoint, it might lose focus on the micro-level.

In sum, for the purpose of this book chapter, we define social impact as any positive and negative results of intended social entrepreneurial activities on their target group and the wider community.

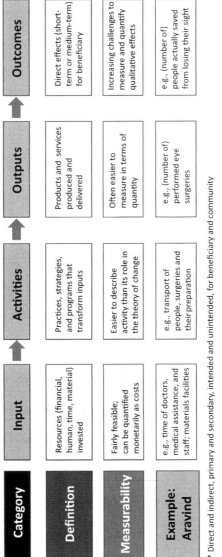

Category	Input	Activities	Outputs	Outcomes	Impact
Definition	Resources (financial, human, time, material) invested	Practices, strategies, and programs that transform inputs	Products and services produced and delivered	Direct effects (short-term or medium-term) for beneficiary	All positive and negative effects* that would have occurred without intervention
Measurability	Fairly feasible; can be quantified monetarily as costs	Easier to describe activity than its role in the theory of change	Often easier to measure in terms of quantity	Increasing challenges to measure and quantify qualitative effects	Very complex and challenging because of multiple dimensions*
Example: Aravind	e.g., time of doctors, medical assistance, and staff; materials facilities	e.g., transport of people, surgeries and their preparation	e.g., (number of) performed eye surgeries	e.g., (number of) people actually saved from losing their sight	e.g., saved costs, social inclusion, increased job opportunities, etc.

* Direct and indirect, primary and secondary, intended and unintended, for beneficiary and community

Figure 7.1 The input-activities-outputs-outcomes-impact model

Source: Authors' illustration adapted from OECD (2002)

7.1.2. Impact—How to Measure It?

Due to the sheer diversity of impact understandings, contexts, social issues, and organizational forms, there are numerous impact measurement tools (Chmelik, Musteen, and Ahsan 2016; Rawhouser, Cummings, and Newbert 2017; Grieco, Michelini, and Iasevoli 2015; Stephan et al. 2016). In this section, we want to use two prominent examples of impact measurement—the Social Return on Investment (SROI) and the Theory of Change—to illustrate how impact measurement is done in practice.

a) Social Return on Investment—A Quantitative Approach

Quantitative impact measurement often emulates conventional financial metrics in that it tries to send very clear numeric signals. Yet, rather than stating how much profit an organization has made, it showcases how match social value was created. As a consequence, various impact measurement tools were adapted from business such as the Social Balanced Score Card, Social Cost-Benefit Analysis, or Social Return on Investment (Arena, Azzone, and Bengo 2015).

The Social Return on Investment (SROI) approach has emerged as a preferred quantitative social impact measurement tool (Millar and Hall 2012; Arena, Azzone, and Bengo 2015). The tool was developed in the early 2000s (nef 2009; Cordes 2017) and is—as its name suggests—an adaption of the Return on Investment calculation (Millar and Hall 2012).

The SROI is based on two key aspects: counterfactuals (Stern et al. 2012) and monetization. Simply put, determining counterfactuals means to determine what would have happened without a specific program or project (Levis 1973; Woolcock 2009). This approach is essential in calculating an SROI because it identifies the social benefits. Some social benefits in the SROI calculation are indeed costs that were saved because a specific scenario did not unfold. Once the social benefits of a program are identified, the next step is to quantify and monetarize them. Here, SROI often uses national statistical data (Social Value UK 2018). Finally, the ratio between cost of the program and benefits is calculated.

To make this approach clearer, let us engage an example of a youth development program in Minnesota (US) outlined by Anton and Temple (2007). This fictional social venture aims to help struggling youth to fulfill their potential and avoid a criminal career. It does so by offering mentoring and similar services. The social benefits here include crime and truancy reduction and improved school performance. To put a monetary value to crime reduction, SROI now applies counterfactual thinking. If we consider what would happen without the program, we can identify a higher probability of youth offenses. Therefore, social benefits of avoiding such counterfactual effects would be reduced court costs as well as reduced costs of treatment for, for example, rehabilitation. In the case of this example, the SROI is

US$4.89, that is, for every dollar spent, the program produces almost five times as much societal value.

The SROI takes a similar approach for different contexts. In the UK, its core proponent, Social Value UK (formerly SROI Network), publishes guides on how to calculate these figures for the UK context (Social Value UK 2017) and suggests how to do so for other countries as well (Social Value UK 2018).

As we will engage in a more detailed discussion in the following two sections, we want to single out only some selected benefits and challenges of the SROI approach at this point. The SROI's arguably greatest advantage is that it allows for comparison between very diverse social ventures (Cordes 2017). Indeed, the literature has documented various success stories in this regard (Ryan and Lyne 2008; Flockhart 2005). Furthermore, some social ventures highlight the potential of SROI for internal organizational learning and decision-making (Millar and Hall 2012) because it clearly points to cost efficiency and effectiveness potentials within the organization. It further provides a good tool to communicate with external stakeholders, especially funders (Millar and Hall 2012). Yet, despite its benefits, the uptake of SROI as an impact measurement tool is low (Nicholls 2005; Millar and Hall 2012).

We conjecture that the SROI's low application rate is largely due to its two core features. First, although counterfactual thinking can be highly potent, it is also reliant on rather speculative assumptions. In a dynamic and complex world, it is actually quite difficult to judge what would have happened otherwise. Furthermore, quantifying such counterfactual effects is only possible if there are relevant statistical information available (e.g., percentage of youth likely to commit crime in certain area). However, there are many countries or issues for which such data is lacking or limited in scope. In these situations, social ventures would have to rely on estimates. Moreover, even if data is available, it is based on past occurrences and the a posteriori assumption that it will continue like this could be false. To overcome this challenge, some social ventures employ randomized control trials to shed light on the potential effects of the specific program by carving out the differences between participants and nonparticipants. However, this approach is still unable to provide necessary information to the social venture on why it works (Jones et al. 2009).

In regard to monetization, some criticism is purely ideological in nature because it criticizes the closeness to business-like behavior (Cordes 2017). However, we argue that monetization faces similar challenges to counterfactuals. It can be very time- and resource-consuming to calculate the financial cost savings of certain achievements because there is often no available relevant data (Bertotti et al. 2011). Furthermore, the scope of calculation is also difficult to determine. Take the example of the youth program. It calculates higher school achievement by assuming that participants will graduate from secondary education and then calculates the average tax revenue per year for employment opportunities. However, it is also possible to argue that youth from socio-economically struggling areas might become role models if they achieve secondary education. The question is then how to monetize such human and social capital effects at the individual and community level. This point is an often-raised critique of SROI (and other quantitative models) because they often do not allow for including 'soft' factors like raised awareness, better self-confidence, or role modeling (Millar and Hall 2012).

Furthermore, it is also questionable whether the conclusion holds true that a social venture with a higher SROI necessarily performs better. There might be various reasons why a social venture's SROI might be lower (e.g., it might pay its staff higher income) or different organizations made different subjective judgments regarding the level and choice of factors included (Lingane and Olsen 2004). SROI also does not provide the social venture or its stakeholders with any information on why and how the chosen approach to problem-solve actually works (McLoughlin et al. 2009).

In short, SROI as an example of a quantitative tool has high potential for comparability but poses challenges to social ventures during implementation.

b) Theory of Change—A Qualitative Approach

Qualitative approaches are often also called evaluation approaches. Many qualitative approaches are explicitly designed for the context of social impact measurement (Arena, Azzone, and Bengo 2015) such as the contingency framework by Ebrahim and Rangan (2010) or the Theory of Change (SIBG 2014).

With the help of the Theory of Change, social ventures aim to understand why their services or products create change, that is, get to the core of the why and how of impact delivery. During the measurement process, a social venture maps out its activities (outputs) and links these to their assumed outcomes and impacts. Based on this initial theory, the social venture then conducts pre- and post-interviews with participants, participant observation, and other forms of data collection. These insights are then used to run interventions to gain an even deeper understanding into which elements of various activities are most relevant to impact delivery as well as to further improve impact delivery.

In comparison to the SROI, the Theory of Change provides insights into how and why an organization is able to deliver impact. Thanks to their qualitative nature, Theory of Change maps allow for richer descriptions that take the specificities of context and the chosen problem-solving approach into account. However, different Theory of Change maps are not comparable as they are idiosyncratic to a specific social venture or even only to part of a social venture. Similar to SROI, a Theory of Change approach is also very time- and resource intensive and becomes more difficult with an increasingly large beneficiary base. Although the SROI requires knowledge on statistical data analysis, the Theory of Change requires qualitative research and evaluation skills.

The purpose of this section was to outline two common, yet specific impact measurement tools as well as to highlight various technical and methodological challenges in measuring impact (Woolcock 2009). Next, we shift the attention to the general discussion about the bright and dark side of using such tools.

7.2. Is Impact Measurement a Blessing or a Curse?

Though many studies aim to understand the available tools and provide some form of systematization (Maas and Liket 2011; Bengo et al. 2016; Grieco, Michelini, and Iasevoli 2015; Rawhouser, Cummings, and Newbert 2017; Arena, Azzone, and Bengo 2015), fewer studies discuss why some social ventures engage in impact measurement whereas others do not (Grieco 2018; Molecke and Pinkse 2017). We thus want to use this section to point to the potential ambivalence, that is, benefits and challenges of applying impact measurement before discussing options to manage this ambivalence in Section 7.3.

7.2.1. Why Social Ventures Should Measure Their Impact

First, measurement increases the level of *comparability between organizations*. The objective of social ventures is to create social change. Therefore, to compare how effective and efficient various social ventures are, there needs to be some form of measurement. In particular, external stakeholders such as venture philanthropists can use this data to make their funding decisions.

Second, impact measurement enables *accountability* of social ventures toward their stakeholders (Arena, Azzone, and Bengo 2015). Social ventures rely on resources from their stakeholders—be it donors, volunteers, governments, or partners. These resource providers might in turn then be interested in knowing how their resources were used and to what effect.

Third, as we already discussed for the SROI, impact measurement can *support internal decision-making* (Arena, Azzone, and Bengo 2015; Millar and Hall 2012). It enables a social venture to identify those activities and programs that create the highest societal benefit as well as those that might not deliver expected impact.

Fourth, recent studies suggest that impact measurement can actually lead to higher impact through *increased motivation*. This research indicates that positive impact measurement results increase the self-efficacy of the social entrepreneur and their venture, which in turn increases their impact (Urban 2015). Put differently, knowing that a program works spurs the social venture on to do even better. Furthermore, as stipulated by goal-setting theory (Locke and Latham 1990), the more formulation of quantifiable and achievable goals can improve motivation and performance. Such goal setting, however, requires the measuring of metrics.

In short, impact measurement can enable comparability, accountability, internal decision-making, and enhanced self-efficacy and motivation.

7.2.2. Why Should Social Ventures Not Measure?

First, as the examples in the previous section highlighted, impact measurement is a difficult activity for any social venture (André and Pache 2016; Ebrahim and Rangan 2010) and as a result is often *time- and resource-intensive*. Because social ventures are often small in size (see Chapter 8) and under-resourced, this can put significant strain on the organization's existing resources and management. In fact, a study by Grieco (2018) revealed that some social ventures are principally willing to engage in impact measurement but do not do so or only irregularly due to lack of resources and capacity.

Second, impact measurement can *reduce innovativeness*. As we mentioned in our definitional Chapter 2, innovation is a key characteristic of social entrepreneurship. However, an emphasis on measuring can shift the focus away from innovation. For one, innovation bears risk and can therefore first consume resources without immediately and reliably yielding any benefits. These risks may skew the results of impact measurement (e.g., increase cost in SROI), which therefore makes them less attractive to the social venture. Furthermore, a focus on measuring might preoccupy the organization so that it has less capacity for innovating.

Third, impact measurement can result in *mission drift*. This can happen for at least two reasons. For one, similar to the above argument about innovation, a strong focus on the measuring process can crowd out a social mission focus. On the other hand, employing impact measurement may shift an organization away from activities whose effect is less measurable or highly complex to those that are more easily measurable. A social venture can thus shift its focus from the actual beneficiaries to the measurement and management of impact (André and Pache 2016). In fact, a study on social ventures who participated in the Global Entrepreneurship Monitor found a negative correlation between impact measurement and social mission (Maas and Grieco 2017).

Fourth, and closely related, impact measurement can lead to *gaps within social entrepreneurship*. As we frequently addressed in this book (see Chapters 2, 4, and 5 especially), social entrepreneurship closes gaps that are not sufficiently filled by the market, the state, or civil society. Therefore, if the field of social entrepreneurship increasingly focuses on impact measurability, there is an inherent risk that social or environmental issues where progress is less easily measured would fall through the grid. Thus, if the emphasis on measurement becomes too strong, social entrepreneurship runs the risk of not fulfilling its societal function.

Fifth, impact measurement struggles to accommodate the sheer *diversity* of social ventures and their solutions (Stephan et al. 2016). Social ventures vary not only in the issues they address but also in how quickly their solutions lead to impact as well as in how concrete or abstract their mission and how complex their solutions are. For instance, it might be challenging to compare the impact of a social venture that issues vaccinations to infants with a social venture that wishes to enhance employment for people living with disabilities.

In short, contra-arguments against impact measurement point to the resource intensity, loss of innovativeness, mission drift, and lack of comparability due to diversity.

Against the background of such potential disadvantages, recent studies seem to indicate that at least some practitioners are actively opposing impact measurement. Grieco (2018) highlights that some social ventures do not consider impact measurement worthwhile. Molecke and Pinkse (2017) found that some social ventures go even further and actively delegitimize formal measurement tools, for example, through using narratives like 'imprudent,' 'incomplete,' or 'irrelevant.' They do so in favor of either no measurement or informal bricolage measurements.

Though some proponents of impact metrics sometimes portray measurement as an inherently desirable objective, the breadth of both advantages and disadvantages underlines our key claim that impact measurement is best understood as an ambivalent tool that deserves to be handled with care. Instead of answering the question of whether or not to measure impact, we therefore ask *for what* kind of problems this tool may be useful and *how* the usage of this tool can be managed in a way that allows handling its underlying ambivalence.

7.3. Managing Ambivalence: Shifting the Question from Whether to How

In his recently published book *The Tyranny of Metrics*, Jerry Z. Muller (2018) dissects the constructive and destructive nature of metrics. Put in the language of this book's conceptual perspective, Muller spells out an ambivalence analysis of metrics. To manage this ambivalence constructively, he argues that a key to make metrics useful for an organization is to clearly identify what it is measuring and how it is using the measurement results.

7.3.1. What to Measure?

We argue that an important point here is that the first question an organization needs to ask itself is what it is measuring. An inherent risk of any measurement approach is that organizations base the definition of their performance indicators not on what is important to measure but on what is easier to measure. In fact, a comparative study of various impact measurements revealed that many "faced construct validity" problems, that is, doubts about to what extent what was measured was a good representation of the 'impact' (Stern et al. 2012). Furthermore, most social ventures seem to evaluate short-term over long-term effects and rather measure outcomes than impact (Stern et al. 2012) despite the relevance of integrating both short- and long-term measurements (Sauka and Welter 2007).

So why is construct validity a potential issue? Although the question of what to measure is of course relevant, it is even more important to ask how closely what is measured is actually related to the core mission. For some organizations, it is easier to achieve this closeness between what they measure and what the mission is about than for others. Take the example of Aravind Eye Care Hospitals in India (Rangan, Thulasiraj, and Rangan 2007; Martin 2011). Aravind undertakes (among many other services nowadays) cataract surgery. If untreated, cataract disease can lead to blindness. Aravind's founder calls it 'needless blindness' because a surgery can resolve the problem permanently (see also Chapter 5 for a discussion of this business model).

Now consider impact measurement in Aravind (see Figure 7.1). It can employ metrics that are easy to measure and at the same time very closely linked to its mission of alleviating needless blindness. Every patient they operate successfully is one step closer to their mission. In other words, every output (i.e., surgery) almost one-to-one equals impact in their case. There is no time delay or complexity issue. To compare, take the example of Women Without Borders (WWB), an organization founded by Austrian Ashoka Fellow Edit Schlaffer (Ashoka 2018). WWB's mission is to engage mothers to prevent radicalization within their families and to empower them as ambassadors for deradicalization in their communities. In places ranging from Austria to Zanzibar, WWB organizes so-called MotherSchools in which trainers guide mothers to become experts against radicalization. When it comes to measuring its impact, WWB might gauge fairly easily the number of women reached and the number of trainings delivered. Though these metrics are clearly linked to WWB's mission, the challenge here is the actual impact related to the long-term family and community effects. To know if the program was indeed successful, the social venture would need to measure its impact not only over a very long time period but also with regard to the indirect effects that accumulate outside the group of the directly targeted group of women. Thus, the social venture can only use proxies to measure its impact.

These two examples illustrate that the more concrete and measurable the objectives of a social venture are and the more direct the interventions contribute to these objectives, the less it needs to rely on remote proxies to measure its impact (Stern et al. 2012). The more distant these proxies become, the less helpful they are for an organization (Muller 2018). As discussed in our conceptual foundations (see Chapter 3), the usefulness of a tool like metrics then also depends on the relevant alternatives available.

If no direct metrics are possible, remote proxies might be the best relevant option to produce quantitative indicators. Yet, as the noise in that information increases with indirect proxies, such metrics, if used at all, need to be used with reflected care.

There are some attempts to provide generic categories of impact measurement for specific types of social ventures (De Ruysscher et al. 2017). Yet, as we have mentioned previously (see subchapter 7.2.2), the field of social entrepreneurship is highly diverse and generic categories might not offer the customization that many social ventures require and desire (Millar and Hall 2012). Moreover, unless they allow for further customization, generic categories are not likely to enable a social venture to closely link its measurement to its mission. An additional point to consider is the sheer number of metrics. The higher the number of metrics, the more costly and complex it becomes to produce them (Muller 2018). At the same time, few but misleading metrics can do more harm in their interpretation than multiple and balanced ones.

In short, instead of debating whether or how many metrics a social venture should measure it is important to critically reflect what should and can be measured. To develop metrics that are closely linked to the social entrepreneur's mission not only requires time and effort. It is also a highly complex task demanding a high level of understanding of what the venture's mission actually entails.

7.3.2. *How Are We Going to Use Measurement Results?*

Because impact measurement is yet another tool a social venture can use to fulfill its mission, the question arises of how the venture uses it in a specific context. As outlined earlier, many voices in the literature point to the benefits of impact measurements for external organizations and other stakeholders. In fact, government agencies and some of the larger funders require continuous performance accountability from those social ventures that they support (Dean 2010). Such external pressure can then lead to mechanisms of coercive isomorphism (DiMaggio and Powell 1983) that leave social ventures little choice but to use certain measurement approaches.

Yet, if social ventures can freely choose what to measure and what to do with the results, what would, then, be their options and a smart way to use them? Inspired by Muller's (2018) discussion of metrics, we can distinguish two very different strategies to *use* metrics. On the one hand, metrics can primarily *serve as information*—without directly and automatically attached consequences. This supposes that decision-makers have individual discretion to interpret what follows from metrics. On the other hand, metrics can be *linked directly to consequences*, thus exercising an incentive and decision function. In terms of incentives, metrics can be linked to *rewards and punishment* for performance. With regard to decision-making, metrics can serve as the criterion to allocate budgets and funding or to decide whether a program will be expanded or discontinued.

When looking at this distinction from our conceptual perspective, linking impact measurement to consequences amounts to a far-reaching sharpening of the metrics tool. Due to its sharpened blade, however, the ambivalence potential of impact measurement strongly increases. For some selected problems, linking metrics to rewards and punishments may well serve to increase transparency, performance, and accountability. Yet linking metrics to consequences can result in at least two substantial negative consequences: gaming effects and poorer decision-making. Both problems can occur in any type of organizations, be it for- or nonprofit. Given the difficulties measuring impact, they are potentially even more relevant for social ventures.

Gaming effects. Linking metrics to rewards and punishments creates strong incentives in an organization. If the only way to improve measured performance is to really increase the actual social impact itself, then these incentives can further the achievement of the social mission. However, as already discussed, the real social impact is typically difficult to measure with real-life metrics just serving as proxies for impact. As a consequence, any metrics measurement can be manipulated. The stronger metrics are linked with high-powered incentives the stronger are incentives for gaming the measurement process to either increase rewards or decrease potential punishments. The level of manipulation can vary. However, our discussion of both SROI and the Theory of Change have already pointed to the fact that most aspects are highly subjective. In other words, people in charge of impact measurement could easily include or exclude certain metrics or chose different proxies or figures to alter the results. Furthermore, both staff and volunteers who understand how impact is calculated could alter their activities to improve key metrics. For instance, if impact measurement looks only at the number of beneficiaries supported and not the quality with which this support was undertaken, this could provide incentives to rush through appointments to increase individual or venture-level performance measures.

Poorer decision-making. Linking metrics with consequences is often used to guide decision-making in business, for example, when using a cash flow analysis to decide whether a product line should be continued or discontinued. However, linking metrics directly with meaningful decisions makes sense only if the relevant indicator really captures all necessary information for this particular decision. Yet, most decisions in the real world depend on multi-causal relations. The danger of linking metrics automatically to decisions lies in the underlying assumption that a single indicator can account for the complexity of a multi-causal problem context of most social ventures. Even if metrics aggregate multiple indicators, it requires judgment to decide which ones to count, how to weigh them, to know their limitations, and to acknowledge additional soft factors that are difficult to measure.

Directly linking metrics to consequences can thus lead to poorer decision-making if it leads to an underestimation of complexity and an erosion or crowding out of judgment. Interestingly, although impact measurement is often discussed as a tool to increase accountability, basing decisions on ambiguous indicators can actually diffuse responsibility and lead to less accountability.

Against this background, the alternative way to use metrics is not to link them automatically with consequences but to use them as information paired with discretion that allows for the development and exercise of *judgment*. A focus on judgment emphasizes that decision-makers can and need to learn to interpret metrics in light of experience. High-powered incentives in terms of rewards and punishment, however, would work against such experienced-based judgment.

It goes without saying that granting discretion to decision-makers is, again, an ambivalent tool. After all, the literature on agency theory (Jensen and Meckling 1976) gives countless examples of how decision-makers can abuse discretionary leeway. In the case of social entrepreneurship, however, most of the staff join the social venture because of its mission (Dempsey and Sanders 2010) and therefore are already willing to work toward the organization's goal (see Section 8.2). Moreover, people who share a common mission can also peer-monitor each other, thus reducing agency problems (Beckmann and Zeyen 2014). In this scenario, reducing discretionary leeway through metrics-based decision-making can actually reduce perceived self-efficacy and reduce motivation.

To summarize, we suggest that impact measurement is an ambivalent tool whose potential dark sides multiply when ambiguous easy-to-manipulate proxies are combined with high-powered incentives. As a consequence, the more ambiguous and proxy-like metrics are, the more it is advisable to use them for information purposes only, above all for an organization's internal dialogue. Just like a dashboard in a car gives drivers useful information without kicking them out of the driver seat, we suggest using metrics above all like an internal dashboard that does not substitute but informs judgment. This does not mean that linking metrics to consequences is per se negative. Yet, as a particularly sharp tool, they need to be handled with extra care.

In short, we argue that the key question in impact measurement should not be whether or not to use it but how to balance cost and benefits and truly carve out the context conditions under which impact measurement helps an organization achieve its mission. Particularly, social ventures that choose to implement social impact measurement need to consider what they wish to measure. Furthermore, if a social venture aims to use impact measurement as part of incentive structures, the social venture needs to clearly consider how to do this without running the risk of crowding out judgment and opening itself up to manipulation.

7.4. Conclusion

On the one hand, this chapter argues that measurement is important to fully understand if the products and services offered lead to the desired societal results. In other words, analogous to financial performance measurements, it supports an organization in making resource-allocation decisions. It further supports purpose-driven ventures in acquiring new resources (donations, volunteers, government funds). On the other hand, performance measurement can unintentionally lead to undesired consequences for social ventures. On top of high costs, ambiguous measurements, and challenges in comparability of diverse ventures, performance measurement can lead to mission drift (Ramus and Vaccaro 2017). This can occur because the organization is overwhelmed with measuring and loses track of its core activities, shifts its focus to activities for which success is more easily measurable, or loses its innovative edge. In turn, some social problems—those less easily quantifiable, slow in showing results or highly interdependent—are less likely to be addressed if impact focus increases too much. To manage the ambivalence of impact measurement, we made the case not only for critically reflecting what can and should be measured. Moreover, we highlighted the relevance of how measurement results are used. Here, we recommended extreme care with regard to linking metrics with consequences and suggest using metrics above all as internal information to inform judgment.

References

Alexander, J., and J. L. Brudney. 2010. "Introduction to the Symposium: Accountability and Performance Measurement: The Evolving Role of Nonprofits in the Hollow State." *Nonprofit and Voluntary Sector Quarterly* 39 (4): 565–70. doi:10.1177/0899764010369662.

Andersson, Fredrik O., and Michael Ford. 2015. "Reframing Social Entrepreneurship Impact: Productive, Unproductive and Destructive Outputs and Outcomes of the Milwaukee School Voucher Programme." *Journal of Social Entrepreneurship* 6 (3). Taylor & Francis: 299–319. doi:10.1080/19420676.2014.981845.

André, Kevin, and Anne-Claire Pache. 2016. "From Caring Entrepreneur to Caring Enterprise: Addressing the Ethical Challenges of Scaling up Social Enterprises." *Journal of Business Ethics* 133 (4): 659–75. doi:10.1007/s10551-014-2445-8.

Anton, Paul A., and Judy Temple. 2007. *Analyzing the Social Return on Investment in Youth Mentoring Programs a Framework for Minnesota*. Saint Paul, MN: Wilder Research.

Arena, Marika, Giovanni Azzone, and Irene Bengo. 2015. "Performance Measurement for Social Enterprises." *Voluntas* 26 (2): 649–72. doi:10.1007/s11266-013-9436-8.

Ashoka. 2018. "Edit Schlaffer | Ashoka | Everyone a Changemaker." July 29. www.ashoka.org/en/fellow/edit-schlaffer#intro.

Beckmann, Markus, and Anica Zeyen. 2014. "Franchising as a Strategy for Combining Small and Large Group Advantages (Logics) in Social Entrepreneurship: A Hayekian Perspective." *Nonprofit and Voluntary Sector Quarterly* 43 (3): 502–22. doi:10.1177/0899764012470758.

Bengo, Irene, Marika Arena, Giovanni Azzone, and Mario Calderini. 2016. "Indicators and Metrics for Social Business: A Review of Current Approaches." *Journal of Social Entrepreneurship* 7 (1). Taylor & Francis: 1–24. doi:10.1080/19420676.2015.1049286.

Bertotti, Marcello, Kevin Sheridan, Patrick Tobi, Adrian Renton, and George Leahy. 2011. "Measuring the Impact of Social Enterprises." *British Journal of Healthcare Management* 17 (4): 152–6. doi:10.12968/bjhc.2011.17.4.152.

Chmelik, Erin, Martina Musteen, and Mujtaba Ahsan. 2016. "Measures of Performance in the Context of International Social Ventures: An Exploratory Study." *Journal of Social Entrepreneurship* 7 (1). Taylor & Francis: 74–100. doi:10.1080 /19420676.2014.997781.

Clark, Catherine, William Rosenzweig, David Long, and Sara Olsen. 2004. "Double Bottom Line Project Report: Assessing Social Impact in Double Bottom Line Ventures." *Business*. doi:10.1016/j.rser.2014.08.006.

Cordes, Joseph J. 2017. "Using Cost-Benefit Analysis and Social Return on Investment to Evaluate the Impact of Social Enterprise: Promises, Implementation, and Limitations." *Evaluation and Program Planning* 64. Elsevier Ltd: 98–104. doi:10.1016/j.evalprogplan.2016.11.008.

Dacin, Peter A., M. Tina Dacin, and Marggret Matear. 2010. "Social Entrepreneurship: Why We Don' t Need a New Theory and How We Move Forward from Here." *Academy of Management Perspectives* 37–58.

Dean, M. 2010. *Governmentality: Power and Rule in Modern Society*. 2nd ed. London: Sage Publications.

Deming, Edwards W. 2000. *The New Economics: For Industry, Government, Education*. 2nd ed. Cambridge, MA: MIT Press.

Dempsey, S. E., and M. L. Sanders. 2010. "Meaningful Work? Nonprofit Marketization and Work/Life Imbalance in Popular Autobiographies of Social Entrepreneurship." *Organization* 17 (4): 437–59. doi:10.1177/1350508410364198.

De Ruysscher, C., C. Claes, T. Lee, F. Cui, J. Van Loon, J. De Maeyer, and R. Schalock. 2017. "A Systems Approach to Social Entrepreneurship." *Voluntas* 28 (6). Springer US: 2530–45. doi:10.1007/s11266-016-9704-5.

Dey, Pascal. 2006. "The Rhetoric of Social Entrepreneurship: Paralogy and New Language Games in Academic Discourse." *Entrepreneurship as Social Change. A Third Movements in Entrepreneurship Book* May: 121–42.

DiMaggio, Paul J., and Walter W. Powell. 1983. "The Iron Cage Revisited: Institutional Isomorphism and Collective Rationality in Organizational Fields." *American Sociological Review* 48 (2): 147–60.

Ebrahim, Alnoor, and Kasturi Rangan. 2010. "The Limits of Nonprofit Impact: A Contingency Framework for Measuring Social Performance. Harvard Business School Working Paper, No. 10–099, May 2010." 10–099.

Emerson, Jed. 2003. "The Blended Value Proposition: Integrating Social and Financial Results." *California Management Review* 45 (4): 35–52.

Flockhart, Andrew. 2005. "Raising the Profile of Social Enterprises: The Use of Social Return on Investment (SROI) and Investment Ready Tools (IRT) to Bridge the Financial Credibility Gap." *Social Enterprise Journal* 1 (1): 29–42. doi:10.1108/17508610580000705.

Grieco, Cecilia. 2018. "What Do Social Entrepreneurs Need to Walk Their Talk? Understanding the Attitude-Behavior Gap in Social Impact Assessment Practice." *Nonprofit Management and Leadership* January–March: 1–18. doi:10.1002/nml.21310.

Grieco, Cecilia, Laura Michelini, and Gennaro Iasevoli. 2015. "Measuring Value Creation in Social Enterprises: A Cluster Analysis of Social Impact Assessment Models." *Nonprofit and Voluntary Sector Quarterly* 44 (6): 1173–93. doi:10.1177/0899764014555986.

Haugh, Helen M., and Alka Talwar. 2016. "Linking Social Entrepreneurship and Social Change: The Mediating Role of Empowerment." *Journal of Business Ethics* 133 (4). Springer Netherlands: 643–58. doi:10.1007/s10551-014-2449-4.

Jensen, Michael C., and William H. Meckling. 1976. "Theory of the Firm: Managerial Behavior, Agency Costs and Ownership Structure." Edited by Michael C Jensen. *Journal of Financial Economics* 3 (4). Elsevier: 305–60. doi:10.1016/0304-405X(76)90026-X.

Jones, Nicola, Harry Jones, Liesbet Steer, and Ajoy Datta. 2009. "Improving Impact Evaluation Production and Use." 300. *ODI Opinion*. ODI Working Papers. London. www.alnap.org/resource/8225.

Levis, D. 1973. *Counterfactuals*. Cambridge, MA: Harvard University Press.

Lingane, Sara, and Alison Olsen. 2004. "Guidelines for Social Return on Investment." *California Management Review* 46 (3): 116–35.

Locke, Edwin A., and Gary P. Latham. 1990. *A Theory of Goal Setting & Task Performance*. Englewood Cliffs, NJ: Prentice Hall, Inc.

Lumpkin, G. T., Todd W. Moss, David M. Gras, Shoko Kato, and Alejandro S. Amezcua. 2013. "Entrepreneurial Processes in Social Contexts: How Are They Different, If at All?" *Small Business Economics* 40 (3): 761–83. doi:10.1007/s11187-011-9399-3.

Maas, Karen, and Cecilia Grieco. 2017. "Distinguishing Game Changers from Boastful Charlatans: Which Social Enterprises Measure Their Impact?" *Journal of Social Entrepreneurship* 8 (1). Taylor & Francis: 110–28. doi:10.1080/19420676.2017.1304435.

Maas, Karen, and Kellie Liket. 2011. "Social Impact Measurement: Classification of Methods." In *Environmental Management Accounting and Supply Chain Management*, 171–202. London: Springer.

Mair, Johanna, and Ignasi Martí. 2006. "Social Entrepreneurship Research: A Source of Explanation, Prediction, and Delight." *Journal of World Business* 41 (1): 36–44. doi:10.1016/j.jwb.2005.09.002.

Martin, Maximilian. (September 1, 2011). *Understanding the True Potential of Hybrid Financing Strategies for Social Entrepreneurs*. Impact Economy Working Papers 2. Available at SSRN: https://ssrn.com/abstract=2209745 or http://dx.doi.org/10.2139/ssrn.2209745

McLoughlin, Jim, Jaime Kaminski, Babak Sodagar, Sabina Khan, Robin Harris, Gustavo Arnaudo, and Sinéad Mc Brearty. 2009. "A Strategic Approach to Social Impact Measurement of Social Enterprises." *Social Enterprise Journal* 5 (2): 154–78. doi:10.1108/17508610910981734.

Millar, R., and K. Hall. 2012. "Social Return On Investment (SROI) and Performance Measurement: The Opportunities and Barriers for Social Enterprises in Health and Social Care. Public Management Review." *Public Management Review* 15 (6): 923–41. doi:10.1080/14719037.2012.698857.

Molecke, Greg, and Jonatan Pinkse. 2017. "Accountability for Social Impact: A Bricolage Perspective on Impact Measurement in Social Enterprises." *Journal of Business Venturing* 32 (5). Elsevier Inc.: 550–68. doi:10.1016/j.jbusvent.2017.05.003.

Moss, Todd W., Jeremy C. Short, G. Tyge Payne, and G. T. Lumpkin. 2011. "Dual Identities in Social Ventures: An Exploratory Study." *Entrepreneurship Theory and Practice* 35 (4): 805–30. doi:10.1111/j.1540-6520.2010.00372.x.

Muller, Jerry Z. 2018. *The Tyranny of Metrics*. Princeton, NJ: Princeton University Press.

nef. 2009. "A Guide to Social Return on Investment."

Nicholls, Alex. 2005. "Measuring Impact in Social Entrepreneurship: New Account-abilities to Stakeholders and Investors?" ESRC Research Seminar. Local Government Research Unit. London.

———. 2008. "Capturing the Performance of the Socially Entrepreneurial Organisation (SEO): An Organisational Legitimacy Approac." In *International Perspectives on Social Entrepreneurship Research*, edited by Joyce Robinson, Johanna Mair, and Kai Hockerts, 27–74. London: Palgrave Macmillan.

OECD. 2002. "Glossary of Key Terms in Evaluation and Results Based Management." *Evaluation and Aid Effectiveness* 38. doi:10.1787/9789264034921-en-fr.

Ramus, Tommaso, and Antonino Vaccaro. 2017. "Stakeholders Matter: How Social Enterprises Address Mission Drift." *Journal of Business Ethics* 143 (2): 307–22. doi:10.1007/s10551-014-2353-y.

Rangan, Kasturi V., R. D. D. Thulasiraj, and V. Kasturi Rangan. 2007. "Making Sight Affordable (Innovations Case Narrative: The Aravind Eye Care System)." *Innovations: Technology, Governance, Globalization* 2 (4). MIT Press: 35–49. doi:10.1162/itgg.2007.2.4.35.

Rawhouser, Hans, Michael Cummings, and Scott L. Newbert. 2017. "Social Impact Measurement: Current Approaches and Future Directions for Social Entrepreneurship Research." *Entrepreneurship Theory and Practice* September: 1–34.

Ryan, Patrick W., and Isaac Lyne. 2008. "Social Enterprise and the Measurement of Social Value: Methodological Issues with the Calculation and Application of the Social Return on Investment." *Education, Knowledge and Economy* 2 (3): 223–37. doi:10.1080/17496890802426253.

Salazar, José, Bryan W. Husted, and Markus Biehl. 2012. "Thoughts on the Evaluation of Corporate Social Performance Through Projects." *Journal of Business Ethics* 105 (2): 175–86. doi:10.1007/s10551-011-0957-z.

Santos, Filipe M. 2009. "A Positive Theory of Social Entrepreneurship." INSEAD Working Papers. Paris.

Sauka, Arnis, and Friederike Welter. 2007. "Productive, Unproductive and Destructive Entrepreneurship in an Advanced Transition Setting: The Example of Latvian Small Enterprises." *Empirical Entrepreneurship in Europe, Cheltenham: Edward Elgar* January: 87–111.

Seelos, Christian, and Johanna Mair. 2009. "Hope for Sustainable Development: How Social Entrepreneurs Make It Happen." In *An Introduction to Social Entrepreneurship: Voice, Preconditions and Context*, edited by Rafael Ziegler, 228–46. Cheltenham, UK: Edward Elgar Publishing.

SIBG. 2014. "How to Measure and Report Social Impact a Guide for Investees Table of Contents Introduction: The Development, Uses and Principles of Social Impact Measurement and How to Use These Guidelines." London, UK: Social Investment Business Group, https://www.sibgroup.org.uk/sites/default/files/files/Measuring_your_social_impact_guidelines_for_investees.pdf

Social Value UK. 2017. "Quantifying the Impact of Investment in Education." London, UK: Social Value UK, www.socialvalueuk.org/app/uploads/2017/10/Impacts-of-education-pdf

———. 2018. "Resources." July 1. http://www.socialvalueuk.org/resources/

Stephan, Ute, Malcolm Patterson, Ciara Kelly, and Johanna Mair. 2016. "Organizations Driving Positive Social Change: A Review and an Integrative Framework of Change Processes." *Journal of Management* 42 (5): 1250–81. doi:10.1177/0149206316633268.

Stern, Elliot, Nicoletta Stame, John Mayne, Kim Forss, Rick Davies, and Barbara Befani. 2012. "Broadening the Range of Designs and Methods for Impact Evaluations." *Department for International Development* 38. Department of International Development Working Papers.

Urban, Boris. 2015. "Evaluation of Social Enterprise Outcomes and Self-Efficacy." *International Journal of Social Economics* 42 (2): 163–78. doi:10.1108/IJSE-03-2013-0071.

Woolcock, Michael. 2009. "Toward a Plurality of Methods in Project Evaluation: A Contextualised Approach to Understanding Impact Trajectories and Efficacy." *Journal of Development Effectiveness* 1 (1): 1–14. doi:10.1080/19439340902727719.

8 Scaling Social Ventures
Growing the Limits or Limiting Growth?

Former US President Bill Clinton has been credited for observing: "Nearly every problem has been solved by someone, somewhere. The challenge of the 21st century is to find out what works and scale it up" (quoted in Heinecke and Mayer 2012, 192). For the purpose of this chapter, we will leave aside a discussion on whether or not humankind actually has solutions available to nearly all of its social or environmental problems. Rather, we will focus on the second part of Bill Clinton's quote and discuss the concept of scaling. As expressed by the quote, scaling strategies are often seen as inherently desirable for social entrepreneurship. After all, social entrepreneurs seek to achieve far-reaching social change, and scaling is needed to achieve and increase this impact. What we want to accentuate, however, is that scaling, though certainly of high significance to the field of social entrepreneurship, is a complex (and, following this book's conceptual perspective, ambivalent) *tool* to achieve the *objective* of social entrepreneurship, that is, social change. In fact, despite the dominant narrative about creating systemic social change (Sen 2007; Ashoka 2018; Skoll foundation 2014; Dacin, Dacin, and Matear 2010; Lee 2015), the reality of social entrepreneurship finds most social ventures to be and stay small in scope—be it in terms of their own size, their impact, or their geographical spread (Bacq, Hartog, and Hoogendoorn 2013; Spiess-Knafl et al. 2013; Blundel and Lyon 2015). So where does this discrepancy between proclaimed objectives and reality come from?

The academic and practitioner literature offers many multi-stepped process models to reach optimal scale, including SCALERS (short for Staffing, Communication, Alliance building, Lobbying, Earnings generating, Replicating, and Stimulating market forces) (Bloom and Chatterji 2009; Bloom and Smith 2010) and PATRI (Purpose, Applicability, Transferability, Readiness, and Implementation) (Tayabali 2014) developed by Ashoka for their Globalizer program. These insights are highly valuable for practitioners who wish to scale. However, they are less helpful to understand why scaling works for some organizations and does not work for so many others.

Our aim is not to provide a comprehensive answer, but we wish to none-theless engage in this discussion and provide some relevant insights and raise questions for future research. To this end, we will employ a four-step approach. First, we will introduce the concept of scaling and the underlying strategies in more detail (Section 8.1). We will then elaborate on two forms of social fran-chising and discuss why and how they had their (relative) successes. We pick social franchising because it is the scaling strategy that receives most interest and is potentially most misunderstood (Section 8.2). Third, we will use the insights from the social franchising cases and other insights from academic literature and real-world cases to discuss contingency factors that influence the choice of scaling strategy and thereby its potential for success or failure (Section 8.3). After discussing how to reduce the limits to growth for social entrepreneurship, Section 8.4 will raise a question that we feel is often overlooked in the discus-sion on scaling. Should we, as Bill Clinton put it, really 'scale it up,' or can there be good reasons for organizations to limit scaling?

8.1. The Concept of Scaling and Its Strategies

The purpose of this section is to provide the conceptual background and ter-minology for this chapter. First, it will discuss the term *scaling* itself. Second, it will then go on to introducing differentiations within the concept.

8.1.1. Why Scaling and Not Growing?

Before outlining the various scaling strategies available to social ventures, we believe it is important to elaborate on why the literature on social entre-preneurship talks about *scaling* (Dees, Anderson, and Wei-Skillern 2004a, 2004b; Zeyen 2014; Dobson et al. 2018; Heinecke and Mayer 2012; Bloom and Chatterji 2009) rather than *growth* as the general business literature does. The difference lies in the focus of the respective terms. Growth refers to organizational growth wherein profits, geographical spread, and/or num-ber of employees of the organization increase. In comparison, scaling does not place the emphasis on *organizational parameters* but on the *social inno-vation* itself (Bloom and Chatterji 2009), that is, it focuses on the *social mission* of social entrepreneurship and its direct and indirect impact which, as Chapter 7 highlighted, typically extend beyond the organization.

This terminological difference becomes clear if we consider the following two scenarios. Although it is possible for a social venture to scale without growing—that is, increase its societal impact while not increasing the size of the organization—it is also conceivable that a social venture grows with-out scaling—that is, it increases the size of the organization through, for example, hiring new staff members, but its achieved impact stagnates. The decoupling of growth and scaling is highly relevant in regards to the scaling strategies (*tools*) available to social ventures.

8.1.2. Three + Three Types of Scaling Strategies

Within the scaling literature are various subcategories of scaling. For instance, on a more abstract level authors distinguish between scaling up (London 2011; Uvin, Jain, and Brown 2000; Gillespie 2004; Lyon and Fernandez 2012), scaling wide (Desa and Koch 2014; London 2011), and scaling deep (London 2011; Desa and Koch 2014). Despite certain differences in nuance among these authors, the overall conceptual differentiation between scaling up, scaling wide, and scaling deep is sufficiently similar.

The differences between these terms reflect different arenas of increasing social impact. The authors distinguish between the type of solution offered and the type of beneficiary served. A social venture scales *deep* if it serves the same beneficiaries but offers them additional services. In this case, increasing social impact is not defined as reaching more people but as reaching the same people on a more holistic level. For instance, most microfinance institutions originally offered only microcredits but have since expanded their business to micro-insurances (Farooqui 2013). If an organization scales *wide*, it keeps its products or services yet tries to identify other potential users for them. For instance, if a social venture offered care services to dementia patients, it would then seek to offer these services to patients with similar diagnoses like Alzheimer's disease. In other words, this scaling strategy increases social impact by enlarging the types of potential beneficiaries. Finally, a social venture that scales *up* keeps both the solution offered as well as the type of beneficiary served but aims to increase the number of beneficiaries. As the first and second scaling type either innovates new services features or adapts applications to new beneficiary segments, they are less about diffusing a given social innovation and more advancing and developing novel solutions. Because the focus of this chapter is not on innovation but the diffusion of innovations, we will predominately refer to scaling up. From a diffusion perspective, scaling up offers the highest potential for fulfilling the social entrepreneurship narrative of alleviating social problems through widespread social change (Meyerson, Berger, and Quinn 2010).

Although there are many different approaches to further breaking down scaling up strategies (Mulgan, Halkett, and Sanders 2007; André and Pache 2016; Jowett and Dyer 2012; Weber, Kröger, and Demirtas 2015), we will use the three-tiered distinction between dissemination, affiliation and branching suggested by Dees, Anderson, and Wei-Skillern (2004b). These three strategies encompass other strategies mentioned in the literature and also offer the widest possible spectrum of tools for scaling social impact (see Table 8.1).

Branching. Branching is the scaling strategy most similar to growth strategies within the for-profit business world. In branching, scaling and growing are most closely coupled. The social venture increases its impact by growing its organization. To achieve this, they may choose to open up a new subsidiary (branch) or merge or acquire other organizations (Lyon and Fernandez

Table 8.1 Three types of scaling

	Dissemination	Affiliation	Branching
Includes strategies such as	• Open source • Provide training to others	• Partnerships • (Social) Franchising	• Open own subsidiaries • Mergers & acquisitions
Role of other organizations	As independent imitators	As contractual partners	No specified role
Speed of scaling	Potentially high	Medium	Low
Need of own resources	Low	Medium	High
Ability to create additional revenues	Low (open source) to medium (training for others)	Medium (through franchising royalties)	Potentially high (in the long term)
Control over service delivery	Low	Medium to high	High
Knowledge flows back to headquarters	Low	Medium (depends on cooperation of partners)	Potentially high (if organized well)

Source: Adapted from Dees, Anderson, and Wei-Skillern (2004b)

2012). For example, Greyston Bakery, the brownie supplier for Ben & Jerry's ice cream, will use branching when they expand their business to the Netherlands (Greyston Bakery 2018).

Dissemination. At the other end of the spectrum, dissemination strategies achieve scale with little to no growth. Dissemination strategies range from training to open source. Training-based dissemination builds on train-the-trainer models and thereby enables *other* organizations to implement the solution. The open source form of dissemination borrows the idea from information technology. There, open source refers to providing other programmers complete and free access to the underlying software code so that they can use and adapt it for their purpose (Fisac-Garcia et al. 2013; Waitzer and Paul 2011). Analogous, social ventures make their service or product blueprints available to the public via websites or other digital depositories. Premium Cola is an example of a social venture that engages both in training-based dissemination as well as in open source because it offers its business model knowledge for free on its website (Kiefer 2017).

Affiliation. Affiliation has characteristics of both dissemination and branching. Rather than opening their own branches, social ventures provide partner organizations with the relevant knowledge to open them on their behalf. Within affiliation strategies, there is a wide range of possible scaling tools including partnerships and (social) franchising. For instance,

Specialisterne (see Chapter 4) uses social franchising as its scaling strategy (Specialisterne 2013).

The three strategies mainly differ in the speed of scaling, the control over service delivery, and the resources required (Dees et al. 2004a; Lyon and Fernandez 2012). Open source dissemination has the potential of high scaling speed whereas branching is often the option with the lowest speed. Furthermore, branching is (often) the most resource-intensive strategy because the social venture has to provide all resources itself. On the other end, dissemination can be the least resource-intensive option because others will implement the idea with their own resources. Thirdly, branching has the potential for the highest level of control whereas dissemination has no or very limited levels of control over implementation and service delivery quality. We deliberately contrasted branching and dissemination because the differences are most clear. In comparison, the speed of scaling, resources required, and level of control available in affiliation strategies greatly depends on its specific type and configuration. This being said, it is nonetheless possible to conjecture that the speed would be lower than that of dissemination and the level of control and resources needed would be higher than in dissemination but lower than in branching. The affiliation strategy that is often described as the "best of two worlds" is social franchising (VanSandt et al. 2010).

8.2. Social Franchising(s)—An Example of a Scaling Strategy

Organizations like Ashoka have particularly been encouraging social ventures to use social franchising to scale. Due to the positive attention this scaling tool receives, we consider it important to analyze it in more detail. To highlight the benefits and challenges of choosing a specific scaling strategy, this subsection will use social franchising as an example to showcase how scaling can work as well as to help us carve out key lessons.

There are two very distinct ways of interpreting social franchising. First, social franchising can be conceived of as an income strategy (Netting and Kettner 1987). For example, Ben & Jerry's ice cream provides free franchise licenses to registered charities (Stephens 2003). These NGOs then use the income from running a commercial franchise outlet to fund their nonprofit activities. The second—and more frequently used—understanding of social franchising is closely linked to that of commercial franchising. Here, franchising contractually grants rights to a franchisee to use the business model or products of the franchisor in exchange for royalties (Combs et al. 2010; Combs, Ketchen, and Short 2011; Combs and Ketchen 2003; Lafontaine and Shaw 1998). In other words, franchising is used not only to fund the organization but also to grow its reach. Then, at its most basic level, social franchising transfers the idea of franchising from the commercial realm to the nonprofit world (Montagu 2002). Because we are interested in the advantages and challenges of certain scaling strategies, we refer to the second understanding of social franchising.

The research on social franchising is still somewhat limited (Schmitz and Scheuerle 2013; Lahme 2018) and leads to inconclusive results. In fact, the findings range from recommending social franchising as a successful scaling tool (Volery and Hackl 2010; Ahlert et al. 2008; Heinecke 2011a; McBride 2018; Heinecke and Mayer 2012) to unclear conclusions (Kistruck et al. 2011) or arguing that it is dysfunctional (Tracey and Jarvis 2007). We believe that these findings are not nuanced enough. Social franchising is not an objective in itself but a *tool*. We therefore need to identify situations or problems for which social franchising is the best scaling strategy given the relevant alternatives (see Chapter 3) such as branching or dissemination. We thus need to ask which context or organizational conditions lead to the respective success or failure of social franchising as a means to scale social ventures. We will address this question in three steps. First, we will outline the theoretical arguments as to why organizations choose franchising. Second, we will dive deeper into the purpose of social franchising in light of the special characteristics of social entrepreneurship and illustrate these with two case examples. In a final step, we will discuss challenges in setting up and successfully running social franchises.

8.2.1. Why Franchise?

Because social franchising is a derivative of commercial franchising, it is useful to highlight theoretical understandings of commercial franchising first. Here, there are two main approaches: resource scarcity theory (Oxenfeldt and Kelly 1969) and agency theory (Eisenhardt 1989).

Resource scarcity theory has two parts to its arguments (Oxenfeldt and Kelly 1969). As the name suggests, resource scarcity theory suggests that organizations choose to franchise only due to their own resource limitations and their subsequent need to tap into others' resources to grow (Part I). However, this theory sees the optimal approach in wholly owned subsidiaries and therefore argues that once sufficient resources are available, the franchisor will start buying back franchise outlets (Part II). Although the first part has been established empirically, the latter has been falsified in many instances (Castrogiovanni, Combs, and Justis 2006). Because social ventures often lack necessary resources and are often underfinanced (Mair and Marti 2009), we argue that a resource scarcity perspective could indeed explain why social ventures use social franchising to scale (Beckmann and Zeyen 2014).

Due to the partly reduced ability to predict empirical realities (Combs and Ketchen 2003), research turned to a second and now much more prevalent theoretical explanation for why organizations franchise. Based on *agency theory*, the franchisor-franchisee relationship is conceptualized as a delegation relationship between the franchisor (principal) and the franchisee(s) (agent). The main argument is that franchising reduces agency costs compared to the use of wholly owned subsidiaries (Combs and Ketchen 2003). Franchising is particularly powerful in reducing ex-ante costs of adverse selection. The argument is that when searching for a branch manager, there will always be a lingering risk that the potential employee (agent) conceals relevant information regardless of how much time and effort is put into the selection process. In franchising, the agent has to pay a considerable fee to join the franchise network. Therefore, the likelihood increases that only those potential franchisees that consider themselves suitable and capable will self-select. As a consequence, agency costs of adverse selection are reduced. Analogous, the fact that franchisees are running the outlet at their own risk and benefit reduces ex post agency costs of moral hazard. In comparison, a branch manager might disengage and not be as motivated because their income would not be dependent (or only partly) on their efforts and they are not in danger of losing a substantial investment. In short, based on agency theory arguments, organizations use franchising because it reduces the cost of running a growing organization while also providing them with additional revenue sources. Here again, it seems logical to conclude that an agency perspective can also explain social franchising (Tracey and Jarvis 2007; Beckmann and Zeyen 2014).

Though the previous conclusions seem highly plausible, they do not consider certain key differences between social and commercial franchising. Social franchisees tend to be organizations (typically nonprofit) rather than income-seeking individuals as is the case in commercial franchising (Montagu 2002). As a consequence, for these franchisees the franchise is only one part of their operation rather than the sole enterprise (Montagu 2002). We thus need to pose the question of how these differences might alter the previous conclusions. At a very concrete level, if the franchisee is also a social venture or nonprofit organization, the likelihood that they will be able to pay high upfront fees or annual royalties is low (Beckmann and Zeyen 2014). Due to these configurational difference, some authors argue that agency theory is in fact not able to explain why social ventures franchise (Volery and Hackl 2010).

However, we consider it shortsighted to end the discussion here. Rather, we believe that it is important to understand social franchising both from an agency as well as a non-agency theory perspective. In fact, we conjecture that this dual approach will highlight both the potential and the challenges of using social franchising as a scaling tool (Zeyen 2014).

8.2.2. *An Agency and Resource Scarcity Theory Perspective on Social Franchising*

Our argument is that agency theory is applicable to explain social franchising but that due to the special characteristics of social entrepreneurship franchising fulfills a different agency function than it does in commercial franchising. As the definitional discussions in Chapter 2 illustrated, the social mission is the core distinguishing factor of social entrepreneurship (Zahra et al. 2009; Dacin, Dacin, and Matear 2010; Lee 2015). Therefore, it is necessary to consider the social mission in any analysis of potential scaling strategies.

Social ventures attract their staff not because of high salaries or career progression opportunities but because of their mission and the call to meaningful work (Dempsey and Sanders 2010). In fact, many social ventures pay below-market wages (Volkmann, Tokarski, and Ernst 2012). Thus, it is the goals and ends of the organization that attract staff and volunteers. The question is then how this end-focused nature of social ventures and their potential franchisees can be integrated into an agency and resource scarcity perspective.

To this end, we will employ a slightly unusual theoretical perspective. In his book *The Fatal Conceit*, Friedrich August von Hayek (1988) analyzed why socialism did not work. Although this debate has no link to our current question, Hayek introduced a distinction between two social orders in modern society that we believe are highly relevant to the study of social entrepreneurship and particularly social franchising (Beckmann and Zeyen 2014 and see Chapter 4). He argues that modern society is simultaneously made up of the macro-cosm (big group) and micro-cosm (small group). Small groups rely on interpersonal relationships, direct face-to-face interactions and are end-connected. In other words, members of a small group know each other well and work together to achieve common goals. This micro-cosm is a heritage of premodern societies. To illustrate, imagine a prehistoric tribe that needs to feed itself. In that situation, they all work together to hunt an animal and prepare it afterward. Importantly, this prehistoric tribe would also know who did not participate and would sanction this by excluding the individual from the feast. In contrast, the macro-cosm is a modern development. Here, interactions are impersonal and rule-based. Individuals within the macro-cosm do not follow the same end but pursue pluralistic goals. To clearly pinpoint the difference, consider a commuter's morning coffee. The person selling the coffee is not necessarily personally interested in whether or not the commuter gets their coffee because they do not know each other. They might work there not to make people happy with coffee but to pay for university tuition. However, both the commuter and the salesperson fulfill their individual ends because of formal rule-based interactions like those governing markets. It is crucial to note that there is no hierarchy between the two social orders but rather both of them are different governance forms, tools so to speak, that occur and are functional in different contexts. Yet, only if the right social order is applied to the appropriate context can society work efficiently and effectively. Take the admittedly weird example of a family using macro-cosm tools to guide their daily interactions. This would mean that rather than giving every child in the house a portion of food, there might be a competition for who gets food and who does not, which would inevitably leave the youngest without food on most days.

So how does this distinction relate to social franchising? We conjecture that many social ventures are built on a small-group logic, that is, they function because people are end-connected rather than rule-connected (Beckmann and Zeyen 2014). Thus, these social ventures require internal micro-cosms to operate successfully. The challenge in scaling this type of social venture then is to protect the small-group logic when expanding geographically because big-group rules will most likely be introduced to coordinate, ensure quality, and streamline intersite communication. Therefore, the very attempt to fulfill the social mission by scaling social impact can be detrimental to the core functioning mechanism of a social venture.

Here, social franchising can be a powerful tool that supports a social venture in separating the required small-group logic of the operating team from the big-group rules that are part of a growing societal impact and organization (Beckmann and Zeyen 2014). Any big-group interactions are then moved to the contractual level between the organizational entities and thereby lifted out of the individual outlet's daily operation.

This reconceptualization of the purpose of social franchising now allows us to reconsider the applicability of both resource scarcity and agency theory. First, the reliance of some social ventures on small-group logics suggests that the scarce resource social franchising provides is not financial but social capital (Beckmann and Zeyen 2014). This also explains why local franchisees tend to be organizations rather than individuals. Organizations have established networks (social capital) that they can draw on in their local areas. Moreover, social franchising would thus allow an organization to scale faster because it can rely on other organizations' social capital (including knowledge about and trust by local beneficiaries, etc.) rather than having to engage in the time-consuming process of building up their own local social capital.

Second, the big-group/small-group separation function of social franchising allows us to link it with agency theory. Here, modern business-like agency interactions—which are sui generis rooted in the macro-cosm—are kept apart from the on-the-ground daily operations of the social venture. Their purpose is rather to ensure that quality standards are met at an *organizational* level and thereby reduce ex post agency costs. A social venture could most likely not afford formal monitoring. Moreover, formal monitoring would go against the organizational identity of and undermine motivation in most small-group-governed social ventures. Yet, as Hayek's micro-cosm concept shows, small groups self-monitor and sanction through regular face-to-face interactions and personal relationships. In other words, the small-group substitutes formal monitoring mechanism, thus reducing ex post agency costs.

To illustrate how this can work in practice, we use the example of Wellcome (Wellcome 2018; Beckmann and Zeyen 2014). Wellcome is a nonprofit social venture headquartered in Hamburg (Germany). Its mission is to support young families in the first six weeks after the birth of a child. To deliver their services, they use volunteers who go into the families' homes and help out. Importantly, this is not a babysitting or nanny service; the volunteers only help out for a couple of hours a week to allow the parents to adjust to their new lives. The volunteers meet regularly among themselves to talk about their experiences (small group, self-monitoring). The model of Wellcome very much relies on the volunteers knowing each other well. So once the organization started growing, Wellcome was faced with the challenge of what to do next. They chose social franchising with important rules for each franchise outlet. First, franchises must organize their volunteers into teams, which must not have more than fifteen women. If a team exceeds this number, it will be split into two new volunteer teams. Generally, fifteen is the highest number of people with whom a person can have valuable, regular, personal relationships. In other words, this rule safeguards the small group. Second, franchisees are typically local organizations that already work with families such as local authorities or welfare organizations. These organizations are the contractual partners of Wellcome and report back any challenges, their performance figures, and other relevant information. However, the volunteers themselves have no point of contact with any of these formal mechanisms. In other words, this arrangement shifts the big-group logic to the interaction between Wellcome's headquarter and the local authority but excludes volunteers. This approach has been highly successful for Wellcome who now operate in excess of 250 franchise outlets within Germany.

8.2.3. A Stewardship Perspective on Social Franchising

The social mission of social ventures can also lead to a second form of social franchising. This form is less based on a small-group logic (e.g., of the volunteers) but rather builds on the motivation of the people involved in management positions. To explain how this social franchising approach works, we will employ stewardship theory (Davis, Schoorma, and Donaldson 1997).

Both agency and stewardship theory analyze delegation relationships. Yet, whereas agency theory views agents (e.g., managers or franchisees) as primarily self-interested and extrinsically motivated, stewardships theory focuses on the scenario that agents are intrinsically motivated, care about what they do, and see themselves as stewards for certain purposes. Against this background, stewardship and agency theory are frequently considered opposites (Fox and Hamilton 1994) to the extent that stewards are described as 'good' and agents as 'bad' (Arthurs and Busenitz 2003). In contrast, we argue that both theoretical viewpoints are complements rather than opposites (Zeyen 2014). Both theories aim to achieve goal congruence between the principal and their agent. The difference is that agency theory aims to create goal congruence through contracts whereas stewardship theory considers it to be present a priori rooted in the intrinsic motivation of the steward-agent. Moreover, ex post stewardship also employs mechanisms to maintain goal congruence. Yet, rather than using formal contractual arrangements, stewardship advocates the use of informal mechanisms of personal power and involvement-oriented management (Davis, Schoorma, and Donaldson 1997). If these mechanisms are not employed properly, stewardship assumes that the a priori pro-organizational behavior of steward-agents will turn to anti-organizational and destructive behaviors. In short, the ex ante assumptions of both theories diverge yet the ex post concerns are parallel (Zeyen 2014).

In the context of social franchising, we outlined how the social mission can reduce agency costs and align goals. Complementary to this perspective, we argue that the social mission may also allow stewardship relationships to occur. In other words, we raise the question of how the social mission and the resulting goal alignment through intrinsic motivation affect the scaling potential of social entrepreneurial franchising.

Stewardship theory describes stewards (both steward-principals and steward-agents) as intrinsically motivated by higher-order needs, other-regarding (Corbetta and Salvato 2004), showing pro-organizational behavior, and responding to personal power (Chrisman et al. 2007; Breton-Miller and Miller 2009; Corbetta and Salvato 2004) and involvement-oriented management (Davis, Schoorma, and Donaldson 1997). Many studies have shown that stewardship relationships can increase performance and reduce managerial costs (Hernandez 2008; Eddleston and Kellermanns 2007; Davis, Schoorma, and Donaldson 1997). Due to these positive results, many advocates of steward-steward relationships consider them superior to principal-agent relationships. Though we do not wish to engage any further in this governance theory debate, we want to use the following discussion to highlight the ambivalence of steward-steward relationships in the context of social franchising.

With the characteristics of stewards in mind, we will now take a closer look at stewardship-based social franchising and will particularly pay attention to challenges that occur due to a steward-steward relationship (Krzeminska and Zeyen 2017). Krzeminska and Zeyen (2017) coined these challenges stewardship costs analogous to the concept of agency costs.

The selection process and stewardship costs: One of the key assumptions in stewardship theory is that stewards are a priori intrinsically motivated. As such it pays less attention to how to keep this motivation ex post. As a consequence, the importance of the ex ante selection process in social franchising increases as only few correctional activities are achievable ex post (Krzeminska and Zeyen 2017). This is particularly the case because steward-agents respond negatively toward external incentives, which in turn may crowd out their intrinsic motivation (Davis, Schoorma, and Donaldson 1997). The selection process further needs to ensure that the steward-agent identifies with the steward-principal and their organization. This identification is in a sense the glue that holds the relationships together. Moreover, the identification is also the channel through which the steward-franchisee will respond to personal power once they entered the franchise. Yet, if a franchisor needs to clearly identify whether a potential social franchisee is not only intrinsically motivated but also identifies entirely with the details of the approach taken within the social franchise, the selection process can become resource- and time-intensive (Krzeminska and Zeyen 2017). The level of complexity is further increased through the possibility of obscuring opinions and motivations (Connelly et al. 2011).

Furthermore, identification can be achieved only through regular personal interactions with the social entrepreneur (franchisor). Due to time constraints of the franchisor, the reliance on stewardship relationships can lead to a deceleration of the scaling process. Finally, an overemphasis on identification and intrinsic motivation during the selection process can overshadow capabilities and expertise (Krzeminska and Zeyen 2017). In short, due to the inherent nature of the social venture and its focus on stewardship relationships, the franchisor can run the risk of adverse selecting either intrinsically motivated franchisees that do not fully understand and identify with the mission and vision of the venture or—what might be worse—select individuals that are stewards but lack expertise and experience to run the outlet successfully.

Managing the steward franchisee: Stewards primarily respond to involvement-oriented management. This in turn affects the potential size of the franchise network (Krzeminska and Zeyen 2017). This type of management style is highly participatory and emphasizes the importance of consensus (Hernandez 2012; Meek et al. 2011) that relies on personalized relationships (Bleeke and Ernst 1993). On top of process concerns, if the number of franchisees increases (e.g., the challenge of reaching consensus increases), there is also the practical issue of maintaining these personalized relationships. This becomes the more challenging, the larger the group and the more geographically spread it is (Krzeminska and Zeyen 2017).

The identification with the mission by stewards guides their decision-making. Thus, if the franchisor changes its operation or shifts away from the original mission, franchisees might respond by shifting their identification entirely toward the beneficiaries. In other words, the potential to realign goals between both parties is highly limited (Krzeminska and Zeyen 2017) (see also Chapter 6 for learning rigidities and reduced adaptiveness of mission-based business models). In short, the intrinsic motivation and mission drive of individuals involved can be a source of both its success and failure.

To illustrate, we refer back to the example of Dialogue Social Enterprises (DSE) previously introduced in this book. The founder Andreas Heinecke describes himself as the "worst salesman" as he deliberately talks about all the challenges of running a DSE franchise outlet in the very first meeting with a potential franchisee (Volery and Hackl 2010). With a stewardship conceptualization lens, we assume that he did so to weed out those candidates that are not in it for the social mission. Moreover, in an interview, Heinecke revealed that it usually took about two years from first contact to the opening of an outlet (Heinecke and Sonne 2012). DSE faced many of the challenges above. Heinecke was the main support for all their global franchise outlets, which involved him traveling a lot to upkeep personal relationships (Heinecke and Sonne 2012). Furthermore, their franchisees continuously outvoted his suggestion to introduce a corporate design, which means that most outlets have different color schemes and fonts. Moreover, due to the lack of monitoring, the Hamburg headquarter of DSE was often not aware of what various franchise outlets were doing. One example here is that Heinecke talked about how successful their Hong Kong outlet was in selling merchandise. Yet, when they asked the outlet what they did differently, they refused an answer. Heinecke described himself during a keynote talk as a "toothless tiger" (Heinecke 2011b). As DSE used only one-page franchise contracts (Volery and Hackl 2010), they had no legal stance to acquire the information. Indeed, DSE used to not refer to it as social franchising but rather as "friendchising" further supporting the notion of intrapersonal relationships (Heinecke 2011b; Krzeminska and Zeyen 2017). To be clear, we do not wish to taint the image of DSE but rather illustrate the challenges that occur when a specific organizational culture and delegation style impact the success of scaling. Although DSE scaled globally, it faced many problems and setbacks, which led to a significant change in its social franchising approach that by now involves very detailed contracts.

Stewardship-based management can be a powerful tool to run an organization efficiently (Davis, Schoorma, and Donaldson 1997; Hernandez 2008; Eddleston and Kellermanns 2007), especially for social ventures. Yet, this management culture poses unique challenges to scaling. For social ventures based on stewardship relationships, social franchising might not be the best tool to reach scale or requires adaptation so that the franchise system overcomes some of the stewardship relationships-specific management challenges outlined earlier.

In sum, our analysis highlighted that there is not *the* social franchising approach but rather various types of social franchising. This distinction is highly relevant because it helps us to understand why the findings in the extant social franchising literature are so diverse. We conjecture that the types of social franchising employed might have varied. Although there are existing differentiations between franchises and social franchises (Asemota and Chahine 2017), they are often based on questions such as what is franchised (e.g., business format versus product franchising) or which legal forms the entities have (nonprofit versus for-profit). Our analysis suggests that it is crucial to go deeper and understand how a social franchise works. Finally, our analysis has shown that social franchising despite its potential for impressive success—like Child and Family Wellness (CFW), a franchise mostly based in Kenya, who reach nearly 500,000 children a year through franchised clinics (McBride 2018)—is just one of many tools to scale and might not be appropriate for all organizations. In fact, it constitutes a toolbox rather than just one uniform tool.

Yet, the most important takeaway from both discussions is that the choice of scaling strategy depends on the unique configuration of the social venture. In fact, both small-group-based franchises and stewardship franchises build on similar core features, that is, the social mission focus of the venture and the motivation of the franchisees and other actors involved. Yet, nuances in their configuration can render the same social franchising tool more successful in some contexts and less appropriate in others.

8.3. Picking the Right Tool from the Scaling Toolbox

For a scaling strategy—just like any strategic decision—to be successful, it needs to fit to the organization's capabilities, its culture, mission, and resource availability. Although this is challenging for any organization to determine, this can be especially challenging for social ventures due to their inherent hybrid nature. For the purpose of this by no means comprehensive discussion, we will divide factors that can impact the choice and respective effectiveness into organizational and context-specific factors.

8.3.1. Organization-Specific Factors in Picking the Right Scaling Tool

Before choosing the most suitable scaling tool, a social venture needs to fulfill two prerequisites. They first have to identify what they wish to scale, that is, do they wish to scale the entire organization or just one program (Chowdhury and Santos 2010; Dees, Anderson, and Wei-Skillern 2004b)? In other words, the social venture needs to understand how it achieves impact. As Chapter 7 has discussed in detail, developing a theory of change and evaluating it is a highly complex and time- and resource-intensive procedure. Yet, if not done properly, a social venture might decide to scale too much or too little of its operations. Second, a social venture needs to be aware of its own organizational culture, management style (like stewardship management), and core business model features (like small-group dependence) (Dees, Anderson, and Wei-Skillern 2004b; Chowdhury and Santos 2010).

The business model: Our discussions on social franchising highlighted the importance of fully understanding an organization's business model (see Chapter 6) when considering potential scaling strategies. For instance, if a social venture has a hybrid business model—that is, aims to achieve social and financial value simultaneously—it is more likely to struggle with growth and scaling. This is because the internal tension created by having to fulfill a dual objective increases with the increase in operations (Doherty, Haugh, and Lyon 2014; Blundel and Lyon 2015). Here, social ventures would need to identify a scaling strategy that helps them to reduce the potential of internal tensions. This becomes even more difficult as any attempts to standardize or rationalize a social venture's operations take away capacity from the founder and can lead to mission drift (André and Pache 2016).

Management and organizational culture: Our stewardship discussion substantiated the importance of linking the scaling strategy to the dominant management and organizational culture. If there is a disconnect, this can lead to significant costs or even to the demise of the organization. As in the case of DSE, the management style and organizational culture of a social venture is often strongly influenced by the entrepreneur (Blundel and Lyon 2015). This is because most small social ventures are entrepreneurial organizations (Mintzberg 2003). In entrepreneurial organizations, the dominance of the entrepreneur's influence on the organization and its culture is likely to shift once the organization grows. For one, this is because of entrepreneurial adjustments to its mission (Desa and Koch 2014) that in turn might impact organizational culture. On the other hand, any social venture that engages in scaling linked to organizational growth needs to be ready for the potential cultural change as the organization moves toward more formal process-orientation and thus bureaucracy (André and Pache 2016). Such shifts can change organizational identity and thereby culture and management style. These interdependent changes increase the challenge of choosing an adaptive scaling strategy as any particular scaling strategy might be the best means to achieve a social venture's end at point A but might become less suitable after internal changes at point B. In fact, these cultural changes can easily lead to people leaving the organization—even the founder as in the case of SAMU social, a French organization that provides care and medical services to homeless people and people in social distress, and its founder Xavier Emmanualli who left the organization as he felt it had become too bureaucratic and too little focused on helping beneficiaries (André and Pache 2016).

Complexity of the solution: Rapid large scale is more easily obtainable the simpler the solution that the social venture provides. In fact, some practitioner organizations that support social ventures in their scaling efforts even argue that an organization wishing to scale first needs to strip down its idea to the essentials (Graham 2018a). Though this sounds easy, it is not. As our discussions in Chapter 7 show, understanding if and why (i.e., theory of change) a solution is working, is highly challenging (Connell and Kubisch 1998; Biggs et al. 2017). Take the example of Evidence Action. Based in Washington, DC, this organization has incredible global scale as it helps millions of people on an annual basis. The reason why it is able to do so is that it offers very simple solutions to very specific problems and then ensures global provision (Graham 2018c). One of its programs is to deworm the world. If in contrast, we consider an example like Sekem, the biodynamic farming social venture in Egypt that also covers education and health services, its social business model and level of expertise is far more complex and would therefore reduce the speed of scaling but also increase the complexity of choosing the right scaling strategy.

Resources needed and available: The lack of resources within social ventures and their potential partners further impacts the choice of scaling strategy (Davies, Haugh, and Chambers 2018). Thus, the availability of resources—be it human, social, or financial—will determine not only the scope and speed of scaling (Bradach 2003, 2010; Chowdhury and Santos 2010; Heinecke and Mayer 2012; Dees, Anderson, and Wei-Skillern 2004a; Bloom and Chatterji 2009) but also the choice of strategy. For instance, internal human resource constraints may be the key influencing factor in choosing a scaling strategy rather than what best suits the organizations' needs. This being said, social entrepreneurs are sometimes able to access informal resources through social bricolage (Zahra et al. 2009). Resources can also be social capital as access to networks (Blundel and Lyon 2015) or the engagement with stakeholders (Bacq and Eddleston 2016).

8.3.2. Context-Specific Factors in Picking the Right Scaling Tool

The context for which and in which a scaling strategy is made is important (Blundel and Lyon 2015; Davies, Haugh, and Chambers 2018).

Situational context conditions: A social venture needs to consider not only its own organization but also the context of both their beneficiaries and any potential partners. To illustrate take the example of micro-franchises discussed by Kistruck and colleagues (2011). They found that contrary to the characteristics of social entrepreneurship, some of the franchisees used their outlets for personal benefits rather than for the benefits of others. This example shows the context-dependence of social ventures. The micro-franchises under investigation operated in rural poor areas in developing countries. As a consequence, these franchisees are less likely to demonstrate stewardship behavior; yet not because they are sui generis 'opportunistic' but because they are in a situation that does not readily allow for stewardship behavior. Stewardship is about other-regarding and higher-order needs satisfaction (Davis, Schoorma, and Donaldson 1997). Thus, if a micro-franchisee lives a subsistence lifestyle, higher-order needs might not be the priority. Furthermore, it can hardly be considered opportunistic behavior if someone puts their families' survival first before helping others. In this situation, it might have been advisable to choose a different franchising model where franchisees are not the beneficiaries but organizations working with the beneficiaries. Alternatively, they could have considered an alternative scaling strategy.

Furthermore, other contextual factors such as legal frameworks and required licenses are also highly relevant (Beckmann and Ney 2013; Aidis 2005) as well as the prevalence of corruption (Aidis 2005)

Public pressures: We have personally witnessed many situations in which social entrepreneurs and their ventures were pressured to scale. Although outside pressure can be highly fruitful, it can also have negative effects on the organization. For one, the organization might not be ready to scale, that is, has not determined what and how to scale. In that situation, they might merely pick a strategy that seems plausible and follow it. Headquartered in Belgium, the case of ViaVia Travellers Café that managed to scale to four countries through experimenting (Dobson et al. 2018) demonstrates that it is indeed possible. Yet, there are numerous examples where outside pressure has led to significant subsequent challenges for a social venture. Furthermore, outside pressures might push an organization to scale that was not only not ready but maybe not even willing to do so. In that situation, a push toward scale can lead to an exit of staff and volunteers.

Isomorphic pressures: The choice of a scaling strategy is inherently ambiguous. In most cases, it is possible to retrospectively analyze only if the choice was correct. Yet, even then it is impossible to know if another strategy might have been more successful. In situations of ambiguity and uncertainty and in contexts of at least moderate institutionalization, actors tend to mimic each other (DiMaggio and Powell 1983). This phenomenon is often referred to as mimetic isomorphic pressures (DiMaggio and Powell 1983). Although following isomorphic pressures does not necessarily lead to bad decision-making, they can also be a pitfall. Within the field of social entrepreneurship, social franchising has been discussed as *the* key scaling strategy that allows for fast impact with only limited resources. In addition, key players (e.g., Ashoka) within the field of social entrepreneurship were supporting this narrative. Following the expectations of powerful actors can then result in what is called coercive isomorphism. In fact, the involvement of large-scale funders can lead to isomorphism in scaling strategies (Aiken 2010) as social ventures try to fulfill their funder's demands (André and Pache 2016). Now that more and more organizations struggle with either maintaining or building up their franchise systems, these external pressures have slightly changed. Nonetheless, these isomorphic pressures can induce social ventures to choose a specific scaling strategy template, such as social franchising, without considering its suitability for their own venture.

If we combine these factors, it becomes apparent how challenging and complex the choice of scaling strategy is. Moreover, it further underpins that any scaling strategy is just a tool to achieve a social venture's end. And as the social venture evolves, so should the tools it uses.

8.4. Limit Scaling!? A Legitimate Question

If we go back to Bill Clinton's quote, we can see that both practitioners and academics are pushing for increased scale. However, as our previous discussions in this chapter have shown, scaling is a highly complex and ambivalent process that can overwhelm an organization. So far, we discussed this ambivalence by focusing on alternative scaling tools and how they can be used. In this last section, we want to go one step further and dare ask the question of whether there can be good reasons to limit scaling or refrain from it in the first place. Although we generally agree that scaling enables social ventures to achieve their social mission and that from an efficiency and effectiveness perspective it is important for these ideas to spread and scale, we want to point out three further issues that can justify limits to scaling.

First, some social innovations are viable and make sense only in a certain niche. Scaling beyond this niche would then either be ineffective or even lead to unintended repercussions for society, thus creating a case for limiting further scaling activities. To illustrate, we want to use the example of the Graduation Approach that was initially developed by BRAC (Graham 2018b; Banerjee et al. 2015)—a highly successful Bangladeshi social venture (Bornstein 2007). The Graduation Approach supports the poorest citizens in developing countries to achieve a sustainable lifestyle, that is, being able to care for themselves and afford essentials. This is done with a large variety of activities ranging from coaching to providing access to bank accounts and certain cash transfers. Because the program was highly successful in Bangladesh, reaching more than 100,000 people (Graham 2018b), it was scaled to various other developing countries including Ethiopia, Ghana, Honduras, India, Pakistan, and Peru (Graham 2018b; Banerjee et al. 2015). The valuation study by Banerjee and collegues (2015) found that one year after completion, the pilots in these six countries who served over 10,000 people exceeded expectations and were creating more value than they cost in five out of six of these countries (Graham 2018b). Therefore, the scaling strategy (affiliation) of BRAC's Graduation Approach seems to have been well chosen and executed. Now, let us return to our argument. As part of the Graduation Approach, participants identify crafts or other jobs that they could do to sustain their livelihood. Ironically, however, this element that makes the program so successful on a small scale could ultimately create new problems if scaled significantly. The problem here is that each training that allows a participant to learn a specific craft creates competition and reduces demand for those who are already active in this craft. As Aude de Montesquiou, a World Bank representative, put it: "How many carpenters can you have?" (Graham 2018b). If too many indivdiuals who follow certain (low-) skilled jobs flood a market, this could impact both incumbants who might be pushed out and even the newcomers if the market gets too crowded. At this stage, it is not clear what a Graduation Approach that takes these aspects into consideration would look like (Graham 2018b). As a consequence, a discussion about limiting scaling makes sense. This is particularly relevant when scaling is driven by outside donor monies that might push into an unsustainable disequilibrium such as too many people who train to become carpenters who would not have done so without the outside money.

Second, scaling can impede innovation. Innovating a solution and diffusing it are not the same thing, with different skills and competencies needed, respectively. A core characteristic of social entrepreneurship is its innovation focus. This is where many innovative entrepreneurs are strong. By emphasizing scaling as well, this innovation focus may get lost. Many scaling strategies require the standardization of processes and activities. Such standardization may improve efficiency but can reduce entrepreneurial freedom for being innovative. Instead of pushing all social ventures to innovate *and* to scale, the overall societal impact might be bigger if we allow social ventures to specialize in what they are particularly good at. Some might then want to innovate and scale, others might want to copy and diffuse what works, whereas others might have good reasons to focus on innovations—and leave the scaling and dynamic effects to others (see also Chapter 4).

Third, scaling might not be in the interest of the social entrepreneur. Although the idealized social entrepreneur wants to create far-reaching system-wide change, many real-life social entrepreneurs (and their teams) care about experiencing their impact directly and personally. In fact, taking an ethics of care perspective, André and Pache (2016) argue that scaling can create significant challenges for a caring organization as it might push the organization away from caring for individual beneficiaries toward those aspects of scaling that can be measured (Zahra et al. 2009). Scaling and growth shift the entrepreneurial founder into more administrative and strategic roles. Though some actually enjoy this development and willingly embrace it to increase positive societal impact, some social entrepreneurs regret the loss in personal interaction with their beneficiaries and experience this as a negative personal impact. Just like in business, some social entrepreneurs are actually quite happy to follow the logic that "small is beautiful" (Schumacher 2011). For social entrepreneurs there might be thus good reasons to limit scaling, even it seems desirable from an outside perspective.

8.5. Conclusion

This chapter shed light on the challenges of scaling. It started off by highlighting different scaling strategies. Following, we took the most popular scaling strategy, social franchising, as a starting point to provide an in-depth discussion on strategic configuration as well as potential pitfalls and challenges when scaling with this tool. Based on these and other insights from the literature, we then point to organization and context-specific factors that influence the choice of scaling strategy. In a last step, we raise the question of whether or not there should be a limit to how much social ventures can scale. Here, one often-neglected point is that the scaling concept focuses on societal impact yet does not explicitly consider the individual needs and wishes of the social entrepreneur. Against this background, Part IV and especially Chapter 9 will shift the perspective and discuss how social entrepreneurship impacts and interacts with the individual on the micro-level.

References

Ahlert, D., M. Ahlert, Hai Van Duong Dinh, Hans Fleisch, Tobias Heussler, Lena Kilee, and Julia Meuter. 2008. *Social Franchising: A Way of Systematic Replication to Increase Social Impact*. Berlin: Bundesverband Deutscher Stiftungen & Internationales Centrum für Franchising und Cooperation.

Aidis, Ruta. 2005. "Institutional Barriers to Small- and Medium-Sized Enterprise Operations in Transition Countries." *Small Business Economics* 25 (4): 305–17. doi:10.1007/s11187-003-6463-7.

Aiken, Mike. 2010. "Taking the Long View: Conceptualizing the Challenges Facing: UK Third Sector Organizations in the Social and Welfare Field." In *Third Sector Organizations Facing Turbulent Environments*, edited by A. Evers and A. Zimme, 295–316. Berlin, Germany: Nomos.

André, Kevin, and Anne-Claire Pache. 2016. "From Caring Entrepreneur to Caring Enterprise: Addressing the Ethical Challenges of Scaling Up Social Enterprises." *Journal of Business Ethics* 133 (4): 659–75. doi:10.1007/s10551-014-2445-8.

Arthurs, Jonathan D., and Lowell W. Busenitz. 2003. "The Boundaries and Limitations of Agency Theory and Stewardship Theory in the Venture Capitalist/Entrepreneur Relationship*." *Entrepreneurship Theory and Practice* 28 (2): 145–62. doi:10.1046/j.1540–6520.2003.00036.x.

Asemota, Joseph, and Teresa Chahine. 2017. "Social Franchising as an Option for Scale." *Voluntas* 28 (6). Springer US: 2734–62. doi:10.1007/s11266-016-9763-7.

Ashoka. 2018. "About Ashoka." May 16. www.ashoka.org/en-gb/about-ashoka-0.

Bacq, Sophie, and Kimberly A. Eddleston. 2016. "A Resource-Based View of Social Entrepreneurship: How Stewardship Culture Benefits Scale of Social Impact." *Journal of Business Ethics*, September. Springer Netherlands, 1–23. doi:10.1007/s10551-016-3317-1.

Bacq, Sophie, Chantal Hartog, and Brigitte Hoogendoorn. 2013. "A Quantitative Comparison of Social and Commercial Entrepreneurship: Toward a More Nuanced Understanding of Social Entrepreneurship Organizations in Context." *Journal of Social Entrepreneurship* 4 (1): 40–68. doi:10.1080/19420676.2012.7 58653.

Banerjee, Abhijit, Esther Duflo, Nathanael Goldberg, Dean Karlan, Robert Osei, William Parienté, Jeremy Shapiro, Bram Thuysbaert, and Christopher Udry. 2015. "A Multifaceted Program Causes Lasting Progress for the Very Poor: Evidence from Six Countries." *Science* 348 (6236). doi:10.1126/science.1260799.

Beckmann, Markus, and Steven Ney. 2013. "Wenn Gute Lösungsansätze Keine Selbstläufer Werden: Vernetzung Als Skalierungsstrategie in Fragmentierten Entscheidungslandschaften Am Beispiel Des Social Labs in Köln." In *Sozialunternehmen in Deutschland: Analysen, Trends Und Handlungsempfehlungen*, edited by Stephan A. Jansen, Rolf G. Heinze, and Markus Beckmann, 253–84. Wiesbaden: Springer Gabler.

Beckmann, Markus, and Anica Zeyen. 2014. "Franchising as a Strategy for Combining Small and Large Group Advantages (Logics) in Social Entrepreneurship: A Hayekian Perspective." *Nonprofit and Voluntary Sector Quarterly* 43 (3): 502–22. doi:10.1177/0899764012470758.

Biggs, Duan, Rosie Cooney, Dilys Roe, Holly T. Dublin, James R. Allan, Dan W. S. Challender, and Diane Skinner. 2017. "Developing a Theory of Change for a Community-Based Response to Illegal Wildlife Trade." *Conservation Biology* 31 (1): 5–12. doi:10.1111/cobi.12796.

Bleeke, Joel, and David Ernst. 1993. *Collaborating to Compete: Using Strategic Alliances and Acquisitions in the Global Marketplace*. New York, NY: John Wiley & Sons.

Bloom, Paul N., and Aaron K. Chatterji. 2009. "Scaling Social Entrepreneurial Impact." *California Management Review* 51 (3): 114–33.

Bloom, Paul N., and Brett R. Smith. 2010. "Identifying the Drivers of Social Entrepreneurial Impact: Theoretical Development and an Exploratory Empirical Test of SCALERS." *Journal of Social Entrepreneurship* 1 (1): 126–45. doi:10.1080/19420670903458042.

Blundel, Richard K., and Fergus Lyon. 2015. "Towards a 'Long View': Historical Perspectives on the Scaling and Replication of Social Ventures." *Journal of Social Entrepreneurship* 6 (1): 80–102. doi:10.1080/19420676.2014.954258.

Bornstein, David. 2007. *How to Change the World: Social Entrepreneurs and the Power of Ideas.* New York, NY: Oxford University Press.

Bradach, Jeffrey. 2003. "Going to Scale: The Challenge of Replicating Social Programs." *Stanford Social Innovation Review* Spring: 19–25.

———. 2010. "Scaling Impact." *Stanford Social Innovation Review* Summer: 27–28.

Breton-Miller, Le, and Danny Miller. 2009. "Agency vs. Stewardship in Public Family Firms." *Entrepreneurship Theory and Practice* 33 (6), 1169–91.

Castrogiovanni, Gary J., James G. Combs, and Robert T. Justis. 2006. "Resource Scarcity and Agency Theory Predictions Concerning the Continued Use of Franchising in Multi-Outlet Networks." *Journal of Small Business Management* 44 (1): 27–44. doi:10.1111/j.1540-627X.2006.00152.x.

Chowdhury, Imran, and Filipe Santos. 2010. "Scaling Social Innovations : The Case of Gram Vikas." In *Scaling Social Impact: New Thinking*, edited by Paul N. Bloom and Edward Skloot, 147–68. New York, NY: Palgrave Macmillan.

Chrisman, James J., Jess H. Chua, Franz W. Kellermanns, and Erick P. C. Chang. 2007. "Are Family Managers Agents or Stewards? An Exploratory Study in Privately Held Family Firms." *Journal of Business Research* 60 (10): 1030–8. doi:10.1016/j.jbusres.2006.12.011.

Combs, James G., and David J. Ketchen. 2003. "Why Do Firms Use Franchising as an Entrepreneurial Strategy? A Meta-Analysis." *Journal of Management* 29 (3): 443–65. doi:10.1016/S0149-2063(03)00019-9.

Combs, James G., David J. Ketchen, C. L. Shook, and J. C. Short. 2010. "Antecedents and Consequences of Franchising: Past Accomplishments and Future Challenges." *Journal of Management* 37 (1): 99–126. doi:10.1177/0149206310386963.

Combs, James G., David J. Ketchen, and Jeremy C. Short. 2011. "Franchising Research: Major Milestones, New Directions, and Its Future Within Entrepreneurship." *Entrepreneurship Theory and Practice* 35 (3): 413–25. doi:10.1111/j.1540-6520.2011.00443.x.

Connell, J. P., and A. C. Kubisch. 1998. "Applying a Theory of Change Approach to the Evaluation of Comprehensive Community Initiatives: Progress, Prospects, and Problems." *New Approach to Evaluating Communities Initiatives* 2: 15–44. doi:ISBN 0-89843-349-9.

Connelly, B. L., S. T. Certo, R. D. Ireland, and C. R. Reutzel. 2011. "Signaling Theory: A Review and Assessment." *Journal of Management* 37 (1): 39–67. doi:10.1177/0149206310388419.

Corbetta, Guido, and Carlo Salvato. 2004. "Self-Serving or Self-Actualizing? Models of Man and Agency Costs in Different Types of Family Firms: A Commentary on 'Comparing the Agency Costs of Family and Non-Family Firms: Conceptual Issues and Exploratory Evidence'." *Entrepreneurship Theory and Practice* 28 (4): 355–62. doi:10.1111/j.1540-6520.2004.00050.x.

Dacin, Peter A., M. Tina Dacin, and Marggret Matear. 2010. "Social Entrepreneurship: Why We Don't Need a New Theory and How We Move Forward from Here." *Academy of Management Perspectives* 37–58.

Davies, Iain Andrew, Helen Haugh, and Liudmila Chambers. 2018. "Barriers to Social Enterprise Growth." *Journal of Small Business Management* online first: 1–21. doi:10.1111/jsbm.12429.

Davis, James H., F. David Schoorma, and Lex Donaldson. 1997. "Towards a Stewardship Theory of Management." *Academy of Management Review* 22 (3): 20–47.

Dees, J Gregory, Beth Battle Anderson, and Jane Wei-Skillern. 2004a. "Pathways to Social Impact: Strategies for Scaling Out Successful Social Innovations." *Stanford Social Innovation Review* 1 (4): 1–15.

———. 2004b. "Scaling Social Impact: Strategies of Spreading Social Innovations." *Stanford Social Innovation Review* 1 (4): 24–32.

Dempsey, S. E., and M. L. Sanders. 2010. "Meaningful Work? Nonprofit Marketization and Work/Life Imbalance in Popular Autobiographies of Social Entrepreneurship." *Organization* 17 (4): 437–59. doi:10.1177/1350508410364198.

Desa, Geoffrey, and James L. Koch. 2014. "Scaling Social Impact: Building Sustainable Social Ventures at the Base-of-the-Pyramid." *Journal of Social Entrepreneurship* 5 (2): 146–74. doi:10.1080/19420676.2013.871325.

DiMaggio, Paul J., and Walter W. Powell. 1983. "The Iron Cage Revisited: Institutional Isomorphism and Collective Rationality in Organizational Fields." *American Sociological Review* 48 (2): 147–60.

Dobson, Kieran, Sarah Boone, Petra Andries, and Alain Daou. 2018. "Successfully Creating and Scaling a Sustainable Social Enterprise Model under Uncertainty: The Case of ViaVia Travellers Cafés." *Journal of Cleaner Production* 172. Elsevier Ltd: 4555–64. doi:10.1016/j.jclepro.2017.09.010.

Doherty, Bob, Helen Haugh, and Fergus Lyon. 2014. "Social Enterprises as Hybrid Organizations: A Review and Research Agenda." *International Journal of Management Reviews* 16 (4): 417–36. doi:10.1111/ijmr.12028.

Eddleston, Kimberly A., and Franz W. Kellermanns. 2007. "Destructive and Productive Family Relationships: A Stewardship Theory Perspective." *Journal of Business Venturing* 22 (4): 545–65. doi:10.1016/j.jbusvent.2006.06.004.

Eisenhardt, M. 1989. "Agency Theory : An Assessment and Review." *Academy of Management Review* 14 (1): 57–74.

Farooqui, Farah. 2013. "Role of Micro Finance Institutions in Micro Insurance." *Global Journal of Management and Studies* 3 (5): 535–40.

Fisac-Garcia, Ramon, Manuel Acevedo-Ruiz, Ana Moreno-Romero, and Thane Kreiner. 2013. "The Role of ICT in Scaling Up the Impact of Social Enterprises." *Journal of Management for Global Sustainability* 1 (2): 83–105. doi:10.13185/JM2013.01205.

Fox, Mark A., and Robert T. Hamilton. 1994. "Ownership and Diversification: Agency Theory or Stewardship Theory." *Journal of Management Studies* 31 (1): 69–81. doi:10.1111/j.1467-6486.1994.tb00333.x.

Gillespie, Stuart. 2004. "Scaling Up Community-Driven Development: A Synthesis of Experience." *International Food Policy Research Institute, Food Consumption and Nutrition Division, FCND Discussion Papers*, no. FCNDP No. 181: 1–44.

Graham, Tom. 2018a. "How to Design for Scale: Lessons for Ambitious New Interventions." *Apolitcal*, May.

————. 2018b. "The Only Scheme Proven to End Poverty—but Too Bespoke to Scale? Pilots Have Worked in 99 Countries, but That Doesn't Mean It Can Reach Billions." *Apolitcal*, May.

————. 2018c. "The World Is Scattered with Pilot Projects Trying to Work Holistically—Q&A with Karen Levy of Evidence Action, the NGO That Delivers Solutions to Hundreds of Millions of People." *Apolitcal*, May. https://apolitical.co/solution_article/the-world-is-scattered-with-pilot-projects-trying-to-work-holistically/.

Greyston Bakery. 2018. "Home." 16th June https://greyston.org/.

Hayek, Friedrich A. 1988. *The Fatal Conceit: The Errors of Socialism*. Edited by W. W. Bartley. Chicago, IL: University of Chicago Press.

Heinecke, Andreas. 2011a. *Franchising as Means to Scale Social Entrepreneurship*. Potsdam, Germany: University of Potsdam.

————. 2011b. "Interview with Andreas Heinecke, Founder of Dialogue Social Enterprise." Interview by Anna Krzeminska, Vienna, Austria: unpublished.

Heinecke, Andreas, and Judith Mayer. 2012. "Strategies for Scaling in Social Entrepreneurship." In *Social Entrepreneurship and Social Business: An Introduction and Discussion with Case Studies*, edited by Christine Volkmann, Kai Tokarski, and K. Ernst, 191–209. Wiesbaden: Gabler Verlag.

Heinecke, Andreas, and Tholkil Sonne. 2012. "Meeting Notes from a Meeting with the Founders of Dialogue Social Enterprise and Specialisterne." Interview by Anna Krzeminska, At the premises of Dialogue in the Dark in Hamburg, Germany: unpublished.

Hernandez, Morela. 2008. "Promoting Stewardship Behavior in Organizations: A Leadership Model." *Journal of Business Ethics* 80 (1): 121–28. doi:10.1007/s10551-007-9440-2.

————. 2012. "Toward an Understanding of the Psychology of Stewardship." *Academy of Management Review* 37 (2): 172–93. doi:10.5465/amr.2010.0363.

Jowett, Alice, and Caroline Dyer. 2012. "Scaling-Up Successfully: Pathways to Replication for Educational NGOs." *International Journal of Educational Development* 32 (6). Elsevier Ltd: 733–42. doi:10.1016/j.ijedudev.2011.12.002.

Kiefer, Christof. 2017. *Re-Imagining Capitalism-Premium Collective—Growth & Impact within a New Business Order*. Copenhagen, Denmark: Copenhagen Business School Press.

Kistruck, Geoffrey M., Justin W. Webb, Christopher J. Sutter, and R. Duane Ireland. 2011. "Microfranchising in Base-of-the-Pyramid Markets: Institutional Challenges and Adaptations to the Franchise Model." *Entrepreneurship Theory and Practice* 35 (3): 503–31. doi:10.1111/j.1540-6520.2011.00446.x.

Krzeminska, Anna, and Anica Zeyen. 2017. "A Stewardship Cost Perspective on the Governance of Delegation Relationships." *Nonprofit and Voluntary Sector Quarterly* 46 (1): 71–91. doi:10.1177/0899764016643610.

Lafontaine, Francine, and Kathryn L. Shaw. 1998. "Franchising Growth and Franchisor Entry and Exit in the U.S. Market: Myth and Reality." *Journal of Business Venturing* 13 (2): 95–112. doi:10.1016/S0883-9026(97)00065-7.

Lahme, Cornelius. 2018. *Social Franchising*. Wiesbaden: Springer Fachmedien Wiesbaden. doi:10.1007/978-3-658-21504-0.

Lee, I. 2015. "A Social Enterprise Business Model for Social Entrepreneurs: Theoretical Foundations and Model Development." *International Journal of Social Entrepreneurship and Innovation* 3 (4). www.indersionceonline.com/doi/abs/10.1504/IJSEI.2015.069351.

London, Ted. 2011. "Building Better Ventures with the Base of the Pyramid: A Roadmap." In *Next Generation Business Strategies for the Base of the Pyramid: New Approaches for Building Mutual Value*, edited by T. London and S. Hart, 19–44. Upper Saddle River, NJ: Prentice Hall, Inc.

Lyon, Fergus, and Heather Fernandez. 2012. "Strategies for Scaling Up Social Enterprise: Lessons from Early Years Providers." *Social Enterprise Journal* 8 (1): 63–77. doi:10.1108/17508611211226593.

Mair, Johanna, and Ignasi Marti. 2009. "Entrepreneurship in and around Institutional Voids: A Case Study from Bangladesh." *Journal of Business Venturing* 24 (5). Elsevier Inc.: 419–35. doi:10.1016/j.jbusvent.2008.04.006.

McBride, Julie. 2018. "Setting the Record Straight on Social Franchising." *The Lancet Global Health* 6 (6). The Author(s). Published by Elsevier Ltd. This is an Open Access article under the CC BY 4.0 license: e611. doi:10.1016/S2214-109X(18)30194-3.

Meek, William R., Beth Davis-Sramek, Melissa S. Baucus, and Richard N. Germain. 2011. "Commitment in Franchising: The Role of Collaborative Communication and a Franchisee's Propensity to Leave." *Entrepreneurship Theory and Practice* 35 (3): 559–81. doi:10.1111/j.1540-6520.2011.00445.x.

Meyerson, Debra E., Alexander Berger, and Rand Quinn. 2010. "Playing the Field: Implications of Scale in the California Charter School Movement." In *Scaling Social Impact*, 65–79. New York, NY: Palgrave Macmillan.

Mintzberg, Henry. 2003. "The Entrepreneurial Organization." In *The Strategy Process: Concepts, Contexts, Cases*, edited by Henry Mintzberg, Joseph Lampel, James Brian Quinn, and Sumantra Goshall, 4th ed., 315–22. Harlow: Prentice Hall, Inc.

Montagu, Dominic. 2002. "Review Article Franchising of Health Services in Low-Income Countries." *Health Policy and Planning* 17 (2): 121–30.

Mulgan, Geoff, Richard Halkett, and Ben Sanders. 2007. *In and Out of Sync: The Challenge of Growing Social Innovations*. Vol. September. London, UK: The Young Foundation.

Netting, F. E., and P. M. Kettner. 1987. "Franchising, Merging, and Profit-Making Ventures: Implications for Health and Human Services." *Nonprofit and Voluntary Sector Quarterly* 16 (4): 15–21. doi:10.1177/089976408701600404.

Oxenfeldt, A. R., and A. O. Kelly. 1969. "Will Successful Franchise Systems Ultimately Become Wholly-Owned Chains?" *Journal of Retailing* 44 (4): 69–87.

Schmitz, Björn, and Thomas Scheuerle. 2013. "Hemmnisse Der Wirkungsskalierung von Sozialunternehmen in Deutschland." In *Sozialunternehmen in Deutschland: Analysen, Trends Und Handlungsempfehlungen*, edited by Stephan A. Jansen, Rolf G. Heinze, and Markus Beckmann, 101–24. Wiesbaden: Springer Gabler. doi:10.1007/978-3-658-01074-4_4.

Schumacher, Ernst Friedrich. 2011. *Small Is Beautiful: A Study of Economics as If People Mattered*. London, UK: Vintage Books.

Sen, Pritha. 2007. "Ashoka's Big Idea: Transforming the World through Social Entrepreneurship." *Futures* 39 (5): 534–53. doi:10.1016/j.futures.2006.10.013.

Skoll foundation. 2014. "About." June 12. http://skoll.org/about/about-skoll/

Specialisterne. 2013. "Welcome to Specialisterne." June 2. http://specialisterne.com/

Spiess-Knafl, Wolfgang, Rieke Schües, Saskia Richter, Thomas Scheuerle, and Björn Schmitz. 2013. "Eine Vermessung Der Landschaft Deutscher Sozialunternehmen." In *Sozialunternehmen in Deutschland: Analysen, Trends Und Handlungsempfehlungen*, edited by Stephan A. Jansen, Rolf G. Heinze, and Markus Beckmann, 21–34. Wiesbaden: Springer Gabler. doi:10.1007/978-3-658-01074-4_1.

Stephens, A. 2003. "Ice Cream with a Mission." *New Statesman* 132: 17–18.

Tayabali, R. 2014. "PATRI Framework for Scaling." *Ashoka Globalize*. many. ashoka. May 20, 2018. org/sites/globalizer.ashoka.org/files/PATRI-Framework. pdf.

Tracey, Paul, and Owen Jarvis. 2007. "Toward a Theory of Social Venture Franchising." *Entrepreneurship Theory and Practice* 31 (5): 667–85.

Uvin, Peter, Pankaj S. Jain, and L. David Brown. 2000. "Think Large and Act Small: Toward a New Paradigm for NGO Scaling Up." *World Development* 28 (8): 1409–19. doi:10.1016/S0305-750X(00)00037-1.

VanSandt, Craig V., Mukesh Sud, Christopher Marmé, and Christopher Marme. 2010. "Enabling the Original Intent: Catalysts for Social Entrepreneurship." *Journal of Business Ethics* 90 (S3): 419–28. doi:10.1007/s10551-010-0419-z.

Volery, Thierry, and Valerie Hackl. 2010. "The Promise of Social Franchising as a Model to Achieve Social Goals." In *Handbook of Research on Social Entrepreneurship*, edited by A. Fayolle and H. Matlay, 155–79. Cheltenham, UK: Edward Elgar.

Volkmann, Christine, Kom Oliver Tokarski, and Kati Ernst. 2012. "Background, Characteristics and Context of Social Entrepreneurship." In *Social Entrepreneurship and Social Business: An Introduction and Discussion with Case Studies*, edited by Christine Volkmann, Kom Oliver Tokarski, and Kati Ernst, 3–30. Wiesbaden: Gabler.

Waitzer, Jon McPhedran, and Roshan Paul. 2011. "Scaling Social Impact: When Everybody Contributes, Everybody Wins." *Innovations: Technology, Governance, Globalization* 6 (2): 143–55. doi:10.1162/INOV_a_00074.

Weber, Christiana, Arne Kröger, and Cihan Demirtas. 2015. "Scaling Social Impact in Europe." Bertelsmann Stiftung, Gütersloh, Germany, 1–72.

Wellcome. 2018. "Wellcome—Hilfe Nach Der Geburt." September 13. https://www. wellcome-online.de/angebote-fuer-familien/praktische-hilfe-nach-der-geburt/

Zahra, Shaker A., Eric Gedajlovic, Donald O. Neubaum, and Joel M. Shulman. 2009. "A Typology of Social Entrepreneurs: Motives, Search Processes and Ethical Challenges." *Journal of Business Venturing* 24 (5): 519–32. doi:10.1016/j. jbusvent.2008.04.007.

Zeyen, Anica. 2014. *Scaling Strategies of Social Entrepreneurship Organizations— an Actor-Motivation Perspective*. Lueneburg: Leuphana University.

Part IV

Social Entrepreneurship and the Micro-level

9 Social Mission, Agency, and Calling

The Impact on Individuals Within and Around Social Ventures

Following our discussion of social entrepreneurship from a macro- and meso-level perspective, this final part of the book will now look at social entrepreneurship and the individual. In particular, this chapter discusses how two of the characteristics of social entrepreneurship (see Chapter 2)—social mission focus and entrepreneurial agency—impact individuals within and around social ventures.

As we have previously deliberated in this book, the *social mission* is a key resource for social ventures because it attracts valuable assets including individuals such as the founder, staff, and volunteers (see Chapter 6). Thus, we argue that for a more comprehensive analysis of social entrepreneurship, it is crucial to shed light on the ambivalent effects of the social mission on individuals involved. We further focus on *agency* as it is enacted by the social entrepreneur. As the examples throughout this book showcase, their agency can lead to impressive innovative solutions (Garud and Karnøe 2003) that create positive social change. What is important for our argument in this chapter is that social entrepreneurs not only take action through their agency but also take on responsibility for their chosen societal issue. Social entrepreneurs often see themselves as stewards responsible for addressing a problem, characterized by a "relentless motivation to change a whole society" (Mair and Noboa 2006, 123).

We propose that the concept of *calling* is a fruitful theoretical tool to analyze this interplay of feeling being social motivated, feeling responsible, and displaying entrepreneurial agency. For the purposes of this book, the calling concept provides a useful framework for a micro-level analysis of the social mission and entrepreneurial agency that allows us to uncover some of the ambivalences within social entrepreneurship. Although calling has been identified among social entrepreneurs (Dempsey and Sanders 2010), there is very limited research on the calling of staff within social ventures. Yet, we argue that many staff and volunteers in the field of social entrepreneurship use the social venture to live their calling. In addition to our dual focus on agency and the social mission, we therefore wish to further extend our analysis to not only encompass the social entrepreneur (as is often the case in the entrepreneurship literature) but to also include other individuals within and around the social venture.

To analyze the ambivalent effects of calling on individuals within and around social ventures, this chapter will first introduce the concept of calling (Section 9.1). It will then discuss its positive effects on both the individual and their organization (Section 9.2). In a third step, the chapter will analyze potential negative micro-level consequences of calling on the social entrepreneur, their staff, and family (Section 9.3).

9.1. Calling—Meaningful Work on a Mission

Calling refers to *deeply meaningful work* (Bunderson and Thompson 2009) that is "a consuming, meaningful passion for a particular career domain or work that a person perceives as her or his purpose in life" (Hirschi 2012, 479). People who perceive a calling are thus drawn to activities that fulfill it (Conklin 2012) and aim to act on it (Duffy and Sedlacek 2007; Duffy et al. 2014).

A closer look at the definitions of calling alludes to an underlying divergence in the ontology (roughly what it is at its core about) and teleology (its development direction) of the term. In its origin, calling referred to a religious calling to a specific profession but has since evolved to include more modern understandings of calling (Elangovan, Pinder, and McLean 2010; Bunderson and Thompson 2009). Generally speaking, it is possible to divide the definitions into three categories: pre-Reformation, post-Reformation or modern classic, and contemporary calling (Anastasiadis and Zeyen 2017; Bunderson and Thompson 2009; Elangovan, Pinder, and McLean 2010). Pre-Reformation calling emerges from outside of an individual (like in the case of the prophets or saints who hear a call from God) and is deeply religious as sacrifices are used to serve the Glory of God. In contrast, contemporary calling is much more ambiguous in its nature. It serves self-interested purposes (such as one's career progression) and mostly originates from within an individual. Although modern classic calling lies between both pre-Reformation and contemporary calling, it has closer ties to the former. Here, individuals also perceive a calling externally and take on sacrifices. However, rather than limiting it to religious purposes, the calling can be for any kind of prosocial purpose (like in the case of voluntary Communist fighters in the Spanish Civil War).

As we are neither interested in purely religiously inspired activities nor in activities that serve purely personal career progression, we will follow a modern classic notion of calling. For the purpose of this book chapter, calling therefore refers to prosocial behaviors and a notion of sacrifice (Berkelaar and Buzzanell 2015; Greene and Robbins 2015; Conway et al. 2015; Bunderson and Thompson 2009; Anastasiadis and Zeyen 2017).

Similar to stewardship theory (for a more detailed discussion see Chapter 8), *prosocial* behavior refers to actions that are directed toward the benefits of others. Because social entrepreneurship has a social mission as its core (Dacin, Dacin, and Matear 2010; Dees 1998 and see Chapter 2), it clearly allows social entrepreneurs and their staff to follow a modern classic calling focused on prosocial behaviors. The notion of *sacrifice* is harder to generalize and narrow down due to its multi-faceted nature. It can range from time sacrifice (e.g., volunteers giving up their free time) to salary cuts (Greene and Robbins 2015; Dempsey and Sanders 2010), or even sacrifices in personal relationships or other parts of personal life (Bunderson and Thompson 2009). Importantly, these sacrifices are not expected of the called individual by others but are often perceived as a core aspect of calling experience by the called themselves. In other words, being able to sacrifice something supports the idea that they are truly doing something for the 'greater good' out of 'genuine intentions' and not just expediency.

A further distinction that the calling literature discusses is that of perceiving versus living a calling (Duffy et al. 2017). The former describes individuals who are aware of their calling but—for whatever reason—are unable to act on it. The call received then remains unanswered. In contrast, the latter refers to individuals who are not only aware of their calling but are also acting on it. We argue that the acting on their calling reflects the notion of agency within the social entrepreneurship debate. Social entrepreneurs perceive their individual calling to, say, support refugees. However, only once they act on this calling and start up a social venture do they also engage in social entrepreneurial agency. Thus, for the purpose of this book chapter, we will only refer to modern classic calling as a lived experience.

9.2. Calling and Its Positive Effects

At its core, the calling literature takes a micro-level viewpoint and predominately analyzes the benefits of following a calling to the called individual (e.g., Berg et al. 2010; Duffy and Sedlacek 2007; Hall and Chandler 2005; Wrzesniewski et al. 1997). These benefits include increased satisfaction with work (Xie et al. 2017; Duffy and Sedlacek 2007; Wrzesniewski et al. 1997) and life (Torrey and Duffy 2012; Douglass, Duffy, and Autin 2016; Wrzesniewski et al. 1997). These increased satisfaction levels are derived from the close link between meaning and work. In other words, called individuals do not just 'have a job' and need to then find meaning outside of work but, metaphorically speaking, kill two birds with one stone. Moreover, calling is a deeply rooted passion and desire to engage in certain behaviors (Hirschi 2012). As such, the objective of the calling becomes part of the called individual's identity. Thus, if someone is able to live their calling, they develop a heightened sense of personal identity (Bunderson and Thompson 2009). This in turn leads to higher levels of perceived life fulfillment among called individuals (Ahn, Dik, and Hornback 2017).

As a result of these increased satisfaction levels, called individuals are less prone to depression and related mental health issues (Oates, Hall, and Anderson 2005; Treadgold 1999). What is more, recent studies indicate that living a calling can actually actively act as a buffer against the effects of burnout and other stress-related diseases (Duffy et al. 2016). In other words, called individuals who experience high stress levels are as satisfied with their life and work as uncalled individuals with low stress levels. Calling can thus have a positive effect on the psychological, emotional, and stress resilience of the called.

In addition, called individuals have higher work performance (Park, Sohn, and Ha 2016). We argue that the enhanced performance is not only a result of their deeply intrinsic motivation but might also further enhance their motivation if they receive praise for their achievements. Moreover, organizations often value their called staff because they require limited managerial intervention as they often go beyond their remit (Bunderson and Thompson 2009). From an organizational perspective, a shared calling can also serve as a means not only to motivate but also to coordinate individuals, a phenomenon that Mintzberg (1989) describes in his description of the 'missionary organization.'

In short, living a calling provides many benefits to called individuals that range from increase life and work satisfaction to reduced risks of mental health problems. Furthermore, they are not only more satisfied personally but also achieve higher levels of productivity in their chosen profession.

9.3. Calling and Its Negative Effects

Though there is a significant amount of literature on the positive effects of calling for both the individual and, to a smaller extend, their employing organization, there is only limited research on potential negative effects of calling (Schabram and Maitlis 2017; Anastasiadis and Zeyen 2017; Bunderson and Thompson 2009; Dempsey and Sanders 2010). Yet despite its often-uncritical appraisal, we argue that calling is yet another phenomenon that can have ambivalent effects with regard to its instrumental consequences, depending on how this 'tool' is handled within the field of social entrepreneurship. Although it might stretch our analogy a bit far to view calling as a 'tool' (after all, you cannot freely choose and change it like a hammer or screwdriver), an instrumental perspective on calling can reveal an interesting look into various directions. For instance, social entrepreneurs use social venture creation as a tool to fulfill their calling objectives whereas they also use the calling of others as a tool to attract them to their organization. Therefore, this section will point to three types of potential challenges associated with calling in the context of social entrepreneurship: well-being effects on the social entrepreneur, well-being effects on others including their staff and families, and dynamic effects on personal learning and development.

9.3.1. Calling and the Social Entrepreneur—Challenges of Well-Being and Long-Term Thinking

For the purpose of brevity, we want to pinpoint one of the potential consequences of living a calling to social entrepreneurs: the neglect of long-term effects on health and well-being. We argue that this oversight of long-term effects on their personal well-being and lifestyle is rooted in the very nature of calling.

As we have outlined in Section 9.1, calling is inherently coupled with sacrifice. Thus, to properly understand calling, we need to understand the notion of sacrifice. In his analysis of many biblical stories, Jordan Peterson (2017) provides an interesting perspective on this notion. Peterson reconceptualizes sacrifice as investment. His argument is that biblical stories of sacrifice (and for that matter within any religion) can be understood as an ongoing long-term investment toward the afterlife or reincarnations. In a way, a sacrifice is like a pact between one's present self and one's future self. Thus, any sacrifice has a certain notion of self-interest attached even if the action in itself is altruistic.

So, how does this religious notion of sacrifice translate to social entrepreneurship? For one, modern classic calling is derived from religiously motivated pre-Reformation calling and has taken on a similar meaning of sacrifice. Besides, it allows us to shed light on some micro-level phenomena within social entrepreneurship. Yet, rather than investing their sacrifice toward a future transcendent afterlife or Nirvana, social entrepreneurs (and their staff) sacrifice their time, income, family life, and health (Dempsey and Sanders 2010) for short-term immanent gains in life and work satisfaction. In fact, one could argue that in this form of calling the mechanism of sacrifice changes its underlying time structure. Instead of being an investment in future well-being, 'sacrifice' then turns into a consumption of present well-being.

From a well-being perspective, increased life satisfaction is certainly not a bad thing. However, if calling builds upon behavior that prioritizes present well-being, calling can turn into an example of time-inconsistent behavior that neglects long-term benefits (Thaler and Sunstein 2008). Put differently, their desire to live their calling 'in the moment' leads social entrepreneurs to intentionally or unintentionally overlook long-term effects of their mission-driven entrepreneurial agency.

For the purpose of brevity, we will outline only two of these long-term effects. First, a short-term focus on calling can have negative long-term health effects. As Duffy and colleagues (Duffy et al. 2016) found, calling can buffer the perceived effects of burnout or stress. However, we conjecture just because life and work satisfaction do not decrease despite high stress levels does not mean that physiological effects will not prevail. Though there are no available statistics, there is some initial empirical evidence (Dempsey and Sanders 2010). In fact, research on calling indicates that people who live their calling struggle to detach themselves from their work after going home, which then leads to worsened sleep patterns and lower morning vigor, thus to a lower level of recovery (Clinton, Conway, and Sturges 2017). Note that people with a calling might be easily willing to embrace such a reduced night's sleep as a short-time sacrifice that is worthwhile for an immediate sense of purpose and belonging. Furthermore, when in the flow of following a calling, people often do not even feel that they are stressed (Kanter and Sherman 2016). Yet, long-term exposure to low levels of recovery can lead to both physical and mental health issues (Hillman and Lack 2013). Furthermore, anecdotal evidence and the fact that organizations such as Ashoka have introduced well-being initiatives further points to the prevalence of this issue (see http://wellbeing.change-makers.com). In addition to physical health challenges, social entrepreneurs who act as caregivers to their beneficiaries can also suffer from emotional draining (André and Pache 2016).

Second, a short-term focus on calling can negatively impact their long-term economic well-being. Many social entrepreneurs live of low wages (Yunus and Weber 2010; Dempsey and Sanders 2010). The reason for this is rooted in the social mission of their venture. Many consider it immoral to demand higher salaries because they believe it more prudent to put as many funds as possible toward the actual mission (Kanter and Sherman 2016). This belief is further heightened because many social ventures are underfunded and might not even have the budget to pay higher salaries. Most social entrepreneurs do not mind this because it is part of their sacrifice for the social mission. Though this is highly admirable, it yet again overlooks long-term consequences of these choices. Low salaries will mean low pensions or, if the work in a country without pension systems, low savings to sustain their life after retirement. Moreover, they might have fewer funds to support their own children through school and university or to pay for medical bills at old age. In short, time-inconsistencies can also occur in an economic dimension. Once the social entrepreneur no longer work and lives their calling, for example, during retirement, the psychological benefits of having followed a calling can fade away while the accumulated opportunity costs remain.

It is important to note that we do not argue that social entrepreneurs are totally ignorant of these effects. In our experience, they rather find it difficult to consider them effectively. During ample conversations, we have personally experienced that, maybe for a lack of alternatives, some social entrepreneurs even prefer to avoid a discussion about such long-term effects.

9.3.2. Calling and Others within and around the Social Venture—Self-Exploitation and Neglect

Although the social entrepreneur is often in the limelight of entrepreneurship research and practice, we now wish to shift the focus toward their staff and family.

a) Social Entrepreneurs, Calling, and Their Staff

Before we start our discussion on the effects of calling on staff, we want to stress that the challenges discussed in the previous section equally apply to most staff within social ventures as they do for the founding social entrepreneur. However, additional effects are more likely to occur among staff than among social entrepreneurs.

First, the experience of living a calling can lead to an exit from the very profession that was chosen to live it (Schabram and Maitlis 2017). If a called individual faces challenges in living their calling (e.g., through funding constraints of an organization), they are likely to follow one of three practice paths identified by Schabram and Maitlis (2017). Though one of these pathways leads to learning, the other two ('identity' and 'contribution') are linked to reduced resilience as well as an inability to develop the required emotional distance from setbacks at work. Calling is coupled with identity (Bunderson and Thompson 2009). Thus, if there are setbacks at work, called individuals fail not only on a work-related issue but also in regard to their personal identity. In other words, failing as a called employee does not only incur potential monetary losses (e.g., if losing one's job leads to income losses) but might also lead to a potential loss of one's identity.

As a result, this can lead to burnout or even exit from the profession (Schabram and Maitlis 2017). Thus, under certain situational conditions, frustrations about the inability to fully live or continue living their calling leads individuals to not only quit their job but their calling altogether. This is highly noteworthy as other studies highlight the dissatisfaction people feel when unable to live their calling (Duffy and Sedlacek 2007). Put differently, for some individuals the expected potential dissatisfaction of not living their calling at all is lower than the experienced decreased satisfaction of trying to live their calling in the light of severe obstacles. This has implications for both the organization as skilled and talented people might leave but also for the individual as their life satisfaction is, at least temporarily, likely to decrease significantly. Also note the difference to calling among social entrepreneurs. Here, the effect of their agency would likely lead to different results. Rather than quitting, they would continue to try and find a solution for the societal issue that they wish to tackle. The social entrepreneur holds decision-making power and can therefore enact their calling better than their staff, who might only have limited decision discretion. In fact, as self-determination theory (Ryan and Deci 2000) highlights, people have enhanced motivation, resilience, and mental health when they experience competence and autonomy, with social entrepreneurs arguably enjoying more autonomy than their hired employees. In their recent study, Hessels, Rietveld, and van der Zwan (2017) similarly found that self-employed entrepreneurs report lower stress levels than wage workers when experiencing self-control. However, they also found that self-employed individuals experience *more* work-related stress when having their own employees because the latter increases job complexity. How social entrepreneurs or their staff differs in their respective experience of calling and ways to handle it thus deserves further research.

Second, calling can leave people vulnerable to potential (un)intentional misuse of their human resources. Empirical evidence suggests that some non-profit organizations mistreat their employees (Foote 2001). For instance, a study on female clergy in the Church of England showed that female vicars would stay despite discrimination and other forms of mistreatment (Greene and Robbins 2015). Other social ventures underpay or do not pay their staff—even if only temporarily (Dempsey and Sanders 2010). If we now imagine similar working conditions in commercial ventures, the question arises why people do not leave the organization and search for alternative employment. Here again, staff remain and self-exploit as a sacrifice to the social mission (Greene and Robbins 2015). Hence, called staff can experience lock-in effects because they might not be happy with their work conditions but on the one hand consider it part of the 'package' and on the other hand might be locked in because they often have limited options to live out their calling in other organizations.

Moreover, it is important to note that some of these working conditions are certainly not of the social ventures' choosing. To illustrate, we will briefly talk about funding and staff salaries. As we discussed in parts II and III, social ventures can achieve business models that can run sustainably on unique resources from the state or private sector, such as earned-income in quasi-markets. This notwithstanding, many social ventures—especially younger ones—rely on project funding from large funders. However, the very nature of project funding is fixed term. Moreover, project funding is often available for only innovative projects rather than for overhead costs (see Part II). Thus, in between projects, many social ventures experience periods in which they have insufficient funds to pay their staff. Furthermore, it is also conceivable that as the social entrepreneur most likely also self-exploits and is highly focused on the social mission, they might not even be aware of challenges for their staff.

As a result of some of these context conditions (e.g., funding structure of the social entrepreneurship field), we argue that some social ventures would not be able to sustain their operations without their staff's calling. In other words, these social ventures do not only rely on their staff's human capital as traditionally defined—talent and skills—but on their calling capital as well. The staff's calling and resulting willingness to self-exploit then becomes a crucial resource for the social venture. Such a model, however, is inherently unsustainable due to the potential of health and work-life related risks for staff. Moreover, such practices raise questions of moral hypocrisy (Foote 2001) as one could argue that mission-driven organizations should not exploit or mistreat their own staff.

b) Social Entrepreneurs, Calling, and Families

Calling among social entrepreneurs and their staff can also impact third parties. Here, we will focus on their families. Many called individuals work long hours (Bunderson and Thompson 2009; Dempsey and Sanders 2010) and are unable to detach once they are at home (Schabram and Maitlis 2017; Clinton, Conway, and Sturges 2017). Thus, they are unlikely to be fully emotionally, mentally, and cognitively available to their spouses and children (Anastasiadis and Zeyen 2017). This unavailability puts strain on these relationships and can lead to estranging among family members, which in a worst case can lead to the divorce or breakdown of a relationship. Calling can become an obsession similar to an addiction for called individuals, which can completely blind them to the negative effects on their family life (Anastasiadis and Zeyen 2017).

Moreover, the very nature of their calling makes it harder for family members to demand more attention. To illustrate, take the following examples. First, imagine, the family of a successful entrepreneur who runs various car dealerships. This entrepreneur is also likely to spend a significant amount of time at work and will strive to grow their business further and further. At some point, their family might demand more attention and point to the fact that they now have a big house, cars, and enough funds for retirement and their children's education. Now take the example of a social entrepreneur who fights against child poverty. For one, their family will find it morally more challenging to demand more attention at the expense of the mission-driven work. They might struggle with the notion that their demand to spend a day out might cause children to starve. Furthermore, both the social entrepreneur and their family will find it harder to define a level of satisficing.[1] It is harder or even impossible to determine when sufficient numbers of children have been saved (for a more detailed discussion of impact see Chapter 7). In other words, it is easier to determine a satisficing level of personal wealth than a satisficing level of societal impact. The flipside of social entrepreneurs' appraised "relentless pursuit of mission" (Kickul and Lyons 2016) is thus that they risk being relentless with themselves.

In short, social entrepreneurs and their staff might engage in dysfunctional behaviors due to their prosocial calling whereas their family members might not only be negatively affected but also find it more challenging to criticize these negative effects.

To overcome some of the challenges outlined in the previous two sections, social ventures can draw on diverse approaches from general business and nonprofit management (Kanter and Sherman 2016) to reduce work-related stress. An approach that is specifically suitable for some social ventures is to encourage caring relationships among organizational members (André and Pache 2016). If members look after each other, they can significantly reduce the likelihood of dysfunctional behavior. These suggestions are based on the idea of ethics of care (Okano 2016; Held 2006; Gilligan 1993). There are various approaches that an organization can take to foster these caring relationships (Madden et al. 2012; McAllister and Bigley 2002; Dutton et al. 2006). For example, one approach is to create caregiver supervisor roles among staff members (Madden et al. 2012). The role of these caregiver supervisors would be to support staff in expressing their emotions through demonstrating empathy (Kahn 2018) or through other-regarding mentoring (Allen 2003). Others argue that this mutual caregiving should not be limited to the immediate supervisor but be institutionalized throughout the organization (Sarason 1985). As recent studies point out that emotional and physical burnout is not simply about the amount of work but also about isolation and loneliness (Seppala and King 2017), such approaches might help to overcome perceived loneliness. We would conjecture that although developing a caring organization can be a fruitful tool for some social ventures, it again has its limits. For one, it is mostly suitable for social ventures in which staff have direct caring responsibilities for their beneficiaries (André and Pache 2016). Therefore, there are numerous social ventures for which these suggestions might not be applicable. Furthermore, this approach hinges on geographical and personal proximity. If organizational members are too far away from each other geographically, it will be harder for them to build up in-depth personal relationships (cf. Hayek 1988, for a more detailed discussion see Chapter 8). Therefore, future research would benefit from a more in-depth discussion of how negative effects of calling on social entrepreneurs' long-term health and lifestyle as well as on their family and staff can be avoided.

9.3.3. *Social Entrepreneurs, Calling, and the Inability to Learn*

A final point that we want to raise in this chapter is the impact of calling on learning and personal development. Although the discussion on individual and family well-being were somewhat static because they mostly ignored changes in personality and calling, this section will take a more dynamic view. Similar to Chapter 6 in which we took an organizational perspective to discuss the adaptiveness of mission-driven business models, this chapter will raise the question of how social entrepreneurs (and their staff) respond in their individual development to changes that question key assumptions that guide their calling. Here, we argue that they excel in one form of learning but struggle with another.

Before substantiating our claim, we briefly repeat key basics of Argyris' (1977) learning theory that distinguishes two forms of learning. The starting point is a decision-making model with two components: the governing variables that include the mental models, goals, values, and beliefs, on the one hand, and the action strategies, techniques, and plans that can be implemented, on the other hand. Figure 9.1 illustrates the key idea. A decision-maker then chooses a certain action that promises to achieve desirable results according to the governing variables. (Note the similarity to the normative assumptions (what is desirable) and positive assumptions (what is possible) in the practical syllogism, see Chapter 3.) If the achieved consequences are not satisfying, however, learning becomes necessary. *Single*-loop learning keeps the underlying assumptions about desired objectives stable and alters the tools used to get there. *Double*-loop learning, in contrast, requires a reflection and potential change of the underlying belief systems. How will social entrepreneurs with a calling engage in these two types of learning?

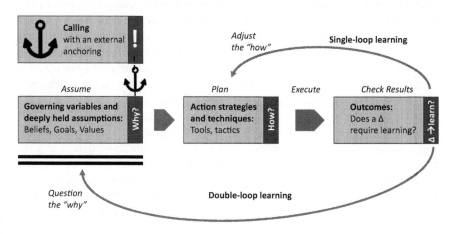

Figure 9.1 (External) calling as inhibiting double-loop learning

Source: Authors' expended illustration adapted from Argyris (1977)

On the one hand, we insinuate that most social entrepreneurs have per-fected single-loop learning. Their "relentless pursuit of mission" allows social entrepreneurs to develop a high level of resilience and perseverance. If social entrepreneurs encounter changes in their environment that do not allow them to pursue their calling in the *way* they originally intended, they change course and identify a new approach. In other words, they do not change their path because they hit a wall but rather, staying with this meta-phor, try to climb over it or dig under it till they find a way to the other side. This distinguishes them from most commercial entrepreneurs. Commercial entrepreneurs would also identify a potential customer need and try to find a solution for it. Yet, if this has failed a couple of times, they would not continue but chose a different path. Social entrepreneurs, however, do not accept 'no' as an answer but as a question how to further innovate their action techniques and solution approaches.

On the other hand, we argue that a strong social entrepreneur's calling can lead to a reduced ability to effectively engage in double-loop learning. As double-loop learning questions more deeply held assumptions, values, and belief systems, it (need not but) may conflict with belief systems that are tightly coupled to one's identity through the mechanism of calling, thus making double-loop learning the less likely the stronger the calling.

Double-loop learning, however, is a prerequisite for development and coping with more significant environmental changes (Argyris 1977). If double-loop learning requires a social entrepreneur to reconsider their call-ing, that is, rather than reconsidering the tools they use, they would need to reconsider the objective they aim to achieve. This is very challenging as most individuals who live a modern classic calling perceive their calling to have come to them from outside (Bunderson and Thompson 2009). They believe that some outside power (religious, spiritual, or other) gave them the duty to serve a specific societal issue. If this outside source defines important governing variables for someone's calling, then questioning these assumptions would amount to giving up pursuit of their calling; a development that might be inconceivable for some as it would involve questioning one's identity, thus risking a loss in purpose, meaning, and life satisfaction.

To illustrate, take again the perhaps controversial example of Evangelical social ventures that promote gay conversion therapy in African countries (see Chapter 4). Arguably, the founders and entrepreneurs of these ventures follow a strong Christian calling, thus hearing their call from the outside source of their Evangelical creed. For this creed, it is a governing variable to believe that homosexuality is sinful and must be fought against. These ventures implement action techniques with the aim of redeeming patients of their perceived abomination. Now consider that the use of electroshock does not lead to the desired results. In fact, while these forms of 'therapy' were used as of the 1950s, they were soon proven to not only be ineffective (the patients kept being gay) but also to lead to severe damage. Despite this drastic feedback, a strong calling makes double-loop learning difficult in this scenario. Note the importance of the outside anchoring of the calling. If a social entrepreneur perceives the opposition to homosexuality as a fundamental(ist) principle, questioning this belief would undermine the entire calling: Accepting homosexuality would mean giving up the Evangelical faith and identity. The only alternative is then to engage in single-loop learning—to hold onto the disapproval of homosexuality and to change the action strategy by searching for new therapy approaches.

Similar to our discussion in Chapter 6, following a calling, particularly when anchored outside the individual, can lead to learning rigidities. In contrast to Chapter 6, which analyzed the effects on organizational adaptiveness, we want to point out that a calling can also result in narrowing personal development and psychological adaptiveness. If double-loop learning is impeded, social entrepreneurs might find it difficult to adapt not only their business models but also their personal life situation, career development, and work-life balance. Particularly when anchored outside of oneself, calling can provide orientation and stability, yet also limit personal development and growth.

9.4. Conclusion

In this chapter, we shifted the perspective from a meso- and macro-level perspective to the micro-level in order to shed light on the impact of social entrepreneurship on individuals. In particular, we focused on the effects of social mission and agency on social entrepreneurs, their staff, and families. To bind these different perspectives together, we first introduced the concept of calling. After outlining the positive effects of calling for individuals, which include enhanced life and work satisfaction, we turned our attention to challenges that derive from living a calling. We first pointed to the potential health and economic well-being risks that may occur due to the consumptive notion of sacrifice inherent in calling. We then pointed to potential negative effects for staff including lock-in effects and mistreatment. In regard to families, we illustrated the double effect of social entrepreneurs' reduced physical and mental availability to their families and their families struggling to express their personal needs at the expense of the social mission. In a final step, we discussed the effects of calling on learning. Here we argue that while a social entrepreneur's calling can lead to perfected single-loop learning, they struggle to engage in double-loop learning necessary to develop in a context of change. In sum, we hope that this chapter showed that calling can increase resilience and productivity of called individuals but at the same time can lead to often overlooked negative consequences as well.

Note

1. Please note the difference between satisfying and satisficing. Satisficing refers to a level that is "good enough" (for a more detailed discussion see Schwartz et al. 2002).

References

Ahn, Jina, Bryan J. Dik, and Ruby Hornback. 2017. "The Experience of Career Change Driven by a Sense of Calling: An Interpretative Phenomenological Analysis Approach." *Journal of Vocational Behavior* 102 July. Elsevier: 48–62. doi:10.1016/j.jvb.2017.07.003.

Allen, Tammy D. 2003. "Mentoring Others: A Dispositional and Motivational Approach." *Journal of Vocational Behavior* 62 (1): 134–54. doi:10.1016/S0001-8791(02)00046-5.

Anastasiadis, Stephanos, and Anica Zeyen. 2017. "Family Values: Calling, Addiction and the Neglected Stakeholder." In *77th Annual Meeting of the Academy of Management Proceedings*, 40. Los Angeles: Academy of Management.

André, Kevin, and Anne-Claire Pache. 2016. "From Caring Entrepreneur to Caring Enterprise: Addressing the Ethical Challenges of Scaling up Social Enterprises." *Journal of Business Ethics* 133 (4): 659–75. doi:10.1007/s10551-014-2445-8.

Argyris, Chris. 1977. "Double Loop Learning in Organizations." *Harvard Business Review* 55 (5): 115–25. doi:10.1007/BF02013415.

Berg, Justin M., Adam M. Grant, and Victoria Johnson. 2010. "When Callings Are Calling: Crafting Work and Leisure in Pursuit of Unanswered Occupational Callings." *Organization Science* 21 (5): 973–94. doi:10.1287/orsc.1090.0497.

Berkelaar, Brenda L., and Patrice M. Buzzanell. 2015. "Bait and Switch or Double-Edged Sword? The (Sometimes) Failed Promises of Calling." *Human Relations* 68 (1): 157–78. doi:10.1177/0018726714526265.

Bunderson, J. Stuart, and Jeffery A. Thompson. 2009. "The Call of the Wild: Zookeepers, Callings, and the Double-Edged Sword of Deeply Meaningful Work." *Administrative Science Quarterly* 54 (1): 32–57. doi:10.2189/asqu.2009.54.1.32.

Clinton, Michael E., Neil Conway, and Jane Sturges. 2017. "'It's Tough Hanging-up a Call': The Relationships between Calling and Work Hours, Psychological Detachment, Sleep Quality, and Morning Vigor." *Journal of Occupational Health Psychology* 22 (1): 28–39. doi:10.1037/ocp0000025.

Conklin, T. A. 2012. "Work Worth Doing: A Phenomenological Study of the Experience of Discovering and Following One's Calling." *Journal of Management Inquiry* 21 (3): 298–317. doi:10.1177/1056492611414426.

Conway, Neil, Michael Clinton, Jane Sturges, and A. L. I. Budjanovcanin. 2015. "Using Self-Determination Theory to Understand the Relationship between Calling Enactment and Daily Well-Being." *Journal of Organizational Behavior* online. doi:10.1002/job.2014.

Dacin, Peter A., M.Tina Dacin, and Marggret Matear. 2010. "Social Entrepreneurship: Why We Don't Need a New Theory and How We Move Forward From Here." *Academy of Management Perspectives*, 24 (3): 37–58.

Dees, J. Gregory. 1998. "The Meaning of 'Social Entrepreneurship'." www.caseat duke.org/documents/dees_sedef.pdf.

Dempsey, S. E., and M. L. Sanders. 2010. "Meaningful Work? Nonprofit Marketization and Work/Life Imbalance in Popular Autobiographies of Social Entrepreneurship." *Organization* 17 (4): 437–59. doi:10.1177/1350508410364198.

Douglass, Richard P., Ryan D. Duffy, and Kelsey L. Autin. 2016. "Living a Calling, Nationality, and Life Satisfaction: A Moderated, Multiple Mediator Model." *Journal of Career Assessment* 24 (2): 253–69. doi:10.1177/1069072715580324.

Duffy, Ryan D., Richard P. Douglass, Kelsey L. Autin, and Blake A. Allan. 2014. "Examining Predictors and Outcomes of a Career Calling among Undergraduate Students." *Journal of Vocational Behavior* 85 (3). Elsevier Inc.: 309–18. doi:10.1016/j.jvb.2014.08.009.

Duffy, Ryan D., Richard P. Douglass, Kelsey L. Autin, Jessica W. England, and Bryan J. Dik. 2016. "Does the Dark Side of a Calling Exist? Examining Potential Negative Effects." *The Journal of Positive Psychology* 9760 February. Routledge: 1–13. doi:10.1080/17439760.2015.1137626.

Duffy, Ryan D., Jessica W. England, Richard P. Douglass, Kelsey L. Autin, and Blake A. Allan. 2017. "Perceiving a Calling and Well-Being: Motivation and Access to Opportunity as Moderators." *Journal of Vocational Behavior* 98. Elsevier Inc.: 127–37. doi:10.1016/j.jvb.2016.11.003.

Duffy, Ryan D., and William E. Sedlacek. 2007. "The Presence of and Search for a Calling: Connections to Career Development." *Journal of Vocational Behavior* 70 (3): 590–601. doi:10.1016/j.jvb.2007.03.007.

Dutton, Jane E., Monica C. Worline, Peter J. Frost, and Jacoba Lilius. 2006. "Explaining Compassion Organizing." *Administrative Science Quarterly* 51 (1): 59–96. doi:10.2189/asqu.51.1.59.

Elangovan, A. R., Craig C. Pinder, and Murdith McLean. 2010. "Callings and Organizational Behavior." *Journal of Vocational Behavior* 76 (3). Elsevier Inc.: 428–40. doi:10.1016/j.jvb.2009.10.009.

Foote, Dorothy. 2001. "The Question of Ethical Hypocrisy in Human Resource Management in the U.K. and Irish Charity Sectors." *Journal of Business Ethics* 34 (1): 25–38. doi:10.1023/A:1011909904150.

Garud, Raghu, and Peter Karnøe. 2003. "Bricolage versus Breakthrough: Distributed and Embedded Agency in Technology Entrepreneurship." *Research Policy* 32 (2): 277–300. doi:10.1016/S0048-7333(02)00100-2.

Gilligan, Carol. 1993. *In a Different Voice: Psychological Theory and Women's Development (with Updated Preface)*. Cambridge, MA: Harvard University Press.

Greene, Anne Marie, and Mandy Robbins. 2015. "The Cost of a Calling? Clergywomen and Work in the Church of England." *Gender, Work and Organization* 22 (4): 405–20. doi:10.1111/gwao.12101.

Hall, Douglas T., and Dawn E. Chandler. 2005. "Psychological Success: When the Career Is a Calling." *Journal of Organizational Behavior* 26 (2): 155–76. doi:10.1002/job.301.

Hayek, Friedrich A. 1988. *The Fatal Conceit: The Errors of Socialism*. Edited by W. W. Bartley. Chicago, IL: University of Chicago Press.

Held, Virginia. 2006. *The Ethics of Care: Personal, Political, Global*. Oxford: Oxford University Press.

Hessels, Jolanda, Cornelius A. Rietveld, and Peter van der Zwan. 2017. "Self-Employment and Work-Related Stress: The Mediating Role of Job Control and Job Demand." *Journal of Business Venturing* 32 (2). Elsevier: 178–96.

Hillman, David R., and Leon C. Lack. 2013. "Public Health Implications of Sleep Loss: The Community Burden." *Medical Journal of Australia* 199 (8): S7–10. doi:10.5694/mja13.10620.

Hirschi, Andreas. 2012. "Callings and Work Engagement: Moderated Mediation Model of Work Meaningfulness, Occupational Identity, and Occupational Self-Efficacy." *Journal of Counseling Psychology* 59 (3): 479–85. doi:10.1037/a0028949.

Kahn, William A. 2018. "Caring for the Caregivers: Patterns of Organizational Caregiving Author (s) : William A. Kahn Source: Administrative Science Quarterly, Vol. 38, No. 4 (December, 1993), pp. 539–63. Published by: Sage Publications, Inc. on Behalf of the Johnson" 38 (4): 539–63.

Kanter, Beth, and Aliza Sherman. 2016. *The Happy, Healthy Nonprofit: Strategies for Impact without Burnout*. Hoboken, NJ: John Wiley & Sons.

Kickul, Jill, and Thomas S. Lyons. 2016. *Understanding Social Entrepreneurship: The Relentless Pursuit of Mission in an Ever Changing World*. New York, NY: Routledge.

Madden, Laura T., Dennis Duchon, Timothy M. Madden, and Donde Ashmos Plowman. 2012. "Emergent Organizational Capacity for Compassion." *Academy of Management Review* 37 (4): 689–708. doi:10.5465/amr.2010.0424.

Mair, Johanna, and Ernesto Noboa. 2006. "Social Entrepreneurship: How Intentions to Create a Social Venture Are Formed." In *Social Entrepreneurship*, edited by Johanna Mair, Jeffrey Robinson, and Kai Hockerts, 121–35. New York, NY: Palgrave Macmillan.

McAllister, D. J., and G. A. Bigley. 2002. "Work Context and the Definition of Self: How Organizational Care Influences Organization-Based Self-Esteem." *Academy of Management Journal* 45 (5): 894–904. doi:10.2307/3069320.

Mintzberg, Henry. 1989. "Ideology and the Missionary Organization." In *Mintzberg on Management: Inside Our Strange World of Organizations*, 221–35. New York, NY: The Free Press.

Oates, Kerris L. M., M. Elizabeth Lewis Hall, and Tamara L. Anderson. 2005. "Calling and Conflict: A Qualitative Exploration of Interrole Conflict and the Sanctification of Work in Christian Mothers in Academia." *Journal of Psychology and Theology* 33 (3): 210–23.

Okano, Yayo. 2016. "Why Has the Ethics of Care Become an Issue of Global Concern?" *International Journal of Japanese Sociology* 25 (1): 85–99. doi:10.1111/ijjs.12048.

Park, J., Y. W. Sohn, and Y. J. Ha. 2016. "South Korean Salespersons' Calling, Job Performance, and Organizational Citizenship Behavior: The Mediating Role of Occupational Self-Efficacy." *Journal of Career Assessment* 24 (3): 415–28. doi:10.1177/1069072715599354.

Peterson, Jordan. 2017. "Biblical Series XII: The Great Sacrifice: Abraham and Isaac Transcript."

Ryan, Richard M., and Edward L. Deci. 2000. "Self-Determination Theory and the Facilitation of Intrinsic Motivation, Social Development, and Well-Being." *American Psychologist* 55 (1). American Psychological Association: 68.

Sarason, Seymour Bernard. 1985. *Caring and Compassion in Clinical Practice: Issues in the Selection, Training, and Behavior of Helping Professionals*. Northvale, NJ: Jason Aronson Inc.

Schabram, Kira, and Sally Maitlis. 2017. "Negotiating the Challenges of a Calling: Emotion and Enacted Sensemaking in Animal Shelter Work." *Academy of Management Journal* 60 (2): 584–609. doi:10.5465/amj.2013.0665.

Schwartz, Barry, Andrew Ward, John Monterosso, Sonja Lyubomirsky, Katherine White, and Darrin R Lehman. 2002. "Maximizing versus Satisficing: Happiness Is a Matter of Choice." *Journal of Personality and Social Psychology* 83 (5). American Psychological Association: 1178.

Seppala, Emma, and Marissa King. 2017. "Burnout at Work Isn't Just about Exhaustion: It's also about Loneliness." *Harvard Business Review* 29.

Thaler, Richard H., and Cass R. Sunstein. 2008. *Nudge: Improving Decisions about Health, Wealth, and Happiness*. New Haven, CT: Yale University Press.

Torrey, Carrie L., and Ryan D. Duffy. 2012. "Calling and Well-Being Among Adults." *Journal of Career Assessment* 20 (4): 415–25. doi:10.1177/1069072712448894.

Treadgold, Richard. 1999. "Transcendent Vocations: Their Relationship to Stress, Depression, and Clarity of Self-Concept." *Journal of Humanistic Psychology* 39 (1): 81–105. doi:10.1177/0022167899391010.

Wrzesniewski, Amy, Clark McCauley, Paul Rozin, and Barry Schwartz. 1997. "Jobs, Careers, and Callings: People's Relations to Their Work." *Journal of Research in Personality* 31 (1): 21–33. doi:10.1006/jrpe.1997.2162.

Xie, Baoguo, Wenxia Zhou, Jason L. Huang, and Mian Xia. 2017. "Using Goal Facilitation Theory to Explain the Relationships between Calling and Organization-Directed Citizenship Behavior and Job Satisfaction." *Journal of Vocational Behavior* 100 (June). Elsevier Inc.: 78–87. doi:10.1016/j.jvb.2017.03.001.

Yunus, Muhammad, and Karl Weber. 2010. *Building Social Business. The New Kind of Capitalism That Serves Humanity's Most Pressing Needs*. New York, NY: Public Affairs.

10 Personality Traits, Abilities, and Intention

Can Mission-Driven Venturing Be Taught?

Given the acclaimed positive effects of social entrepreneurship (e.g., Bornstein 2007), there has been an ongoing discussion on how to encourage more people to become social entrepreneurs. This debate mirrors a debate within the commercial entrepreneurship literature (McKeown et al. 2006). Proposed approaches include entrepreneurial ecosystems as well as entrepreneurship education. Although an ecosystem perspective (e.g., Suresh and Ramraj 2012) highlights the role of supportive institutions, funding, and partner organizations (see Chapter 5), the debate about social entrepreneurship education highlights the question as to how the personalities, skill sets, and intentions of social entrepreneurship can be enhanced.

For the purpose of this book chapter, we will focus on social entrepreneurship *education* because this puts the prospective entrepreneur at its center and therefore is in line with our micro-level discussion. Thus, as social entrepreneurship education aims to foster and support people to become entrepreneurs, we need to first understand the factors that influence individuals to become social entrepreneurs. DeTienne and Chandler (2004, 254) argue that "entrepreneurship is not about who the entrepreneur is, but what the entrepreneur does." We thus need to combine a perspective on the personality (*is*) of social entrepreneurs with an analysis of their skills and intentions (*doing*) to gain a full picture of who they are. Moreover, we need to further distinguish two levels: the *entrepreneur* in general and the *social entrepreneur* and their specificities in particular.

Against this background, we will build our argument in four steps. First, we will briefly review the literature on traits, skills, and intentions within (social) entrepreneurship (Section 10.1). Second, we will discuss (social) entrepreneurship education with a focus on the what and how (Section 10.2). Third, we will argue that given our experience, there are limits to the positive effects that social entrepreneurship education can achieve (Section 10.3). Fourth, we will go one step further and take a more critical view at social entrepreneurship education as an ambivalent tool to create impact on both the individuals taught and society at large. Here, we suggest to consider value not in the short-term (start up a venture) but in the long-term (develop management and soft-skills).

10.1. Traits, Skills, and Intentions—What Makes Up a (Social) Entrepreneur?

Generally speaking, the literature on (social) entrepreneurs distinguishes three categories of characteristics: their personality traits, their skills, and their intentions. We will follow this categorization and discuss each separately.

10.1.1. Personality Traits and (Social) Entrepreneurs

We will first briefly outline personality traits in the context of commercial entrepreneurship and will then discuss differences to social entrepreneurship.

a) The Big Five Personality Traits and Entrepreneurs

Psychological research has identified five key personality traits, which are referred to as the Big Five. These are openness to experience, conscientiousness, extraversion, agreeableness, and neuroticism (Judge et al. 1999; Gosling, Rentfrow, and Swann 2003). A key argument within the literature on entrepreneurship is that entrepreneurs possess a certain configuration of these personality traits that enables them to recognize and exploit opportunities (for a detailed meta-analysis see Rauch and Frese (2007)). We will first briefly outline the content of the Big Five and then discuss how they relate to (social) entrepreneurship. Each trait represents a continuum between two extremes.

Openness to experience refers to the continuum of curiosity and caution (Judge et al. 1999; Gosling, Rentfrow, and Swann 2003). This trait describes the level of preference for novelty and variety. A higher level of openness (i.e., curiosity) links with a preference for unusual experience and a willingness to take risks. Furthermore, people with higher scores prefer variations in their daily life whereas low scores reflect a preference for strict routines.

Conscientiousness depicts the continuum from efficient and organized to easy-going and careless (Judge et al. 1999; Gosling, Rentfrow, and Swann 2003). It highlights the tendency to prefer planned over spontaneous activities. High levels of conscientiousness are often coupled with stubborn and obsessive behaviors and a preference for achievement and dutifulness. In contrast, low scorers are more flexible and may appear unreliable (Toegel and Barsoux 2012).

Extraversion refers to the continuum of outgoing and energetic versus solitary and reserved (Judge et al. 1999; Gosling, Rentfrow, and Swann 2003). People with high levels of extraversion often have high energy, portray positive emotions, and seek stimulation through the company of others (Toegel and Barsoux 2012). As a consequence, they tend to dominate social settings (Friedman and Schustack 1999).

Agreeableness constitutes a continuum that ranges from friendly and compassionate to challenging and detached (Judge et al. 1999; Gosling, Rentfrow, and Swann 2003). This trait points to the tendency of individuals to show compassion, be trusting and helpful. High levels can be perceived as naive whereas low levels as argumentative (Toegel and Barsoux 2012)

Neuroticism outlines a continuum from nervous and insecure to secure and confident (Judge et al. 1999; Gosling, Rentfrow, and Swann 2003). This personality trait is closely coupled to psychological stress, emotional stability, and impulse control (Friedman and Schustack 1999). High levels of stability lead to calm and stable personalities. In contrast, people with low levels of stability are excitable and tend to be more dynamic (Toegel and Barsoux 2012).

The question now arises which combination of these traits are more likely to predict entrepreneurial behavior. In their meta-analysis, Rauch and Frese (2007) identified key traits that lead to entrepreneurial behaviors. These are the need for achievement, innovativeness, confidence, stress tolerance, need for autonomy, and proactiveness (Rauch and Frese 2007). Though it is not possible to perfectly match these subtraits to the Big Five, we conjecture that their findings suggest certain tendencies within each of the Big Five. A need for achievement indicates higher levels of *conscientiousness* whereas innovativeness suggests higher levels of *openness to experience* as does proactiveness. Confidence and stress resilience indicate higher levels of psychological stability (*neuroticism*). Need for autonomy is harder to place but could indicate a link to *agreeableness*. In short, there seem to be relevant links between (the Big Five) personality and a tendency toward entrepreneurial behavior in general, although the specificities of these links are still debated and call for further research.

b) Personality Traits and How Social Entrepreneurs Are Different

Social entrepreneurs combine entrepreneurial traits with their prosocial motivation (Lanteri 2015; Ernst 2012; Bacq and Janssen 2011). As a consequence, social entrepreneurs share some personality traits with commercial entrepreneurs but have additional traits less pronounced in the commercial entrepreneur population.

Social entrepreneurs *share* risk-taking propensity (Man, Lau, and Chan 2002; Stewart et al. 1998; Peredo and McLean 2006; Zahra et al. 2009; Almarri and Meewella 2015; Ernst 2012), proactive behavior (Ernst 2012; Weerawardena and Mort 2006), and innovativeness (Ernst 2012; Austin, Stevenson, and Wei-Skillern 2006). They further share a need for achievement (Ernst 2012) and independence (Shane, Kolvereid, and Westhead 1991; Carter et al. 2003; Ernst 2012).

The key *difference* between social and commercial entrepreneurs lies in their prosocial traits. Social entrepreneurs show prosocial traits like empathy and a sense of social responsibility (Ernst 2012) as well as compassion (Dees 1998; Miller, Wesley, and Williams 2012).

We conjecture that these prosocial traits also cause their higher level of agreeableness (Hwee Nga and Shamuganathan 2010). This seems to particularly manifest itself in a greater tendency to trust others (Jenner and Oprescu 2016; Petrovskaya and Mirakyan 2018). The literature further points to their 'moral imperative' (Harris, Sapienza, and Bowie 2009) and integrity (Petrovskaya and Mirakyan 2018).

In short, social entrepreneurs have a dual nature with regard to their personality traits (Lanteri 2015; Ernst 2012). As Part III illustrated, this dual nature of their personality seems to then translate into the hybridity of their ventures.

10.1.2. Skills and (Social) Entrepreneurs

Both commercial and social entrepreneurs have to master a large variety of skills. For the purpose of brevity, we will highlight only some of these skills. We will particularly focus on core skills for social entrepreneurs.

A core skill type for any entrepreneur are personal entrepreneurial skills (Hisrich and Peters 1998) such as the ability to recognize opportunities (Dees 1998; Tracey and Phillips 2007; Thompson, Alvy, and Lees 2000).

Furthermore, research stresses the importance of *social and communication skills* for entrepreneurs (Baron and Markman 2000; Dacin, Dacin, and Matear 2010). Social skills are a prerequisite for effective communication with partners or customers (Litzky, Godshalk, and Walton-Bongers 2010). In the context of social entrepreneurship, the need for well-developed social and communication skills seems to be even higher. This is because social entrepreneurs do not only have to converse with a variety of stakeholders (Almarri and Meewella 2015) but also need to be able to cross institutional logics between these stakeholders (Pache and Chowdhury 2012). Institutional logics influence beliefs, values, and assumptions that in turn impact decision-making (Greenwood et al. 2009). To cross these logics, social entrepreneurs need to not only be aware of these variations in logics but understand their underlying assumptions and translate messages from one logic into another. Take the example of a social entrepreneur who works with both commercial ventures and nonprofit organizations. Companies are typically following a market logic of competition whereas nonprofits often have a family logic (Greenwood et al. 2009). Thus, if a social entrepreneur envisions a cooperation between all three organizations, they need to be able to provide arguments from both a market and a family logic. In other words, they need to be able to sell both their mission and organization (Miller, Wesley, and Williams 2012) in diverse ways. These skills are the more important as research indicates that social entrepreneurs have a high tendency to collaborate (Jenner and Oprescu 2016), which thus requires the necessary skill sets to engage in these activities (Almarri and Meewella 2015; Arroyo-López 2011).

Analogous to commercial entrepreneurs, social entrepreneurs also require *business and management skills* (Hisrich and Peters 1998). However, they need to further be able to manage a hybrid organization, that is, an organization with a double (or even triple) bottom line and a resulting hybrid organizational identity (Tracey and Phillips 2007). This inherent hybridity of social ventures also means that social entrepreneurs need to be able to bridge between different types of capital (Mair, Battilana, and Cardenas 2012). Furthermore, managing accountability (Tracey and Phillips 2007) and the ability to measure outcome (Miller, Wesley, and Williams 2012) are further social entrepreneurship-specific management skills. As a consequence of these additional management challenges, social ventures tend to rely on a broader range of general business and management skills than their commercial counterparts (Estrin, Mickiewicz, and Stephan 2016).

In sum, social entrepreneurs require a large variety of skills to balance the dual objective of their organization, to interact with diverse stakeholders and to effectively create social change.

10.1.3. Intentions, Antecedents, and (Social) Entrepreneurs

A final component of the entrepreneur is entrepreneurial intention, that is, the desire to start (Krueger, Reilly, and Carsrud 2000) or own a venture (Crant 1996). In psychology, intention is considered the best predictor of actual behaviors (Ajzen 1991; Bagozzi, Baumgartner, and Yi 1989). This is why entrepreneurship research often refers to this component to identify and predict entrepreneurial action. In other words, traits influence the propensity toward entrepreneurial action (the *is*) whereas skills represent the ability to act on it (the potential to do); entrepreneurial intention then informs us if an individual will act on their entrepreneurial characteristics (*doing*).

Mair and Noboa (2006) were the first to apply entrepreneurial intention to the field of social entrepreneurship. They developed four antecedents of social entrepreneurial intention: *empathy* as a proxy for attitudes toward behavior, *moral judgment* as a proxy for social norms, *self-efficacy* as a proxy for internal behavioral control, and *perceived presence of social support*[1] as a proxy for external behavioral control (for detailed measures see Hockerts 2015). They further propose that these antecedents positively influence social entrepreneurship intentions through their effects on perceived feasibility (have I got the skills to be an entrepreneur?) and perceived desirability (do I want to be an entrepreneur?) (Shapero and Sokol 1982). More specifically, their propositions suggest that perceived desirability is influenced by the effects of empathy and moral judgment whereas self-efficacy and perceived social support influence perceived feasibility (Mair and Noboa 2006). Despite their clear findings, later studies resulted in more ambiguous findings. For instance, Ernst (2011) found that an increased level of empathy can actually reduce entrepreneurial intention.

In later studies, Hockerts (2017) excluded perceived feasibility and desirability as mediating factors because his analysis yielded that they are not two but one factor. Instead, he introduced the antecedent *prior experience*. He found that prior experience is a good predictor of social entrepreneurial intention. Furthermore, he found that self-efficacy is the strongest predictor of entrepreneurial intention and also most responsive to prior experience (Hockerts 2017).

As this antecedent has also long since been recognized as a key trigger for commercial entrepreneurial intention (Bae et al. 2014; Chen, Greene, and Crick 1998; Douglas 2013; Segal et al. 2002; Tiwari, Bhat, and Tikoria 2017), we will take a closer look at self-efficacy. Self-efficacy is the belief that one is able to accomplish a certain activity (Chen, Greene, and Crick 1998; McGee et al. 2009). It can originate from four different sources: (1) enactive mastery experience, that is, experiencing own performance accomplishments, (2) vicarious experience, that is, learning through experience of others, (3) verbal persuasion, that is, behaviors encouraged by others, and (4) emotional arousal, that is, getting excited about an activity (Bandura 1982, 1986).

Interestingly, research indicates that some social entrepreneurs have a lower level of self-efficacy than their commercial counterparts (Harding and Cowling 2006), especially in regard to their entrepreneurial skills (Bacq, Hartog, and Hoogendoorn 2016). Yet, a recent study by Clark, Newbert, and Quigley (2018) suggests that nascent entrepreneurs who seek to start a for-profit social venture actually have higher levels of self-efficacy than commercial entrepreneurs. Thus, although research supports the importance of self-efficacy as a predictor for social entrepreneurial intention (Hockerts 2017), it seems inconclusive what level of self-efficacy is present within the social entrepreneur population.

In sum, this section highlighted some of the specific characteristics of social entrepreneurs such as their heightened levels of empathy and compassion and their higher willingness to trust. It further pointed to entrepreneurship-specific skills as well as skills that are specific to the field of social entrepreneurship. Finally, this subsection discussed the importance of social entrepreneurial intention and its reliance on prior experience and self-efficacy. The next step is now to identify how (social) entrepreneurship education can foster and enhance these traits and skills.

10.2. What Social Entrepreneurship Education Can Do

The prevalence of entrepreneurship education has significantly increased since the 1990s to an extent that it is now mainstream in most business schools (Kuratko 2005). Entrepreneurship education refers to "any pedagogical [program] or process of education for entrepreneurial attitudes and skills" (Fayolle, Gailly, and Lassas-Clerc 2006, 702). There are different types of entrepreneurship education. Some of these are tailored toward different stages of development (Bridge and O'Neill 2012; Gorman, Hanlon, and King 1997) whereas others target different audiences (Liñán 2004). For the purpose of this book chapter, we will focus on university-level entrepreneurship education. This form of entrepreneurship education is often awareness building entrepreneurship education (Liñán 2004), that is, these programs are designed to develop entrepreneurial skills and support students in their entrepreneurial career path (Garavan and O'Cinneide 1994). Though there is a large body of research on commercial entrepreneurship education (for reviews see Pittaway and Cope 2007; Mwasalwiba 2010), there is only limited research on social entrepreneurship education (see Tracey and Phillips 2007; Miller, Wesley, and Williams 2012).

To gain a better understanding of social entrepreneurship education, we will proceed in four steps. First, we will review the purpose of entrepreneurship education (*why*) and the reasoning for why it might be effective. Second, we will then briefly review the content of such education—*what* do and can we teach—as well as, third, the mode of delivery roots suitable to social entrepreneurship education—*how* can and do we need to teach. Fourth, we will conclude this chapter by critically discussing the why, what, and how.

10.2.1. The Purpose of Entrepreneurship Education and Why It Might Work

To a large extent, entrepreneurship education focuses on developing entrepreneurial intention (Pittaway and Cope 2007; Peterman and Kennedy 2003) by increasing its perceived feasibility and desirability (Peterman and Kennedy 2003). There are two main theoretical arguments for why entrepreneurship education leads to an increased entrepreneurial intention amongst students (Bae et al. 2014).

First, some scholars use human capital theory (Becker 1964) to explain the underlying assumption about the effectiveness of entrepreneurship education. Human capital is the combination of knowledge and skills that individuals acquire through attending education institutions or through on-the-job training (Becker 1964). This human capital is seen as a precondition for entrepreneurial intention (Davidsson and Honig 2003). Because universities have skills development and knowledge transfer as their core tasks, it is therefore conceivable that entrepreneurship education can increase entrepreneurial intention through human capital development.

Second, another strand of research uses self-efficacy theory (Chen, Greene, and Crick 1998). The idea is that entrepreneurship education is able to positively influence the students' self-efficacy (Wilson, Kickul, and Marlino 2007) by providing the four sources of experiences for self-efficacy (Bandura 1982, 1986 and see following section for more detail).

Due to the hopes placed on entrepreneurship education (creating economic benefits, solving societal problems), a key question within the field is its effectiveness. The measurement of the effectiveness of entrepreneurship education is challenging as it has short-, mid-, and long-term effects (Henry, Hill, and Leitch 2005). Short-term effects might be the actual formation of entrepreneurial intentions, whereas mid-term effects are the actual founding of start-ups with then long-term effects referring to the start-ups' organizational survival and growth as well as the willingness and ability of the entrepreneur to stay with the organization in the long run.

Analogous to the core purpose of entrepreneurship education, the majority of studies use intention as a proxy for entrepreneurship (for a review see Nabi et al. 2016; Bae et al. 2014; Béchard and Grégoire 2005). Studies indicate that the relationship between entrepreneurship education and entrepreneurship intention is stronger for academic-focused interventions than for training-focused interventions (Martin, McNally, and Kay 2013).

This notwithstanding, there are two challenges with this type of effectiveness measurement. First, intention is a short-term measure and highly subjective, which renders it unreliable (Nabi et al. 2016). To overcome this issue, recent studies suggest the inclusion of various stakeholders in the development of entrepreneurship education effectiveness studies (Duval-Couetil 2013). These stakeholders should include the students, successful and failed entrepreneurs, as well as academics who teach the classes.

Second, and more significantly, reviews of studies on the effectiveness of entrepreneurship education lead to inconclusive results (Bae et al. 2014; Béchard and Grégoire 2005; Solomon et al. 2008; Mwasalwiba 2010). This is in part due to methodological challenges. For instance, in some cases the correlations could be the reverse (Martin, McNally, and Kay 2013). However, most notably are the findings that if preselection is taken into account, there is no relationship between entrepreneurship education and entrepreneurial intention. Put differently, those students who attend entrepreneurship classes self-select because they already have a propensity toward entrepreneurial behavior and higher levels of entrepreneurial intentions before taking the class (Bae et al. 2014).

10.2.2. *What to Teach to Make It Work*

Despite the inconclusive results in regard to the effectiveness of entrepreneurship education, we now turn our attention to what entrepreneurship education teaches. A key aspect here is the question of what can be taught. Many scholars argue that although skills can be taught, it is much more challenging to teach certain traits (Henry, Hill, and Leitch 2005).

Miller and colleagues (2012) conducted a study among social entrepreneurship educators and practitioners to identify the key topics for social entrepreneurship education. They found that both practitioners and educators consider it essential to teach prospective graduate entrepreneurs the ability to measure outcomes, the ability to formulate strategy, the ability to develop collaborative relationships, and the ability to problem-solve. Furthermore, teaching innovation and creativity as well as the creation and evaluation of effective business plans are equally considered essential by both groups.

Furthermore, they also identified topics that practitioners consider important but that have lower prevalence in the classroom. These include the ability to sell and market the organization, developing a sense of moral imperative (which, interestingly, was seen as particularly relevant for *for*-profit social ventures), the ability to communicate with customers, suppliers, and other stakeholders, the ability to challenge traditional thinking, and the ability to display leadership and to develop teams and employees (Miller, Wesley, and Williams 2012). As the majority of social entrepreneurship education is delivered in business schools (Mirabella and Young 2012), it is conceivable that some of the skills (e.g., developing teams and leadership) are taught in other classes (Miller, Wesley, and Williams 2012).

Finally, some components of the curricula are considered of lower relevance to practitioners. These are the ability to identify social problems as well as the desire and ability to grow the organization. Interestingly, optimism was dismissed as a priority skill by nonprofit and for-profit social entrepreneurs but considered essential by hybrid social entrepreneurs (Miller, Wesley, and Williams 2012).

At this point, we want to draw attention to two main points. First, the outlined study supports a finding by Mirabella and Young (2012) that the vast majority of social entrepreneurship education is linked to business and management. It thereby ignores other relevant skills such as those outlined in the previous section. Second, although, from a conceptual perspective, the espoused goal of entrepreneurship education is mostly about intention, the actual content of social entrepreneurship education in the classroom is less about the direct formation of intention but more about specific skills development. We argue that this can influence social entrepreneurship intention indirectly through the increase in perceived feasibility, because students feel more capable to manage a social venture. Yet, a focus on skill development only seems less likely to influence their confidence or the perceived desirability of social entrepreneurship.

10.2.3. How to Teach Social Entrepreneurship

Despite the inconclusive results about the impact of entrepreneurship education on entrepreneurial intention (Bae et al. 2014), the assumption that there is a positive relationship influenced the design of many entrepreneurship programs. In particular, we can observe that many teaching methods are designed to enhance self-efficacy in their students. In other words, we argue that while the content addresses skills, the delivery mode addresses self-efficacy. To elaborate, we will take a closer look at teaching tools through the lens of the four sources of self-efficacy (Bandura 1982, 1986). Table 10.1 summarizes this comparison.

Table 10.1 Four sources of self-efficacy and social entrepreneurship teaching approaches

Source of Self-Efficacy	General Definition	Concrete Application in SE Education	Literature on Application
Enacted experience	To experience own performance accomplishments	• Pitch competitions • Business simulations • 5-dollar business, Waste exercise • Service learning	Mwasalwiba (2010); Litzky, Godshalk, and Walton-Bongers (2010); Seelig (2014); Mueller, Brahm, and Neck (2015)
Vicarious experience	Learning through the experience of others	• Guest speakers • Case studies Videos • Site visits, internships	Honig (2004) Tracey and Phillips (2007) Mwasalwiba (2010)
Verbal persuasion	Behavior and confidence encouraged by others	• Portrayal of success stories with emphasis on social desirability • Narrative of "you can and should do it"	For a criticism of the "social-desirability of SE"-narrative, see Chapter 11 and Dey and Lehner (2017)
Emotional arousal	Getting excited, creating a sense of affectedness	• Reduce personal distance to social issues through field trips and personal encounters • Include emotional elements (testimonials, ceremonies) • Service learning with community partners to create emotional commitment	Litzky, Godshalk, and Walton-Bongers (2010); Mueller, Brahm, and Neck (2015)

Source: Authors' work, based on the distinction by Bandura (1982, 1986)

Enacted experiences: These activities create situations in which students can experience small successes, which are designed to encourage enhanced future performance. These might include pitch competitions in which students can present their own venture ideas in front of academics or invited guest. Business simulations are also frequently used (Mwasalwiba 2010). Enacted experiences can also include small challenges such as the 5-Dollar or Waste challenge (Seelig 2014). In the former, students are given five dollars (or an equivalent in their respective national currency) and a short set time frame. Their task is then to create as much profit with this initial seed fund as possible without adding any additional funds. The waste exercise is a variation of this where students are given products that are usually considered worthless or of low value such as coat hangers or toilet paper. Again, their task is to create something with it. Yet, rather than making profit this exercise is about creating any kind of value—be it financial, social, environmental, or aesthetic. Regardless of the specific nature of these exercises, they enable students to engage in effectuation (Perry, Chandler, and Markova 2012) and to have small-scale entrepreneurial success stories to tell. We have used both pitch competitions and the waste exercise in our own classes and can attest to the positive influence they have on students. While each student group goes through a stage of confusion and frustration when engaging in the waste exercise, they are the prouder of their achievements afterward.

Vicarious experience: This element of entrepreneurship education tools is probably most developed. Here, educators invite guest speakers—often entrepreneurs or those who work closely with them—to report on their own experience (Honig 2004; Tracey and Phillips 2007). Other courses use case studies, videos, or site visits (Mwasalwiba 2010). Tracey and Phillips (2007) argue that in the context of social entrepreneurship education, it is even more valuable if students develop their own case studies. In our own classrooms, we go a step further and invite social entrepreneurs to join the students as part of a live case study, that is, students work with the social entrepreneur on a current challenge.

Verbal persuasion: We argue that this element is indirectly included in many social entrepreneurship classrooms. Through case studies and practitioner reports that tell of the fun of being a social entrepreneur (cf. Dey and Lehner 2017) as well as about the emotional rewards that stem from prosocial work, students can experience verbal persuasion.

Emotional arousal: Creating emotional arousal is a key to creating entrepreneurial intention, especially in the context of social entrepreneurship. Although social entrepreneurs are often described as compassionate (Dees 1998; Miller, Wesley, and Williams 2012) or as having high levels of empathy (André and Pache 2016; Petrovskaya and Mirakyan 2018), both alone are not sufficient to turn an empathetic person into someone who will take entrepreneurial action (André and Pache 2016). Personal distance to the subject matter as well as pessimism about the potential to change the situation can hinder individuals from acting on their empathy (André and Pache 2016). Against this background, we believe that creating an emotional response, thus shrinking the distance to a social issue, can increase emotional arousal. Moreover, by showing how others have done it (see vicarious experience), students can further reduce their potential pessimism.

As we discussed in the section on skills, social entrepreneurs need to cross institutional logics (Pache and Chowdhury 2012). To help students develop these skills, social entrepreneurship education uses interdisciplinary, transdisciplinary, and service-learning-based teaching in addition to the above. As a consequence, in comparison to its commercial counterpart (Mwasalwiba 2010), social entrepreneurship education often involves forms of service learning and community outreach (Litzky, Godshalk, and Walton-Bongers 2010; Mueller, Brahm, and Neck 2015). Service learning refers to a form of teaching wherein students actively work within a mission-driven organization in parallel to attending classes. This form of micro-placement often entails a project that students work on, which often is used for assessment. In our teaching experience, linking social ventures and students through such forms of service learning allows both a deeper and more realistic dive into the realities of social entrepreneurship as well as a higher level of motivation, commitment, and self-efficacy for the students who appreciate that their work contributes to solving real-life challenges.

Although all of these teaching tools hold the potential of developing knowledge, skills, and entrepreneurial intention, their *scalability* is limited for at least three reasons. First, our own experience has shown us that it is not possible to run highly innovative and interactive modes of teaching (for example, live case studies, social entrepreneurship project labs, or service learning) in classes exceeding forty students. However, most universities have large numbers of undergraduate and postgraduate students. Therefore, it is difficult to offer such classes to even a small fraction of the student body.

Second, these types of courses often require significant resources. On the one hand, service learning and experiential learning require more one-to-one attention to students or student groups. This is not least because of the frustrations that students experience due to the uncommonly uncertain and ambiguous nature of the tasks. Thus, office hours are then spent less on content but on rebuilding confidence and advising students on how to cope with uncertainty. Furthermore, to conduct community outreach programs, educators need to build networks and connections, manage the relationships, coordinate schedules, and manage expectations.

Third, successfully running such modules may go beyond the skill set of some educators. To create a successful learning environment when engaging in these innovative forms of teaching, it is important to create a community of practice to ensure psychological safety for the student and to acknowledge the learners' identities (Howorth, Smith, and Parkinson 2012). However, developing such learning communities of practice or developing and engaging with community outreach programs is a skill that not all educators inherently possess. Therefore, this raises questions of how to best educate the educator (Miller, Wesley, and Williams 2012).

In addition to scale limitations, these teaching modes also face *institutional* challenges regarding the organization of (higher) education. In particular, they might be incompatible with the logic and structure of their hosting university or other higher education institution. For one, if social entrepreneurship is not taught as a stand-alone course but is rather integrated into other programs (Tracey and Phillips 2007), higher education structures need to be able to accommodate that. Another aspect here is the question of assessment. Assessment needs to allow for equal opportunity and fair comparison not only within but also between cohorts. However, if we take the example of service learning, this can be challenging. Depending on the partner organization and their project, students might engage in very different activities and hence learning. Moreover, service learning and problem-focused projects typically enable the students to work and learn in teams. Yet, despite this importance of group learning, the formal assessment often requires individual grades, thus raising additional challenges (Lejk, Wyvill, and Farrow 1996). Furthermore, if the focus of social entrepreneurship education is to foster social entrepreneurial intention, the question is then how to incorporate this into assessment. A classic coursework assignment or exam would not suffice. However, many universities do not allow more innovative forms of assessments such as diaries, vlogs, or reflection essays due to the inherent challenge of comparability.

10.2.4. What Social Entrepreneurship Education Cannot Do

In a final step, we would now like to shift the viewpoint and ask what social entrepreneurship education cannot do (well). In our own experience as social entrepreneurship educators, we have witnessed that successful social entrepreneurs often bring together three ingredients: a) a (somewhat relentless) prosocial motivation to solve a problem, b) a concrete knowledge and a good understanding of a specific social problem, and c) in-depth skills or expertise that helps solve the problem.

To illustrate take the example of Specialisterne's founder Thorkil Sonne. Specialisterne is a social enterprise that provides meaningful work for people living with autism (for a more detailed discussion see Chapters 4 and 7). Thorkil Sonne's son has a high-functioning form of autism that is coupled with a unique ability to spot errors in long sequences of numbers and letters. Due to his personal situation, Sonne thus had an in-depth understanding of the realities of autism (b)). When his son became older, Sonne started worrying about his future because most people with autism do not find a job that suits their needs and are therefore forced to retire straight after graduating from school. As a father, Sonne had a strong and relentless motivation to address this problem (a)). Thanks to his professional expertise in the software industry, he realized that this son (and others with similar talents) would be able to provide a highly valuable service. Sonne thus had in-depth knowledge to develop a workable solution that reflects the specificities of the software industry (c)). Indeed, Specialisterne's software testers have a much higher likelihood of spotting bugs in software codes than their non-autistic counterparts (Specialisterne 2013). Thus, the success of Specialisterne was only possible because Thorkil Sonne was not only aware of his son's needs but also of the needs of software companies.

Successful social entrepreneurs thus often build upon specific motivations, problem knowledge, and additional expertise that, in addition, need to match. We argue that social entrepreneurship education cannot force such configurations to form in the classroom.

1. For one, it is difficult to teach prosocial motivation, particularly of the relentless, almost possessed personal type. Though it is possible to enhance or funnel someone's general prosocial motivation, it would be difficult to persuade someone within the timeframe of a course to develop such a specific mission. Furthermore, there are ethical questions as to whether such persuasion would be appropriate in classroom.
2. Our experience of teaching social entrepreneurship at various international universities points to the fact that most students do not have the necessary understanding or experience of their chosen social mission. Yet, prior experience is a crucial (Hockerts 2017). Moreover, the social entrepreneurial process often starts through experiences within people's personal or professional lives (Belz and Binder 2017; Bacq, Hartog, and Hoogendoorn 2016). Indeed, for social entrepreneurs, opportunity recognition is something deeply personal and affective in nature (André and Pache 2016). So if social entrepreneurs recognize opportunities in contexts they understand (Bacq, Hartog, and Hoogendoorn 2016), how can students access such knowledge in the protected space of the classroom?
3. The aspect that is more easily teachable are skills to implement ideas. Put differently, we argue that for instance a master's in social entrepreneurship makes less sense than a master's in social enterprise or nonprofit management. Moreover, because social entrepreneurship education may prepare students to apply entrepreneurial strategies in their professional development much later in life, we would suggest that social entrepreneurship education is run as a complimentary course for other disciplines such as medicine or social work. Students of these subjects would have the necessary subject expertise and could then acquire essential management and entrepreneurial skills to use in their later professional roles.

10.3. Unintended Effects of Social Entrepreneurship Education

The previous discussion highlights that social entrepreneurship education faces challenges in achieving the intended outcomes with regard to teaching the specific traits, skills, and intentions characteristic for social entrepreneurs. In this section, we shift gears and take a more critical look at the tool of social entrepreneurship education. In fact, we argue that the uncritical promotion and usage of this tool runs the risk of creating unintended negative consequences. We will point to one micro-level and two macro-level consequences as a means of demonstrating such unintended consequences of social entrepreneurship education.

First, on a micro-level, social entrepreneurship education can lead to unsatisfied 'wanna-be' social entrepreneurs. Due to the focus on creating social entrepreneurial intention, students might develop a distorted sense of perceived desirability and perceived feasibility. This can lead to at least two challenges. First, graduates might start their entrepreneurial journey with heightened enthusiasm to then realize that they do not have either the characteristics or skills to succeed as a social entrepreneur. Even if they possess an entrepreneurial nature and have the motivation to persevere, they might lack the required expertise to succeed.

We have witnessed this challenge many times. Students are often highly enthusiastic to follow a vague idea of becoming a social entrepreneur. Yet, when asked about the specific problem they intend to solve, they find it difficult to identify (and stick relentlessly to) an actual, specific societal problem. What is more, even if they identify an issue, they often have no prior experience in the field. We insinuate that we are not the only educators who have experienced this. We would even go so far as to argue that the divergence regarding the perceived importance of teaching *identifying social problems* between social entrepreneurship practitioners and educators (Miller, Wesley, and Williams 2012) stems from this effect. We conjecture that the reason why practitioners see this point as less relevant is that they are, by definition, steeped in a specific problem for which they have the expertise and which they might have come across much earlier through their professional or personal lives (Belz and Binder 2017). Educators, on the other hand, seem to experience that students need to be made aware that the identification and understanding of a social problem is anything but trivial. As a result, if students lack the knowledge about and skills to address specific problems, the mere intention to engage in social entrepreneurship may be frustrating for graduates and can negatively impact their emotional and psychological well-being. In short, the more social entrepreneurship education creates empathic intentions that lack actual problem-solving skills, the more intentions can turn into frustrations later on.

On a macro-level, this oversupply of social-entrepreneurs-to-be can have another effect. The dominant narrative that everyone needs to innovate and be a changemaker (Sen 2007; see, critically, Seelos and Mair 2012) can push people away from other mission-driven vocations. In fact, a recent study by Bacq, Hartog, and Hoogendoorn (2016) found that some new social entrepreneurs have a very weak entrepreneurial profile, indicating that entrepreneurship might not actually suit them. Although we need social entrepreneurs, we also need those that support social entrepreneurs and other nonprofit organizations with functional skills such as marketing or accounting. In other words, the enthusiasm that social entrepreneurship education creates for founding a social venture can lead to misallocation of talent on a macro-level. If social entrepreneurship education portrays being a social entrepreneur as being inherently desirable (and superior to other careers in non-entrepreneurial organizations that appear "univocally disadvantageous" (Dey 2006, 129), then people who are not really fit to pursue this path might chose it nevertheless. A decreased fit between talent and work position, however, can, in the extreme, lead to a suboptimal utilization of resources from a macro perspective and reduced well-being from a micro-perspective.

Furthermore, social entrepreneurship education can limit innovation. A recent study found that out of five necessary skills for running a social venture, nearly 75 percent of the content taught in business schools focuses exclusively on market skills thus neglecting other skills such as political or philanthropic skills (Mirabella and Young 2012). As the majority of social entrepreneurship education is conducted within business schools, this focus can have significant impact on the field of social entrepreneurship. This becomes clear if we conceptualize this focus on market skills as an implicit assumption (and value judgment) that these skills are more important than leadership, political, philanthropic, or general business skills.

Therefore, if the majority of university students who participate in social entrepreneurship education courses predominately learn about market skills, they are likely to take this on as the leading principle. In turn, this can lead to normative isomorphism (DiMaggio and Powell 1983). In this type of isomorphism, organizations become more similar due to the professional training that their staff members received outside the organization. Thus, if most social-entrepreneurs-to-be experience similar education, the likelihood that the resulting ventures is similar is high. This is not a problem per se. Yet, it can limit the innovation power of social entrepreneurship because certain forms of social entrepreneurship (e.g., purely nonprofit) might appear less desirable for these graduates. However, as we have shown extensively in Chapter 6, some social entrepreneurial business models early on use nonprofit and voluntary sector resources that might be inaccessible when following a predominately market logic.

To be clear, we do not aim to argue against the notion of social entrepreneurship education. As we are both social entrepreneurship educators ourselves, we are aware of its great potential for social entrepreneurship as a field and society at large. Rather we point out that social entrepreneurship education needs to highlight that entrepreneurship is simply one tool to solve societal issues and engage with mission-driven venturing. Therefore, social entrepreneurship education needs to clearly outline that there are other options such as working for governmental or third sector organizations or in commercial ventures that may or may not cooperate with social entrepreneurs.

Put differently, we call for a reconfiguration of the notion of what constitutes effective social entrepreneurship education. Rather than measuring it in the increased intention to become an entrepreneur (cf. Bae et al. 2014) or in the number of start-ups founded (Mwasalwiba 2010), we argue that it is equally legitimate (and individually and socially helpful) if students realize that social entrepreneurial agency is *not* for them or that they have developed the skills and knowledge to work for a social venture as an employee, cooperate with a social entrepreneur working for different types of organization, or find meaningful work or purpose in a completely different domain, also outside the job.

10.4. Conclusion

In this chapter, we continued our discussion of micro-level effects of social entrepreneurship. Here, we engaged with a core theme in entrepreneurship research and aimed to understand who the social entrepreneur is and how they differ from commercial entrepreneurs. We identified that they share entrepreneurial traits but have additional characteristics such as increased propensity to trust and higher levels of empathy and compassion. In our discussion on social entrepreneurial skills, we showcased that social entrepreneurs especially require social and communication skills as well as additional business and management skills that cater to the hybrid nature of their ventures. After outlining social entrepreneurial intention, we then turned our attention to social entrepreneurship education. Here, we first discussed its purpose of creating entrepreneurial intention and then turned to its content. In our discussion on how to teach social entrepreneurship, we pointed to innovative teaching techniques designed to enhance self-efficacy in students. We argued that these techniques suffer from limits to scale and an incompatibility with existing higher education structures. In a final step, we outlined how social entrepreneurship can negatively impact graduate entrepreneur well-being and lead to misallocation of talent and normative isomorphism on a macro-level.

Note

1. Relevance of social appraisal is also supported by Baierl and colleagues (2014).

References

Ajzen, Icek. 1991. "The Theory of Planned Behavior." Edited by P. A. M. Lange, Arie W. Kruglanski, and E. Tory Higgins. *Organizational Behavior and Human Decision Processes*, Dissertation Abstracts International: Section B: The Sciences and Engineering, 50 (2). Elsevier: 179–211. doi:10.1016/0749-5978(91)90020-T.

Almarri, Jasem, and John Meewella. 2015. "Social Entrepreneurship and Islamic Philanthropy." *International Journal of Business and Globalisation* 15 (3): 405–24. doi:10.1504/IJBG.2015.071.

André, Kevin, and Anne-Claire Pache. 2016. "From Caring Entrepreneur to Caring Enterprise: Addressing the Ethical Challenges of Scaling up Social Enterprises." *Journal of Business Ethics* 133 (4): 659–75. doi:10.1007/s10551-014-2445-8.

Arroyo-López, Pilar. 2011. "The Role of the Social Entrepreneur as Coordinator of a Social Network." *International Journal of Entrepreneurship and Small Business* 14 (2): 271–85.

Austin, James, Howard Stevenson, and Jane Wei-Skillern. 2006. "Social and Commercial Entrepreneurship: Same, Different, or Both?" *Entrepreneurship Theory and Practice* 47 (3): 1–22. doi:10.5700/rausp1055.

Bacq, Sophie, Chantal Hartog, and Brigitte Hoogendoorn. 2016. "Beyond the Moral Portrayal of Social Entrepreneurs: An Empirical Approach to Who They Are and What Drives Them." *Journal of Business Ethics* 133 (4). Springer Netherlands: 703–18. doi:10.1007/s10551-014-2446-7.

Bacq, Sophie, and F. Janssen. 2011. "The Multiple Faces of Social Entrepreneurship: A Review of Definitional Issues Based on Geographical and Thematic Criteria." *Entrepreneurship & Regional Development* 23 (5–6): 373–403. doi:10.1080/089 85626.2011.577242.

Bae, Tae Jun, Shanshan Qian, Chao Miao, and James O. Fiet. 2014. "The Relationship Between Entrepreneurship Education and Entrepreneurial Intentions: A Meta-Analytic Review." *Entrepreneurship: Theory and Practice* 38 (2): 217–54. doi:10.1111/etap.12095.

Bagozzi, Richard P., Johann Baumgartner, and Youjae Yi. 1989. "An Investigation into the Role of Intentions as Mediators of the Attitude-Behavior Relationship." *Journal of Economic Psychology* 10 (1): 35–62. doi:10.1016/0167-4870(89)90056-1.

Baierl, Ronny, Dietmar Grichnik, Matthias Spörrle, and Isabell M. Welpe. 2014. "Antecedents of Social Entrepreneurial Intentions: The Role of an Individual's General Social Appraisal." *Journal of Social Entrepreneurship* 5 (2). Taylor & Francis: 123–45. doi:10.1080/19420676.2013.871324.

Bandura, Albert. 1982. "Self-Efficacy Mechanism in Human Agency." *American Psychologist* 37 (2): 122–47. doi:10.1037/0003-066X.37.2.122.

———. 1986. "The Explanatory and Predictive Scope of Self-Efficacy Theory." *Journal of Social and Clinical Psychology* 4 (3): 359–73. doi:10.1521/jscp.1986. 4.3.359.

Baron, R. A., and G. D. Markman. 2000. "Beyond Social Capital: How Social Skills Can Enhance Entrepreneurs' Success." *Academy of Management Perspectives* 14 (1): 106–16. doi:10.5465/AME.2000.2909843.

Béchard, Jean-Pierre, and Denis Grégoire. 2005. "Entrepreneurship Education Research Revisited: The Case of Higher Education." *Academy of Management Learning & Education* 4 (1): 22–43. doi:10.5465/AMLE.2005.16132536.

Becker, Gary S. 1964. *Human Capital Theory*. Chicago, IL: University of Chicago Press.

Belz, Frank Martin, and Julia Katharina Binder. 2017. "Sustainable Entrepreneurship: A Convergent Process Model." *Business Strategy and the Environment* 26 (1): 1–17. doi:10.1002/bse.1887.

Bornstein, David. 2007. *How to Change the World: Social Entrepreneurs and the Power of Ideas*. New York, NY: Oxford University Press.

Bridge, Simon, and Ken O'Neill. 2012. *Understanding Enterprise: Entrepreneurship and Small Business*. London, UK: Macmillan International Higher Education.

Carter, Nancy M., William B. Gartner, Kelly G. Shaver, and Elizabeth J. Gatewood. 2003. "The Career Reasons of Nascent Entrepreneurs." *Journal of Business Venturing* 18 (1): 13–39. doi:10.1016/S0883-9026(02)00078-2.

Chen, Chao C., Patricia Gene Greene, and Ann Crick. 1998. "Does Entrepreneurial Self-Efficacy Distinguish Entrepreneurs from Managers?" *Journal of Business Venturing* 13 (4): 295–316. doi:10.1016/S0883-9026(97)00029-3.

Clark, Kevin D., Scott L. Newbert, and Narda R. Quigley. 2018. "The Motivational Drivers Underlying For-Profit Venture Creation: Comparing Social and Commercial Entrepreneurs." *International Small Business Journal: Researching Entrepreneurship* 36 (2): 220–41. doi:10.1177/0266242617731139.

Crant, M. J. 1996. "The Proactive Personality Scale as a Predictor of Entrepreneurial Intentions." *Journal of Small Business Management* 34 (3): 8–42. doi:10.1287/isre.13.2.205.83.

Dacin, Peter A., M. Tina Dacin, and Marggret Matear. 2010. "Social Entrepreneurship: Why We Don't Need a New Theory and How We Move Forward From Here." *Academy of Management Perspectives*, 37–58.

Davidsson, Per, and Benson Honig. 2003. "The Role of Social and Human Capital among Nascent Entrepreneurs." *Journal of Business Venturing* 18 (3): 301–31. doi:10.1016/S0883-9026(02)00097-6.

Dees, J. Gregory. 1998. "The Meaning of 'Social Entrepreneurship'." www.case atduke.org/documents/dees_sedef.pdf.

DeTienne, D. R., and Gaylen N. Chandler. 2004. "Opportunity Identification and Its Role in the Entrepreneurial Classroom: A Pedagogical Approach and Empirical Test." *Academy of Management Learning & Education* 3 (3): 242–57. doi:10.5465/AMLE.2004.14242103.

Dey, Pascal. 2006. "The Rhetoric of Social Entrepreneurship: Paralogy and New Language Games in Academic Discourse." *Entrepreneurship as Social Change. A Third Movements in Entrepreneurship Book* January: 121–42.

Dey, Pascal, and Othmar Lehner. 2017. "Registering Ideology in the Creation of Social Entrepreneurs: Intermediary Organizations, 'Ideal Subject' and the Promise of Enjoyment." *Journal of Business Ethics* 142 (4). Springer Netherlands: 753–67. doi:10.1007/s10551-016-3112-z.

DiMaggio, Paul J., and Walter W. Powell. 1983. "The Iron Cage Revisited: Institutional Isomorphism and Collective Rationality in Organizational Fields." *American Sociological Review* 48 (2): 147–60.

Douglas, Evan J. 2013. "Reconstructing Entrepreneurial Intentions to Identify Predisposition for Growth." *Journal of Business Venturing* 28 (5). Elsevier Inc.: 633–51. doi:10.1016/j.jbusvent.2012.07.005.

Duval-Couetil, Nathalie. 2013. "Assessing the Impact of Entrepreneurship Education Programs: Challenges and Approaches." *Journal of Small Business Management* 51 (3): 394–409. doi:10.1111/jsbm.12024.

Ernst, Kati. 2011. "Heart over Mind—An Empirical Analysis of Social Entrepreneurial Intention Formation on the Basis of the Theory of Planned Behaviour." Doctoral Thesis. Wuppertal, Germany: University of Wuppertal. http://nbn-resolving.de/urn/resolver.pl?urn=urn:nbn:de:hbz:468-20120327-142543-6.

———. 2012. "Social Entrepreneurs and Their Personality." In *Social Entrepreneurship and Social Business*, 51–64. Wiesbaden, Germany: Springer Gabler.

Estrin, Saul, Tomasz Mickiewicz, and Ute Stephan. 2016. "Human Capital in Social and Commercial Entrepreneurship." *Journal of Business Venturing* 31 (4). Elsevier Inc.: 449–67. doi:10.1016/j.jbusvent.2016.05.003.

Fayolle, Alain, Benot Gailly, and Narjisse Lassas-Clerc. 2006. "Assessing the Impact of Entrepreneurship Education Programmes: A New Methodology." *Journal of European Industrial Training* 30 (9): 701–20. doi:10.1108/03090590610715022.

Friedman, Howard S., and Miriam W. Schustack. 1999. *Personality: Classic Theories and Modern Research*. Boston, MA: Allyn and Bacon.

Garavan, Thomas N., and Barra O'Cinneide. 1994. "Entrepreneurship Education and Training Programmes." *Journal of European Industrial Training* 18 (8): 3–12. doi:10.1108/03090599410068024.

Gorman, G., D. Hanlon, and W. King. 1997. "Some Research Perspectives on Entrepreneurship Education, Enterprise Education and Education for Small Business Management: A Ten-Year Literature Review." *International Small Business Journal* 15 (3): 56–77. doi:10.1177/0266242697153004.

Gosling, Samuel D., Peter J. Rentfrow, and William B. Swann. 2003. "A Very Brief Measure of the Big-Five Personality Domains." *Journal of Research in Personality* 37 (6): 504–28. doi:10.1016/S0092-6566(03)00046-1.

Greenwood, R., A. M. Diaz, S. X. Li, and J. C. Lorente. 2009. "The Multiplicity of Institutional Logics and the Heterogeneity of Organizational Responses." *Organization Science* 21 (2): 521–39. doi:10.1287/orsc.1090.0453.

Harding, R., and M. Cowling. 2006. *Social Entrepreneurship Monitor*. London, UK: London Business School.

Harris, Jared D., Harry J. Sapienza, and Norman E. Bowie. 2009. "Ethics and Entrepreneurship." *Journal of Business Venturing* 24 (5). Elsevier Inc.: 407–18. doi:10.1016/j.jbusvent.2009.06.001.

Henry, Colette, Francis Hill, and Claire Leitch. 2005. "Entrepreneurship Education and Training: Can Entrepreneurship Be Taught? Part II." *Education + Training* 47 (3): 158–69.

Hisrich, R. D., and M. P. Peters. 1998. *Entrepreneurship*. Eth ed. Boston, MA: Irwin McGraw-Hill.

Hockerts, Kai. 2015. "The Social Entrepreneurial Antecedents Scale (SEAS): A Validation Study." *Social Enterprise Journal* 11 (3): 260–80. doi:10.1108/SEJ-05-2014-0026.

———. 2017. "Determinants of Social Entrepreneurial Intentions." *Entrepreneurship: Theory and Practice* 41 (1): 105–30. doi:10.1111/etap.12171.

Honig, Benson. 2004. "Entrepreneurship Education: Toward a Model of Contingency-Based Business Planning." *Academy of Management Learning & Education* 3 (3): 258–73. doi:10.5465/AMLE.2004.14242112.

Howorth, Carole, Susan M. Smith, and Caroline Parkinson. 2012. "Social Learning and Social Entrepreneurship Education." *Academy of Management Learning & Education* 11 (3): 371–89. doi:10.5465/amle.2011.0022.

Hwee Nga, Joyce Koe, and Gomathi Shamuganathan. 2010. "The Influence of Personality Traits and Demographic Factors on Social Entrepreneurship Start Up Intentions." *Journal of Business Ethics* 95 (2): 259–82. doi:10.1007/s10551-009-0358-8.

Jenner, Peter, and Florin Oprescu. 2016. "The Sectorial Trust of Social Enterprise: Friend or Foe?" *Journal of Social Entrepreneurship* 7 (2). Taylor & Francis: 236–61. doi:10.1080/19420676.2016.1158732.

Judge, Timothy A., Chad A. Higgins, Carl J. Thoresen, and Murray R. Barrick. 1999. "The Big Five Personality Traits, General Mental Ability, and Career Success across the Life Span." *Personnel Psychology* 52 (3): 621–52. doi:10.1111/j.1744-6570.1999.tb00174.x.

Krueger, Norris F., Michael D. Reilly, and Alan L. Carsrud. 2000. "Competing Models of Entrepreneurial Intentions." *Journal of Business Venturing* 15 (5–6): 411–32. doi:10.1016/S0883-9026(98)00033-0.

Kuratko, D. F. 2005. "The Emergence of Entrepreneurship Education: Development, Trends, and Challenges." *Entrepreneurship Theory and Practice* 29 (5): 577–98. doi:10.1111/j.1540-6520.2005.00099.x.

Lanteri, Alessandro. 2015. "The Creation of Social Enterprises: Some Lessons from Lebanon." *Journal of Social Entrepreneurship* 6 (1). Taylor & Francis: 42–69. doi:10.1080/19420676.2014.954256.

Lejk, Mark, Michael Wyvill, and Stephen Farrow. 1996. "A Survey of Methods of Deriving Individual Grades from Group Assessments." *Assessment and Evaluation in Higher Education* 21 (3): 267–80. doi:10.1080/0260293960210306.

Liñán, Francisco. 2004. "Intention-Based Models of Entrepreneurship Education." *Piccolla Impresa/Small Business* 3 January: 1–30.

Litzky, Barrie E., Veronica M. Godshalk, and Cynthia Walton-Bongers. 2010. "Social Entrepreneurship and Community Leadership." *Journal of Management Education* 34 (1): 142–62. doi:10.1177/1052562909338038.

Mair, Johanna, Julie Battilana, and Julian Cardenas. 2012. "Organizing for Society: A Typology of Social Entrepreneuring Models." *Journal of Business Ethics* 111 (3): 353–73. doi:10.1007/s10551-012-1414-3.

Mair, Johanna, and Ernesto Noboa. 2006. "Social Entrepreneurship: How Intentions to Create a Social Venture Are Formed." In *Social Entrepreneurship*, edited by Johanna Mair, Jeffrey Robinson, and Kai Hockerts, 121–35. New York, NY: Palgrave Macmillan.

Man, Thomas W. Y., Theresa Lau, and K. F. Chan. 2002. "The Competitiveness of Small and Medium Enterprises." *Journal of Business Venturing* 17 (2): 123–42. doi:10.1016/S0883-9026(00)00058-6.

Martin, Bruce C., Jeffrey J. McNally, and Michael J. Kay. 2013. "Examining the Formation of Human Capital in Entrepreneurship: A Meta-Analysis of Entrepreneurship Education Outcomes." *Journal of Business Venturing* 28 (2). Elsevier Inc.: 211–24. doi:10.1016/j.jbusvent.2012.03.002.

McGee, Jeffrey E., Mark Peterson, Stephen L. Mueller, and Jennifer M. Sequeira. 2009. "Entrepreneurial Self-Efficacy: Refining the Measure." *Entrepreneurship Theory and Practice* 33 (4): 965–88. doi:10.1111/j.1540-6520.2009.00304.x.

McKeown, Julie, Cindy Millman, Srikanth Reddy Sursani, Kelly Smith, and Lynn M. Martin. 2006. "Graduate Entrepreneurship Education in the United Kingdom." *Education + Training* 48 (8–9): 597–613. doi:10.1108/00400910610710038.

Miller, Toyah L., Curtis L. Wesley, and Denise E. Williams. 2012. "Educating the Minds of Caring Hearts: Comparing the Views of Practitioners and Educators on the Importance of Social Entrepreneurship Competencies." *Academy of Management Learning and Education* 11 (3): 349–70. doi:10.5465/amle.2011.0017.

Mirabella, Roseanne, and Dennis R. Young. 2012. "The Development of Education for Social Entrepreneurship and Nonprofit Management: Diverging or Converging Paths?" *Nonprofit Management and Leadership* 23 (1). Wiley Online Library: 43–57.

Mueller, Susan, Taiga Brahm, and Heidi Neck. 2015. "Service Learning in Social Entrepreneurship Education: Why Students Want to Become Social Entrepreneurs and How to Address Their Motives." *Journal of Enterprising Culture* 23 (3): 357–80. doi:10.1142/S0218495815500120.

Mwasalwiba, Ernest Samwel. 2010. "Entrepreneurship Education: A Review of Its Objectives, Teaching Methods, and Impact Indicators. Education and Training." *Education + Training* 52 (1): 20–47. doi:10.1108/00400911011017663.

Nabi, G., F. Liñán, N. Krueger, A. Fayolle, and A. Walmsley. 2016. "The Impact of Entrepreneurship Education in Higher Education: A Systematic Review and Research Agenda." *Academy of Management Learning & Education* 16 (2): 277–99. doi:10.5465/amle.2015.0026.

Pache, A. C., and I. Chowdhury. 2012. "Social Entrepreneurs as Institutionally Embedded Entrepreneurs: Toward a New Model of Social Entrepreneurship Education." *Academy of Management Learning & Education* 11 (3): 494–510. doi:10.5465/amle.2011.0019.

Peredo, Ana María, and Murdith McLean. 2006. "Social Entrepreneurship: A Critical Review of the Concept." *Journal of World Business* 41 (1): 56–65. doi:10.1016/j.jwb.2005.10.007.

Perry, John T., Gaylen N. Chandler, and Gergana Markova. 2012. "Entrepreneurial Effectuation: A Review and Suggestions for Future Research." *Entrepreneurship Theory and Practice* 36 (4): 837–61. doi:10.1111/j.1540-6520.2010.00435.x.

Peterman, Nicole E., and Jessica Kennedy. 2003. "Enterprise Education: Influencing Students' Perceptions of Entrepreneurship." *Entrepreneurship Theory and Practice* 28 (2): 129–44. doi:10.1046/j.1540-6520.2003.00035.x.

Petrovskaya, Irina, and Araksya Mirakyan. 2018. "A Mission of Service: Social Entrepreneur as a Servant Leader." *International Journal of Entrepreneurial Behaviour and Research* 24 (3): 755–67. doi:10.1108/IJEBR-02-2016-0057.

Pittaway, Luke, and Jason Cope. 2007. "Entrepreneurship Education: A Systematic Review of the Evidence." *International Small Business Journal* 25 (5): 479–510. doi:10.1177/0266242607080656.

Rauch, Andreas, and Michael Frese. 2007. "Let's Put the Person Back into Entrepreneurship Research: A Meta-Analysis on the Relationship between Business Owners' Personality Traits, Business Creation, and Success." *European Journal of Work and Organizational Psychology* 16 (4): 353–85. doi:10.1080/13594320701595438.

Seelig, Tina. 2014. *What I Wish I Knew When I Was 20: A Crach Course on Making Your Place in the World*. New York, NY: HarperCollins.

Seelos, Christian, and Johanna Mair. 2012. "Innovation Is Not the Holy Grail." *Stanford Social Innovation Review* Fall: 44–9.

Segal, Gerry, Dan Borgia, Jerry Schoenfeld, and Jerry Schoenfeld. 2002. "Using Social Cognitive Career Theory to Enhance Students' Entrepreneurial Interests and Goals." *Academy of Entrepreneurship Journal* 13: 69–73.

Sen, Pritha. 2007. "Ashoka's Big Idea: Transforming the World through Social Entrepreneurship." *Futures* 39 (5): 534–53. doi:10.1016/j.futures.2006.10.013.

Shane, Scott, Lars Kolvereid, and Paul Westhead. 1991. "An Exploratory Examination of the Reasons Leading to New Firm Formation across Country and Gender." *Journal of Business Venturing* 6 (6). Elsevier: 431–46.

Shapero, Albert, and Lisa Sokol. 1982. "The Social Dimensions of Entrepreneurship." *Ncyclopedia of Entrepreneurship*, 72–90.

Solomon, George, Pat H. Dickson, George T. Solomon, and K. Mark Weaver. 2008. "Entrepreneurial Selection and Success: Does Education Matter?" *Journal of Small Business and Enterprise Development* 15 (2): 239–58. doi:10.1108/14626000810871655.

Specialisterne. 2013. "Welcome to Specialisterne." June 2. http://specialisterne.com/

Stewart, Wayne H., Warren E. Watson, Joann C. Carland, and James W. Carland. 1998. "A Procluvity for Entrepreneurship: A Comparison of Entrepreneurs, Small Business Owners, and Corporate Managers." *Journal of Business Venturingine* 14 (2): 189–214.

Suresh, Jayshree, and R. Ramraj. 2012. "Entrepreneurial Ecosystem: Case Study on the Influence of Environmental Factors on Entrepreneurial Success." *European Journal of Business and Management* 4 (16): 95–102.

Thompson, John L., Geoff Alvy, and Ann Lees. 2000. "Social Entrepreneurship— A New Look at the People and the Potential." *Management Decision* 38 (5): 328–38. doi:10.1108/00251740010340517.

Tiwari, Preeti, Anil K. Bhat, and Jyoti Tikoria. 2017. "The Role of Emotional Intelligence and Self-Efficacy on Social Entrepreneurial Attitudes and Social Entrepreneurial Intentions." *Journal of Social Entrepreneurship* 8 (2). Taylor & Francis: 165–85. doi:10.1080/19420676.2017.1371628.

Toegel, Ginka, and Jean-Louis Barsoux. 2012. "How to Become a Better Leader." *MIT Sloan Management Review* 6 (10): 67–70, 72.

Tracey, Paul, and Nelson William Phillips. 2007. "The Distinctive Challenge of Educating Social Entrepreneurs : A Postscript and Rejoinder to the Special Issue on Entrepreneurship Education." *Academy of Management Learning & Education* 6 (2): 264–71. doi:10.5465/AMLE.2007.25223465.

Weerawardena, Jay, and Gillian Sullivan Mort. 2006. "Investigating Social Entrepreneurship: A Multidimensional Model." *Journal of World Business* 41 (1): 21–35. doi:10.1016/j.jwb.2005.09.001.

Wilson, Fiona, Jill Kickul, and Deborah Marlino. 2007. "Gender, Entrepreneurial Self-Efficacy, and Entrepreneurial Career Intentions: Implications for Entrepreneurship Education." *Entrepreneurship Theory and Practice* 31 (3): 387–406. doi:10.1111/j.1540-6520.2007.00179.x.

Zahra, Shaker A., Eric Gedajlovic, Donald O. Neubaum, and Joel M. Shulman. 2009. "A Typology of Social Entrepreneurs: Motives, Search Processes and Ethical Challenges." *Journal of Business Venturing* 24 (5): 519–32. doi:10.1016/j.jbusvent.2008.04.007.

11 Narratives, Hagiographies, and Future Perspectives

In our final book chapter, we will engage in a critical discussion about the dominant *narrative* within the field of social entrepreneurship. Within the academic and practitioner discourse are ample examples of accounts of social entrepreneurs as hero-like individuals. Social entrepreneurs are described as 'hero entrepreneurs' (Nicholls 2010) or even as the "real-life superheroes of our society" (Kickul and Lyons 2016, 2) who have an extraordinary character (Bornstein 2007; Elkington and Hartigan 2008). Although we do not deny the impressive feats by some social entrepreneurs, we argue that putting social entrepreneurs on a pedestal or lifting them up to be super-humans or portraying their achievements as "God-like acts of redemption" (Dey 2006, 127) can bear destructive risks for the field of social entrepreneurship.

Narratives and discourse—that is, the way we talk about something—have constitutive and performative effects (Dey 2006). In other words, our language guides our thinking and in turn our behaviors. Thus, if we talk about social entrepreneurship solely in one specific way, we risk developing blind spots. Yet, these blind spots might hold valuable information and insight for advancing the field of social entrepreneurship. To unearth some of these blind spots, we will take apart the narrative of hero-like individuals. To this end, our final chapter will not provide a conventional summary of the book but rather use the critical reflection of the social entrepreneurship narrative to point to avenues for future research and trends within the field of social entrepreneurship. We will first (Section 11.1) allude to the potential negative implications of heroization and hagiographies. We will then (Section 11.2) turn to the risks of overemphasizing the importance of a social entrepreneur as an individual. In a final step (Section 11.3), we will combine these insights to develop implications for future research and practice. Moreover, we will apply a critical perspective to ourselves and briefly discuss our use of stereotypical archetypes throughout the book.

11.1. Hagiographies, Heroes, and Success Bias of All Is Always Good

Heroes are people that need to be worshiped and raised above everyone else. This hero-like narrative paints a picture of social entrepreneurship as having "univocally positive effects" (Dey 2006, 121). As a consequence, many biographical accounts of social entrepreneurs read more like hagiographies, that is, biographies of saints. However, social entrepreneurs are people and—just like everyone else—they and their actions are not without faults. Moreover, as we have discussed in detail in our theoretical framework (Chapter 3) as well as from a macro-level perspective (Chapters 4 and 5), social entrepreneurship is only one of many tools for society.

Some might argue that this heroization is only a figure of speech to indicate that social entrepreneurs aim for higher-order objectives. However, a narrative of heroism does not only imply noble mission but also implies success. As a consequence, this normative prejudgment about social entrepreneurs does not allow for the notion of failure (Light 2006). Nobody becomes a hero for failing to achieve their mission. Superheroes always save the day.

So why in fact is it a problem to acknowledge only success and reject the notion of failure? Following the logic of this book, we will briefly outline potential negative consequences of a hero-like narrative and success bias on the micro-, meso-, and macro-levels.

Micro-level effects: On a micro-level, such narrative can lead to at least two effects. First, it can create *false illusions* of what it is like to be a social entrepreneur. In particular, it can inadvertently deceive prospective social entrepreneurs as it constructs an illusion of simplicity. Many stories about social entrepreneurs and their venturing journey avoid detailed descriptions of their failures along the way. Moreover, they also neglect other effects such as their unique skills, traits (see Chapter 10), and social capital, timing, and frankly luck. Ample examples in the entrepreneurship history show that some of the greatest successes were accidents (e.g., penicillin) or that some ideas flopped the first time (e.g., Apple's launch of its first tablet computer). Other successful entrepreneurs such as Walt Disney actually went insolvent or nearly so a couple of times before they finally had their breakthrough. Moreover, it also creates false illusions about success potential. Fifty percent of ventures do not survive their fifth year of operation, and 70 percent do not make it to their tenth anniversary (Henry 2017). And even these figures are misleading as they only consider those ventures that made it past the ideation and formalization stage. There are estimates that only one in 3,000 ideas actually makes it there. In short, it is much more likely to fail than to succeed.

However, the disillusioning nature of the hero narrative—success is possible if you just try hard enough—might distort perceived feasibility and perceived desirability, which in turn can lead to an unrealistic level of self-efficacy (see Chapter 10). Despite the fact that later-on failure is more likely to be the norm than the exception, individuals might then interpret the lack of success as a personal failure. As a consequence, society might find itself in a position where there are more disillusioned and frustrated social entrepreneurs-wannabes than necessary.

Second, we suggest that heroization of existing social entrepreneurs can also negatively impact their *beneficiaries*. We conjecture that these arise from the ambivalent consequences of praise and worship implied by the hero narrative. Constant appraisal can affect expectations. McMullen and Bergman (2018) found that social entrepreneurs can develop a psychological feeling of entitlement in regard to gratitude of their beneficiaries. The social entrepreneur thus starts to expect and even demand gratitude. Although we do not contest that many beneficiaries are grateful, we argue that an expectation of gratitude implies inferiority and dependence (see the 'medical treatment' analogy in Dey 2006). This hierarchical distinction between those who know what the solution is and those that need the help can lead to lack of confidence in beneficiaries.

Meso-level effects: Heroization can impede *learning* due to groupthink and impeded double-loop learning. As we discussed in Chapter 6, a social venture is able to change its business model only if all organizational members partake. However, a continuous portrayal of the social entrepreneur as a hero might lead them to become overconfident in their own judgment. They might then be less open to suggestions by other organizational members. Moreover, organizational members might not even offer criticism because they are likely to identify not only with the social mission but also with the social entrepreneur (see discussions on stewardship in Chapter 8). Thus, the social venture might endure groupthink as a result (Boesso and Kumar 2009). In addition, the underlying assumption that the social entrepreneur is a hero and their achievements universally good (Dey 2006)—that is, does things right—is likely to block double-loop learning (Argyris 1977). This is because the narrative does not allow for questioning the assumption of being right and doing good.

Second, the hero narrative might also push some social ventures to *scale* before their time or too quickly. Chapter 8 showed that some social ventures need to carefully consider their choice of scaling strategies as well as if scaling is the right option for their venture in the first place. However, a felt pressure to live up to their hero status might create decision biases toward quick and large scale.

Third, a hero narrative and success bias can negatively impact *accountability*. As there are no concrete standards of impact measurement (see Chapter 7), the pressure to showcase that the social venture is indeed doing 'univocally good' and is living up to its public expectation might create ambivalent incentives. For one, it creates coercive isomorphisms (DiMaggio and Powell 1983) to conduct impact measurement to show achievements. On the other hand, it can lead to intentional or unintentional manipulation of these measurements (see Chapter 7).

Macro-level: The assumption of universal goodness may *misallocate resources*. As we discussed in Chapters 4 and 5, social entrepreneurship is one tool of many to solve societal problems. However, in many situations, it is only the second-best solution. Yet, a narrative based on success bias might overshadow such insights and even lead to a discursive downgrading of other societal tools such as the state, governments, or non-entrepreneurial civil society organizations (Dey 2006). In short, it crowds out productive questions about under which conditions and for what problems social entrepreneurship is an appropriate tool but a priori insinuates that social entrepreneurship is the solution.

Second, success narratives do not only impede individual or organizational but also societal learning. A point in case is research on social entrepreneurship. From a *research* point of view a focus on heroization and success offers limited potential for academic discussions (Hoogendoorn, Pennings, and Thurik 2010). The literature on (social) entrepreneurship, however, tends to only discuss success stories. As Spoelstra (2010, 95) aptly phrases it: "Only happy ends apparently deserve the term 'innovation'" and academic analysis. Thus, if we only study the stories of heroes we run the risk of only studying success (Andersson and Ford 2015). To use an analogy by Davidsson (2005), this is like studying gamblers by only looking at those who win. This would likely lead us to wrong conclusions and suggestions for changes to the meso- and macro-environments (cf. Andersson and Ford 2015).

In the business and entrepreneurship literature, the methodological challenge of avoiding survivor bias and covering unsuccessful cases, too, is well-known (Ţurcan et al. 2010). Yet, the very narrative of social entrepreneurship and its focus on fascinating stories renders avoiding survivor bias difficult. In fact, despite the recognition of the importance of failure within the general entrepreneurship literature (Olaison and Sørensen 2014; Politis and Gabrielsson 2009), there is a significant lack of such research in the field of social entrepreneurship (Dacin, Dacin, and Tracey 2011). Although this could potentially add "a faddish flavour to social entrepreneurship" (Andersson and Ford 2015, 303), it also misallocates academic resources.

11.2. The Lone Wolf—The Narratives on Individuals

We now turn our attention to the second part of the narrative—the focus on an individual social entrepreneur. According to this narrative, social entrepreneurs are individuals—one person who engages in entrepreneurial agency for the benefit of society (Bacq, Hartog, and Hoogendoorn 2016). Analogous to the previous subsection, we will point to some of the consequences of this emphasis on a sole social entrepreneur on all three levels.

Micro-level effects: An overemphasis or even sole emphasis on individual social entrepreneurial agency can create certain *pressure* on the individual. The feeling that "I have to do this or nobody else does it" can lead to unhealthy work patterns (Dempsey and Sanders 2010, and see Chapter 9) and in turn negatively impact a social entrepreneur's mental and physical health. What is more, in combination with the focus on hagiographies, social entrepreneurs might not get the help they need in time. After all, who has ever heard of a superhero or saint that goes to therapy?

Second, for prospective social entrepreneurs, it paints a *misleading picture of the entrepreneurial process*. In particular, it neglects that many social ventures are founded by entrepreneurial teams (for an introduction see Stewart 1989) or as part of collective entrepreneurial endeavors (Ratten 2014; Morgan 2016). Chapter 10 discussed the necessity of social entrepreneurs to have a social mission, an in-depth understanding of that social mission, and expertise and skills to implement a solution. Here, entrepreneurial teams can be a helpful tool because team members can complement each other in their skills. However, if the dominant narrative of social entrepreneurs as individuals is depicted in the media as well as in social entrepreneurship education, prospective social entrepreneurs might be less inclined to engage in team or collective entrepreneurship, because it is not the 'proper' way of doing it. Ironically, even some of the individual social entrepreneurs awarded Ashoka Fellowships are actually members of social entrepreneurial teams. However, to feed into the narrative of individual changemakers, only one team member receives the fellowship and public recognition. As a consequence, the narrative of individual social entrepreneurs runs the risk of reducing the desirability of team and collective entrepreneurship.

Meso-level effects: The focus on outstanding individuals creates hierarchies between organizational members, which can lead, in the extreme, to interpersonal conflicts. This is particularly challenging as many mission-driven employees and staff prefer an involvement-oriented management style (cf. Davis, Schoorma, and Donaldson 1997 and Chapter 8). Similarly to our argumentation in the previous subchapter, the social entrepreneur might become overconfident in their abilities. If they then reduce the involvement of their staff and volunteers, they run the risk of creating frustration within their organization.

Macro-level effects: A focus on the individual can lead to a *misallocation of entrepreneurial resources*. Baumol (1990) starts his arguments with the assumption that the potential number of entrepreneurs within a given population is fairly stable and cannot be expended easily. Chapter 10 supports this notion as research on the effectiveness of (social) entrepreneurship education is inconclusive and suffers from selection biases. However, trying to transform individuals into social entrepreneurs might even misallocate individual talent and other resources into want-to-be-start-ups and entrepreneurial venturing simply for the sake of it, with individuals following this path as a fancy, individualistic lifestyle choice. However, not all of these want-to-be-social-entrepreneurs might be suited to cope with the idiosyncratic challenges of the field or have the relevant skills or expertise levels (see Chapter 10). Therefore, a focus on individual life(style) stories may shift resources away from more traditional entrepreneurship or non-entrepreneurial mission-driven careers.

11.3. Future Perspectives on Social Entrepreneurship

So, what can we take away from our narrative critique in particular and our book in general? This last subchapter of our book will outline some avenues for future research as well as implications for future practice. Rather than aiming to provide a comprehensive list, we will focus on two main areas.

11.3.1. *Everything Is a Tool—Be Critical*

Based on our admittedly brief critique of the social entrepreneurship narrative as the endeavor of hero-like individuals, we call for a far more nuanced academic and practitioner discussion. We claim that it is crucial for the progression of the field to go beyond a normatively clouded portrayal of the key actors (for similar critiques see Dey 2006; Andersson and Ford 2015). Only if the field of social entrepreneurship acknowledges its failures are we able to learn how to improve ecosystems, social entrepreneurship education, organizational support systems, or other management-related tools. Understanding failure is a great source of information. We, of course, acknowledge the challenges in studying failure, but believe that this might be an area in which practice and academia could work more closely together as both sides have a vested interest here.

Moreover, failure within social entrepreneurship does not need to mean the demise of an organization or the inability to even start the social venture in the first place but can also mean small-scale failures—questions such as why successful social ventures are suddenly less successful. To give two examples, Wellcome (see Chapter 8) and Specialisterne (see Chapters 4 and 10) are two social ventures that we have long since used as good practice examples in our classrooms. For the purpose of this book, we checked their websites to identify their current number of franchise outlets. Here we noticed that over the last two years, Wellcome's franchise outlets reduced from 250 to 230 and Specialisterne's German outlet is no longer in business. There might be numerous reasons for these developments. Yet, only if we allow the notion of (partial) failure as a possibility (cf. Light 2006) and perceive social entrepreneurship as an open development (and not as teleological story of infinite progress) are we even able to conceive more nuanced research and practice questions.

We hope that the application of our theoretical framework (Chapter 3) to various elements of social entrepreneurship has demonstrated that social entrepreneurship not only is not inherently good and univocally desirable but neither are its tools. In our book, we could highlight only some of the inherent normative ambivalences of social entrepreneurship that derive from variations within situational contexts. Future research and practice should try to better understand these ambivalences and how to overcome them, that is, how to alter situations to achieve more desirable outcomes. Furthermore, there are many more of these ambivalences that require uncovering and solving. We hope that our book provides a useful contribution for the broader debate about both the bright and dark sides of social entrepreneurship as well as ways to handle them.

11.3.2. It's Not Dichotomous but Rather Blurry

In this book, we have often used or developed idealized dichotomies. In our experience, this is useful to gain conceptual clarity about different logics and dynamics. However, we fully acknowledge that treating features like *having a social mission*, *being innovative*, or *following multiple logics* as binary issues for which only the pure, ideal types are possible, does not do justice to the complexity of real-life phenomena. In fact, in the real world, many if not all of these distinctions describe phenomena that lie on a spectrum with dynamic shades of gray.

This point is highly relevant, both for future research and future practice. We have the impression that the boundaries between certain phenomena become increasingly blurred. For instance, take the examples of Corporate Social Responsibility (for a conceptual review see Garriga and Melé 2004), Corporate Citizenship (Matten and Crane 2005; Pies, Hielscher, and Beckmann 2009), or Corporate Sustainability (for a review see Engert, Rauter, and Baumgartner 2016). Many traditional for-profit ventures now try to create societal impact as well. Their approach to social value creation might be different but becomes increasingly similar as well. This is not least due to increasing collaborations between social ventures and for-profit companies. Moreover, some for-profit companies incorporate social entrepreneurship in the form of social intrapreneurship (Kistruck and Beamish 2010; Nandan, London, and Bent-Goodley 2015).

Similarly, in entrepreneurship it is often not clear where to draw the boundary between social entrepreneurship and corporate entrepreneurship (Sharma and Chrisman 2007)—or whether the attempt to draw such a boundary makes sense in the first place. For instance, Zeyen (2014) found support for this point in an interview study with eighty commercial and social entrepreneurs. The in-depth analysis of the motivations of these entrepreneurs yielded no dichotomy but rather a taxonomy of entrepreneur types. Within each taxonomy, there were representatives of both commercial and social entrepreneurs.

Finally, social entrepreneurship needs to consider both team and collective entrepreneurship as well as blurring boundaries between other related fields of mission-driven activities. As our discussion Chapter 4 indicated, the boundaries between social entrepreneurship and social movements or activities might be less clear than often considered.

In a way, the hybrid concept of social entrepreneurship may just be one tip of a bigger hybridity iceberg. Against this background, our discussion might have implications for other debates—and other debates have interesting implications for social entrepreneurship. Future research can investigate both this general phenomenon of hybridization as well as the links and overlaps between social entrepreneurship, management, sustainability, nonprofit management, and business ethics. By wedding the latter with social entrepreneurship, this book was one step into this direction. And we hope to inspire more advances by the fellow research community.

References

Andersson, Fredrik O., and Michael Ford. 2015. "Reframing Social Entrepreneurship Impact: Productive, Unproductive and Destructive Outputs and Outcomes of the Milwaukee School Voucher Programme." *Journal of Social Entrepreneurship* 6 (3). Taylor & Francis: 299–319. doi:10.1080/19420676.2014.981845.

Argyris, Chris. 1977. "Double Loop Learning in Organizations." *Harvard Business Review* 55 (5): 115–25. doi:10.1007/BF02013415.

Bacq, Sophie, Chantal Hartog, and Brigitte Hoogendoorn. 2016. "Beyond the Moral Portrayal of Social Entrepreneurs: An Empirical Approach to Who They Are and What Drives Them." *Journal of Business Ethics* 133 (4). Springer Netherlands: 703–18. doi:10.1007/s10551-014-2446-7.

Baumol, William J. 1990. "Entrepreneurship: Productive, Unproductive, and Destructive." *Journal of Political Economy* 98 (5): 893–921.

Boesso, Giacomo, and Kamalesh Kumar. 2009. "An Investigation of Stakeholder Prioritization and Engagement: Who or What Really Counts." *Journal of Accounting & Organizational Change* 5 (1): 62–80. doi:10.1108/18325910910932214.

Bornstein, David. 2007. *How to Change the World: Social Entrepreneurs and the Power of Ideas*. New York, NY: Oxford University Press.

Dacin, M. Tina, Peter A. Dacin, and Paul Tracey. 2011. "Social Entrepreneurship: A Critique and Future Directions." *Organization Science* 22 (5): 1203–13. doi:10.1287/orsc.1100.0620.

Davidsson, Per. 2005. "Nascent Entrepreneurship: Empirical Studies and Developments." *Foundations and Trends® in Entrepreneurship* 2 (1): 1–76. doi:10.1561/0300000005.

Davis, James H., F. David Schoorma, and Lex Donaldson. 1997. "Towards a Stewardship Theory of Management." *Academy of Management Review* 22 (3): 20–47.

Dempsey, S. E., and M. L. Sanders. 2010. "Meaningful Work? Nonprofit Marketization and Work/Life Imbalance in Popular Autobiographies of Social Entrepreneurship." *Organization* 17 (4): 437–59. doi:10.1177/1350508410364198.

Dey, Pascal. 2006. "The Rhetoric of Social Entrepreneurship: Paralogy and New Language Games in Academic Discourse." *Entrepreneurship as Social Change: A Third Movements in Entrepreneurship Book* May: 121–42.

DiMaggio, Paul J., and Walter W. Powell. 1983. "The Iron Cage Revisited: Institutional Isomorphism and Collective Rationality In Organizational Fields." *American Sociological Review* 48 (2): 147–60.

Elkington, John, and Pamela Hartigan. 2008. *The Power of Unreasonable People: How Social Entrepreneurs Create Markets That Change the World*. Boston, MA: Harvard Business Press.

Engert, Sabrina, Romana Rauter, and Rupert J. Baumgartner. 2016. "Exploring the Integration of Corporate Sustainability into Strategic Management: A Literature Review." *Journal of Cleaner Production* 112. Elsevier Ltd: 2833–50. doi:10.1016/j.jclepro.2015.08.031.

Garriga, Elisabet, and Domènec Melé. 2004. "Corporate Social Responsibility Theories: Mapping the Territory Social Responsibility Corporate Theories: Mapping the Territory." *Journal of Business Ethics* 53 (1–2): 51–71. doi:10.1787/9789264122352-de.

Henry, Patrick. 2017. "Why Some Startups Succeed (and Why Most Fail)." *Entrepreneur*, February.

Hoogendoorn, Brigitte, Enrico Pennings, and Roy Thurik. 2010. "What Do We Know about Social Entrepreneurship: An Analysis of Empirical Research RE-PORT SERIES." ERS-2009–044-ORG. ERIM Report Series Research In Management. Rotterdam, NL.

Kickul, Jill, and Thomas S. Lyons. 2016. *Understanding Social Entrepreneurship: The Relentless Pursuit of Mission in an Ever Changing World.* New York, NY: Routledge.

Kistruck, Geoffrey M., and Paul W. Beamish. 2010. "The Interplay of Form, Structure, and Embeddedness in Social Intrapreneurship." *Entrepreneurship Theory and Practice* 34 (4): 735–61. doi:10.1111/j.1540-6520.2010.00371.x.

Light, Paul C. 2006. "Reshaping Social Entrepreneurship." *Stanford Social Innovation Review* Fall: 47–51.

Matten, Dirk, and Andrew Crane. 2005. "Corporate Citizenship: Towards an Extended Theoretical Framework." *Academy of Management Review* 30 (1): 166–79. doi:10.2307/20159101.

McMullen, Jeffery S., and Brian J. Bergman. 2018. "The Promise and Problems of Price Subsidization in Social Entrepreneurship." In *Business Horizons* 61 (4): 609–21. doi:10.1016/j.bushor.2018.03.009.

Morgan, Kevin. 2016. "Collective Entrepreneurship: The Basque Model of Innovation." *European Planning Studies* 24 (8). Taylor & Francis: 1544–60. doi:10.108 0/09654313.2016.1151483.

Nandan, Monica, Manuel London, and Tricia Bent-Goodley. 2015. "Social Workers as Social Change Agents: Social Innovation, Social Intrapreneurship, and Social Entrepreneurship." *Human Service Organizations Management, Leadership & Governance* 39 (1). Routledge: 38–56. doi:10.1080/23303131.2014.955236.

Nicholls, Alex. 2010. "The Legitimacy of Social Entrepreneurship: Reflexive Isomorphism in a Pre-Paradigmatic Field." *Entrepreneurship Theory and Practice* 34 (4): 611–33.

Olaison, Lena, and Bent Meier Sørensen. 2014. "The Abject of Entrepreneurship: Failure, Fiasco, Fraud." *International Journal of Entrepreneurial Behaviour and Research* 20 (2): 193–211. doi:10.1108/IJEBR-09-2013-0143.

Pies, Ingo, Stefan Hielscher, and Markus Beckmann. 2009. "Moral Commiments and the Societal Role of Business: An Ordonomic Approach to Corporate Citizenship." *Business Ethics Quarterly* 19 (3): 375–401.

Politis, Diamanto, and Jonas Gabrielsson. 2009. "Entrepreneurs' Attitudes towards Failure: An Experiential Learning Approach." *International Journal of Entrepreneurial Behaviour and Research* 15 (4): 364–83. doi:10.1108/13552550910967921.

Ratten, Vanessa. 2014. "Future Research Directions for Collective Entrepreneurship in Developing Countries: A Small and Medium-Sized Enterprise Perspective." *International Journal of Entrepreneurship and Small Business* 22 (2): 266. doi:10.1504/IJESB.2014.062505.

Sharma, Pramodita, and Sankaran James J. Chrisman. 2007. "Toward a Reconciliation of the Definitional Issues in the Field of Corporate Entrepreneurship." In *Entrepreneurship – Concepts, Theory and Perspective*, 83–103. Berlin, Germany: Springer.

Spoelstra, Sverre. 2010. "Business Miracles." *Culture and Organization* 16 (1): 87–101. doi:10.1080/14759550903558136.

Stewart, Alex. 1989. *Team Entrepreneurship*. London, UK: Sage Publications.

Ţurcan, Romeo V., Markus M. Mäkelä, Olav J. Sørensen, and Mikko Rönkkö. 2010. "Mitigating Theoretical and Coverage Biases in the Design of Theory-Building Research: An Example from International Entrepreneurship." *International Entrepreneurship and Management Journal* 6 (4): 399–417. doi:10.1007/s11365-009-0122-7.

Zeyen, Anica. 2014. *Scaling Strategies of Social Entrepreneurship Organizations—an Actor-Motivation Perspective*. Lueneburg: Leuphana University.

Index

Page numbers in *italic* indicate a figure on the corresponding page

Made in the USA
Monee, IL
19 August 2024